ADVANCES IN
EXPERIMENTAL
SOCIAL PSYCHOLOGY

VOLUME 18

CONTRIBUTORS TO VOLUME 18

Mary M. Connors

Mary Anne Fitzpatrick

Albert A. Harrison

Chester A. Insko

David A. Kenny

S. S. Komorita

Lawrence La Voie

Mark Snyder

ADVANCES IN

Experimental

Social Psychology

EDITED BY

Leonard Berkowitz
DEPARTMENT OF PSYCHOLOGY
UNIVERSITY OF WISCONSIN—MADISON
MADISON, WISCONSIN

VOLUME 18

 1984

ACADEMIC PRESS, INC.
(Harcourt Brace Jovanovich, Publishers)
Orlando   San Diego   New York   London
Toronto   Montreal   Sydney   Tokyo

ACADEMIC PRESS, INC.
Orlando, Florida 32887

United Kingdom Edition published by
ACADEMIC PRESS, INC. (LONDON) LTD.
24/28 Oval Road, London NW1 7DX

LIBRARY OF CONGRESS CATALOG CARD NUMBER: 64-23452

ISBN 0-12-015218-5

PRINTED IN THE UNITED STATES OF AMERICA

84 85 86 87   9 8 7 6 5 4 3 2 1

CONTENTS

The Social Relations Model

David A. Kenny and Lawrence La Voie

Coalition Bargaining

S. S. Komorita

When Belief Creates Reality

Mark Snyder

CONTRIBUTORS

Numbers in parentheses indicate the pages on which the authors' contributions begin.

Mary M. Connors (49), *Ames Research Center, National Aeronautics and Space Administration, Moffett Field, California 94035*

Mary Anne Fitzpatrick (1), *Department of Communication Arts, University of Wisconsin, Madison, Wisconsin 53706*

Albert A. Harrison (49), *Department of Psychology, University of California, Davis, Davis, California 95616*

Chester A. Insko (89), *Department of Psychology, University of North Carolina, Chapel Hill, North Carolina 27514*

David A. Kenny (141), *Department of Psychology, University of Connecticut, Storrs, Connecticut 06268*

S. S. Komorita (183), *Department of Psychology, University of Illinois, Champaign, Illinois 61820*

Lawrence La Voie (141), *Department of Psychology, University of Miami, Coral Gables, Florida 33124*

Mark Snyder (247), *Department of Psychology, University of Minnesota, Minneapolis, Minnesota 55455*

A TYPOLOGICAL APPROACH TO MARITAL INTERACTION: RECENT THEORY AND RESEARCH

Mary Anne Fitzpatrick

DEPARTMENT OF COMMUNICATION ARTS
UNIVERSITY OF WISCONSIN
MADISON, WISCONSIN

ADVANCES IN EXPERIMENTAL
SOCIAL PSYCHOLOGY, VOL. 18

I. Introduction

A. PURPOSE

Marriage and divorce are pervasive aspects of life in American society. Over 95% of the adult population is or has been married (Rawlings, 1978). Even though some estimates suggest that 40% of all marriages end in divorce (Glick & Norton, 1976), about 80% of those who divorce marry again (Reiss, 1972). Understanding the forces which hold a marriage together and those which encourage dissolution is of great value in this time of record high marriage, divorce, and remarriage rates.

Scholars in a variety of academic disciplines pursue the search for the causes of the success or failure of marriage. Historians (Gadlin, 1977; Shorter, 1975), sociologists (Burgess, 1981; Nye, 1976), psychologists (Gottman, 1979; Weiss, 1975), and clinicians (Jacobson & Martin, 1976; Olson, 1976) offer a variety of explanations for marital satisfaction and marital stability. From these different perspectives, however, emerges a surprisingly consistent viewpoint. That is, in our culture subjectively experienced contentment in a marriage is the primary determinant of whether a marriage will remain stable or intact (Lewis & Spanier, 1979). Furthermore, the communication that takes place between a husband and wife leads to this contentment or satisfaction.

The purpose of this article is not to present a comprehensive discussion of the merits or shortcomings of the research and theory on marital interaction but to introduce a typology of marital relationships. The typology is based on the assumption that only by describing relationships in reference to dimensions defined a priori as important aspects of marital life can we understand the communication that occurs in those relationships, as well as the outcomes emerging from a couple's communicative exchanges. This article describes the development of an empirical typology of marital relationships. We examine the basis for typological construction, the development of the measurement, and the early validation work linking the types to other variables of interest. Finally, the relationship between marital types and communication behavior is presented.

B. THE CONSTRUCTION OF AN EMPIRICAL TYPOLOGY

The primary goal of a typology is to construct an orderly scheme for the classification and description of social phenomena (Reynolds, 1971; Zetterberg, 1965). Although there are a variety of ways to approach typological construction, the most useful one is a polythetic method of classification (Bailey, 1975; Fitzpatrick, 1976; Sneath & Sokal, 1973). In a polythetic approach to classification, the logical model is tested by a statistical one in which types are assumed to constitute a subpopulation with a certain probability distribution (Fleiss & Zubin, 1969; Wolfe, 1970). The polythetic model replaces the present or absent orientation of the classic, monothetic model with an ordering procedure in which the dimensions of the typology are ordered from high to low on a continuous scale. This procedure permits more subtle distinctions among types (Sneath & Sokal, 1973).

A polythetic classification scheme places individuals in the same type when they possess a large number of shared characteristics. Members of a given type, though not identical on every dimension, do share a similar pattern of characteristics. A polythetic model is more parsimonious than the classical methods of typology building because it is based on empirical data. Consequently, it does not define empirically null types.

The empirical model of the classification of plants, animals, individuals, societies, or cultures demands that the measures on which a typology is based be objective, repeatable, and explicit (Sneath & Sokal, 1973). The variables which define the dimensions of a typology must be of central theoretical importance. The establishment of these significant dimensions can then interact with the empirical test of them. Typal categories emerge when measurements are taken on important dimensions which describe the phenomena of interest.

In general, the study of interpersonal relationships has suffered from a lack of a descriptive phase in the scientific investigation of relationships (Gottman, 1979; Hinde, 1979). Theories have emerged without a well-described set of phenomena and, as Gottman (1979, p. 292) elegantly states, "the result resembles the theorizing of medieval alchemists." It is the premise of this article that a firm descriptive basis for the study of intimate relationships requires, however, procedures for classifying couples, the actual assignment of couples to types, and the validation of the types in terms of external attributes (Hempel, 1965).

Section II reviews some of the major typologies that have been proposed to describe marital relationships.

II. A Typological Approach

A. CRITIQUE OF PREVIOUS APPROACHES

Numerous attempts have been made to establish relationship typologies (see Fitzpatrick, 1976, for a review). Most of these attempts have been made either by observers working in clinical settings (e.g., Lederer & Jackson, 1968; Shostrom & Kavanaugh, 1971), by investigators reflecting on interaction data collected for other purposes (e.g., Goodrich, 1968; Olson, 1981; Ryder, 1970), or by theoreticians working with the benefit of little or no empirical support (e.g., Adams, 1971; Bernard, 1972; Burgess & Wallin, 1953; Cuber & Harroff, 1965).

There are four problems with the existing systems. First, most of the typologies lack comprehensiveness because they focus on one or two dimensions as ways to categorize couples (e.g., Burgess & Wallin, 1953; Farber, 1962). Second, the schemata developed through post hoc data examination or speculation by the researcher have limited utility because they offer other researchers no reliable way to categorize couples (e.g., Goodrich, 1968; Ryder, 1970). Third, typologies generated from interaction data categorize relationships on small samples of behavior collected in laboratory situations (e.g., Olson, 1981; Schaap, 1982). Fourth, for the typologies that are empirically based, little is known about relationship types other than the means of classification (e.g., Ravich & Wyden, 1974).

For the theorist attempting to develop a typology of relationships, the first task is to develop a series of measures that can tap significant dimensions of relationships. Having developed these measures, the researcher must detect in some empirical manner the existence of subgroups on the relational dimensions. In detecting these subgroups, no assumptions should initially be made concerning their nature, number, size, or discriminating aspects. All of these should emerge from an examination of the data. The goal is to develop types of couples who cluster, simultaneously, at distinct points on many conceptually important dimensions.

B. THE BASIC DIMENSIONS

The first step in the development of this empirical typology of relationships was the delineation of an important set of dimensions of relational life. Numerous theorists maintain that couples evolve particular patterns of interaction with one another through the various ways that they use the physical aspects of their life together to achieve specific goals. Through the organization of the commonplaces of space, time, and energy, couples and families gain access to a degree of affect, a level of power, and a sense of meaning in their lives. The major dimensions in relational life are space, time, energy, affect, power, and meaning (Haley, 1963; Henry, 1965; Hess & Handel, 1959; Kantor & Lehr, 1975; Rapoport & Rapoport, 1971).

To measure these dimensions, we developed a preliminary questionnaire with an initial pool of more than 200 items (Fitzpatrick, 1976). Each item corresponded either to an access (energy, space, time) or a target (affect, power, meaning) dimension (Kantor & Lehr, 1975). Additionally, 25 of the initial items

were specifically designed to assess a person's stand on the importance of autonomy and interdependence in a relationship (Bochner, 1976).

The initial set of items was examined for clarity and consistency by a small
set of couples as well as by several expert judges familiar with the work of
Kantor and Lehr (1975). When the redundant and unclear items were eliminated,
184 remained. The final questionnaire consisted of approximately 25 items associated with each of the six dimensions. The remaining items tapped the autono-
my/interdependence issue. The large number of items included in the initial
questionnaire offered some assurance that the relational dimensions would be
adequately sampled. This was particularly important in the initial work.

The resulting scale, named the Relational Dimensions Instrument (RDI),
was pilot tested on more than 1000 married individuals. Through factor and item
analyses of these responses, the original scale was reduced to a reliable 64-item,
eight-factor instrument (Fitzpatrick, 1976). The factor structure was subsequently revalidated on another random sample of 448 married individuals. The
factors that emerged from these analyses were the Ideology of Traditionalism,
the Ideology of Uncertainty and Change, Sharing, Autonomy, Undifferentiated
Space, Temporal Regularity, Conflict Avoidance, and Assertiveness. Table I
lists some representative items from each dimension of the RDI. The entire scale,
including factor loadings and reliabilities, is reported in full in Fitzpatrick and
Indvik (1982).

The factor and item analyses of the RDI indicated that the six original
dimensions of energy, space, time, affect, power, and meaning are highly correlated dimensions of family relations. Sharing, for example, although primarily
an affect dimension, includes some items that tap the organization of the house-
hold (space) and the scheduling of daily activities (time) to promote companionship between spouses. In addition to the mixing of access and target dimensions across the subscales of the RDI, it is interesting to note that none of the
energy items emerged on the final version of the scale. It may be that the concept
of energy in relationships is too abstract to be assessed through the self-reports of
individuals.

A second-order factor analysis of the RDI indicated that these eight factors
represent three major conceptual dimensions of relational life. The first is *auton-
omy/interdependence*. Although close relationships are said to be marked by a
growing sense of interdependence (Levinger, 1977), the problem of how to
achieve a satisfying degree of connectedness (Bochner, 1976; Hess & Handel,
1959) is generally acknowledged as a basic problem in all human relationships.
Each spouse tries to cast the relationship in a form that satisfies the ways in
which he or she wants to be together yet needs to be apart. Relational connectedness is examined by the amount of sharing and companionship in the marriage as
well as by a couple's organization of time and space. The more interdependent
the couple, the higher the level of companionship, the more time they spend

TABLE I

REPRESENTATIVE STATEMENTS FROM THE RELATIONAL DIMENSIONS INSTRUMENT

Ideology of Traditionalism
  A woman should take her husband's last name when she marries
  Our wedding ceremony was (will be) very important to us
  Our society as we see it needs to regain faith in the law and in our institution

Ideology of Uncertainty and Change
  In marriage/close relationships there should be no constraints or restrictions on individual freedom
  The ideal relationship is one marked by novelty, humor, and spontaneity
  In a relationship, each individual should be permitted to establish the daily rhythm and time schedule that suits him/her best

Sharing
  We tell each other how much we love or care about each other
  My spouse/mate reassures and comforts me when I am feeling low
  I think that we joke around and have more fun than most couples

Autonomy
  I have my own private workspace (study, workshop, utility room, etc)
  My spouse has his/her own private workspace (workshop, utility, etc)
  I think it is important for one to have some private space which is all his/her own and separate from one's mate

Undifferentiated Space
  I feel free to interrupt my spouse/mate when he/she is concentrating on something if he/she is in my presence
  I open my spouse/mate's personal mail without asking permission
  I feel free to invite guests home without informing my spouse/mate

Temporal Regularity
  We eat our meals (i.e., the ones at home) at the same time every day
  In our house, we keep a fairly regular daily time schedule
  We serve the main meal at the same time every day

Conflict Avoidance
  If I can avoid arguing about some problems, they will disappear
  In our relationship, we feel that it is better to engage in conflicts than to avoid them
  It is better to hide one's true feelings in order to avoid hurting your spouse/mate

Assertiveness
  My spouse/mate *forces* me to do things that I do not want to do
  We are likely to argue in front of friends or in public places
  My spouse/mate tries to persuade me to do something that I do not want to do

---

together, and the more they organize their space to promote togetherness and interaction.

The second dimension is *conventional/nonconventional ideology*. The beliefs, standards, and values that individuals hold concerning their relationship and family are a major factor guiding not only the interactions with the spouse but also the judgments individuals make about these interactions and their outcomes. Values concerning relationships can range from those stressing the importance of stability and predictability to those emphasizing the importance of change and uncertainty. Individuals and couples vary in their beliefs on such ideological matters.

The third dimension is *conflict engagement/conflict avoidance*. It is inevitable that individuals in ongoing relationships experience conflict. The ways to approach the resolution of differences, however, range from total conflict avoidance to active engagement in conflict interactions (Raush, Barry, Hertel, & Swain, 1974). Individuals and couples differ as to the degree that they perceive such openness to conflict as an important characteristic of marital communication. Couples vary as to their willingness to engage in conflict and their degree of assertiveness with one another.

C. THE RELATIONAL DEFINITIONS

The second step in the development of this empirical typology of relationships was the clustering of individuals according to their responses to the RDI (Bailey, 1975; Blashfield, 1976). An individual's eight scores on the subscales of the Relational Dimensions Instrument were submitted to a linear typal analysis (Overall & Klett, 1972) followed by a discriminant analysis. Such a procedure allows a researcher to find and name the patterns used by individuals to describe the relationships.

In the initial phase of the research, the number of unique relational definitions was an empirical unknown. The number and characteristics of relational definitions thus emerged from an empirical examination of the responses that individuals assigned to these dimensions. Data from over 1000 married individuals were input into the typal analysis in order to uncover the basic definitions. The definitions emerged from a specific empirical clustering of cases on the eight reliably measured factors.

A variety of different solutions for the number of definitions that would provide the best fit for these data were examined. Of those that were attempted, the linear typal analysis suggested that the three-cluster solution provided the clearest explanation of the data. The three-cluster solution yielded the most unambiguous assignment of subjects to clusters. Each subject was assigned a weighted loading based on the degree to which his or her profile corresponded to each of the three pure relational definitions.

For each sample drawn throughout this program of research, the rectangular matrix of typal loadings was examined to assess the goodness of fit of the three-cluster solution and to assign subjects to a definition. Not only must each group be relatively homogeneous with respect to the eight factors, but also each individual should clearly resemble one, and only one, cluster. The criteria used to assign the subjects to clusters were a primary loading above .30 and a secondary loading at least .10 smaller than the primary loading. Across the various samples, only 8% failed to meet these criteria. In cases of these complex loadings, individuals were assigned to the cluster with the highest loading.

To verify the classification of individuals to clusters, discriminant analysis was also used to assign individuals to clusters. This independent classification was compared to that produced by the linear typal analysis. An examination of the results of these analyses across samples indicated that never less than 94%, and usually up to 97%, of the cases were assigned to the identical group by both procedures. These discriminant analyses also suggest that the three-cluster solution is appropriate (Cattell, Coulter, & Tsujioka, 1966).

According to their scores on the RDI, three discrete relational definitions, or ways to describe the marital relationship, were identified. These definitions are *traditional, independent,* and *separate.* Table II summarizes the responses to the RDI of five different samples totaling 1672 individuals.

Traditionals hold conventional ideological values about relationships. These conventional values place more emphasis on stability in a relationship than on spontaneity. A conventional orientation stresses traditional societal customs, for example, a woman should take her husband's last name when she marries, and infidelity is always inexcusable. A traditional exhibits interdependence in his/her marriage. The interdependence of a traditional is marked by a high degree of sharing and companionship in the marriage. This companionship is strongly reinforced by the traditional's use of time and space. A regular daily time schedule and the low level of support for autonomous physical space in the home facilitates companionship. Traditionals also report that although they are not assertive, they tend not to avoid conflict with their spouses.

Independents hold fairly nonconventional values about relational and family life. At the opposite end of an ideological continuum from a traditional orientation, an independent believes that relationships should not constrain an individual's freedom in any way. The independent maintains a high level of companionship and sharing in his/her marriage but it is of a qualitatively different kind than that of a traditional. Although he/she tries to stay psychologically close to his/her spouse, an independent maintains separate physical spaces to control accessibility. In addition, an independent has a difficult time maintaining a

TABLE II

Means on the Relational Dimensions Instrument across Five Samples[a,b]

Relational definition	Relational definition		
	Traditional	Independent	Separate
Ideological Views			
Ideology of Traditionalism	4.97_a	3.93_b	4.88_a
Ideology of Uncertainty	3.52_a	4.35_b	4.19_b
Autonomy/Interdependence			
Sharing	5.01_a	4.73_b	4.07_c
Autonomy	3.20_b	4.39_a	4.40_a
Undifferentiated Space	4.44_a	4.41_a	3.88_b
Temporal Regularity	4.71_a	3.23_b	4.41_a
Conflict			
Conflict Avoidance	3.94_b	3.60_b	4.54_a
Assertiveness	2.80_b	3.54_a	3.27_a

[a]Means with different subscripts across relational definitions differ from each other at the .10 level by the Scheffé procedure. Relational Dimensions Instrument ratings are on a 7-point scale.
[b]$N = 1672$.

regular daily time schedule. Independents report some assertiveness in their relationship with their spouses and tend not to avoid conflicts.

A separate seems to hold two opposing ideological views on relationships at the same time. While a separate is as conventional in reference to marital and family issues as a traditional, he/she simultaneously supports the values upheld by independents and stresses individual freedom over relationship maintenance. Supporting two opposing sets of values suggests that the separates are ambivalent about their relational values. They may espouse one set publicly while believing another privately. The separates have significantly less companionship and sharing in their marriage. They attempt to keep a psychological distance in their relationship to the spouse and they try to maintain some autonomy through their use of space. The major way that a separate indicates interdependence in the marriage is by keeping a regular daily schedule. Separates, although they report some attempts at persuasion and assertiveness toward the spouse, indicate that they avoid open marital conflicts.

D. THE RELATIONAL TYPES: COMPARISON OF HUSBAND
AND WIFE PERSPECTIVES

The third step in the development of this empirical typology of relationships was to compare the individual definitions of the husbands and wives. Great care was taken when the scales were administered to ensure no collaboration between husbands and wives on their answers. Consequently, when spouses are placed in different clusters, it means that they disagree on important dimensions of the marriage.

By comparing the husband and wife's perspectives on their marriage, couple types are identified.[1] From these three individually based relational definitions, nine relational types can be logically constructed. The first three types are the Pure types in which the husband and wife independently agree on a definition of their relationship. Husbands and wives who share the same ideological views of relationships, who experience the same level of autonomy and interdependence in their marriage, and share the same level of conflict expression, end up in the same cluster. These couples are categorized in one of the three Pure types. These types are *Traditional, Independent,* and *Separate.*

Spouses who disagree on major aspects of these basic dimensions end up in different clusters. These couples are categorized in one of the six Mixed types in which the husband and wife describe their relationship differently. The major Mixed type uncovered in the early research is the *Separate/Traditional* in which the husband defines the marriage as separate while his wife defines the same relationship as traditional.

Of the 700 couples who completed the Relational Dimensions Instrument in the early phases of the research, 60% were unambiguously classified into one of the three Pure types. In other words, 60% of the husbands and wives agree on the basic definitions of their marriage while 40% of these couples define their relationship differently. Parallel to this finding is that of Bernard (1972) who suggests that often the husband's description of a marriage is significantly different from that of his wife. "His" marriage is significantly different from "her" marriage in 40% of the couples who have completed the RDI. The distribution of the couple types across five samples appears in Table III.

Of the 700 couples represented in Table III, 20% are Traditionals, 22% are Independents, and 17% are Separates. Approximately 30% of the remaining Mixed marriages involve a separate partner or one who is emotionally divorced from the marriage. Contrary to the assumption that it is more likely for the husband to be estranged in a marriage and unable to communicate with his spouse (Balswick & Peek, 1971; Slater, 1970), there are as many wives as husbands categorized as separates.

Although it appeared in the early stages of the research that Separate/Traditional couples were the most frequently occurring Mixed type, this finding

---

[1]By convention, relational definitions are not capitalized although couple type designations are. In addition, in discussing Mixed couples, the definition of the husband precedes that of the wife. A Separate/Independent couple consequently is one in which the husband defines the relationship as separate while his wife sees the relationship as independent.

TABLE III

PROPORTIONS OF PURE AND MIXED COUPLE TYPES DISTRIBUTED
ACROSS 700 COUPLES[a]

Husband type	Wife type		
	Traditional	Independent	Separate
Traditional	.20	.07	.07
Independent	.06	.22	.09
Separate	.07	.06	.17

[a]The samples from which this table is derived are reported in full in
Fitzpatrick (1976), Fitzpatrick and Indvik (1982), Fitzpatrick, Best, Mabry,
and Indvik (1984), and Vance (1981).

has not held up across the samples. In the total sample, no Mixed type occurs
with any greater frequency than the others.

E. SAMPLING OF COUPLE TYPES

Three sampling strategies were utilized in the research reported in this
article. The first was convenience sampling. Questionnaires were distributed in
political and social groups, in hospitals, schools, factories, and offices. This
strategy was used in the early stages of the research in order to isolate the major
patterns in the data and to develop a reliable scale (Fitzpatrick, 1976, 1977;
Fitzpatrick & Best, 1979).

The second strategy utilized was a stratified sampling technique. Neighborhoods within a standard metropolitan statistical area were categorized according to seven demographic criteria such as income and type of housing. Fourteen
neighborhoods were randomly selected and their statistical profiles were checked
against what was known about the entire metropolitan area. These profiles were
found to be representative of the stratification of that metropolitan area. A street
directory was then used to randomly select households for interviews (Fitzpatrick
& Indvik, 1982).

The third sampling strategy involved the random selection of married couples for participation in research from lists provided by organizations such as
political groups, churches, and university housing offices (Fitzpatrick, Tenney,
& Witteman, 1983; Vance, 1981; Williamson, 1983).

We cannot generalize to the population at large from these samples because
they are not all random samples of couples. Indeed, it is difficult to generate a
random sample of couples since it takes only one partner's refusal to participate

in the research to invalidate the data as couple data. Although we cannot say with assurance that 20% of the married population have Traditional marriages, we can examine some demographic indicators from the stratified random sample (Fitzpatrick & Indvik, 1982) to see if the couple types describe marriages at different points in the life cycle of the family.

In the stratified sample of 224 couples, there were no significant differences among the couple types on any of the demographic indicators used in the research. Couple types did not differ on number of years married, on whether or not the husband or wife was married before, on number of children, on religion of either spouse, or on level of schooling, employment, or income (Fitzpatrick, 1984a). There was no significant relationship between this set of demographic variables and the type of marriage that a couple had evolved. The variance in couple type cannot be explained by a couple's place in the social structure.

The facts that marriages can be classified in one of three basic ways, that husbands and wives can be compared as to how they categorize their relationships, and that such classifications are not merely psychological manifestations of demographic differences are useless unless the scheme allows a researcher to discriminate these types on a number of different attributes of relationships. Section III examines the connection between the couple types and other aspects of relationships.

III. Early Validation Studies

Mathematically placing couples into relational types is an elegant but useless exercise unless membership within a type can predict other variables of theoretical interest. Few previous typologies have attempted validation by linking types of relationships to other theoretical concepts. Typologies are of merely incidental interest unless they can be associated with a wide variety of behaviors aside from those which are used to define the categories. We now turn to the early validation work on the relational typology.

A. EXPRESSIVITY AND INSTRUMENTALITY

The first validation study examined instrumental and expressive communication in the Pure couple types (Fitzpatrick, 1977). Although communication is acknowledged as vital to the growth and development of relationships (Lederer & Jackson, 1968; Bach & Wyden, 1969; Clinebell & Clinebell, 1970; Schauble & Hill, 1976), two very different views emerge about what characteristics of communication are enhancing to prolonged interpersonal relationships. These two views are the expressive and the instrumental.

The *expressivist* school of human communication, derived from the work of humanistic psychologists such as Maslow (1968), Rogers (1961), and Jourard (1971), maintains that the open disclosure of spontaneously experienced feelings, thoughts, and wishes to at least one "significant other" is necessary for the development of a healthy personality. The viewpoint has been translated by advocates of expressivism into the suggestion that a complete sharing of feelings and perceptions with one's partner promotes successful relationships (Bernard, 1972; Giffin & Patton, 1974; Rossiter & Pearce, 1975; Steward & D'Angelo, 1975).

The *instrumental* school of human communication favors carefully monitoring what is said to others in order to solve a problem or to accomplish a task (Hart & Burks, 1972; Hart, Eadie, & Carlson, 1975; Phillips & Metzger, 1976). The major function of an interaction is not necessarily to express oneself openly but rather to achieve specific interaction goals. Indeed, the willingness to calculate responses prior to communicating with another most clearly distinguishes instrumental from expressive communication.

Instrumental and expressive communication styles both within and outside the marriage were examined. A couple may, for example, be very open with one another yet reserved in discussing their feelings or opinions with others in general. Expressive marital communication was measured by the perceived amount of self and spouse disclosure and the open expression of feelings between partners. Instrumental marital communication was measured by the willingness of one partner to inhibit the expression of thoughts or feelings that he/she experienced when communicating with the spouse (Swenson, 1961, 1968; Swenson & Gilner, 1964, 1973; Fitzpatrick, 1976).

The general approach to instrumental and expressive communication was measured by the Rhetsen scale (Hart *et al.*, 1975). The expressive component of this scale measures the degree to which respondents agree that under all circumstances individuals should "tell it like it is." The instrumental component of this measure asks whether the respondent is willing to restrain what he/she says in conversations with others in order to avoid hurting them. Data were available only for the Pure couple types in this study. Sixteen Independent, 17 Separate, and 10 Traditional couples completed these questionnaires.

A multivariate analysis of variance was computed with couple types as the independent variable and the six communication measures as the dependent variables. The overall F test for the equality of the mean vectors, using the Wilks' lambda criterion, was significant [$F(12, 70) = 4.63, p < .0001$]. Table IV lists the observed means and the differences among the Pure couple types on each communication measure.

The most expressive marital communication style is that of the Traditionals.

TABLE IV

MEAN SELF-REPORT OF COMMUNICATION STYLE BY PURE COUPLE TYPE[a]

Communication style	Couple type		
	Traditional	Independent	Separate
Marital			
Expression of positive feelings	2.17_a	1.90_b	1.86_b
Inhibition of expression of positive feelings	1.39_b	1.39_b	1.71_a
Self-disclosure	2.51_a	2.33_a	2.07_b
Spouse disclosure	2.51_a	2.21_b	2.01_b
General			
Expressivity	$.72_b$	1.02_a	1.26_a
Instrumentality	1.92_a	1.40_b	1.99_a

[a]Means with different subscripts across couple types differ from each other at the .05 level by the Newman–Keuls' procedures. Marital communication style ratings are on a 3-point scale while general communication style ratings are on a 4-point scale.

Traditionals are more likely to express their feelings to their spouse and perceive a good deal of self-disclosure in their marriage. With individuals other than the spouse, however, the Traditionals are the least expressive of the couple types and tend to be very instrumental in their nonmarital communication.

The Independents are also relatively expressive in communicating with their spouse, though they rate their spouses as disclosing to them less than the Traditionals. Independents retain their own expressivity with individuals other than their spouses. Less likely than the other couple types to be instrumental in their communication, Independents are more expressive with outsiders than are Traditionals.

The Separates have the least expressive marital communication style of the couple types. Inhibiting the expression of their feelings on a variety of issues, Separates disclose less to their spouses and see their spouses disclosing less to them than the other couple types. Outside the relationship, the Separates are more expressive than the Traditionals but do try to restrain their communication with others.

The Pure couple types differ from one another in their perceptions of their marital communication behavior as well as in their evaluations of their own general communication style.

B. SEX ROLE ORIENTATIONS

The central biosocial issue in a marital relationship is how couples interpret the meaning of maleness and femaleness (Hess & Handel, 1959). These interpretations are generally studied under the rubric of sex roles. The male sex role is associated with task completion, problem solving, and concern for oneself as an individual. The female sex role is associated with nurturance, concern for others, and relationships with others (Bem, Martyna, & Watson, 1976).

There are a variety of ways in which these roles may have significant implications for the maintenance of long-term relationships. At the very least, these roles prescribe what is and what is not appropriate behavior for males and females in their relationships as well as in the larger social milieu. The present study includes both normative and perceptual approaches to sex roles. Couple types are compared on how they believe males and females (Brogan & Kutner, 1976; Broverman, Vogel, Broverman, Clarkson, & Rosenkrantz, 1972; Hochschild, 1973) should behave as well as on how they see themselves behaving in their relationships (Bem, 1974).

The sample consisted of 224 couples drawn at random from the Milwaukee, Wisconsin Standard Metropolitan Statistical Area (SMSA) (Fitzpatrick & Indvik, 1982). Fifty-one Independent couples, 54 Traditional couples, 17 Separate couples, 17 Separate/Traditional couples, and 85 additional Mixed couples comprised the sample. To explore the normative conceptions of male and female behavior, the Sex Role Orientation (SRO) scale developed by Brogan and Kutner (1976) was utilized. This 36-item, Likert-type scale was designed to assess appropriate male and female behavior patterns rather than perceptions of the "typical" traits, behaviors, or interests of men and women. Three reliable factors emerged from the factor analysis of this instrument. The first factor, *conventional orientation,* supports a fairly conservative approach to appropriate behavior for males and females. The second factor, *sex reversed orientation,* suggests that both sexes should be able to adopt roles previously prohibited to them. The third factor, *personal orientation,* maintains that individuals should govern their behavior by personal preferences and not social conventions.

A multivariate analysis of variance was computed with the couple type as the independent variable (Independent, Traditional, Separate, Separate/ Traditional, and Mixed) and the three SRO factors as the dependent variables. The overall F test of the equality for the mean vectors, using the Wilks' lambda criterion, was significant [$F(12, 1077) = 7.10, p < .0001$] indicating that the types are clearly discriminated by their sex role orientations.

An examination of the group centroids, the standardized discriminant function coefficients, and the means on the dependent measures indicates that the Separates, the Traditionals, and the Separate/Traditionals share the same value orientation to appropriate male and female behaviors. All three types are strongly opposed to sex reversed or personal preference orientations and favor traditional sex role orientations. The Independents, on the other hand, are clearly opposed to such a conventional role orientation. Supportive of a personal or more flexible orientation, Independents also favor the more liberal sex reversed orientation.

To explore the Mixed types, a separate analysis was conducted with five Mixed types as the independent variable and the three SRO factors as the dependent variables. Although the multivariate analysis of variance was significant $[F(12, 399) = 2.08, p < .02]$, the only Mixed type that can be discriminated on the function is the Traditional/Separate couple type. This couple is strongly supportive of conventional orientations to role behaviors and opposed to sex reversed and personal approaches. The other Mixed types score between the Traditional/Separate and the Independent couples on these measures. When an independent is married to either a traditional or a separate, these couples neither agree on a relational definition nor have they negotiated clear role values and expectations for appropriate male and female behavior.

To examine how individuals see their own interpersonal behavior, husbands and wives were asked to complete the Bem Sex Role Inventory (BSRI) (Bem, 1974). The BSRI has individuals rate themselves on 20 "masculine" traits (e.g., dominance) and 20 "feminine" traits (e.g., nurturance). Individuals are subsequently categorized into one of four groups: masculine (high masculinity/low femininity), feminine (low masculinity/high femininity), androgynous (high masculinity/high femininity), and undifferentiated (low masculinity/low femininity).

Husbands and wives were compared on how they perceived their own interpersonal behavior relative to masculinity and femininity. For the husbands, neither couple type $[\chi^2(8) = 13.78, p > .09]$ nor individual relational definition $[\chi^2(4) = 6.55, p > .20]$ related to how he characterized himself. Most husbands in this sample rated their own behavior as masculine sex typed. The largest proportion of husbands in every relational type falls into the masculine grouping.

In contrast to the husbands, a comparison of the five relational types with the perceptual sex role orientation for the wives was significant $[\chi^2(8) = 17.43, p < .03]$. The wives in this sample tend toward sex typing, although androgyny is equally likely for the independent wife, as is undifferentiation for the separate wife. How these wives view themselves, however, depends on the kind of marriage they have.

Couple types can be clearly discriminated on their normative and perceptual approaches to sex roles. Regardless of their normative orientation, the husbands in this sample saw themselves as rarely nurturant, passive or, dependent, always dominant and task oriented. Although marital type does not predict the husband's self-definition, it is clearly related to how these wives see themselves. The marital type, and not an individual relational definition, predicts how a wife rates her own interpersonal traits.

C. COORIENTATIONAL ACCURACY

Communicators must have an accurate understanding of how their spouses view themselves. Effective communication in the marital relationship demands that each partner correctly perceives how the mate views him/herself on core aspects of the personality. One set of personality traits germane to the marital relationship are those relating to masculinity and femininity. Marital partners have individualized views about their own sex typing. This study examined how spouses rate one another on dimensions of masculinity and femininity and how accurate these ratings are. Two hundred seven couples participated in this research (Fitzpatrick, 1984b; Fitzpatrick & Indvik, 1982). Spouses were asked to complete the BSRI as they believed their spouse would answer for himself or herself. Each spouse's perception was then compared to the individual's self-perception as a measure of coorientational accuracy.

The accuracy measure utilized in this research is a correlational profile measure developed by Wackman (1969). This measure takes into account some of the methodological critiques of the research in person perception offered by Cronbach (1955) by factoring out a projective accuracy component. Once the correlation profile measure was computed for each individual, the profile scores for husbands and wives were correlated and averaged. This average was compared to an average generated by a random male and female pairing. The actual husband and wife correlation was significantly larger (Indvik, 1978; Indvik & Fitzpatrick, 1982) than that of the random pairing.

In order to show that it is a relational type and not an individual relational definition that can explain a dyadic level variable like accuracy, we computed two one-way analyses of variance with husband and wife's relational definitions as the independent variable and accuracy as the dependent variable. Neither the independent relational definitions of the husbands [$F(2, 204) = 2.331$, $p > .099$] nor those of the wives [$F(2, 204) = 2.16$, $p > .1117$] were capable of predicting accuracy. Women were not more accurate than men [$F(1, 412) = 1.29$, $p > .05$], nor were those who had been married longer more accurate in perceiving the spouse [$F(1, 412) = .75$, $p > .05$]. Since accuracy scores for Mixed couple types for both husbands [$F(4, 78) = 2.11$, $p > .09$] and wives [$F(4, 78) = .384$, $p > .81$] were not significantly different from one another, they were collapsed into one group for each set.

A one-way analysis of variance with relational type as the independent variable and husband's accuracy score as the dependent variable was not significant [$F(4, 202) = 1.47$, $p > .21$], indicating that the husbands in each of the types were equally accurate in predicting how their wives viewed their own masculine and feminine traits. A one-way analysis of variance with relational types as the independent variable and the wife's accuracy score as the dependent variable was significant [$F(4, 202) = 2.46$, $p < .05$].

Table V presents the means for accuracy for the husbands and wives in each relational type and the correlation between spouses' accuracy scores. Although the findings for husbands were not significant, the overall pattern of the means displayed in Table V strongly supports a couple type interpretation.

Separate/Traditional couples score higher than the other types on accuracy,

TABLE V

Means and Correlations of Husband and Wife Accuracy Scores
across Pure and Mixed Relational Types[a]

	Couple type				
	Traditional	Independent	Separate	Separate/Traditional	Mixed
Mean husband accuracy	.56	.48	.43	.57	.51
Mean wife accuracy	.58$_b$	.55$_b$	.42$_c$	.62$_a$	.51$_b$
Correlation between husband and wife	.527*	.360*	.645*	.455	.480*

[a]There are no significant differences among husbands in predicting their wives. Mean accuracy scores with different subscripts across relational types are significantly different at the .05 level with the Newman–Keuls' procedure. Asterisks indicate that the correlations within couple type for husband and wife accuracy scores are significant at the .05 level. The small correlation for Independents was statistically significant because there are 51 Independents in contrast to 17 Separate/Traditionals.

while the least accurate of the couple types are the Separates. Traditional, Independent, and Mixed couple types seem to do equally well in predicting their mates. The highest correlations between the husband and wife accuracy scores occur with the Traditional and Separate couples. In the Traditional marriage, both partners do very well in predicting how the spouse rates himself or herself on these attributes, while in the Separate marriage, both partners do poorly in predicting their spouse's self-rating.

Although the wives in the various relational types tend to be more accurate in predicting their mates, there are strong, positive correlations between partners' accuracy scores. Few of these relationships have couples who markedly differ in their level of accuracy. Only the Separate/Traditionals exhibit a nonsignificant husband–wife correlation. These husbands and wives are, however, the most accurate of their respective sexes in predicting the mate.

D. DYADIC ADJUSTMENT

One of the key questions asked in any study of marriage is how satisfied or adjusted are given couples. The purpose of this study was to examine each couple type's level of dyadic adjustment (Fitzpatrick & Best, 1979). We are concerned with happiness or the subjective feelings of the partners concerning the state of their relationship. Dyadic adjustment, or related concepts bearing names such as satisfaction, integration, success, or happiness, is the most widely studied dependent variable in marital and family research (Hicks & Platt, 1970).

Dyadic adjustment is viewed as a process whose outcome is defined by the degree of consensus, cohesion, affection, and satisfaction in the relationship (Spanier, 1976). Consensus is the extent of agreement that couples maintain on issues of importance in the relationship. Cohesion refers to how often a couple engages in positve interaction with one another such as laughing and talking together, calmly discussing something, and working cooperatively on a project. Affection taps how frequently a couple openly expresses affection to one another. Satisfaction examines not only whether a couple wishes to remain together but also the number and intensity of conflicts they experience in the relationship. A marriage is considered adjusted to the extent that couples exhibit consensus, cohesion, affection, and satisfaction in their relationship. The dependent variables were measures of dyadic functioning based on the 32-item Dyadic Adjustment Scale developed by Spanier (1976).

Sixty-eight couples participated in this study. Subjects were recruited from political and social groups in the community. There were 16 Independents. 17 Separates, 10 Traditionals, 10 Separate/Traditionals, and 15 Mixed couple types.

A multivariate analysis of variance was computed with relational type as the independent variable and the four dyadic adjustment measures as the dependent variables. The overall F test for the equality of mean vectors was significant $[F(12, 246) = 7.81, p < .0001]$. Table VI lists the observed means for each of the dependent variables.

The data in Table VI indicate that each couple type displays a specific kind of dyadic adjustment. Traditionals are the most cohesive of the couples and experience a high degree of consensus, affection, and satisfaction. Separates

TABLE VI

MEANS FOR DYADIC ADJUSTMENT MEASURES ACROSS PURE AND MIXED RELATIONAL TYPES[a]

Dyadic adjustment	Couple type				
	Traditional	Independent	Separate	Separate/Traditional	Mixed
Consensus	67.20_{ac}	59.88_b	63.80_{ac}	62.28_{bcd}	61.24_{bcd}
Affection	13.70_{ad}	12.41_{bc}	12.60_{bc}	13.89_{ad}	13.55_{ad}
Satisfaction	53.50_{ad}	46.69_{bc}	46.47_{bc}	51.00_{ad}	48.74_{bc}
Cohesion	23.55_a	20.25_b	18.97_c	20.22_b	19.97_{bc}

[a]Means with different subscripts across couple types differ from each other at the .10 level by the Scheffé procedure. There are 13 consensus items, 4 affection items, 10 satisfaction items, and 5 cohesion items.

experience as much consensus on a variety of issues as do the Traditionals yet along with the Independents and the Mixed couple types report significantly less satisfaction and cohesion in their marriage. Both Separate/Traditional and Mixed couples report the same high degree of affection in their marriages as do the Traditionals, yet only the Separate/Traditionals are as satisfied as Traditional couples.

To visualize the differences among the couples on dyadic adjustment, a discriminant function analysis was calculated in order to plot the group centroids (Stevens, 1972). The first [$\chi^2(12) = 81.03, p < .0001$], second [$\chi^2(6) = 39.17, p < .0001$], and third [$\chi^2(2) = 14.67, p < .0007$] discriminant functions were significant, indicating that the couples could be separated on three dimensions. The first dimension can be labeled satisfaction, the second consensus, and the third cohesion (Bochner & Fitzpatrick, 1980). Figure 1 shows the Traditionals set apart from the other types by the relatively higher satisfaction, consensus, and cohesion in their relationship. The Separate/Traditionals and the Traditionals share the same level of satisfaction in their relationships, while the Separates are close to the Traditionals in consensus. All other aspects of dyadic adjustment being equal, Mixed types have the same level of consensus as the Separate/Traditionals. The Independents, although their satisfaction and consensus may

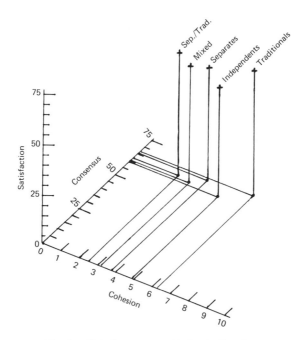

Fig. 1.   Plot of group centroids for dyadic adjustment.

be lower than that of the Traditionals, are close to the Traditionals on cohesiveness in the relationship. Although Fig. 1 indicates significant differences among the types, it is interesting to note that despite their differences, the Pure types cluster more closely to one another than they do to the Mixed couple types.

E. SUMMARY

The reliable assignment of couples to marital types is capable of predicting how couples view their level of instrumental and expressive communication, normative approaches to sex roles, personal definitions of their own masculinity and femininity, coorientational accuracy, and dyadic adjustment. Psychological gender and accuracy, which were not significantly associated with the husband's relational type, were also not associated with either spouse's individual definitions. These two variables were, however, significantly associated with marital type, albeit only for wives.

The Traditional relationship is one marked by a good deal of self-disclosure between spouses, yet reticence and reserve with outsiders. Traditionals can express their feelings to one another. These couples have very conventional approaches to male and female sex roles and see their own personalities as matching the cultural stereotypes for appropriate masculine and feminine behavior. Traditional husbands and wives are accurate in predicting how each rates himself/herself on a variety of personality characteristics. Finally, Traditionals experience a high level of dyadic adjustment.

Independent spouses see themselves as uninhibited in expressing their feelings to their spouses but do not see their spouses as self-disclosing as much to them. The spontaneity that Independents see themselves manifesting in their marital relationship carries over to their relationships with others. Independents have very liberal approaches to sex roles, although the Independent husband tends to be masculine sex typed while his wife is androgynous. Independent wives are quite accurate in predicting how their husbands define themselves although their husbands do significantly less well at predicting the wives' self-definitions. The dyadic adjustment of these couples is generally lower than that of the other couple types. The main source of the dyadic adjustment that does exist for these couples is cohesion.

Separates see their relationship as one which involves relatively less self-disclosure than the other relationships. Separates are relatively inhibited in expressing their positive feelings to one another although they can be somewhat more expressive with those outside the relationship. As conventional in their normative sex roles as the Traditionals, Separate husbands are masculine sex typed while the wife in this relationship sees herself as possessing neither positive instrumental nor expressive traits. There is a high correlation between the abilities of each Separate partner to predict the self-definition of the other. The problem is that both husbands and wives do less well in predicting one another than any other type. The Separate wife is the only wife bested by her husband in predictive ability. This finding corroborates others that suggest that if the marriage is to be satisfactory the wife must be able to predict accurately how the husband sees himself (Luckey, 1960; Stuckert, 1963). Indeed, the only source of dyadic adjustment for the Separate involves the high perceived consensus that these couples have on relational issues.

The Separate/Traditional couple is the only Mixed type that consistently can be discriminated from the other Mixed types. Separate/Traditionals represent a type of couple—the withdrawn husband and the companionate wife—frequently discussed by other researchers (Komarovsky, 1964; Slater, 1970). Separate/Traditionals have the same conventional orientation to male and female roles in society as do the Traditionals and are even more sex stereotyped in their interpersonal behavior. The most accurate of the couple types in predicting one another's self-ratings on a series of personality traits, Separate/Traditionals also experience a high degree of dyadic adjustment. Separate/Traditionals are very satisfied with their relationships, and are very affectionate toward one another.

In general, the Mixed couple types other than the Separate/Traditionals are more similar to one another than they are different. Although couples in these marriages disagree on basic aspects of their relationship, they are capable of openly expressing affection for one another. These husbands and wives do better than the Separates at predicting how their spouses view themselves, although they are not as accurate as the Separate/Traditionals and the other Pure types.

The only discriminations that can be made among these Mixed types are in reference to sex roles. Traditional/Separates have more conventional sex role orientations than the other Mixed types. In addition, a separate wife married to either a traditional or an independent husband rates herself as possessing neither positive feminine nor positive masculine characteristics.

The couple types appear to be validated across a number of measures related to marital functioning. Given shared method variance, however, it is generally much easier to predict self-reports from other self-reports. Even statistically significant relationships between the original dimensions used to type couples and their evaluations of their communication and behavior are of less ultimate utility than a consideration of the relationship between couple type and actual verbal and nonverbal communication behaviors.

IV. Communication in Couple Types

A. CASUAL INTERACTION BETWEEN SPOUSES

To examine casual interaction between spouses, 51 couples were audiotaped as they interacted with one another waiting for an experiment to begin

(Fitzpatrick, Vance, & Witteman, 1984). The middle 4 minutes of this interaction segment were transcribed and coded with the Stiles system (1978). The Stiles system codes psychological thought units in conversation into one of eight major categories: disclosure, edification, advisement, confirmation, question, acknowledgment, interpretation, and reflection. The average frequency counts for the eight communication categories were analyzed with log-linear analysis which indicated that the model specifying the sex by couple type, and couple type by communication category, was the best fit to the data [likelihood ratio $\chi^2(47) = 25.35, p > .99$].

Over 56% of the interactions coded for these couples during this 4-minute segment fell into either the disclosure or edification category (Vance, 1981). In other words, these couples primarily disclosed their attitudes, feelings, or opinions to one another, or they expressed what they believed to be objective information to one another from their own experience. Independents accounted for the most disclosure during this segment (23%) while Separate/Traditionals utilized this category the least (15%) of the couple types. The Separates accounted for only 13% of the edification statements during these interactions while the Separate/Traditionals accounted for 35% of the edification statements.

In addition to examining the differences in the usage of these eight categories by the couple types, the couples' roles in the interactions were examined. The conversations were scored for attentiveness, acquiescence, and presumptuousness (Stiles, 1978).

Speakers are verbally attentive to one another to the degree to which they are concerned with their partner as a source of experience in conversation. Asking questions of the other, for example, is one way that speakers have of using the other as a source of experience in conversation and drawing attention away from the self. The results indicated that the Separates were the most attentive of the couples and the Separate/Traditionals the least attentive of the couples during these casual conversations.

Speakers are acquiescent to one another to the degree that they use the other as a frame of reference in conversation. Confirming the other's statements or verbally reflecting what the other has said are examples of ways in which speakers acquiesce to one another in conversations. The results indicated that the Separate/Traditionals are significantly more acquiescent than the other couple types in casual conversations with their spouses.

Speakers are presumptuous to the degree that they assume that they understand their partners. Advising the partner or interpreting what has been said are examples of presumptuousness on the part of a speaker. The results indicated that the Separate/Traditionals are significantly less presumptuous than the other couple types in casual interactions with their spouses.

The Separates spoke less frequently to their spouses during this time segment than did the other couple types. The communication avoidance exhibited by the Separates reflects an avoidance of the spouse rather than any inherent displeasure with the task per se. There were no differences across the husbands in how much they enjoyed the conversations [$F(4, 49) = .823$], nor in how much they felt their wives enjoyed the conversations [$F(4, 49) = 1.17$], nor for the wives in evaluating their own enjoyment [$F(4, 49) = .219$], nor in evaluating the enjoyment of their husbands [$F(4, 49) = .226$]. In addition, the avoidance of communication cannot be accounted for by differential levels of anxiety across couple types. Fallis, Fitzpatrick, and Friestad (1984) coded six verbal and non-verbal indicators of anxiety during these experimental sessions and found no significant differences among the couple types on these measures.

In casual conversations, Separates speak less to one another than do the other couple types. In the conversations Separates do have, both partners avoid speaking from their own point of view; hence, they are more attentive to their mates. Traditionals, Independents, and Mixed couple types, although they also presume to understand their spouses' frame of reference, tend to speak from their own experience significantly more than the Separates. These couples are less attentive in conversations than the Separates.

The casual interaction style of the Separate/Traditionals is the most unusual of the couple types. Separate/Traditionals are the least attentive of the couples because they frequently discuss their own experiences, thoughts, and feelings. Separate/Traditionals are acquiescent to their spouses and attempt to include the spouse in their conversational references. In addition, the Separate/Traditionals were the least presumptuous of the couples in that they did not mind read nor presume to speak for their spouses. Rather, they indicated by their conversational choices that they did not necessarily feel they understood their spouse's frame of reference.

B. CONFLICT IN MARRIAGE

Olson (1981) has estimated that in the last decade about 10% of the family research has utilized behavioral methods in which the interaction of family members is observed and coded. Most of the observational research conducted on the marital dyad has focused on how couples resolve their differences. The successful resolution of differences is considered necessary for effective marital functioning (Gottman, 1979).

There are three types of communication strategies used in conflict: avoidance, competition, and cooperation (Sillars, 1981). Individuals avoid conflict by using a number of communicative acts designed to move the discussion away from the matter at hand. Topic shifting, denying that any difficulty exists, and speaking abstractly about an issue are a few examples of conflict avoidance. A competitive strategy includes those communicative acts which involve faulting or blaming the partner for the disagreement. A cooperative strategy includes those acts which are designed to seek mutually beneficial outcomes in an interpersonal conflict. Emphasizing commonalities, initiating problem solving, and accepting responsibility are a few examples of cooperative communicative acts (see Sillars, 1980, for a complete description of the coding scheme).

Couples were asked to engage in a role play surrounding issues of disagreement between them (Fitzpatrick, Fallis, & Vance, 1982). Since few Mixed types emerged in this sample, only the communication of the Pure types was analyzed: 12 Traditional couples, 5 Independent couples, and 10 Separate couples comprised this sample. In comparing the three Pure couple types by the proportion of their communication acts coded as avoidance, cooperation, or competitive categories, we find significant differences [$\chi^2(4) = 11.78$, $p < .025$]. The Traditionals use significantly fewer avoidance acts than the other couple types, whereas the Independents use significantly more verbal avoidance acts. These results were surprising because the Separates report that they avoid conflicts with their spouses significantly more than do the other couple types. An examination of the nonverbal behavior of the Separates, however, elucidated these findings. As in the casual interactions, Separates spoke to one another significantly less than did the other Pure couple types. In addition, the Separates were significantly less likely than the other couples to attempt to interrupt one another during conversations. Separates avoided conflict with their spouses by speaking to them less frequently than did the other couples and by exerting care in their conversations not to interrupt the spouse during these discussions.

While the pattern of avoidance usage by Traditionals and Separates falls in line with previous reports of the couples on their communication, the behavioral reliance of the Independents on avoidance acts, contrary to their self-reports, is surprising. A more extensive examination of avoidance, cooperation, and competitive communication sheds light on this matter. Sillars, Pike, Redman, and Jones (1983) recruited 40 couples and gave them packets and instructions for discussions of their marital conflicts. The couples' discussions were audiotaped and the issues that the couples identified as salient were coded. In general, the results support the previous analyses in that the major discriminations among the Pure types were the avoidance messages. While there were no differences among the three Pure types on the use of competitive and cooperative messages, the Traditionals used significantly fewer avoidance messages than the other types. The Separates and the Independents were, however, discriminated by the specific avoidance acts that they did use.

The Independents had fewer instances of outright denial that a conflict existed and fewer noncontinuations of previous topics than expected by chance and more instances of level shifting in these conflict discussions. The Separates had significantly more instances of outright denial and noncontinuity and significantly fewer instances of level shifting than expected by chance during these discussions. When the Separates avoided conflict they did so with blatant communication acts. Separates refused to discuss their interpersonal difficulties with their spouses. The Independents, however, when they used an avoidance strategy, favored more subtle acts such as humor and shifting the level of the conversation.

Although they may be in total disagreement and conflict with a spouse over a highly salient issue, the Separates refuse to acknowledge that any conflict exists. They blatantly deny problems and do what they can conversationally to drop the topic of disagreement. Independents, when they do attempt to avoid discussing a salient problem, use nonhostile humor or try to move the conversation off the track by speaking about the problem in an abstract or intellectual manner or focusing on the process of discussion and not on the content of the problem.

The coding of vocal tones of these couples using Gottman's (1979) system sheds further light on these differential avoidance patterns. When Traditionals openly discussed their conflicts with their spouses, they managed to do so in a neutral tone of voice. As Separates blatantly avoided discussing problems with their spouses, they also maintained a neutral vocal affect. Independents, however, avoided the discussion of a problem yet spoke to their spouses with a distinctly negative tone.

An alternative approach to the study of conflict in marriage is to examine how couples go about gaining compliance from a spouse for a course of action. A number of analyses of compliance gaining techniques have focused on the persuasive techniques which individuals believe they use to gain their own way in relationships (Marwell & Schmitt, 1967; Fitzpatrick & Winke, 1979; Falbo & Peplau, 1980). Rather than rely on what individuals say they do, this study examined what couples actually say to one another in compliance gaining situations.

Broadly speaking, the coding scheme isolates nine major message strategies that individuals use to gain compliance from others. In attempting to persuade the spouse, a speaker can use messages directly focused on the self (me strategy), on the other (you strategy), or on the relationship (us strategy). The speaker can suggest that the force to comply comes from the nature of the action required (activity strategy) or from an enabling agent outside the relationship (external strategy). A speaker may test the waters with nonevaluative questions (information search), simply request compliance (direct), or attempt to dominate the other (power plays). Finally, a speaker may offer a variety of different types of alternatives (compromise) in an attempt to gain compliance.

Fifty-one couples were videotaped as they role played for 30 minutes situations in which each spouse had to gain compliance from the other for competing courses of action (Fitzpatrick et al., 1983). Thirteen Traditional, 10 Separate, 6 Independent, 5 Separate/Traditional, and 17 Mixed couple types participated in this experiment. There were no differences across couple types in self-reports of comfort, naturalness, or typicality of their role play behavior. The Traditionals, however, spent less time in the compliance gaining role play than the other couple types. Traditionals reported that they rarely attempted to gain direct compliance from one another in their typical interactions. Traditionals approached issues as negotiable ones rather than with a preset idea of the specific outcomes they wished to achieve (Fisher & Ury, 1983).

The average frequency counts for the sex by couple type by nine major compliance gaining categories were analyzed by log-linear analysis (Bishop, Feinberg, & Holland, 1975). This analysis indicated that the model specifying the sex by couple type and couple type by communication behavior represented the best fit for the model [likelihood ratio $\chi^2(40) = 46.89$, $p > .21$]. The interaction term of sex by couple type was included in all the models because that is fixed by the sampling plan. No interpretation of this interaction is thus warranted (Bishop et al., 1975; Swafford, 1980). The Freeman–Tukey deviates for the nine communication behaviors within each couple type were examined to see which cells accounted for the major differences in the model. Table VII lists the proportions of compliance gaining strategies used by the couples.

Traditionals use significantly fewer me, you, external, or power strategies when they are attempting to persuade their spouses to agree to a certain course of action or a given activity. Traditionals place their persuasive energy into discussing the advantages or disadvantages of a particular activity and are more likely to ask their spouses directly to comply with them, to search for information from the spouse about his or her wants or needs, and to offer to compromise.

The compliance gaining behavior of the Independents is markedly different

TABLE VII

PROPORTIONS OF NINE COMPLIANCE GAINING STRATEGIES USED BY THE COUPLE TYPES[a]

| Strategies | Couple type | | | | |
	Traditional	Independent	Separate	Separate/Traditional	Mixed
Me	.142(−)**	.185(−)*	.203	.292(+)**	.178(−)**
You	.140(−)**	.198(+)*	.223(+)*	.289(+)**	.149(−)**
Us	.172	.138	.155(−)*	.328(+)**	.207
Activity	.257(+)**	.164(−)*	.193(−)*	.164(−)**	.221(+)*
External	.170(−)*	.170(−)*	.264(+)**	.217	.179(−)*
Search	.196(+)*	.242(+)**	.170(−)*	.176(−)*	.216(+)*
Power	.147(−)*	.239(+)*	.248(+)*	.110(−)**	.257(+)*
Direct	.198(+)*	.182(−)*	.185(−)*	.210(−)*	.225(+)*
Compromise	.203(+)*	.203(+)*	.212(+)*	.127(−)**	.254(+)**

[a]The proportions sum to one across the rows of the table. These indicate the differences among the couple types in their usage of the nine compliance gaining messages. One asterisk signifies that the Freeman–Tukey deviate associated with the frequency in each cell is $p < .05$. A double asterisk indicates $p < .01$. Positive or negative signs in parentheses indicate whether the observed value is more or less, respectively, than that expected by chance.

from that of the Traditionals. Independents seem to demand compliance from their spouses in that they rely on you strategies and power plays when attempting to persuade their mates. Independents are less likely to use me, activity, external, or direct strategies when they are engaged in persuading their spouses. They are, however, likely to offer compromises and to try to search out the needs and wants of their spouse.

Separates attempt to persuade their spouses to follow a given course of action by citing the external reasons why they should comply, by compromising, and by using messages focused on the other rather than on the self. Separates are unlikely to use direct requests or to focus on the attributes of the activity itself. Separates are also less likely to use messages which focus on the requirements of the relationship as a reason for compliance, and they tend not to seek information about the needs or desires of their spouses.

The Separate/Traditionals use messages which stress requests for compliance because of themselves, their spouses, and the relationship. Separate/Traditionals have a unique compliance gaining style in that they do not discuss the activity, they do not use power strategies, they are not direct, and they tend not to ask the spouse about their needs or desires. In addition, these couples are not likely to offer compromises when they attempt to gain compliance from one another.

The Mixed couple types tend to use activity focused messages, power plays, direct requests, and compromises when they attempt to gain compliance from their spouses. These Mixed types are not likely to use me strategies, you strategies, or external strategies when they try to persuade their spouse to follow a given course of action.

The studies reported in this section indicate that the husbands and wives in the various couple types resolve the conflicts that arise in their marriages in substantially different ways. They differ behaviorally, both in their willingness to engage in or to avoid conflicts and in the degree of verbal assertiveness they use in attempting to persuade the spouse to take a particular action.

C. CONTROL IN MARRIAGE

Since the coining of the term the "principle of least interest," which states that the individual in a relationship who has the least interest in maintaining that relationship has the most power (Waller & Hill, 1951, pp. 190–192), the study of power bases, processes, and outcomes has been the focus of interest in much marital research (Cromwell & Olson, 1975). The bases of power are generally considered the resources that an individual brings into an interaction. Outcomes are defined as whose decision prevailed. Of interest in this section are power processes, generally termed control (Folger, 1978; Millar & Rogers, 1976).

Control focuses on the interaction of couples during various stages of discussions, decision making, problem solving, conflict resolution, and crisis management. Conversationally, the control dimension involves who has the right to define, delimit, and direct the actions of the dyad at any given time (Ericson & Rogers, 1973; Millar & Rogers, 1976).

Communication coding schemes (e.g., Mark, 1971; Millar & Rogers, 1976; Sluzki & Beavin, 1977) designed to measure control in conversations begin with the assumption that all messages not only convey content but also make a statement about the nature of the relationship between the conversational participants. Any given message may be categorized into one of three alternatives (Millar & Rogers, 1976). A message that asserts control over the definition of the relationship between the communicators is called a one-up messsage (↑). A message that signals acceptance of the other's control move is called a one-down message (↓). A message that avoids either the assertion or acceptance of control is called a one-across message (→).

Messages, however, cannot be analyzed in isolation. Theoretically, the focus of analysis is the message pair or interact (Raush, Greif, & Nugent, 1979). A message sent by one spouse, for example, yields useful information about the control processes only when one takes into consideration how the other spouse responded to it.

The structural concepts generated by pairing of messages are complementarity, symmetry, and transition. Complementary transactions are those in which the control move of one spouse is completely accepted by the other spouse; for example, a submissive act by one spouse is followed by an assertive act by the other spouse. Symmetrical transactions are those in which interactants exchange the same control move. In competitive symmetry, both partners attempt to assert control while in submissive symmetry both are attempting to be supportive of the other. In neutralized symmetry, control is an issue for neither party. Transitory transactions are those in which at least one spouse attempts to neutralize the issue of control in a given exchange.

In the first study, 43 couples were tape-recorded in their homes as they discussed two issues, one highly salient and one less salient, on which they disagreed (Fitzpatrick, Best, Mabry, & Indvik, 1984). Fourteen couples were categorized as Traditionals, 8 as Independents, 10 as Separates. The remaining 11 were evenly distributed among the Mixed couple types and these 11 were combined for analysis purposes.

Couples' discussion data for the highly salient and the less salient disagreements were reliably coded using the relational communication coding scheme. This scheme codes individual messages and then allows the messages to form the structural concepts of symmetry, complementarity, and transition. A complete description of the coding procedures can be found in Millar and Rogers (1976).

The analysis of the couple types by specific interaction codes was significant for the high-salient [$\chi^2(15) = 44.21, p < .05$] and the low-salient [$\chi^2(15) = 55.17, p < .05$] issue discussion, indicating significant differences among the couple types in both the high- and low-salient conditions. Across all couples, the majority of the interacts used in the conflict discussions were categorized as either complementary or competitively symmetrical. Figure 2 shows that regardless of the importance of the disagreement Independents engaged in more competitively symmetrical exchanges than did the other couple types. Competitively symmetrical exchanges represent one spouse refusing to give in to the control moves of the other spouse. One-up moves are countered with one-up moves. Regardless of the importance of the issue under discussion, the Separates used proportionally fewer competitively symmetrical exchanges than the other couple types. Separates are far less likely to fight for their rights to control a segment of the conversation.

The issue under discussion affected the Traditionals and the Mixed types in their use of competitively symmetrical exchanges. Traditionals decrease their use of competitive symmetry when the disagreement between them is unimportant while the Mixed types marginally increase their use of this exchange pattern when the issue is less salient.

Figure 3 indicates that accepting the control moves of the spouse, or complementarity, reflects a different pattern than does competitive symmetry. Across both conditions, Separates used significantly higher proportions of complementary transactions than did the other couple types. The Independents used the same proportion of complementary exchanges in the highly salient disagreement as

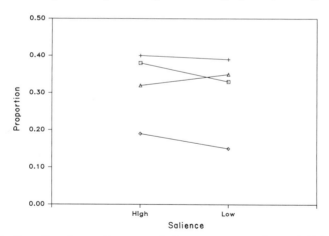

Fig. 2.   Proportion of competitive symmetrical interacts across couple types in high versus low salient conflicts. +—+, Independent; □—□, Traditional; △—△, Mixed; ◇—◇, Separate. [From Fitzpatrick, M. A. Predicting couple's communication from couple's self reports. In R. Bostrom (Ed.), *Communication Yearbook 7* (pp. 41–54). Beverly Hills: Sage, 1983. Reproduced by permission of Sage Publications, Inc.]

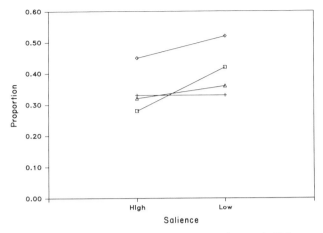

Fig. 3. Proportion of complementary interacts across couple types in high versus low salient conflicts. +—+, Independent; □—□, Traditional; △—△, Mixed; ◇—◇, Separate. [From Fitzpatrick, M. A. Predicting couple's communication from couple's self reports. In R. Bostrom (Ed.), *Communication Yearbook 7* (pp. 41–54). Beverly Hills: Sage, 1983. Reproduced by permission of Sage Publications, Inc.]

when the disagreement was of less concern to them, while the Traditionals and the Mixed increased their use of complementarity when the issue was less important.

In order to extend the results concerning communication and control in the couple types, 40 couples were randomly drawn from a list of volunteers from a church group and a university sample (Williamson, 1983). Eleven Separates, seven Independents, three Traditionals, and the rest Mixed types participated in this study.[2]

There were two discussion conditions. In one, couples discussed their most recent significant conflict. In the other, couples discussed a neutral topic. These tasks were counterbalanced. The tapes were transcribed and the messages were coded with an alternative relational control scheme (Ellis, Fisher, Drecksel, Hoch, & Werbel, 1976). This scheme codes the structural concepts of symmetry, complementarity, and transition but allows for different levels of intensity for "one-up" and "one-down" messages.

The data for the two discussion topics for each couple type were analyzed in two major ways. First, a frequency analysis of the individual messages was computed. This was accomplished by a log-linear analysis for each of the major message types (Bishop *et al.*, 1975). The second was the sequential analysis of

[2]Since few Traditional couples emerged in this sample, there were not enough communication behaviors to complete the lag sequential analyses. Only the first-order interacts for Traditionals are discussed.

the messages. This involved examining the structure of the interaction utilizing Markov and lag sequential analyses. The Markov analysis allowed the test of the three assumptions concerning stationarity, order effects, and homogeneity of these interaction data. The lag sequential analysis allowed probing the data over time (Allison & Liker, 1982).

The Markov analysis indicated that the interaction process for these couples in both the neutral and conflict condition is not time dependent and is best represented as a first-order process. More importantly, two different tests for homogeneity indicated that there are significant differences between the interaction that occurs in the Pure and Mixed couple types. Specifically, the Independents, Separates, and Traditionals are homogeneous within couple type yet exhibit different interaction patterns between types. In addition, all Mixed couples exhibit the same interaction patterns. This indicates that the interaction of the Mixed types can be analyzed together. The Markov tests yield strong support for the assumption that different kinds of Pure couple types communicate in very different ways. In addition, these results indicate that disagreements between couples in basic aspects of their relational definition may be of greater theoretical significance in predicting communication in couples than the content of disagreement.

Control is very much an issue across these couple types. The interaction data indicate that there are no submissive symmetrical interacts ($\Downarrow$) in these couples in which both partners accede to the control moves of the other. In some discussions for some couples, both will move out of a control mode with neutralized symmetrical patterns ($\rightarrow\rightarrow$), but both will not simultaneously submit to the directions of the other. Depending upon the issue under discussion and the couple type discussing it, the Pure types cycle through strong and weak complementarity ($\Updownarrow$; $\Updownarrow$), competitive symmetry ($\Uparrow$), and neutralized symmetry ($\rightarrow\rightarrow$), yet they do not use any transition interacts. Only the Mixed types, and only at the end of a control sequence, use the transition categories. The assertion of control in conversation is important for all of these couples, and few relinquish control to a spouse.

Sections IV, C, 1–4 summarize the results of both the frequency and lag sequential analyses of the neutral and conflict interaction tasks (Williamson, 1983).

1. Traditionals

In the neutral discussion condition, Traditionals use very few intense communication control behaviors. In discussing a neutral topic with the spouse, the Traditionals use virtually no strong one-up or strong one-down messages, favoring instead weak one-up, weak one-down, and one-across behaviors. Traditionals use more one-across messages in the neutral discussion than any other couple type. Sequential interaction patterns of a weakened form of complementarity and neutralized symmetry predominate in the Traditionals' casual discussions with one another.

In the conflict conditions, Traditionals rely more on the intense control moves. They slightly increase their strong one-up messages, particularly statements of personal nonsupport, yet also use more strong one-down statements and attempt to extend ideas brought up by the spouse. Sequential interaction patterns, however, of competitive symmetry and neutralized symmetry predominate in the Traditionals' conflict discussions. No complementary interacts are observed in Traditional communication during a conflict situation.

The results of studies on both communication and control indicate that Traditionals change their interaction patterns with the spouse when moving from a casual conversation to a salient disagreement. Although Traditionals use neutralized symmetrical interacts in both types of discussions, when the issue is serious they also use competitive symmetry, while their neutral discussions are marked by weak complementarity. Traditionals struggle for control when the issue is a serious one but readily yield control to a spouse when the issue is a trivial one.

2. Independents

In both conditions, the Independents use significantly more strong one-up acts than the other couple types. Independents also use the same number of one-across and weak one-up acts in both conditions. The only difference between the overall frequency of communication behaviors of the Independents during the two discussions is that Independents tend to use more weak one-down messages in the neutral condition. The first-order sequential interaction patterns of the Independents remain exactly the same in both conditions. Competitive symmetry, neutralized symmetry, and weakened forms of complementarity predominate in each condition. In both conditions, furthermore, the spouse who initiates the competitive cycle with a strong one-up move ends with a strong one-up move. In conflict, the interactional sequences of the Independents are longer than the sequences in casual conversations. This may indicate more patterning in the Independents' conflict interactions. In conflict, neutralized symmetry moves toward strong one-up acts that end the sequence, and weak complementarity extends out for a number of conversational lags yet ends with a weak one-up move.

Independents engage in competitive symmetrical exchanges in their neutral as well as in their conflict discussions with the spouse. The struggle for control in the Independent relationships occurs regardless of topic. The conflict behavior of the Independents appears more patterned, however, than their neutral discussion behavior. Regardless of the communication act that begins a sequence, the conflict interaction of the Independents ends with one-up moves. The last word for the Independent in conflict is always an attempt to assert control over the spouse.

3. Separates

The Separates utilize virtually no strong one-up acts in the neutral condition and only slightly increase the use of these acts in the conflict condition through the use of more acts of personal nonsupport. In the conflict condition, Separates tend to use more one-across statements. Sequential patterns of weak complementarity predominate in Separates' communication in both the neutral and the conflict condition, as does neutralized symmetry.

In the neutral condition, the Separates' interaction is marked by weak complementarity and neutralized symmetry. In the conflict condition, Separates move to strong complementarity while still maintaining the interaction patterns of weak complementarity and neutralized symmetry. In conflict, the Separates are even more willing to give in to the relational control attempts of a spouse. They are the only couple type marked by patterns of strong complementarity in any discussion condition.

4. Mixed Types

Despite some differences among these couple types in the frequency of some of the individual communication categories, the interaction patterns across the six Mixed types were similar. Both the neutral and conflict discussions of the Mixed couple types show extremely strong patterns of competitive symmetry. Like the Independents, the Mixed types refuse to relinquish control regardless of the issue under discussion.

Neutralized symmetrical interacts end in one-across moves when the Mixed couples are casually discussing a topic. In this way, one spouse attempts to dismiss the issue of control. When they are in conflict, however, these couples end sequences of neutrality with a strong one-up move. In neutral discussions, Mixed couples also exhibit interactional patterns of weak complementarity tending toward one-across messages. In conflict, the weaker forms of competitive symmetry tend to end in one-across messages. At the end of these sequences any weak one-down message a spouse might make is suppressed.

The Mixed types resemble the Independents in that they use strong patterns of competitive symmetry even when the conversation is casual. Mixed types differ from the Independents in two basic patterns. One, although the conversations of the Mixed type couples are intense struggles for relational control, they end with one-across moves. In contrast, the conversations of the Independents end with strong one-up messages. Two, Mixed couples appear even more patterned in their interaction sequences than the Independents, for their interaction can be predicted for substantially longer lags than that of the Independents.

D. SUMMARY OF THE COMMUNICATION BEHAVIOR IN COUPLE TYPES

The couple type predicts not only the self-reports of couples concerning aspects of their relationship but the actual exchange of messages between marital partners. Both the verbal and nonverbal behavior of these couples differs not only in their conflict interactions but also in casual conversations with one another.

Traditionals confront one another over issues of significance in their relationship. Traditionals report that they actually have fewer disagreements than the other couple types. When they do disagree, however, on important matters, they tend not to avoid discussing those issues. Traditionals seem capable of discussing these salient issues in a relatively neutral manner. Traditionals are not as likely to attempt to seek compliance from one another, for they view the negotiation of issues in a broader perspective. When Traditionals do attempt to exert influence on one another, however, they are likely to be very direct in their requests for compliance. One of the major strategies that Traditionals use is to stress the positive characteristics of the actions they want to take. In conflict, the Traditionals struggle for the right to control how an issue is to be defined yet give in to a spouse when the issue is not as important. Traditionals do reference their own thoughts, feelings, and attitudes in casual conversations with their spouses but also make presumptive attributions in conversations about how their spouse may be thinking or feeling. In general, the Traditionals exhibit some flexibility in their communication with one another. They change their style depending on the issue discussed.

In casual conversations with their spouses, Independents also reference their own thoughts, feelings, and ideas and tend to make presumptive attributions about the thoughts and feelings of their mates. In conflict, Independents attempt to avoid discussion of significant issues of disagreement by making jokes or not following through on a conflict topic brought up by a spouse. This avoidance on the verbal level, however, is undercut by the paralinguistic cues of Independents. When discussing issues of significant disagreement, Independents do so in a decidedly negative tone of voice. On the control level of a conversation, whether it be in discussing an issue of significance or insignificance on which Independent couples disagree, these spouses are locked in a struggle to manage the direction of the conversation. One-up messages are matched with one-up messages for long cycles in Independent conversations. In attempting to gain compliance from a spouse, Independents rely on power plays and make demands when they attempt to achieve compliance from their spouses. The patterns of Independent communication suggest that the Independents are conflict habituated and in general fairly assertive in their relationship.

One of the more notable aspects of the Separates' communication is that they speak to one another in both casual and conflict discussions significantly less than do the other couples. Separates also tend to have longer latencies in their conversations and tend to interrupt one another less frequently. In casual conversations Separates do not speak about themselves when they speak to their spouses, although they are likely to make presumptive attributions about the spouse's frame of mind. Separates blatantly avoid conflict with their mates and seem to do so with little affect, either positive or negative. If they try to gain compliance from a spouse for a course of action, Separates rarely simply request it; rather, they are likely to plead external reasons for requesting compliance, such as career or societal pressure, or to use power plays. Separates will accede control to one another with an intensity that matches whatever the spouse has started. If the mate offers a strong one-up message, the Separate is more than likely to respond with a strong one-down move, especially if the partners are discussing a serious issue of disagreement. The patterns of communication used by the Separates, in both casual and conflict interaction, suggest a lack of ease or spontaneity in their communication.

The Mixed couple types are composed of those husbands and wives who define their relationship differently. In many of the self-report studies, the only Mixed couple type that could be discriminated consistently from the other Mixed types was the couple in which the husband was a separate and the wife a traditional. In some of the interaction studies, this Separate/Traditional couple also exhibited differential communication behaviors. Separate/Traditionals appear to have an unusual casual interaction style. Although both partners often speak about their own experience, they do not presume to understand the thoughts, feelings, or attitudes of their spouses. Indeed, the Separate/Traditionals acquiesce to one another in casual conversations. If they are attempting to persuade one another to take a particular course of action, these couples can be quite energetic. Separate/Traditionals use themselves, the spouse, or the relationship as reasons why the mate should comply. Interestingly, these couples are the least likely of the types to compromise or ask the spouse for information about their own position, yet they also do not rely on external reasons, power plays, direct requests, or any inherent attributes of a given activity when asking the spouse to comply. At the control level of a conversation, Separate/Traditionals negotiate control in essentially the same manner as the other Mixed types. On both serious and nonserious issues, Separate/Traditionals do not relinquish control to the spouse.

The casual style of the other Mixed types more closely resembles that of the Traditionals and the Independents. In other words, the Mixed types tend to speak from their own frame of reference, and tend to presume to understand the spouse's point of view. The Mixed types are noted for their attempts to compromise when trying to gain compliance from their mates, although they also use power plays during persuasive attempts. Mixed types use strong patterns of competitive symmetry in both casual and conflict interaction, although they do end sequences of interaction with a one-across message.

V. Conclusions and Future Research

The data across these self-report and behavioral studies support the proposition that the definition that couples hold of their marriage in reference to their levels of autonomy/interdependence, their ideological views on relationships, and their level of openness to conflict expression can predict their normative positions on sex roles, evaluations of their own personality traits, coorientational accuracy, dyadic adjustment, and a variety of verbal and nonverbal behaviors during casual and conflict interactions with their spouses. These findings were obtained across a variety of different samples with a number of different self-report scales and interaction coding schemes.

Across these studies, we see a high correspondence between what these couples say about their relationships and how they interact. Although couples may not be able to predict moment-by-moment interaction patterns, they are capable of estimating the frequency of certain types of communication events that occur between them. The estimates by these individuals of how frequently they attempt to express their disagreements with the spouse and how often they are assertive with the spouse seem to be borne out by the laboratory data. A typological definition yields an estimate of how couples communicate with one another when they disagree, while the behavioral coding of their interaction gives us a richer picture of what couples actually say and do under specific conditons.

Traditional couples share the same conventional value orientation and indicate that they agree with their spouse on most major issues. For these reasons, they probably have few serious conflicts. Traditionals are defined, however, as very expressive yet not very assertive with one another. Behaviorally, we see the limits placed on the expressivity of the Traditionals. First, Traditionals tend not to self-disclose to one another when they know their conversations are being taped. Second, Traditionals do argue with their spouse but only over important issues. When Traditionals say that they do not avoid conflict, they mean that they confront one another over significant matters and they usually do so in private. Finally, Traditionals are not very assertive with one another. When given the opportunity, Traditionals are less likely than the other couples to try to force their positions on their spouses.

Independents share the same value orientation; it is an orientation that stresses individuality, spontaneity, and personal growth. Ideologically, the Independents have agreed to disagree as a basic value of relational life. Since Independents report that they do indeed disagree over many issues, they are likely to have many conflicts. Independent couples see themselves as both willing to engage in conflict and very assertive toward one another. Behaviorally, we see few limits placed on the expressivity of the Independents. Not only did Independents self-disclose as they were being taped, but they also actively engaged in conflict with their mates over both significant and nonsignificant issues. In discussing some major areas of disagreement, Independents do try at times to control their expressivity by using some communication behaviors to change the topic under discussion. Even as they are avoiding a disagreeable topic, however, Independents indicate the tension in the interaction by their negative tone of voice. When given the opportunity to try to gain compliance from their spouses, Independents proved to be very assertive toward one another.

Separate couples define themselves as conflict avoiders who are, however, capable of being assertive with one another. Since the Separates agree with one another on a number of issues, they probably have few conflicts. Behaviorally, the Separates have been shown to avoid self-disclosing to their spouses, to avoid conflict even when they have defined the disagreement as a serious one, and to avoid communicating with the spouse in general. When given the opportunity to try to persuade the spouse to comply with their wishes, the Separates show themselves to be assertive. Although not very open about their feelings, Separates do try to persuade the spouse to go along with them. Often, they rely on external reasons as to why their spouse should comply with their wishes.

The Separate/Traditional couple is one in which the husband tries to avoid conflict while his wife attempts to discuss significant areas of disagreement. He tends to be assertive toward her although she is not equally assertive with him. Despite the fact that this husband is less interdependent than his traditional counterpart, this couple shares a number of the same values and agrees on a number of issues. The Separate/Traditional relationship is often discriminated from other Mixed relationships because of the special nature of this relational combination. The disagreement between this husband and wife on important aspects of their relationship falls within societal norms for appropriate male and female behavior. The members of this couple are not only the most sex typed but also have a very conservative orientation to male and female roles. Consequently, the lack of interdependence by this husband and his attempt to avoid communication with his spouse are compensated for by his traditional, feminine sex typed wife. The burden of expressivity and the responsibility for the marriage is borne by this wife. Separate/Traditionals do not self-disclose to one another in public, although they openly share their opinions. These couples also tend not to assume they understand one another. Both partners attempt to assert influence on one another, but they rely on the self, the other, or even the relationship as reasons why their mate should comply.

The remaining Mixed couple types are composed of couples who disagree on basic aspects of their relationship. While the Independents have agreed to disagree with one another and attempt to preserve a spontaneity in their relationship, the Mixed types have established no such agreement. Like the Independents, the Mixed types struggle for control in conflict interactions. In casual conversations with their spouses, however, the Mixed couples are more likely than the Independents to end a sequence with a message that is neither assertive nor submissive. The research reported in this article suggests that the major defining characteristic of the Mixed types is that they disagree with one another on significant aspects of their relationship. In many of the self-report and behavioral studies, no differences were uncovered among the Mixed types on the variables of interest. For these Mixed types, it is the disagreement between a couple on important defining characteristics of the marriage and not the content of the disagreement that makes a difference in their interaction patterns. Future research needs to explore other potential interaction differences among the Mixed couple types. Of particular interest would be under what conditions specific differences in a couple's ideological values, levels of interdependence, and attitudes toward the expression of conflict differentially affected their communication.

These data raise a variety of other empirical and theoretical issues which should be addressed in future research. One way to organize these issues is to consider how this typology of relationships meets the fundamental goals of science and what steps could be taken within the typology to further these goals of description, prediction, control, and explanation (Reynolds, 1971; Rudner, 1966).

A. DESCRIPTION

Currently, the typology of marital relationships offers an excellent descriptive base for the delineation of types of relationships. The typology categorizes couples by conceptually important dimensions of relationships that go beyond labels frequently used in research. In most research on marital interaction couples are divided into those who are satisfied with their marriage and those who are dissatisfied with their marriage. Some research contrasts couples who are currently married with those seeking counseling and/or those who are divorced. On balance, these distinctions are not well conceptualized, for they tend to group many disparate relationships under the same label. One couple may be highly satisfied with their relationship for a variety of institutional reasons unrelated to the personal relationship that they have evolved with one another, while another couple may be equally satisfied for reasons intrinsic to the relationship (Cuber & Harroff, 1965). Similarly, one couple undergoing marital counseling may be less dysfunctional on many indexes than a couple currently married who has never sought such help. To describe the interaction processes that occur in relationships, better discriminations than those provided by satisfaction or stability distinctions are needed.

The reports of couples concerning how interdependent or companionate they see themselves to be, what they believe constitute important relational values, and how open to conflict they are in their marriage describe the private culture of these relationships in greater detail than other approaches.

B. PREDICTION

The relational typology has done extremely well in predicting a number of attributes of relationships as well as the communication that takes place in relationships. There are two directions that future research should take to increase the predictive ability of the relational typology. The first involves studying developmental change through time and the second involves affiliative messages.

All of the data collected on the relational typology have been cross-sectional. Longitudinal studies should be conducted to examine how the relational types or an individual's definition changes through time. Mixed couple types, for example, could represent couples caught in a specific stage in their relationship during which they are attempting to redefine their relationship. Alternately, the Separates could be Traditional couples who have decreased their level of companionship and sharing and their openness to conflict while maintaining some commitment to a conventional ideology.

To test the change through time of these relational types, couples could be followed over a short time period around what may be hypothesized to be a stress point in the relationship (e.g., the birth of a child). During these times, couples may be expected to begin a process of relational redefinition that would be indicated by changing responses to the dimensions of the RDI.

Change in typal definitions could also be studied by following couples through dating and courtship stages. The typological framework is built on currently married couples and does not define empirically null types. Considering the missing cells, there is no basic relational definition, for example, in which a couple espouses a nonconventional value orientation yet demonstrates little interdependence. Dating couples exhibiting such patterns would be predicted to either evolve into one of the basic definitions or dissolve their relationship. Indeed, research by Huston and colleagues (Cate, Huston, and Nesselroade, 1983) on trajectories of courtship progress indicates that the dimensions of interdependence and conflict do seem to discriminate courting couples. In addition to studying changing relational definitions through time, the predictive ability of the typology could profit from an examination of affiliative messages in couples. Although couples have reported different levels of affection toward one another (Fitzpatrick & Best, 1979) and exhibited different vocal affects in discussing conflicts (Sillars *et al.*, 1983), future research needs to be done in coding the verbal and nonverbal affiliative messages that couples use in communicating with one another (Fitzpatrick & Fallis, 1983). Research has demonstrated that satisfied and dissatisfied couples demonstrate significantly different cycles of positive and negative affiliative behaviors (Gottman, 1979). The typology allows more specific predictions of such positivity and negativity across the couple types. The positivity and negativity of couples toward one another across a variety of verbal and nonverbal indexes is an important manifestation of the type of relationship a couple has evolved.

C. CONTROL

By systematizing a substantial body of information about each couple type, the typology offers the potential for control, for it has obvious clinical and counseling applications. With the RDI and the norms based on the previous samples, couples can be efficiently classified according to their typical modes of functioning. The information concerning agreement or disagreement that couples manifest on the RDI can be fruitfully utilized by clinicians to develop an understanding of couples and the approaches they bring to their marriages.

Caution must be exercised in attempting to use this typology in applied settings. The typology is built from the couple's perspectives on their marriage, considering each of the dimensions in turn. When couples are shown vignettes of the relational types, however, and asked which most closely represents their marriage, the majority incorrectly identify themselves. Those who are incorrect most often chose the Traditional relationship as the one most closely representing their marriage (Williamson, 1983). Because the Traditional relationship has also been judged the ideal relationship by a sample of undergraduate students (Fitzpatrick, 1981), it seems that when asked for overall evaluations of their marriage, couples place themselves in different, idealized clusters than their responses to the specific relational dimensions indicate.

Clinicians and researchers cannot rely on global self-reports or a limited number of indicators to make subtle discriminations among couples. In applied settings, a consideration of a number of relational dimensions would prove fruitful for those interested in helping couples.

D. EXPLANATION

There is little scientific explanation offered by the typology in its current state. The promise of a typology, however, lies in its ability to eventually generate theoretical propositions which can be tested (Reynolds, 1971). The relational typology can be viewed as a useful first step in the construction of a theory of communication in intimate relationships.

In biology, early taxonomic methods used morphological characteristics to type species. Each type became associated with a large bundle of empirically connected traits. The morphological basis gradually began to be replaced with a phylogenetic basis, more deeply embedded in the theory of evolution. The various species are now defined in phylogenetic and genetic terms, although the original morphological characteristics still provide criteria for the assignment of organisms to species. Without the original description and taxonomy of the species, it is possible that the phylogenetic basis could not have emerged (Sneath & Sokal, 1973).

As the firm descriptive base for the classification of species eventually led to more abstract theoretical developments, so, too, it is hoped that a firm descriptive base for the classification of couples will lead to the development of a theory of communication in relationships. Such a theory might consider how the ideological views of couples as well as their established patterns of interdependence constrain their communicative choices, as well as lead to specific levels of dyadic adjustment in relationships. The specifics of relational types can be used to specify multivariate hypotheses (Hage, 1972, pp. 47–50), or techniques of causal modeling could be employed.

The typology may prove to be a heuristic tool in the development of a theory of intimate communication, or it may remain a powerful tool for collating and describing relationships. Whether axioms of communication can emerge from this typological approach remains to be seen. As it currently stands, the relationship typology is a rigorous, nonartifactual way to systematize what we know about communication in individuals' marriages.

ACKNOWLEDGMENT

The preparation of this article was aided substantially by grants to the author from the Wisconsin Alumni Research Foundation.

REFERENCES

Adams, B. N. *The American family: A sociological interpretation.* Chicago: Markham, 1971.
Allison, P. D., & Liker, J. K. Analyzing sequential categorical data on dyadic interaction: A comment on Gottman. *Psychological Bulletin*, 1982, **91**, 393–403.
Bach, G. R., & Wyden, P. *The intimate enemy: How to fight fair in love and marriage.* New York: Morrow, 1969.

Bailey, K. D. Cluster analysis. In D. R. Heise (Ed.), *Sociological methodology*. San Francisco: Jossey-Bass, 1975, 59–128.

Balswick, J. O., & Peek, C. W. The inexpressive male: A tragedy of American society. *Family Coordinator*, 1971, **20,** 363–368.

Bem, S. L. The measurement of psychological androgyny. *Journal of Consulting and Clinical Psychology*, 1974, **42,** 155–162.

Bem, S. L., Martyna, W., & Watson, C. Sex typing and androgyny: Further explorations of the expressive domain. *Journal of Personality and Social Psychology*, 1976, **34,** 1016–1023.

Bernard, J. S. *The future of marriage*. New York: Bantam, 1972.

Bishop, Y. M., Feinberg, S. E., & Holland, P. W. *Discrete multivariate analysis: Theory and practice*. Cambridge, Massachusetts: MIT Press, 1975.

Blashfield, R. K. Mixture model tests of cluster analysis: Accuracy of four agglomerative hierarchical methods. *Psychological Bulletin*, 1976, **83,** 377–388.

Bochner, A. Conceptual frontiers in the study of communication in families: An introduction to the literature. *Human Communication Research*, 1976, **2,** 381–397.

Bochner, A., & Fitzpatrick, M. A. Multivariate analysis of variance: Techniques, models and applications in communication research. In P. Monge & J. Cappella (Eds.), *Multivariate techniques in human communication research*. New York: Academic Press, 1980, 143–174.

Brogan, D., & Kutner, N. G. Measuring sex-role orientation: A normative approach. *Journal of Marriage and the Family*, 1976, **38,** 31–40.

Broverman, I. K., Vogel. S. R., Broverman, D. M., Clarkson, F. E., & Rosenkrantz, P. S. Sex-role stereotypes: A current appraisal. *Journal of Social Issues*, 1972, **28,** 59–78.

Burgess, E. W., & Wallin, P. *Courtship, engagement and marriage*. Chicago: Lippincott, 1953.

Burgess, R. L. Relationships in marriage and the family. In S. Duck & R. Gilmour (Eds.), *Personal relationships: Vol. 1*. New York: Academic Press, 1981.

Cate, R., Huston, T. L., & Nesselroade, J. R. *Premarital relationships: Toward the identification of alternative pathways to marriage*. Unpublished manuscript, Oregon State University, 1983.

Cattell, R. B., Coulter, M. A., & Tsujioka, B. The taxonomic recognition of types and functional emergents. In R. B. Cattell (Ed.), *Handbook of multivariate experimental psychology*. Chicago: Rand McNally, 1966, 285–306.

Clinebell, H. J., & Clinebell, C. H. *The intimate marriage*. New York: Harper & Row, 1970.

Cromwell, R. E., & Olson, D. H. Multidisciplinary perspectives on power. In R. E. Cromwell & D. H. Olson (Eds.), *Power in families*. New York: Wiley, 1975, 15–37.

Cronbach, L. J. Processes affecting scores on ''understanding of others'' and ''assumed similarity.'' *Psychological Bulletin*, 1955, **52,** 177–193.

Cuber, J. F., & Harroff, P. B. *Sex and the significant Americans: A study of sexual behavior among the affluent*. Baltimore: Penguin, 1965.

Ellis, D., Fisher, B., Drecksel, G., Hoch, D., & Werbel, W. *Codebook relational control scheme*. Unpublished manuscript, University of Utah, 1976.

Ericson, P. M., & Rogers, L. E. New procedures for analyzing relational communication. *Family Process*, 1973, **12,** 245–267.

Falbo, T., & Peplau, L. A. Power strategies in intimate relationships. *Journal of Personality and Social Psychology*, 1980, **38,** 618–628.

Fallis, S. I., Fitzpatrick, M. A., & Friestad, M. *Nonverbal anxiety indicators in marital interaction research*. 1984, submitted.

Farber, B. Types of family organization. In A. Rose (Ed.), *Human behavior and social processes*. Boston: Houghton Mifflin, 1962, 285–306.

Fisher, R., & Ury, W. *Getting to yes: Negotiating agreements without giving in*. New York: Penguin, 1983.

Fitzpatrick, M. A. *A typological approach to communication in relationships*. Unpublished PhD dissertation, Temple, 1976.

Fitzpatrick, M. A. A typological approach to communication in relationships. In B. Rubin (Ed.), *Communication yearbook 1*. Rutgers: Transaction Press, 1977.

Fitzpatrick, M. A. A typological approach to enduring relationships: Children as audience to the parental relationships. *Journal of Comparative Family Studies*, 1981, **12**, 81–94.

Fitzpatrick, M. A. Predicting couple's communication from couple's self reports. In R. Bostrom (Ed.), *Communication yearbook 7* (pp. 41–54). Beverly Hills: Sage, 1983.

Fitzpatrick, M. A. A typology of relationships. *Journal of Communication*, 1984, in press. (a)

Fitzpatrick, M. A. Coorientational accuracy in couple types. In L. Larsen & J. White (Eds.), *Interpersonal phenomenology of the family*, 1984, in preparation. (b)

Fitzpatrick, M. A., & Best, P. Dyadic adjustment in traditional, independent, and separate relationships: A validation study. *Communication Monographs*, 1979, **46**, 167–178.

Fitzpatrick, M. A., Best, P., Mabry, E., & Indvik, J. *An integration of two approaches to relational conflict*, 1984, submitted.

Fitzpatrick, M. A., & Fallis, S. *Affiliative behavior in relational types: The development of a coding scheme and initial validation*. Paper presented at the Second International Conference on Language and Social Psychology, Bristol, England, July 1983.

Fitzpatrick, M. A., Fallis, S., & Vance, L. Multifunctional coding of conflict resolution strategies in marital dyads. *Family Relations*, 1982, **31**, 61–70.

Fitzpatrick, M. A., & Indvik, J. *What you see may not be what you have: Communicative accuracy in marital types*. Paper presented at the Speech Communication Association Convention, San Antonio, 1979.

Fitzpatrick, M. A., & Indvik, J. The instrumental and expressive domains of marital communication. *Human Communication Research*, 1982, **8**, 195–213.

Fitzpatrick, M. A., Tenney, B., & Witteman, H. *Compliance-gaining in marital interaction*. Paper presented at the International Communication Association Conference, Dallas, 1983.

Fitzpatrick, M. A., Vance, L., & Witteman, H. Interpersonal communication in the casual interaction of marital partners. *Language and Social Psychology*, 1984, in press.

Fitzpatrick, M. A., & Winke, J. "You always hurt the one you love": Strategies and tactics in interpersonal conflicts. *Communication Quarterly*, 1979, **47**, 3–11.

Fleiss, J. L., & Zubin, J. On the methods and theory of clustering. *Multivariate Behavioral Research*, 1969, **4**, 235–250.

Folger, J. *The communicative indicants of power, dominance and submission*. Unpublished dissertation, University of Wisconsin, 1978.

Gadlin, H. Private lives and public order: A critical view of the history of intimate relations in the United States. In G. Levinger & H. L. Rausch (Eds.), *Close relationships: Perspectives on the meaning of intimacy*. Amherst: University of Massachusetts, 1977, 33–72.

Giffin, K., & Patton, B. R. *Personal communication in human relations*. Columbus, Ohio: Merrill, 1974.

Glick, P., & Norton, A. *Number, timing and duration of marriage and divorce in the United States: June, 1975*. U.S. Bureau of the Census, *Current Population Reports*, Series P-20, No. 297. Washington, D.C.: U.S. Government Printing Office, 1976.

Goodrich, W. Toward a taxonomy of marriage. In J. Marman (Ed.), *Modern psychoanalysis: New directions and perspectives*. New York: Basic Books, 1968.

Gottman, J. M. *Marital interaction: Experimental investigations*. New York: Academic Press, 1979.

Hage, J. *Techniques and problems of theory construction in sociology*. New York: Wiley, 1972.

Haley, J. *Strategies of psychotherapy*. New York: Grune & Stratton, 1963.

Hart, R., & Burks, D. Rhetorical sensitivity and social interaction. *Speech Monographs*, 1972, **39**, 75–91.

Hart, R., Eadie, W., & Carlson, R. *Rhetorical sensitivity and communication competence*. Paper presented at the Annual Convention of the Speech Communication Association, December 1975.

Hempel, C. G. *Aspects of scientific explanation.* New York: Free Press, 1965.

Henry, J. *Pathways to madness.* New York: Vantage Books, 1965.

Hess, R., & Handel, G. *Family worlds.* Chicago: University of Chicago Press, 1959.

Hicks, M. W., & Platt, M. Marital happiness and stability: A review of the research in the sixties. *Journal of Marriage and the Family,* 1970, **32,** 553–574.

Hinde, R. A. *Towards understanding relationships.* New York: Academic Press, 1979.

Hochschild, A. R. A review of sex role research. *American Journal of Sociology,* 1973, **78,** 1011–1029.

Indvik, J. *A coorientational study of perceptual competence in enduring relationships.* Unpublished master's thesis, University of Wisconsin, Milwaukee, 1978.

Indvik, J., & Fitzpatrick, M. A. "If you could read my mind love": Understanding and misunderstanding in the marital dyad. *Family Relations,* 1982, **31,** 43–51.

Jacobson, N. S., & Martin, B. Behavioral marriage therapy: Current status. *Psychological Bulletin,* 1976, **83,** 540–556.

Jourard, S. *The transparent self.* New York: Van Nostrand-Reinhold, 1971.

Kantor, D., & Lehr, W. *Inside the family.* San Francisco: Jossey-Bass, 1975.

Komarovsky, M. *Blue collar marriage.* New York: Random House, 1964.

Lederer, W. J., & Jackson, D. D. *The mirages of marriage.* New York: Norton, 1968.

Levinger, S The embrace of lives: Changing and unchanging. In G. Levinger & H. Raush (Eds.), *Close relationships: Perspectives on the meaning of intimacy.* Amherst: University of Massachusetts, 1977, 1–16.

Lewis, R. A., & Spanier, G. Theorizing about the quality and the stability of marriage. In W. Burr, R. Hill, F. I. Nye, & I. R. Reiss (Eds.), *Contemporary theories about the family: Research based theories* (Vol. 1). New York: Free Press, 1979, 268–295.

Luckey, E. B. Marital satisfaction and congruent self spouse concepts. *Social Forces,* 1960, **39,** 153–157.

Mark, R. A. Coding communication at the relationship level. *Journal of Communication,* 1971, **21,** 221–232.

Marwell, G., & Schmitt, D. R. Dimensions of compliance gaining behavior: An empirical analysis. *Sociometry,* 1967, **30,** 350–364.

Maslow, A. H. *Toward a psychology of being* (2nd ed.). Princeton, New Jersey: Van Nostrand, 1968.

Millar, F., & Rogers, E. A relational approach to interpersonal communication. In G. Miller (Ed.), *Explorations in interpersonal communication.* Beverly Hills: Sage, 1976, 87–103.

Nye, F. I. *Role structure and analysis of the family.* Beverly Hills: Sage, 1976.

Olson, D. H. L. Treating relationships: Trends and overview. In D. H. L. Olson (Ed.), *Treating relationships.* Lake Mills, Iowa: Graphic Publishing, 1976.

Olson, D. H. L. Family typologies: Bridging family research and family therapy. In E. E. Filsinger & R. A. Lewis (Eds.), *Assessing marriage: New behavioral approaches.* Beverly Hills: Sage, 1981, 74–89.

Overall, J. E., & Klett, C. J. *Applied multivariate analysis.* New York: McGraw-Hill, 1972.

Phillips, G. M., & Metzger, N. J. *Intimate communication.* Boston: Allyn & Bacon, 1976.

Rapoport, R., & Rapoport, R. N. *Dual-career families.* Baltimore: Penguin, 1971.

Raush, H. L., Barry, W. A., Hertel, R. K., & Swain, M. A. *Communication, conflict, and marriage.* San Francisco: Jossey-Bass, 1974.

Raush, H. L., Greif, A. C., & Nugent, J. Communication in couples and families. In W. Burr, R. Hill, F. I. Nye, & I. L. Reiss (Eds.), *Contemporary theories about the family: Research based theories* (Vol. 1). New York: Free Press, 1979, 468–492.

Ravich, R., & Wyden, B. *Predictable pairing: The structures of human atoms.* New York: Wyden, 1974.

Rawlings, S. Perspectives on American husbands and wives. *Current Population Reports,* Special Studies, Series P-23, No. 77. Washington, D.C.: U.S. Department of Commerce, 1978.

Reiss, I. Prologue: The family system and its probable future. In I. Reiss (Ed.), *Readings on the family system.* New York: Holt, Rinehart & Winston, 1972, 1–7.

Reynolds, P. D. *A primer in theory construction.* Indianapolis: Bobbs-Merrill, 1971.

Rogers, C. *On becoming a person: A therapist's view of psychotherapy.* Boston: Houghton Mifflin, 1961.

Rossiter, C. M., & Pearce, W. B. *Communicating personally: A theory of interpersonal and human relationships.* Indianapolis: Bobbs-Merrill, 1975.

Rudner, R. S. *Philosophy of social science.* Englewood Cliffs, New Jersey: Prentice-Hall, 1966.

Ryder, R. G. A topography of early marriage. *Family Process,* 1970, **9,** 385–402.

Schaap, C. *Communication and adjustment.* Lisse, Netherlands: Swets & Zeitlinger, B. V., 1982.

Schauble, P. G., & Hill, C. G. A laboratory approach to treatment in marriage counseling: Training in communication skills. *Family Coordinator,* 1976, **25,** 277–284.

Scheffé, H. A method for judging all contrasts in the analysis of variance. *Biometrika,* 1953, **40,** 87–104.

Shorter, E. *The making of the modern family.* New York: Basic Books, 1975.

Shostrom, E., & Kavanaugh, J. *Between men and women: The dynamics of interpersonal relationships.* Los Angeles: Nash, 1971.

Sillars, A. L. Communication and attributions in interpersonal conflict. Unpublished PhD dissertation, University of Wisconsin—Madison, 1980.

Sillars, A. L. Attributions and interpersonal conflict resolution. In J. H. Harvey, W. J. Ickes, & R. F. Kidd (Eds.), *New directions in attribution research* (Vol. 3), Hillsdale, New Jersey: Erlbaum, 1981, 279–305.

Sillars, A. L., Pike, G. R., Redman, K., & Jones, T. S. Communication and conflict in marriage: One style is not satisfying to all. In R. Bostrom (Ed.), *Communication yearbook 7* (pp. 414–431). Beverly Hills: Sage, 1983.

Slater, P. E. *The pursuit of loneliness: American culture at the breaking point.* Boston: Beacon, 1970.

Sluzki, C., & Beavin, J. Symmetry and complementarity: An operational definition and a typology of dyads. In P. Watzlawick & J. Weakland (Eds.), *The interactional view.* New York: Norton, 1977, 71–87.

Sneath, P. H. A., & Sokal, R. R. *Numerical taxonomy: The principles and practice of numerical classification.* San Francisco: Freeman, 1973.

Spanier, G. B. Measuring dyadic adjustment: New scales for assessing the quality of marriage and similar dyads. *Journal of Marriage and the Family,* 1976, **38,** 15–28.

Stevens, J. P. Four methods of analyzing between variation for the K-group MANOVA problem. *Multivariate Behavioral Research,* 1972, **7,** 499–522.

Stewart, J., & D'Angelo, G. *Together: Communicating interpersonally.* Reading, Massachusetts: Addison-Wesley, 1975.

Stiles, W. B. *Manual for a taxonomy of verbal response modes.* Chapel Hill, North Carolina: Institute for Research in Social Science, 1978.

Stuckert, R. P. Role perception and marital satisfaction: A configurational approach. *Marriage and Family Living,* 1963, **25,** 415–419.

Swafford, M. Three parametric techniques for contingency table analysis: A nontechnical commentary. *American Sociological Review,* 1980, **45,** 664–690.

Swenson, C. H. Love: A self-report analysis with college students. *Journal of Individual Psychology,* 1961, **17,** 167–171.

Swenson, C. H. *Manual and test booklet for the Love Scale.* Unpublished manuscript, Purdue University, 1968.

Swenson, C. H., & Gilner, F. Factor analysis of self-report statements of love relationships. *Journal of Individual Psychology*, 1964, **20,** 186–188.

Swenson, C. H., & Gilner, F. *Scale of the feelings and behaviors of love*. Unpublished manuscript, Purdue University, 1973.

Vance, L. E. *Dimensions of autonomy/interdependence reflected in casual marital interaction*. Unpublished master's thesis, University of Wisconsin—Madison, 1981.

Wackman, D. A proposal for a new measure of coorientational accuracy. Paper presented at the Association for Education in Journalism, Berkeley, California, 1969.

Waller, W. W., & Hill, R. *The family: A dynamic interpretation*. New York: Holt, Rinehart & Winston, 1951.

Weiss, R. S. *Marital separation*. New York: Basic Books, 1975.

Williamson, R. *Relational control and communication in marital types*. Unpublished PhD dissertation, University of Wisconsin, 1983.

Wolfe, J. H. Pattern clustering by multivariate mixture analysis. *Multivariate Behavioral Research,* 1970, **5,** 329–350.

Zetterberg, H. *On theory and verification in sociology*. Totowa, New Jersey: Bedminster, 1965.

GROUPS IN EXOTIC ENVIRONMENTS[1]

Albert A. Harrison

DEPARTMENT OF PSYCHOLOGY
UNIVERSITY OF CALIFORNIA, DAVIS
DAVIS, CALIFORNIA

Mary M. Connors

AMES RESEARCH CENTER
NATIONAL AERONAUTICS AND SPACE
ADMINISTRATION
MOFFETT FIELD, CALIFORNIA

[1]Preparation of this report was supported in part by the National Aeronautics and Space Administration (Contract NASA NCA 2-OR-180-803); reproduction in whole or in part is permitted for any purpose of the United States Government. The views presented in this report are those of the authors and do not necessarily reflect the views or policies of the National Aeronautics and Space Administration or any other governmental agency. We are indebted to Faren Akins, Joseph McGrath, and John Vohs who read and commented upon earlier versions of this material.

49

ADVANCES IN EXPERIMENTAL
SOCIAL PSYCHOLOGY, VOL. 18

No longer does any place on earth or in the skies seem permanently immune from human intrusion. Over the past few decades, it has become increasingly possible for groups of people to enter remote, harsh, and potentially lethal environments. The successes of these groups represent in part a triumph of science and engineering, and in part a triumph of the adventurers themselves. In addition to challenging people's physical and technical abilities, such environments challenge their psychological and social abilities as well. In anticipation of a half year with a companion in outer space, Russian cosmonaut Valeriy Ryumin (quoted in Oberg, 1981, p. 213) mused "Didn't O. Henry say that all one needs to effect a murder is to lock two men in a cabin eighteen feet by twenty feet and keep them there for two months?"

I. Introduction

This article focuses on groups of people in polar camps, submarines, space capsules, and other exotic environments that are defined by the characteristics of isolation, confinement, and risk. Although such environments may seem to represent little more than curiosities, in combination they form a considerable aggregate, and their number is increasing over time. Submarines, certain remote bases, and encampments behind enemy lines constitute exotic environments in the military. Supertankers, which never pull into port, some weather stations and observatories, and remote mining and manufacturing facilities are a few civilian settings that are characterized by isolation, confinement, and risk. Every year Antarctica is the site of multitudinous parties. In the past decade, the Russians have made great strides toward the habitation of space (Oberg, 1981), and, after a 6-year hiatus following Skylab and the Apollo–Soyuz rendezvous of 1975, the flight of the space shuttle Columbia reopened the United States' manned space program in 1981.

Personal accounts and case histories of people in exotic environments have been available for decades, but in the early 1960s there was a pronounced rise in attempts to conduct serious research. To a large extent, these projects were sparked by an increase in the number and salience of underseas, polar, and outer space environments. A partial description of some of these environments appears in Table I.

First, underseas environments gained attention when conventional diesel submarines, which could remain submerged for a maximum of 3 days, were replaced with nuclear submarines, which could remain submerged for months. The deployment of these nuclear submarines on extended duration missions prompted a series of studies of the mental health of submariners (Earls, 1969; Serxner, 1969; Weybrew, 1961, 1963; Weybrew & Noddin, 1979a,b). Additional interest in undersea environments was generated in the mid-1960s when underwater research habitats were established, in part to discover new ways to

TABLE I

REPRESENTATIVE EXOTIC ENVIRONMENTS

Environment	Group size	Confinement duration
Antarctica		
Small stations		
(Byrd, Hallett, South Pole)	4–40	90–450 days
Large stations		
(McMurdo)	150–2500	90–450 days
Underwater		
Ben Franklin	6	30 days
Sealab	4–10	Up to 15 days
Tektite	4–5	Up to 60 days
Polaris	140	90 days or more
Trident	143	Over 90 days
Outer space		
U.S.A.		
Mercury	1	Up to 2 days
Gemini	2	Up to 14 days
Apollo	3	Up to 11 days
Skylab	3	Up to 84 days
Space shuttle	7	Up to 30 days
USSR		
Vostok	1	Up to 5 days
Vokshod	2 or 3	Up to 1 day
Soyuz/Salyut	2 or 3	Up to 185 days

exploit ocean resources, and in part to stimulate some of the living conditions expected in outer space (Cunningham, 1977). These latter extremely dangerous vessels have proved useful as natural laboratories for social psychological research (Bakeman & Helmreich, 1975; Radloff, 1973; Radloff & Helmreich, 1968; Vinograd, 1974).

Second, Antarctica loomed important in plans for the International Geophysical Year (1957–1958). Since that time, many nations have sponsored antarctic expeditions. Members of such expeditions have frequently been drawn upon to participate in research aimed at understanding the effects of polar environments on cognitive functioning, performance, mental health, and social behavior (Gunderson, 1963, 1968, 1973; Gunderson & Mahan, 1966; Gunderson & Nelson, 1963, 1965, 1966; Natani & Shurley, 1974; Nelson, 1965; Shurley, Natani, & Sengel, 1977; Taylor, 1969, 1980; White, Taylor, & McCormick, 1983).

The third stimulant has been the human penetration of outer space. The earliest missions (Mercury, Vostok) which involved isolates soon gave way to missions involving dyads (Gemini, Soyuz) and then groups of three (Apollo, Salyut). The present United States space shuttle supports a crew of seven, and will soon facilitate the construction of a permanent orbiting space station. Over the years of space exploration there has been an increase not only in crew size but also in crew heterogeneity and mission duration. The actual and projected consequences of these changes have gained attention from both Americans (Berry, 1973; Bluth, 1979a, 1980, 1981a,b; Connors, Harrison, & Akins, 1984; Haythorn, McGrath, Hollander, Latané, Helmreich, & Radloff, 1972; Helmreich, 1983; Helmreich, Wilhelm, & Runge, 1980; Kanas & Fedderson, 1971; Kubis, 1972; Sells & Gunderson, 1972) and Russians (Ceausu, Miasnikov, & Kozerenko, 1982; Gazenko, Myasniknov, Ioseliani, Kozetenko, & Uskov, 1977; Lebedev, 1980; Leonov & Lebedev, 1975).

In addition to prompting *in situ* studies, the increased prominence of underseas, polar, and outer space environments has encouraged simulation research (Altman, 1973; Altman & Haythorn, 1965, 1967a,b; Altman, Taylor, & Wheeler, 1971; Brady, Bigelow, Emurian, & Williams, 1974; Brady & Emurian, 1979, 1983; Emurian, Emurian, Bigelow, & Brady, 1976; Emurian, Emurian, & Brady, 1982; Haythorn, 1970, 1973; Haythorn & Altman 1967a,b; Haythorn, Altman, & Myers, 1966; Smith & Haythorn, 1972). Both field and simulation studies vary greatly in terms of scientific rigor. For example, much of the available information on astronauts and cosmonauts is of the anecdotal or case history variety, and simulation research includes simple feasibility studies undertaken by government contractors as well as carefully designed experiments (Vinograd, 1974). We agree with S. Smith (1969) who, in a review of research on isolated and confined groups through the mid-1960s, noted that whereas many studies are limited by the lack of control groups or give little assurance that important extraneous variables have been controlled, they remain of interest, particularly for purposes of generating hypotheses and suggesting directions for additional research.

Our article proceeds in Section I with a consideration of some of the ways exotic environments differ from everyday environments and some commonly reported reactions to these differences. We then consider the topics of group composition, group structure, and group dynamics. Finally, we note that whereas there has been an expansion in the number and variety of such environments, the accrual of hard behavioral data has not kept pace. We identify possible reasons for this state of affairs, and suggest some possible remedies.

A. DISCONTINUITIES WITH EVERYDAY LIFE

Compared to everyday environments, exotic environments are marked by severe climates, danger, limited facilities and supplies, isolation from family and friends, and enforced interaction with others. As we shall see, the available literature suggests certain common reactions to this constellation of environmental attributes.

1. Physical Climate

Typically, exotic environments are characterized by harsh physical climates. The world outdoors is hostile to, if not totally unsupportive of, life. Neither the depths of the ocean nor the void of space sustains unprotected life for more than minutes, and death may not take appreciably longer in the extreme frigidity of the polar regions. Although protective clothing and life support gear may make it possible to "sally forth" from the habitat, such equipment is often uncomfortable and cumbersome and makes the simplest tasks difficult and exhausting (Sloan, 1979). The world outside may be essentially unchanging (as in the case of underseas and outer space locations) or given to dramatic seasonal shifts (as in the case of polar locations) which can themselves have an adverse impact on people (Bohlen, 1979; Myers & Davies, 1978).

Although the habitat is engineered to support life, it does not necessarily do so with comfort. Propulsion and life support systems may take substantial room and generate a high level of ambient noise. Temperature and humidity can be difficult to control. Imperfect filtration systems coupled with limited hygienic facilities often make the atmosphere aromatically unpleasant. Finally, if the habitat is effectively sealed off from the outside or is located in an unchanging external environment, it may lack temporal cues (*Zeitgebers*) that normally help regulate behavior.

2. Danger

Exotic environments are typically dangerous environments. Life depends on the integrity of the habitat (which cannot be engineered to withstand all contingencies), on the absence of fire and other disasters, and on the proper performance of complex and sometimes temperamental propulsion and life support systems. Coping with any emergency that does arise may require an abrupt shift from a state of lethargy induced by a monotonous daily routine to the highest level of mental and physical activity (Natani, 1980). Furthermore, exotic environments can be dangerous to enter or leave; for example, safe decompression can require 6 days to return to the surface from 600 feet undersea (Radloff, 1973).

3. Limited Facilities and Supplies

Exotic environments are characterized by primitive living conditions. Although these environments may contain highly advanced scientific equipment, the living quarters themselves tend to be cramped and austere. Supplies are necessarily limited, and may be of poor quality. In many cases, people within exotic environments seek compensation in the form of high-quality foodstuffs (S. Smith, 1969; Smith & Haythorn, 1972). However, meals that include fresh foods are unusual, and in some cases hot food cannot be prepared. Garments are typically simple and may have to be worn, without cleaning, for weeks at a time. Medical care may be primitive, with specialized medical care impossible to get. Normally common luxuries are likely to be scarce, prohibitively expensive, or unobtainable at any price.

4. Social Privations

Exotic environments pose two sets of social frustrations. The first are those associated with isolation from the larger community, including reduction in social support from family and friends, the loss of many customary social comparison points, and a constriction in the range of social roles. The second type of frustrations are those associated with confinement with a relatively small number of other individuals. These include accelerated acquaintance processes, limited personal space, an inability to escape companions who have annoying traits or mannerisms, and an inability to keep conflicting individuals apart.

B. COMMONLY REPORTED REACTIONS

Observation of people in underseas, polar, and space environments suggests certain common emotional and behavioral correlates. These correlates, which include intellectual impairment, motivational decline, somatic complaints, and changes in mood, are not invariably reported, nor, when reported, are they necessarily pronounced. When reported, these correlates may be more illusory than real, because the absence of a control group or normative data makes base rates difficult or impossible to ascertain. Nonetheless, these correlates have been reported with sufficient regularity that they are not easily ignored.

Typically, explanations of these correlates are based upon environmental causation theories. That is, as a result of exotic conditions, capable and well-adjusted people begin to show signs of maladjustment (Whelan, 1976). However, there is also evidence supporting alternative environmental drift explanations which state that exotic environments attract people who already have psychological liabilities (Kehoe & Abbott, 1975; Law, 1960; Parkin, 1974).

1. Intellectual Impairment

Decreased alertness, a loss of concentration, memory failure, and perceptual distortions have been reported among submariners (Earls, 1969; Serxner, 1968) and polar explorers (Mullin, 1960; W. M. Smith, 1966; Taylor, 1980). In one recent study, White et al., (1983) compared the performances of Scott Base personnel and a control group located at Trentham, New Zealand. For both groups, information processing time at a mental paper-folding task increased over successive administrations, but the rate of increase was greater for the antarctic group, thus confirming anecdotal reports of a mental "slowing down" that occurs in Antarctica. Decreased attention and concentration have been a source of concern to cosmonauts (Leonov & Lebedev, 1975; Oberg, 1981), and, reportedly, astronauts have forgotten to execute procedures that had been rehearsed for months or even years (Bluth, 1979a, 1980, 1981a,b; Cunningham, 1977; McNeal & Bluth, 1981). Recently, Helmreich (1983) has proposed that exotic environments may promote mindlessness, a passive form of information processing which involves the use of previously formed cognitive categories rather than the drawing of new distinctions (Langer, 1978). Mindlessness could prove particularly maladaptive under emergency conditions, or when problems arise that demand creative solutions.

2. Motivational Decline

Prolonged stays in exotic environments can eventuate in motivational decline. As polar missions progress, participants are likely to show increased fatigue, inertia, and apathy (Mullin, 1960; Gunderson & Nelson, 1963; Natani & Shurley, 1974). Among polar scientists and support personnel, feelings of satisfaction with one's work and a sense of group accomplishments have declined (Gunderson & Nelson, 1963), and feelings of helplessness and worthlessness have increased (Pope & Rogers, 1968). The intially high motivation of submariners sometimes decreases as the mission continues (Rohrer, 1961), and a "diminution of vitality" has been reported within a small group confined to a fallout shelter (Cleveland, Boyd, Sheer, & Reitman, 1963). Declining or vacillating motivation has also been reported among explorers in space (Bluth, 1980, 1981a,b; Cooper, 1976, 1979; Cunningham, 1977; Oberg, 1981). However, the shifts in motivation are difficult to interpret because of the lack of comparable data from nonisolated, nonconfined groups.

3. Somatic Complaints

Sleep disturbances, sometimes serious, have been noted among members of polar expeditions (Law, 1960; Mullin, 1960; Gunderson & Nelson, 1963; Natani & Shurley, 1974), among submariners (Beare, Bondi, Biersner, & Naitor, 1981; Earls, 1969; Detre, Weybrew, & Kupfer, 1972), among space travelers (Cunningham, 1977; Oberg, 1981; McNeal & Bluth, 1981), and among participants in simulation studies (Brady & Emurian, 1983). Headaches, nose and chest colds, and digestive problems such as upset stomachs and constipation are common within an entire range of exotic environments (Cunningham, 1977; Earls, 1969; Hammes & Osborne, 1965; Oberg, 1981; McNeal & Bluth, 1981; Natani & Shurley, 1974). Although the incidence of such problems seems high, there is again a lack of high-quality base rate data.

4. Changes in Mood

Although some observers report either no deterioration in mood and morale over time (Radloff & Helmreich, 1968) or continuing deterioration (Gunderson & Mahan, 1966; Gunderson & Nelson, 1966), others suggest more complex temporal dynamics (Vinograd, 1974). Three sequential stages have been identified by Rohrer (1961). The first, heightened anxiety, is brought about by a recognition of the dangers inherent in the situation. The second stage, depression, emerges as the group settles into its daily routine. The third stage, anticipation, is characterized by boisterousness and aggressiveness and occurs as the end of the mission approaches. Our reading of the literature, most of which consists of uncontrolled longitudinal studies, suggests that shifts from one stage to another depend more on the relative than on the absolute passage of time; typically, mood and morale reach nadir somewhere between the one-half and two-thirds mark of the mission (see Vinograd, 1974). More recently, Lebedev (1980) has proposed a seven-stage model that includes both preconfinement and postconfinement reactions.

C. SUMMARY AND DIRECTIONS FOR FUTURE RESEARCH

Events during the 1950s and 1960s sparked interest in conducting serious behavioral research within environments characterized by harsh climates, danger, limited facilities and supplies, and social frustrations. Although many environments have such characteristics, virtually all of the available field research to date has involved groups in submarines, polar, and outer space settings. Groups in many other exotic locations have been ignored. Groups in offshore and arctic oil drilling stations, certain remote pumping stations (for example, along the California aqueduct), and supertankers are examples, as are groups of astronomers, archaeologists, wildlife biologists, fire fighters, and forest rangers who spend substantial uninterrupted time in jungle, desert, and other wilderness areas. The historical events of the 1950s and 1960s focused attention on a very limited range of exotic environments and an obvious task which now confronts us is to expand this range to include additional military, commercial, scientific, and recreational locations.

Commonly reported within the environments studied have been intellectual impairment, motivational decline, somatic dysfunction, and variations in mood. However, these generally deleterious effects have not been universally reported and, when reported, appear to differ in form and intensity. It is extremely difficult to assess the significance of these effects, because only rarely are there comparable data from control groups. Certainly, future efforts to understand the effects of isolation and confinement would profit by vigorous attempts to gain baseline data.

Differences in reported reactions to exotic environments may reflect differences among observers or differences among populations, but they may also reflect important ways in which exotic environments differ from one another. Only a few systematic attempts have been made to take environmental differences into account. Sells has compared a number of different exotic environments to outer space environments in an attempt to determine the best analogs of spaceflight (Sells, 1966) and has also developed a general taxonomy of exotic settings (Sells, 1973). Abstracts compiled under the direction of Vinograd (1974) organize studies not only by general type of environment but also by selected variables such as length of confinement and size of group. Different exotic environments have nonidentical constellations of attributes and may therefore produce nonidentical constellations of effects. At this time, it seems worthwhile to apply multivariate procedures to link specific environmental attributes to their specific behavioral effects. Finally, we need to find ways to ameliorate specific adverse effects.

II. Group Composition

A prominent theme in the literature is the selection of group members who are compatible with one another in the sense that each person show qualities and acts in ways that others deem appropriate under the prevailing conditions. The general rule seems to be that the more numerous the socially desirable traits that group members show the better they will get along with one another and get the job done. After enumerating many of the sterling qualities prescribed for saturation divers (intellectual brilliance, courage, perseverance, social adaptability, and humility), Biersner (1984) concluded that "those who are most suited to work at watery depths should be able to walk on the surface as well."

A. DEMOGRAPHIC FACTORS

For the most part, groups studied in exotic environments have been composed of relatively young white males. It is likely that in the future, groups in such environments will be more heterogeneous in gender, age, race, and other demographic characteristics. Law and custom now encourage social diversity in terms of gender, age, and ethnicity. Furthermore, as more such settings are generated, and as they come to require larger numbers of inhabitants, we will have to look beyond a narrow segment of the population merely to staff them adequately.

1. Gender

Changing social conditions are encouraging the integration of women into many exotic environments. Women have visited remote polar regions, worked in underwater habitats, and participated in fallout shelter studies, and, in 1963, cosmonaut Valentina Tereshkova was one of the first people to enter outer space. By 1984, desegregation of the military was proceeding apace, women were appearing in increased numbers at polar research stations, at least eight women astronauts had entered training, and two more women, one Russian and one American, had flown in space.

Thus far, there has been little or nothing in the way of systematic field studies of all female or mixed gender groups; however, two recent laboratory studies of isolated and confined groups have included gender as a variable. One of these studies found that the same conditions that sparked conflict within all-male groups and between the groups and the experimenters did not provoke comparable responses from an all-female group (Brady & Emurian, 1983). Another study found that the introduction of a female into an all-male group produced destabilizing effects and raised questions of hierarchy and leadership that did not appear when a male newcomer was introduced (Brady & Emurian, 1983).

2. Age and Seniority

Inhabitants of exotic environments have ranged in age from their late teens to their early 50s or beyond. Provided that one is fit to withstand environmental rigors and to make positive contributions to the group, being older than one's coadventurers does not seem to raise serious problems. Observations of groups in underseas environments suggest that mature group members may serve as parent surrogates to younger group members and thereby serve a useful leadership function (Radloff & Helmreich, 1968). Simulation research by Smith and Haythorn (1972) also suggests that maturity is of value. Dyads and triads composed of navy men had either junior leaders, who had been in the service a few days or weeks longer than the other group members, or senior leaders, who had been in the service considerably longer and who had higher ratings than the other group members. Compared to the junior-led groups, senior-led groups showed less hostility over the 21 days of confinement. Smith and Haythorn suggest that the senior leaders were more readily accepted in recognition of their greater experience and maturity.

3. Race or Ethnicity

Since the United States' armed forces were desegregated in 1948, we would expect at least some Navy submarine crews and antarctic support units to be ethnically mixed. Polar research groups are often of international composition: there was a joint United States–USSR space mission during 1975, and, during the late 1970s, the Russians began a guest cosmonaut program involving international crews. In 1983, the United States sent its first black astronaut aloft, and there was a United States–European Space Agency Mission. Despite many such opportunities, ethnic or racial mix has not been a major variable in studies of group composition.

B. SOCIALLY DESIRABLE TRAITS

Competence, emotional stability, and social versatility are among the traits that have gained the attention of observers of isolated and confined groups. The general thesis is that whereas such traits may be of value in any setting, they are of particular value under conditions of isolation, confinement, and risk.

1. Competence and Motivation

Groups in exotic environments typically have a strong task or mission orientation. They also recognize that, under dangerous conditions, incompetence, disinterest, or carelessness can pose a threat to life and limb. Thus, strenuous efforts are undertaken to ensure that each group member has the ability and motivation to get his or her job done.

The available evidence suggests that actual or perceived deficits in ability or motivation generate adverse peer reaction. High task motivation has accom-

panied "good years" in Antarctica (Gunderson & Nelson, 1965), and both personal motivation and perceptions of the group's achievements have been found to relate to satisfaction with antarctic assignments (Shears & Gunderson, 1966). Studies undertaken by the Alaskan Air Command suggest that marginal task performance is correlated with poor adjustment and dissatisfaction (Vinograd, 1974), and Day (1969) has described the adverse reactions generated by crew members in the days of sail who failed to fulfill their shipboard duties.

Helmreich and associates have identified achievement motivation as a potentially important factor in isolated and confined groups (Helmreich, 1983; Helmreich et al., 1980). They suggest that the classical conception of achievement motivation as a preference for engaging in achievement-related activities subsumes three independent factors: work orientation, which refers to motivation to work hard because work is intrinsically satisfying; mastery orientation, which refers to motivation to continually improve one's own best performance; and competition, which refers to motivation to outperform others. Helmreich notes that experiments in everyday environments suggest that people who show high work and mastery needs but low competitiveness perform best. Noncompetitive achievers may be of particular value in exotic environments where a premium is placed upon accomplishment, but where competition might increase a level of conflict that is already high due to environmentally imposed stress.

2. Emotional Stability

A highly emotional individual who is a mere annoyance under everyday conditions could be downright dangerous in an exotic environment. Antarctic personnel place high premium on having calm, even-tempered, emotionally mature companions (Doll & Gunderson, 1971; Law, 1969; Taylor, 1969), as do astronauts and cosmonauts (Cunningham, 1977; Jones & Annes, 1983; Leonov & Lebedev, 1975; Oberg, 1981).

Anecdotal evidence suggests that minor maladjustment may be fairly common in exotic environments. Mild depression is reported frequently among polar parties (Gunderson & Nelson, 1963; Law, 1960; Nardini, Herman, & Rasmussen, 1962; Natani & Shurley, 1974), submarine crews (Earls, 1969; Serxner, 1968), and space crews (Bluth 1979a, 1981a,b; Cunningham, 1977; Oberg, 1981). The Smith and Haythorn (1972) study, which involved relatively prolonged preisolation and postisolation observations, found that the isolation and confinement experience was associated with psychological stress and anxiety. However, it also appears that the incidence of major psychiatric disorders in polar parties (Gunderson, 1963, 1968) and aboard submarines (Serxner, 1968; Weybrew & Noddin, 1979a,b) is not particularly high. Submariners tend to show better mental health than do sailors on surface ships (Weybrew & Noddin, 1979b), and both types of sailors appear to compare favorably with the population at large.

A relative lack of serious psychiatric problems in confined groups may reflect intensive personnel selection procedures and also an absence of the "secondary gains" (exemption from unpleasant duties, and so forth) that so often reinforce aberrant behaviors in everyday environments. Because mentally disturbed individuals pose a serious threat to the welfare of a group situated in an exotic environment, deviant tendencies may be suppressed by extremely strong and effective forms of social control. Still another possibility is that the relatively low incidence of mental illness is artifactual: psychiatric disorders may be under-reported because they can reflect poorly on the sponsoring agency and on the leader of the group.

3. Social Versatility

Group members who are socially versatile, in the sense that they appropriately regulate the quantity and type of their interactions with others, are expected to be more compatible than members who are either consistently introverted or extroverted or members whose social behaviors are drawn from a narrow behavioral repertoire. Group members who can regulate their affiliative tendencies depending upon the situation and other people's needs and moods may be more valuable than group members who are so introverted as to provide little stimulation for others or group members who attempt to force themselves upon others.

Also notable in the present context are androgynous individuals who are versatile in the sense that they have the capacities for both task-oriented and socioemotionally oriented activities (Helmreich, 1983; Helmreich et al., 1980). Group members who are exclusively task oriented could hurt other people's feelings and exacerbate tensions that are already high due to the stresses imposed by isolation and confinement. Group members who are exclusively socioemotionally oriented may be perceived as falling short of the high performance standards set by so many isolated and confined groups. Group members who are capable of both types of activities can help the group reach its objectives while contributing to the overall quality of social life. Thus far, hypotheses to the effect that socially versatile people form compatible groups remain to be tested under conditions of isolation, confinement, and risk.

C. INTERPERSONAL COMPLEMENTARITY

Also affecting compatibility are those attributes and behaviors whose effects can be gauged only while considering the attributes and behaviors of others within the group. Haythorn, Altman, and associates have developed the well-known theme that different people's needs may fit together in such a way as to affect overall compatibility within a group (Altman, 1973; Haythorn, 1970,

1973). This particular version of need compatibility theory involves three patterns of needs: congruent needs, which are similar or identical needs such that the satisfaction of one person's need results in the satisfaction of the other person's need (for example, affiliation and affiliation); complementary needs, which are different appearing needs such that the satisfaction of one person's need also satisfies the other person's need (for example, dominance and submission); and competitive needs, such that the satisfaction of one person's need results in the aggravation of the other person's need (for example, dominance and dominance).

In one set of carefully designed simulation studies, isolated and confined subjects were paired to form dyads varying in compatibility along dimensions of dogmatism, dominance, need for achievement, and need for affiliation (Altman, 1973; Altman & Haythorn, 1965, 1967a,b; Haythorn, 1970, 1973; Haythorn & Altman, 1967a,b; Haythorn et al., 1966). Group members' abilities to adapt to one another during 8 days of confinement were found to be a direct function of need compatibility. All of the isolated dyads who experienced serious difficulties had been composed in such a way as to be incompatible. Isolation and confinement appeared to exacerbate the effects of need complementarity, since none of the nonisolated control dyads composed of individuals with incompatible needs showed similar problems of adjustment. In another study, dyads and triads were composed of subjects who were computer matched to be either maximally compatible or maximally incompatible along dimensions of control, affection, and need for achievement (Smith & Haythorn, 1972). During the 21-day confinement period, the members of the hypothetically compatible groups adapted better to one another than did the members of the incompatible groups. Rather than expressing hostility toward one another, members of the compatible groups directed their irritation toward the environment.

The studies also found that need incompatibility boosted performance under experimental conditions. If we assume that isolation and confinement yield a low level of arousal and that incompatible needs are arousing, this finding can be interpreted in terms of the inverted U relationship between arousal and performance (e.g., Haythorn, 1973). That is, incompatible needs may produce an arousal increment that moves the overall level from the zone of underarousal toward the zone of optimality. An important implication is that need incompatibility coupled with other sources of arousal (for example, an emergency situation) could impair performance by boosting overall arousal into the zone of overarousal.

D. GROUP SIZE AND COMPATIBILITY

The available evidence suggests that relatively large groups fare better than relatively small groups (S. Smith, 1969). A comparison of isolated individuals with isolated groups reveals that, when companions are present, dramatic sensory deprivation effects are eliminated (S. Smith, 1969). The evidence from field studies is sketchy, and complicated by the fact that relatively large groups may be stationed at comfortable main bases, whereas relatively small groups may be quartered in more primitive settings. However, Doll and Gunderson (1971) found that antarctic groups consisting of 8–10 members reported less compatibility and more hostility than groups consisting of 20–30 members, and Nardini *et al.* (1962) found more emotional and interpersonal problems at stations composed of 15–40 men than at still larger antarctic bases. The Georgia fallout shelter studies, which imposed very Spartan conditions on unselected but unusually large groups, had very low defection rates (Hammes, Ahearn, & Keith, 1965; Hammes & Osborne, 1965; Hammes & Watson, 1965).

Group size was an independent variable in the Smith and Haythorn (1972) 21-day simulation study. Results showed that when there was at least 200 cubic feet per person, members of triads adapted to one another better than did members of dyads. In comparison to members of two-man groups, members of three-man groups reported less stress and anxiety and complained less as the study progressed. The chief advantage of having two partners rather than one appeared to be the enrichment of the social environment. However, the advantage of this enrichment was negated or reversed when the amount of space per person was reduced to 70 cubic feet.

E. SUMMARY AND DIRECTIONS FOR FUTURE RESEARCH

The problem of assembling people who are able to relate to one another and remain productive was selected as a major research topic early in the study of exotic environments, and has received substantial emphasis ever since. Among the factors considered have been demographic variables; individual differences in ability, motivation, and personality; and the interplay of different people's personal qualities. This heavy emphasis upon studying members' characteristics has diverted attention from other means for understanding group behavior, such as through examining social structure or the allocation of rewards.

Demographic variables include gender, age, and race or ethnicity. These variables should gain salience as affirmative action values and the need to recruit large numbers of people force recruiters to search beyond the population of young white males. At present, there are very few hard data regarding the effects of varying the gender, age, and race or ethnicity of the people who comprise exotic environment groups. Furthermore, it is unlikely that such data will be available in useful form until substantial numbers of women and minorities begin appearing in exotic environments. The dynamics involved when one or two token individuals gain membership are so different from the dynamics involved when true integration is achieved that it is essentially impossible to generalize from the former situation to the latter.

Actual differences among people of differing gender, age, and race or ethnicity may be of secondary importance to the differences as perceived or imagined by other group members, some of whom may be prejudiced. For example, as reported by Cunningham (1977) and Oberg (1981), some astronauts and cosmonauts have expressed the view that women are basically unsuited for space (Cunningham, 1977; Oberg, 1981), and we have heard negativity toward women expressed by antarctic hands. However, it is worth noting that some of the conditions associated with prejudice reduction (Amir, 1969) are also associated with exotic environments. First, despite different backgrounds, group members may show considerable attitudinal similarity on a number of issues, such as polar biology, space exploration, or national defense. Second, in some (but by no means all) exotic environments, prejudice-enhancing status differentials may be minimal. Additionally, a high degree of interdependence and a strong need to cooperate in pursuit of common goals are likely to be present.

Only a relatively small number of abilities and traits have been studied. With the exception of need achievement and androgyny (which have not been examined under conditions of isolation and confinement) the range has not expanded appreciably since the 1960s. Furthermore, some of the abilities and traits that have been studied remain narrowly defined. For example, competence is typically defined in terms of technical skills. But, because group success may be equally, or more, dependent upon interpersonal skills, it would be useful to supplement studies of task competence with studies of socioemotional competence (Haythorn et al., 1972; Natani, 1980). Similarly, our understanding of need complementarity involves relatively few dimensions. It also might be useful to supplement studies of complementary needs with studies of complementary skills and abilities (Haythorn, 1970, 1973; Haythorn et al.. 1972). Also of potential use are the personality characteristics associated with navy divers (Biersner, 1984; Biersner & LaRocco, 1983).

Finally, while there is evidence of a positive correlation between group size and social compatibility, this relationship is neither well documented nor well understood. With the exception of the Smith and Haythorn study, few or no studies have involved systematically varying group size while holding other factors constant, and the Smith and Haythorn study was limited to a comparison of dyads and triads. A basic remaining research question is identifying the form of the relationship between group size and social compatibility.

III.   Social Structure

Structural concepts such as positions, roles, and norms refer to variables outside of the individual which constrain behavior and impose coordination among the members of a group. Social structure gains importance as social entities become large (Perrow, 1979). It is necessary to be a little less "choosey" when trying to assemble a large group, and it may be prohibitively expensive to accord each member of a large group the same level of training that can be offered to a very limited number of people. Furthermore, at some point, the problem of coordinating individuals is supplemented by the problem of coordinating groups. The remedy, suggests Perrow (1979), is to rely on external, structural controls to achieve a high degree of mutually accommodative behavior and to coordinate task-related activities.

A. POWER STRUCTURES

Social power refers to the influence that one person is capable of exerting on another. Power structures refer to the distribution of power to regulate individual conduct and coordinate activities within and between groups. The hierarchical or pyramidal form of organization, which typifies so many contemporary governmental and private organizations, also typifies both military and civilian groups in submarine, polar, and outer space environments. Although several writers have questioned the universal applicability of the hierarchical model in exotic environments (Helmreich, 1983; Helmreich et al., 1980; Nelson, 1965, 1973) there have been few or no systematic attempts to explore alternatives.

B. WORK ROLES

As in everyday life, people in exotic environments are assigned specific tasks. Contemporary United States' antarctic bases, for example, typically involve three types of roles: administrative, scientific, and support. Officers and crews of supertankers have well-defined roles; except for cargo capacity, supertankers are sufficiently similar to each other that a sailor on one can immediately assume a comparable role on another (Mostert, 1975). Future United States' spaceflights are likely to involve five types of roles: flight operations, scientific–investigative, environmental support, personnel support (Kanas & Fedderson, 1971), and production (Helmreich, 1983). A common practice is to spell out each role in elaborate detail.

Role overload can easily occur in exotic environments (Helmreich, Wilhelm, Tanner, Sieber, & Burgenbach, 1979). Tasks that are relatively easy to perform under normal conditions may consume great time and energy underwater or under conditions of zero gravity in space (Cooper, 1976; Sloan, 1979). Yet, the fact that an exotic environment can accommodate just so many people coupled with pressures to accomplish as much as possible in the course of a mission encourages the assignment of heavy combinations of roles (Helmreich *et al.*, 1979). People who accept multiple roles may not be fully aware of the demands that each role will place on their energy and time (Helmreich *et al.*, 1979). Even if aware of potential overburdening, people may nonetheless accept multiple roles because of a high need to achieve, a "can do" self-image, real or imagined career considerations, or a lack of assertiveness to decline. Usual attempts to adjust to overload, such as by omitting certain tasks, backlogging chores, and increasing tolerance for errors, involve inefficiency, a decrement in performance, and wear and tear on the organism (Miller, 1960).

C. PRESCRIBED AND EMERGENT ROLES

As noted in an observational study of a group on an antarctic trek, prescribed or formal roles may be supplemented or even replaced by informal roles that emerge in the course of social interaction (W. M. Smith, 1966). There are at least three reasons that this might happen (Katz & Kahn, 1978). First, prescribed roles may not make adequate allowance for the satisfaction of personal needs. For example, emotional well being may require some behavioral variety which could be inhibited by strict adherence to prescribed roles. Second, prescribed roles are based on anticipated conditions. In exotic environments, people may encounter unanticipated conditions that necessitate developing new ways of coping. Third, roles are prescribed on the basis of conditions that are in effect at a given point in time. A change in conditions may make certain roles obsolete, force the rapid development of new roles, or force one person to perform another person's duties.

D. SUMMARY AND DIRECTIONS FOR FUTURE RESEARCH

Groups in exotic environments, like other groups, can be analyzed in terms of positions, roles, and other structural concepts. Although structural concepts are beginning to appear in discussions of groups in exotic environments, there is very little in the way of actual research: one study of role overload in the course of a simulated space mission (Helmreich *et al.*, 1979), and one of emergent norms in an antarctic setting (W. M. Smith, 1966). Macroscopic analyses based upon structural concepts are likely to gain favor as it becomes necessary to deal with increasingly large groups, for example, as the small teams that operate contemporary space vehicles give way to complex organizations aboard permanent orbiting space stations.

At present, the hierarchical power structure is the prevalent organizational form in exotic environments. As others have noted, although this model works well for military personnel, it may not work well for scientific personnel who staff underseas research vessels and polar stations and who comprise an ever larger percentage of the astronaut corps, nor for the production workers who presently staff offshore oil rigs and who will eventually work in outer space (Helmreich, 1983). Alternatives to the hierarchical model include the community democracy model and the labor relations model as discussed by Whyte (1967). Under the community democracy model, authority is deemphasized. Each group member participates in a decision-making process that is organized along one-person/one-vote or discussion-to-consensus procedures. The labor relations model openly combines hierarchical and participative elements. Under this latter model, one group has the authority to make and enforce decisions while the other group has the right to be heard. Each group takes the other side seriously, and bargaining and negotiation are important. The nature of the personnel, the type of work performed, and group goals are among the variables that should influence the choice or evolution of a power structure. Both Russians and Americans, for example, report success with procedures whereby decisions regarding the mission itself are made under the hierarchical model, and decisions regarding off-duty activities, living arrangements, and the like are made following democratic procedures (Leonov & Lebedev, 1975; Nelson, 1973).

Other questions surround the optimal degree of role specification. Although there is a clear need to prevent confusion regarding the distribution of authority and tasks, there is also a need to provide people with the latitude to respond to changing conditions and to satisfy their personal needs. Sharply defined roles can discourage functional as well as dysfunctional behaviors [for example, Leonov & Lebedev (1975) report that two members of a polar exploration party refused to help put out a fire because it "wasn't part of their job"], generate reactance, and, as Katz and Kahn (1978) remind us, place a lid on the maximum level of contributions that people are willing to make. We thus need a better understanding of the optimal balance between prescribed and discretionary role components given different populations, goals, and scenarios. Finally, we need to know more about the causes and consequences of role overload in exotic environments.

IV. Group Dynamics

In this section we turn to a discussion of some of the processes that go on within exotic environment groups and between such groups and other social entities.

A. LEADERSHIP

Leadership can be construed as a social influence process whereby leaders organize, direct, and coordinate followers (Hollander, 1978). As one might expect, the most common prescription is for strong leadership postures. Weak leadership has been blamed for failures in the course of certain polar expeditions (Leonov & Lebedev, 1975), and for increased friction and decreased morale in the course of fallout shelter confinement (Hammes *et al.*, 1965; Hammes & Osborne, 1965; Hammes & Watson, 1965). A finding of the Smith and Haythorn (1972) study was that groups whose leaders were relatively senior in terms of military rating adapted better to confinement than did groups whose leaders lacked seniority. The benefits of senior leadership were greater for triads than dyads, and for groups that had been composed to be incompatible than for groups that had been composed to be compatible.

Almost all of the discussions of leadership in exotic environments follow in the leadership-trait tradition that is based upon the premise that individuals who possess specified qualities or traits are better leaders than people who do not. For example, Leonov and Lebedev's (1975) analysis of leadership focuses almost exclusively on dispositional differences between effective and ineffective leaders, and Kubis (1972) describes the effective space crew commander as competent, goal oriented, and interpersonally sensitive. Conspicuously absent is discussion of the various contingency factors that distinguish contemporary leadership theories.

B. COHESIVENESS

Cohesiveness refers to the degree of solidarity or unity within a group. The causes of cohesiveness are typically sought in the costs and rewards of group membership. Costs provide the focal point for the cognitive dissonance analysis, which suggests that the adverse conditions and suffering associated with group membership generate dissonance, which is subsequently reduced by increased attractiveness of the group (Aronson & Mills, 1959). There often is a high price attached to membership in an exotic environment group. After meeting selection standards much higher than those set for surface sailors, submariners must complete about 18 months of difficult lessons and dangerous exercises; final acceptance depends upon passing an exam administered by an already qualified crew (Earls, 1969). Following a rigorous selection process, candidates for outer space undergo an array of discomforts and stresses (Cunningham, 1977; Oberg, 1981; Wolfe, 1979). Illustrative is an exercise intended to yield cosmonauts who perform well under stress. After jumping from an airplane, the candidate must "pick" a lock or complete some other task before the parachute may be opened (Oberg, 1981).

The rewards of group membership provide the focal antecedents for theorists such as Cartwright (1968), who has defined cohesiveness as the sum of the satisfactions which membership accords the members of the group. Despite the associated hardships, many exotic environments do provide substantial rewards (Law, 1960; Natani & Shurley, 1974). These include (1) an opportunity to become totally immersed in one's work, (2) an opportunity to be judged on the basis of performance rather than on the basis of extraneous factors such as age or race, (3) a socially uncomplicated existence, (4) a financially uncomplicated existence, (5) an opportunity to build self-esteem, and (6) adventure. Additionally, people who venture forth may gain considerable social recognition. Illustrative is the immense popularity of the early polar explorers, and, more recently, of the first people into outer space.

According to one analysis, as exotic environments become safer and more numerous, both the costs of participation (deprivation, crowding, danger, and so forth) and the rewards of participation (enhanced self-esteem, social recognition, and so forth) are likely to decrease (Helmreich et al., 1980; Radloff & Helmreich, 1968). The analysis also suggests that for the next few years, at least, costs will decrease at a slower rate than rewards, and that the increasing difference in favor of costs will adversely affect morale. For example, compared to the space capsules of the 1960s, the space capsules of today are large, well-equipped habitats with superior supplies and facilities. But do these improvements compensate for the lesser degree of recognition accorded newcomers to space?

Several writers have noted that the manipulation of reward structures may be an effective means for increasing cohesiveness. One proposal, based on the famous camp studies of Sherif, Harvey, White, Hood, and Sherif (1961), is to promote superordinate goals, that is, structure the situation so that group members perceive certain outcomes as of overriding importance and attainable only through cooperative activity (Haythorn et al., 1972; Haythorn, 1973; Helmreich, 1983). More recently, Brady and associates have manipulated reward structures within triads isolated and confined within a laboratory (Brady & Emurian, 1979, 1983). In one study, subjects in a cooperative condition, which required that all three subjects earn access to the group area before it became available for use by anyone, showed greater cohesiveness than did subjects in triads whose members could gain access to the group area individually (Emurian et al., 1976; Emurian, Emurian, & Brady, 1978). Other studies found higher cohesiveness under "appetitive" reinforcement schedules, where subjects cooperated to gain rewards, than under "aversive" reinforcement schedules which required them to act in concert to prevent losses (Emurian et al., 1982).

Although cohesive groups also may be efficient and effective, the relationship between cohesiveness and performance is not simple. First, cohesiveness is likely to be associated with a high level of performance only when group norms support production-related activities and high group achievement. Second, good performance can be a cause of, rather than a result of, cohesiveness.

By means of closed circuit television, Bakeman and Helmreich (1975) conducted longitudinal studies of several crews aboard Tektite. Behavioral measures of cohesiveness and performance were obtained at the beginning and at the end of each mission. Cross-lagged correlational analyses were performed. The correlation between cohesiveness early in the mission and performance later in the mission was negligible, but the correlation between performance early in the mission and cohesiveness later on was substantial. This pattern of results suggests that, in this study, variations in performance led to variations in cohesiveness, rather than the other way around.

C. PERSONAL SPACE

Since the mid-1960s, social psychologists have devoted increasing attention to the general topic of personal space, that is, the use of physical areas, markers, and props to regulate and define social interaction. Although there is an extensive general literature in this area, most studies have involved airport waiting rooms, libraries, college dorms, cafeterias, and the like that are occupied by their typical users for brief periods of time and characterized by easy egress. Exotic environments, on the other hand, are typically occupied by the same users for prolonged periods and are not easily escaped. Hence, there may be greater pressures on exotic environments' occupants to regulate their distance from one another, and their ability to do so effectively may have greater implications for group success.

A simulation study by Altman, Haythorn, and colleagues involved experimental dyads who were kept isolated and confined on an around the clock basis, and control dyads who spent normal working hours in a comparable confinement chamber but who were otherwise free to come and go. Within each condition, dyads had been composed in such a way as to vary in terms of need compatibility. In general, isolation and confinement led to increasing withdrawal and increased territorial behaviors. Territoriality appeared first with respect to relatively fixed personal areas (beds, workspaces) and then extended to movable objects (chairs). However, withdrawal and territoriality depended in part on the type of needs that conflicted; incompatibility in terms of ''sociocentric'' needs which were directly associated with interpersonal matters led to increased withdrawal and territoriality, whereas incompatibility on other needs did not (Altman & Haythorn, 1965, 1967a,b; Haythorn & Altman, 1967a,b; Haythorn et al., 1966). Another study showed that nonaborting dyads, that is, those who remained intact for the full period of confinement, showed different patterns of behavior than did aborting dyads, that is, those who sought early release. Members of the nonaborting dyads established norms regarding interpersonal distance early on. Members of the aborting dyads initially showed very low levels of interest in interpersonal distance norms, but frantically tried to establish such norms as their interpersonal relations deteriorated. These findings suggest that the early but slow evolution of norms regarding personal space serves an adaptive function for isolated and confined groups (Altman *et al.*, 1971; Taylor, Wheeler, & Altman, 1968; Taylor, Altman, Wheeler, & Kushner, 1969).

D. COMPLIANCE AND CONFORMITY

Social pressure intended to encourage adherence to group norms promotes common goals and helps achieve coordination within the group. In exotic environments, group members who fail to do their jobs may endanger everyone else. Because of this, pressures to comply or conform may be very strong within isolated and confined groups. A common mechanism of social control, rejection of the deviant, can have a damaging effect on the deviant as well as rob the group of the services of one of its members. Ostracism of members of isolated and confined groups has been associated with the "long eye" syndrome which involves loss of energy, poor appetite, weeping, repetitive behaviors, suspiciousness, and, on occasion, active hallucinations (Haggard, 1964). Some of the adaptive mechanisms that are available in everyday environments to mitigate the effects of ostracism are unavailable in exotic environments. The group cannot replace the deviant; the deviant cannot retreat from the group.

The social stability that is brought about as a result of pressures to comply with the demands of people who are in positions of authority or by pressures to adhere to group norms may be bought at the expense of creativity and effective problem solving. For example, as Helmreich (1983) has noted, groups in exotic environments are subject to some of the conditions associated with "groupthink" (Janis, 1971), a state of affairs in which efforts to maintain group harmony undermine critical thought and the quality of decisions. These conditions include (1) a preoccupation with maintaining amiability, (2) highly limited communication with outsiders, and (3) decision making under threat.

Subservience may prove maladaptive in emergency situations where leaders attempt to exert their authority to gain prompt acceptance of a course of action. Despite their expertise, leaders may lack the information necessary to make a wise decision or fail to process the available information correctly. The necessary inputs might be available from other members of the group. A number of aviation accidents or near accidents have been identified as avoidable if knowledgeable crew members had drawn the pilot's attention to unnoticed conditions or had openly questioned the pilot's instructions (Murphy, 1980; Yanowitch, 1977).

E. CONFLICT

A common hypothesis is that exotic environments heighten interpersonal conflict (Berry, 1973; Haythorn *et al.*, 1972; Kanas & Fedderson, 1971; Leonov

& Lebedev, 1975; S. Smith, 1969; Vinograd, 1974). This conflict may occur within the group, or it may involve the group and an interfacing agency. The worst case scenario is that heavy stress coupled with the absence of customary safety valves (for example, the option of leaving the group) can escalate minor disputes to that point where the group will collapse.

1. Intragroup Conflicts

Anger and touchiness have been noted among members of polar expeditions (Law, 1960; Gunderson & Nelson, 1963; Natani & Shurley, 1974), submariners (Rohrer, 1961), fallout shelter confinees (Cleveland *et al.*, 1963), participants in laboratory simulations of exotic environments (Haythorn, 1970, 1973; Vinograd, 1974), and space crews (Cooper, 1976, 1979; Oberg, 1981; Stockton & Wilford, 1981). On occasion, battle lines have been drawn between occupants of different types of roles (Doll & Gunderson, 1971; Natani & Shurley, 1974). Although these conflicts usually involve minor issues, such as musical selections (Doll & Gunderson, 1971), they occasionally have major consequences. In one incident, crew members of an antarctic research vessel threw a 2-years' collection of biological specimens overboard to make room for more beverages in the freezer (Bluth, 1981a). The fact that certain roles are perceived as more important than others also may contribute to conflict. Some of the military test pilots who initiated the conquest of space have expressed hostility toward the ''hyphenated astronauts'' who joined to play scientific and other nonpiloting roles (Cunningham, 1977; Wolfe, 1979). Although anger, hostility, and touchiness occur in exotic environments, it is not clear that the relative frequency or intensity is substantially greater than in nonexotic settings.

People within exotic environments have themselves evolved behavior patterns which help to contain conflicts. One such pattern is to avoid competitive games such as cards which could give rise to escalating disagreements. Another pattern is to deliberately avoid emotional communications: Flinn, Monroe, Cramer, and Hagen (1961) found that most of the activities of subjects within a space simulator fell within the neutral categories of Bales' Interaction Process Analysis. Other safety mechanisms include social withdrawal or cocooning and a redirection of hostility toward things or toward outsiders (Haythorn, 1970, 1973; S. Smith, 1969; Smith & Haythorn, 1972).

2. Conflicts with External Parties

Most exotic environments are not totally isolated, because there are telecommunications links with the outside. For example, most military units are linked with command centers by some form of radioteletype, polar explorers communicate with home by means of amateur radio, and the Russians have tried two-way television contact with their cosmonauts.

Considerable anecdotal evidence suggests that relationships with external authorities can assume a negative cast. Early simulation studies found that isolated and confined groups directed hostility toward outsiders (Kanas & Fedderson, 1971; Kubis, 1972; S. Smith, 1969; Vinograd, 1974). Negative attitudes toward monitors were expressed during a 1-year simulation study conducted in the USSR (Lenov & Lebedev, 1975). Cunningham (1977) reports low-grade but continuing conflict between the members of the first (nonlunar) Apollo crew and mission control. More recently, a sharp exchange was reported between mission control and the crew of the Columbia (Stockton & Wilford, 1981), and it is believed that the members of a Salyut crew deliberately broke off communications with Earth for about a day (Oberg, 1981).

A well-publicized incident involved the crew of the third manned Skylab mission (Skylab IV) and mission control (Bluth, 1979b; Cooper, 1976, 1979). The relations between the two groups were strained for the first half of the mission. The climax came when the crew took a day off from its scheduled work activities. Whether or not this constituted a "rebellion" (Cooper, 1979) or a "necessary readjustment" (Bluth, 1979b), the incident does need to be well understood. Several explanations have been offered. First, the crew's time may have been overprogrammed (Bluth, 1979b; Cooper, 1976, 1979; Weick, 1977). Whereas the preprogrammed work pace might have been maintained for a brief period of time, it could not be maintained for a period of 3 months. Second, early during the mission, the commander decided against advising Earth that motion sickness had occurred, a decision sharply criticized by mission control. Thus, the friction may have reflected competing interpretations as to who was in charge— the commander on the spot, or external authorities. Third, imperfections and shortcomings in supplies generated frustrations which also may have contributed to the conflict (Cooper, 1976). Finally, Emurian et al. (1982) note that the members of the Skylab crew behaved similarly to "aversively" controlled subjects in their simulation experiments.

In general, communications links with family and friends are presented as beneficial, and the common prescription is to encourage frequent and extended personal communication (e.g., Berry, 1973; Oberg, 1981). The Russians have taken particular pains to help cosmonauts retain contact with family and friends; in addition, Soviet control centers have arranged for them to communicate with entertainers, scientists, politicians, and other "interesting personalities" (Oberg, 1981). Russian research suggests that as mission length increases, so do cosmonauts' attempts to initiate and extend communication with outsiders (Gazenko et al., 1977). However, there are also some potential disadvantages associated with external communication. First, some individuals may attempt to monopolize the communications system and thereby provoke conflicts with other group members (McGuire & Tolchin, 1969). Second, the failure of someone at home to communicate on schedule can cause fear and worry (Pope & Rogers, 1968).

Third, anxious people may remain "glued to the telephone" and neglect other duties (Radloff & Helmreich, 1968). Fourth, the messages received by isolates tend to be bland and unsatisfying (Law, 1960; McGuire & Tolchin, 1961; Earls, 1969). Fifth, the pleasure of a conversation with significant others may be offset by postcommunication letdown or depression (McGuire & Tolchin, 1961). Finally, not all conversations are pleasant.

Departure for an exotic environment is likely to place stress upon the participants' families (Hunter & Nice, 1978; Jones & Annes, 1983). Submariners' wives are likely to be more anxious and depressed (Beckman, Marsella, & Finney, 1979; Pearlman, 1970) and more susceptible to physical illness (Snyder, 1978) during husband-absent than during husband-present periods. During the period of separation, spouses left behind may be taxed to their limits as they assume responsibility for all family decisions, take over the budget, perform their absent spouses' parenting role, and so forth. Harbored resentments may surface during reunion. To the extent that the spouse left at home adjusts to new responsibility and autonomy, there may be an awkward period of reassimilation.

F. SUMMARY AND DIRECTIONS FOR FUTURE RESEARCH

Studies of groups in exotic environments have touched upon many of the topics that are traditional within the area of group dynamics. Progress has varied tremendously from area to area. Although leadership is perennially popular in discussions of groups in exotic environments, it is perhaps the substantive area that is in the greatest state of disrepair. For years, even elementary textbooks in social psychology have emphasized that leadership reflects a complex interplay of factors associated with leaders, followers, and situations or tasks. Discussions of leadership in exotic environments remain dominated by the leadership trait approach. One prime candidate for advancing research on leadership is Fiedler's (1967, 1971, 1978) contingency theory, which states that leadership style (task versus socioemotional orientation) and situational favorability (acceptance by the group, goal structure and clarity, and leader power) combine to determine leadership effectiveness. Other candidates include the Vroom and Yetton (1973) normative model and Hersey and Blanchard's (1982) theory of situational leadership.

The past decade *has* seen advances in the study of cohesiveness. Early theorizing that cohesiveness is affected by the distribution of rewards has been substantiated by the continuing research program of Brady, Emurian, and associates (Brady & Emurian, 1979, 1983). Among other things, these investigators have shown that cooperative reward structures promote cohesiveness under conditions of isolation and confinement, and that cooperation to gain rewards promotes greater cohesiveness than cooperation to prevent loss. Helmreich and

Bakeman's (1975) field study suggests that a high level of group performance contributes to the cohesiveness of isolated and confined groups. Personal space is of interest because physical space is likely to be precious within exotic environments, and because easy withdrawal from such environments is seldom an option. The early studies of Altman, Haythorn, Taylor, and colleagues [reviewed by Altman (1973) and Haythorn (1973)] remain preeminent. Their findings that isolation and confinement promote both social withdrawal and territorial behaviors, that group composition affects withdrawal and territoriality, and that the early evolution of social norms helps groups adjust to isolation and confinement provide a strong empirical base for future efforts.

In general, it is hypothesized that isolation and confinement are associated with strong pressures to conform, harsh treatment of deviants, and strong emotional reactions to rejection. Experimental verification is lacking. Recently, a case has been made for studying the effects of isolation and confinement on decision making. These studies, too, remain to be carried out. Also of interest is gaining a better understanding of the optimal balance between conformity and independence in different exotic settings.

Finally, there remain many issues surrounding social conflict. First of all, it is difficult to assess the frequency and severity of conflict within isolated and confined groups. The assumption seems to be that even low levels of conflict are significant when they occur in exotic environments. The same level of negative affect that would be unremarkable within a college dormitory or within a middle-class home provokes extended discussion when it occurs in Antarctica or outer space. Conflict may be underreported because aggressive behavior is socially undesirable, leaders might not want to create the impression that they ''can't control their men,'' and belligerents might not want to be identified as unfit for future assignments. Alternatively, retired adventurers may exaggerate reports of conflict to amuse and delight their listeners. How may conflict be minimized or curtailed? Both Kubis (1972) and Berry (1973) have advocated direct training in human relations, and Shurley et al. (1977) propose that role rotation can help eliminate conflict along occupational lines through encouraging mutual problem solving, promoting the breakdown of invidious status distinctions, and underscoring the importance of each role within the group. Among the remedies proposed for conflict with external parties are rigorous selection procedures intended to weed out individuals with deviant tendencies, limiting time in isolation, and using veterans of the isolation experience as support personnel (Natani, 1980). Once again, the past decade has seen new hypotheses outpace data collection. Finally, we suggest studying the reactions of families of people who venture into exotic environments, for family reactions may impact adjustment to exotic environments as well as readjustment to the home community following completion of a mission.

V. Toward a Revitalization of Research

Events of the 1950s and early 1960s spurred research on groups in exotic environments, but these efforts have long since peaked and declined. Numerous simulation studies were undertaken during the early years of space travel as various aerospace firms sought to ascertain the feasibility of various vehicle designs, and it was during the late 1960s that the Altman, Haythorn, and Smith studies were concluded. In the early 1970s, Brady and Emurian and their associates resumed realistic simulation research. Studies of personal adjustment and social dynamics in Antarctica began in the early 1960s, and reached the high water mark within the decade. Scientific studies of submariners, aquanauts, and divers continue to appear (Biersner, 1984; Biersner & LaRocco, 1983; Weybrew & Noddin, 1979a,b), but tend to focus on individual rather than on social dynamics.

Although the past 10 years or so have seen nomothetic data collection slow to a trickle, new case histories and new hypotheses have appeared. Observations of astronauts and cosmonauts are on the increase, at least by insightful journalists and historians. Several authors have identified variables that may have important implications for groups in exotic environments, but the associated empirical research (if any) has involved people in everyday settings. We suspect that attitudinal, technical, and conceptual barriers need to be surmounted before exotic environment research will regain a firm empirical footing.

A. ATTITUDINAL BARRIERS

There are many reasons that sponsors and members of groups in exotic environments might disfavor psychological research. The fact that such groups typically accomplish their missions may promote the view that psychological research is not really necessary. Many individuals, with backgrounds in the "hard" sciences, engineering, and the military, may see "soft" sciences such as psychology as useless. (Psychologists may have contributed to this impression by failing to develop a good track record.) Inquisitive researchers may threaten the group (perhaps by reporting grumbling, incompetent performances, deviant activities, or other behaviors that could lower the group's prestige) or specific individuals (for example, by reporting information that disqualifies an individual from coveted future missions). There may be feelings within the group that certain kinds of questions (for example, who dislikes whom) are best left unasked, and fears that real or imagined weaknesses will be paraded before the public. Moreover, when this type of research has implications for national security, secrecy may be deemed appropriate.

We believe that a better understanding of groups in exotic environments is both necessary and desirable. Even though very few groups have been destroyed by psychological or social factors, it is better to gain an understanding of such factors now than to wait until after catastrophe strikes (Helmreich, 1983). Furthermore, settling for survival conditions is settling for too little. The same conditions that can be endured during a brief visit to a place like outer space may not be endured during a more protracted stay (Cooper, 1976). As more and more people spend greater amounts of time in exotic environments, increased attention needs to be directed toward improving the overall quality of life and accommodating higher level needs such as for belongingness, esteem, and self-actualization (Connors et al., 1984; Haythorn et al., 1972; Helmreich, 1983). Group members need guarantees that if psychological research is supported it will be conducted in ways which will minimize embarassment and distress, and that there is at least some chance that useful results will be obtained. The selling of psychology and the fostering of rapport are prerequisites for furthering psychology in many settings (Helmreich, 1975, 1983), and exotic environments provide no exception to this rule.

B. TECHNICAL BARRIERS

Empirical studies of groups in exotic environments fall into one of two categories: simulation studies and field studies. Simulation studies typically involve a high degree of experimental control and quantitative dependent measures. However, simulations often exclude salient aspects of isolation, confinement, deprivation, and risk, and involve, as subjects, the kinds of people who volunteer for experiments rather than the kinds of people who volunteer for exotic environments. To some extent, adequate funding can help simulation researchers minimize some of these problems. Although it may be difficult to obtain funding for studies concerned exclusively with psychological and social variables, it may be possible to "piggyback" such research onto high-priority projects that address medical and human engineering problems.

Field studies involve authentic settings and people, but logistical problems typically make it difficult to gain direct access to the group or to preserve methodological rigor. For example, there are severe limitations on the number of people who can be accommodated within an exotic environment, and, compared to the cook or the electronics technician, the psychologist is an obvious candidate for omission. In such cases, researchers may be able to find volunteer assistants among the group membership, but volunteers all too often have limited research skills. Indirect surveillance by such means as postmission interviews and questionnaires; the scrutiny of diaries, logs, and organizational records; and post hoc site visits to explore unobtrusive records of the group's stay can be feasible and inexpensive alternatives (Nelson, 1973). Unfortunately, indirect observation may encourage selective reporting or force people to rely on very imperfect impressions and memories. Remote surveillance is another possibility. When remote surveillance gear can be accommodated within the environment, the action may take place out of the gear's range, the quality of transmissions may be poor, and malfunctions are all too common (Radloff & Helmreich, 1968; Radloff, 1973).

Although formidable, technical barriers are not insurmountable, and certain developments augur well for future research. Today's exotic environments accommodate more people than yesterday's; perhaps there is even room for a psychologist who is willing to perform two roles (e.g., psychologist–cook), one of which is of acknowledged benefit to the group. Increased miniaturization and other improvements in the field of electronics have improved the feasibility of remote surveillance. The sheer number of opportunities for field studies is on the increase, simply because the number of exotic settings is increasing.

C. CONCEPTUAL BARRIERS

A certain amount of intellectual inertia needs to be overcome to revitalize exotic environment research. Many of the parameters for such research were established 20 years ago. We now need to recognize that the conditions that prevailed in the exotic environments of yesterday do not necessarily prevail today. The groups that are entering some such environments are greater in size and heterogeneity, and, in some cases, the periods of isolation and confinement are longer. Furthermore, the environments themselves are changing. The exotic habitats of the 1960s (such as Nautilus submarines and Gemini spacecraft) have been replaced (e.g., by Trident submarines and space shuttles), and, as we noted in Section I, new, or at least unstudied, environments have appeared. All of these developments raise new questions and suggest new ways to proceed.

Moreover, the behavioral and social sciences have changed substantially since the research pattern initially was set. Many variables and concepts have been introduced into the literature that are of potential value, but which remain to be studied in the context of isolated and confined groups. Examples of these (such as androgyny, "groupthink," and mindlessness) have appeared throughout this article. Also, developments in social and organizational psychology have made it possible to approach perennially popular topics in new ways. The best example of this is leadership. Future studies of leadership in exotic environments can extend beyond leadership traits and include situational variables which are a component of every contemporary theoretical approach.

Additionally, consideration needs to be given to developing broad range theories which are capable of integrating results and guiding future research. Two theoretical models, the ecological and the behavioral, have already entered the literature. Open systems theory may also be of use.

1. The Ecological Model

The ecological model, as explicated by Altman (1973), arose in large part from simulation studies of isolated and confined groups. This model posits a fundamental interdependence among group members and between group members and their environments, and is concerned with both the processes and products of social interaction. Interpersonal processes are viewed as occurring at several levels including verbal communication, nonverbal communication through interpersonal distancing, and the manipulation of environmental props. Acts that occur at different levels can substitute for one another, compensate for one another, or have additive effects. The products of social interaction include level of intimacy, degree of interpersonal accommodation, interpersonal attraction, conflict, and the like.

The ecological model encompasses an unusually wide array of variables; in many cases, a variable can serve as either a cause or an effect. For example, the environment can both determine and reflect interpersonal dynamics. Salient as independent variables are environmental variables, structural variables, personality variables, and interpersonal variables such as attitudinal similarities and need compatibility. Salient as dependent variables are those that reflect the course and quality of relations within the group. Here the key concept is social penetration, which refers to the processes through which people get to know and accommodate one another and the degree to which acquaintance and accommodation have occurred. Penetration proceeds along two dimensions: a breadth dimension, defined by the number of different facets or components of the self that enter in, and a depth dimension, defined by the extent to which the knowledge shared is detailed and intimate.

Although spawned largely by studies of isolated and confined groups, the ecological model is in fact a general theory of interpersonal dynamics and is quite suitable for comparing interpersonal relations under normal and exotic conditions. In the everyday world, social penetration is a gradual process that involves some balance among breadth and depth dimensions. Because each person has many social ties, problems in one relationship can be assuaged by turning to other relationships. Isolation and confinement speed the pace of social penetration and reduce tolerance for interpersonal errors (Altman, 1973).

2. The Behavioral Model

Drawing on the work of Skinner (1969), Brady and associates have developed a highly behavioristic approach to the study of isolated and confined groups

(Brady *et al.*, 1974; Brady & Emurian, 1979, 1983). The basic building block is Skinner's three-term contingency analysis, which involves occasions, behaviors, and consequences. These three terms are used to account for emotional and motivational functions; at the risk of oversimplification, emotion is linked most closely to occasion (stimuli affect emotional states) and motivation to consequences (rewards affect motivation). Emotional and motivational functions are analyzed in terms of three dimensions: a "somatic," or internal–external dimension; an "associative," learning, or occasion–consequence dimension; and a "hedonic" or appetitive–aversive dimension. Although the Skinnerian emphasis may suggest a "black box" approach, the model has a biological flavor, and includes such variables as genetic and constitutional endowment; proprioceptive, interoceptive, and chemoreceptive inputs; and sensory–efferent, autonomic, and neuroendocrinal outputs (Brady & Emurian, 1979, p. 89). External factors and internal factors, both historical and contemporary, combine to determine behavior which has both private (internal) and public (observable) aspects.

A key part of the model's application is through the use of programmed environments, which require that tasks be undertaken and completed in set sequences. That is, the environment is engineered in such a way that on specified occasions specified responses yield specified outcomes. The model is highly reductionistic; studies based upon it typically involve the manipulation of one variable at a time, relatively molecular behaviors, and painstaking replication. The model's proponents argue that whereas proceeding in such a fashion is time consuming, it is only through the experimental analysis of objective behaviors in controlled settings that true progress is possible.

3. Toward an Open Systems Approach

Both the ecological and behavioral models are rich models whose surfaces have barely been scratched. However, they are formulated in such a way as to be more applicable to small groups than to larger social entities. As exotic environments encompass larger and larger numbers of people, small group phenomena will be joined by organizational level phenomena. It may then become useful to supplement these models with models that can be applied at a macroscopic level.

The seeds for such a model can be found in early work by Sells (1966) and Sells and Gunderson (1972), who proposed a "systems" approach to studying groups in exotic environments. Specifically, these authors argued that space missions and the like are best viewed as consisting of highly interdependent components (objectives and goals, philosophy and value system, personnel composition, organization, technology, physical environment, cultural and social environment, and temporal characteristics) such that variations in one component typically have repercussions in the other components. The goal for planners is to achieve systems congruence, a state of affairs such that all parts are compatible and mutually reinforcing. Sells and Gunderson (1972) describe their model as "frankly a structural model" (p. 181) and "static" (p. 207), and note that "this model should be expanded and refined to take more account of changing conditions (dynamics), covariation of elements in different phases, and specification of system functions (operations)" (p. 208).

Perhaps useful for furthering this approach is open systems theory as set forth by Katz and Kahn (1978). This theory began in the late 1950s as an attempt to integrate all of the behavioral and social sciences. It posits that individuals, groups, organizations, and societies constitute systems. Each system can be viewed in terms of five component subsystems that vary in ascendancy and salience: production, maintenance, supportive, adaptive, and managerial. Certain descriptive terms and dynamic principles hold true for all systems; for example, systems growth and decline follow a predictable course. By describing systems as open, full acknowledgment is given to intergroup relations and to the importance of the sponsoring agencies. Open systems theory takes over where standard social psychological analyses stop; that is, where the objects of analysis are large social entities that subsume a number of functionally differentiated subgroups. Thus, open systems theory becomes increasingly attractive as the number of people who staff any given exotic environment extends beyond the small group range.

D. CONCLUSIONS

At the same time that exotic environments are becoming more salient, behavioral research on groups in exotic environments has almost ground to a halt. To conclude our discussion of groups in exotic environments, we considered certain barriers to further advancement. First, people who are involved in such groups may view psychological research as useless or counterproductive. We must be both assertive and sensitive to such people's needs when trying to enlist their cooperation. Second, although it is always difficult to conduct good research, the problems seem to multiply when studying isolated and confined people. We must demonstrate resourcefulness and ingenuity, avoid premature commitment to a narrow range of settings and methods, and keep in mind that convergent methods typically overcome the objections associated with individual techniques. Third, we need to break out of the conceptual molds that were formed many years ago. The exotic environments of yesteryear have changed substantially, and many new exotic environments are available for study. Social and organizational psychology have changed immensely, and many new developments can be taken into account. Finally, we noted that two theoretical models, the ecological and the behavioral, have evolved around isolation and con-

82   ALBERT A. HARRISON AND MARY M. CONNORS

finement research. As group level phenomena are supplemented by organizational level phenomena, open systems theory may be put to good use.

REFERENCES

Altman, I. An ecological approach to the functioning of isolated and confined groups. In J. E. Rasmussen (Ed.), *Man in isolation and confinement* (pp. 241–270). Chicago: Aldine, 1973. 241–270.

Altman, I., & Haythorn, W. W. Interpersonal exchange in isolation. *Sociometry,* 1965, **28,** 411–426.

Altman, I., & Haythorn, W. W. The ecology of isolated groups. *Behavioral Science,* 1967, **12,** 169–182. (a)

Altman, I., & Haythorn. W. W. The effects of social isolation and group composition on performance. *Human Relations,* 1967, **20,** 313–339. (b)

Altman, I., Taylor, D. A., & Wheeler, L. Ecological aspects of group behavior in social isolation. *Journal of Applied Social Psychology,* 1971, **1,** 76–100.

Amir, Y. Contact hypothesis in ethnic relations. *Psychological Bulletin,* 1969, **71,** 319–342.

Aronson, E., & Mills, J. The effect of severity of initiation on liking for a group. *Journal of Abnormal and Social Psychology,* 1959, **59,** 177–181.

Bakeman, R., & Helmreich, R. Cohesiveness and performance: Covariation and causality in an undersea environment. *Journal of Experimental Social Psychology,* 1975, **11,** 478–489.

Beare, A. N., Bondi, K. R., Biersner, R. J., & Naitor, P. Work and rest on nuclear submarines. *Ergonomics,* 1981, **24,** 593–610.

Beckman, K., Marsella, A. J., & Finney, R. Depression in the wives of nuclear submarine personnel. *American Journal of Psychiatry,* 1979, **136,** 524–526.

Berry, C. A. A view of human problems to be addressed for long duration space flights. *Aerospace Medicine,* 1973, **44,** 1136–1146.

Biersner, R. J. Psychological evaluation and selection of divers. In C. W. Schilling & C. B. Carlston (Eds.), *Physician's guide to diving medicine.* New York: Plenum, 1984.

Biersner, R. J., & LaRocco, J. M. Personality characteristics of US Navy divers. *Journal of Occupational Psychology,* 1983, **56,** 329–334.

Bluth, B. J. Consciousness alteration in space. *Space manufacturing 3, proceedings of the 4th Princeton/AIAA Conference.* New York: American Institute of Aeronautics and Astronautics, 1979, 525–532. (a)

Bluth, B. J. The truth about the skylab crew "revolt." *L-5 News,* September, 1979, 12–13. (b)

Bluth, B. J. Social and psychological problems of extended space missions. *AIAA international meeting & technical display "Global Technology 2000."* New York: American Institute of Aeronautics and Astronautics, 1980.

Bluth, B. J. Sociological aspects of permanent manned occupancy of space. *AIAA Student Journal,* Fall, 1981, **48,** 11–15. (a)

Bluth, B. J. Soviet space stress. *Science 81,* 1981, **2,** 30–35. (b)

Bohlen, J. G. Biological rhythms: Human responses in the polar environment. *Yearbook of Physical Anthropology,* 1979, **22,** 47–79.

Brady, J. V., Bigelow, G., Emurian, H., & Williams, D. M. Design of a programmed environment for the experimental analysis of social behavior. In D. H. Carson (Ed.), *Man–environment interactions: Evaluations and applications. 7: Social ecology* (pp. 187–208). Milwaukee, Wisconsin: Environmental Design Research Association, 1974.

Brady, J. V., & Emurian, H. H. Behavioral analysis of motivational and emotional interactions in a programmed environment. In H. E. Howe & R. A. Dienstaber (Eds.), *Nebraska Symposium on Motivation, 1978.* Lincoln, Nebraska: University of Nebraska Press, 1979.

Brady, J. V., & Emurian, H. H. Experimental studies of small groups in programmed environments. *Journal of the Washington Academy of Sciences,* 1983, **73**(1), 1–15.

Cartwright, D. The nature of group cohesiveness. In D. Cartwright & A. Zander (Eds.), *Group dynamics: Research and theory* (3rd ed.). New York: Harper & Row, 1968.

Ceausu, V., Miasnikov, V. I., & Kozerenko, O. P. Psychic activity under conditions of space flight. *Revue Roumaine Des Sciences Sociales—Serie de Psychologie,* 1982, **26**(2), 101–118.

Cheston, T. S., & Winter, D. L. *Human factors in outer space production.* Boulder, Colorado: Westview Press, 1980.

Cleveland, S. E., Boyd, I., Sheer, D., & Reitman, E. E. Effects of fallout shelter confinement on family adjustment. *Archives of General Psychiatry,* 1963, **8**, 38–46.

Connors, M. M., Harrison, A. A., & Akins, F. R. *Living aloft: Human requirements for extended spaceflight.* Washington, D.C.: NASA RP, 1984.

Cooper, H. S. F., Jr. *A house in space.* New York: Bantam Books, 1976.

Cooper, H. S. F., Jr. Comments on B. J. Bluth's "The truth about the skylab crew 'revolt.'" *L-5 News,* September, 1979, 13.

Cunningham, W. *The all-American boys.* New York: Macmillan, 1977.

Day, R. M. *Ships laws: Normative structure for isolated groups.* Fort Worth, Texas: Texas Christian University Institute of Behavioral Research, 1969.

Detre, T., Weybrew, B. B., & Kupfer, D. J. The relationship of sleep changes to psychological symptoms in highly selected young male adults. *Psychophysiology,* 1972, **9**(1), 135.

Doll, R. E., & Gunderson, E. K. E. Group size, occupational status, and psychological symptomatology in an extreme environment. *Journal of Clinical Psychology,* 1971, **27**(2), 196–198.

Earls, J. H. Human adjustment to an exotic environment: The nuclear submarine. *Archives of General Psychiatry,* 1969, **20**(1), 117–123.

Emurian, H. H., Emurian, C. S., Bigelow, G. E., & Brady, J. V. The effects of a cooperation contingency on behavior in a continuous three-person environment. *Journal of the Experimental Analysis of Behavior,* 1976, **25**, 293–302.

Emurian, H. H., Emurian, C. S., & Brady, J. V. The effects of a pairing contingency on behavior in a three-person programmed environment. *Journal of the Experimental Analysis of Behavior,* 1978, **29**, 319–329.

Emurian, H. H., Emurian, C. S., & Brady, J. V. Appetitive and aversive reinforcement schedule effects on behavior: A systematic replication. *Basic and Applied Social Psychology,* 1982, **3**(1), 39–52.

Fiedler, F. E. *A theory of leadership effectiveness.* New York: McGraw-Hill, 1967.

Fiedler, F. E. Validation and extension of the contingency model of leadership effectiveness: A review of empirical findings. *Psychological Bulletin,* 1971, **76**, 128–148.

Fiedler, F. E. Recent developments in research on the contingency model. In L. Berkowitz (Ed.), *Group processes* (pp. 209–228). New York: Academic Press, 1978.

Flinn, D. E., Monroe, J. T., Cramer, E. H., & Hagen, D. H. Observations in the SAM two-man space cabin simulator. Behavioral factors in selection and performance. *Aerospace Medicine,* 1961, **32**, 610–615.

Gazenko, O. G., Myasnikov, V. I., Ioseliani, K. K., Kozetenko, O. P., & Uskov, F. N. *Important problems of space psychology.* Moscow: Institute of Biomedical Research, 1977.

Gunderson, E. K. E. Emotional symptoms in extremely isolated groups. *Archives of General Psychiatry,* 1963, **9**, 362–368.

Gunderson, E. K. E. Mental health problems in Antarctica. *Archives of Environmental Health,* 1968, **17**, 558–564.

Gunderson, E. K. E. Individual behavior in confined or isolated groups. In J. E. Rasmussen (Ed.), *Man in isolation and confinement* (pp. 145–164). Chicago: Aldine, 1973.

Gunderson, E. K. E., & Mahan, J. L. Cultural and psychological differences among occupational groups. *Journal of Psychology*, 1966, **62**, 287–304.

Gunderson, E. K. E., & Nelson, P. D. Adaptations of small groups to extreme environments. *Aerospace Medicine*, 1963, **34**, 1111–1115.

Gunderson, E. K. E., & Nelson, P. D. Biographical predictors of performance in an extreme environment. *Journal of Psychology*, 1965, **61**, 59–67.

Gunderson, E. K. E., & Nelson, P. D. Criterion measures of extremely isolated groups. *Personnel Psychology*, 1966. **19**(1), 67–80.

Haggard, E. A. Isolation and personality. In P. Worchel & D. Byrne (Eds.), *Personality change* (pp. 433–469). New York: Wiley, 1964.

Hammes, J. A., Ahearn, T. R., & Keith, J. R., Jr. A chronology of two weeks fallout shelter confinement. *Journal of Clinical Psychology*, 1965, **21**, 452–456.

Hammes, J. A., & Osborne, R. T. Survival research in group isolation studies. *Journal of Applied Psychology*, 1965, **49**, 418–421.

Hammes, J. A., & Watson, J. A. Behavior patterns of groups experimentally confined. *Perceptual and Motor Skills*, 1965, **20**, 1269–1272.

Haythorn, W. W. Interpersonal stress in isolated groups. In J. E. McGrath (Ed.), *Social and psychological factors in stress* (pp. 159–176). New York: Holt, Rinehart & Winston, 1970.

Haythorn, W. W. The miniworld of isolation: Laboratory studies. In J. E. Rasmussen (Ed.), *Man in isolation and confinement* (pp. 219–241). Chicago: Aldine, 1973.

Haythorn, W. W., & Altman, I. Personality factors in isolated environments. In M. H. Appley & R. Trumbull, (Eds.), *Psychological stress: Issues in research* (pp. 363–399). New York: Appleton-Century-Crofts, 1967. (a)

Haythorn, W. W., & Altman, I. Together in isolation. *Transaction*, 1967, **4**, 18–23. (b)

Haythorn, W. W., Altman, I., & Myers, T. Emotional symptomatology and subjective stress in isolated pairs of men. *Journal of Experimental Research in Personality*, 1966, **1**(4), 290–305.

Haythorn, W. W., McGrath, J. J., Hollander, E. P., Latané, B., Helmreich, R., & Radloff, R. Group processes and interpersonal interaction. In Space Science Board–NASA, *Human factors in long duration spaceflight* (pp. 160–178). Washington, DC: National Academy of Sciences, 1972.

Helmreich, R. L. Applied social psychology: The unfulfilled promise. *Personality and Social Psychology Bulletin*, 1975, **1**, 548–561.

Helmreich, R. L. Applying psychology in outer space: Unfulfilled promises revisited. *American Psychologist*, 1983, **38**, 445–450.

Helmreich, R. L., Wilhelm, J. A., & Runge, T. E. Psychological considerations in future space missions. In S. Cheston & D. Winter (Eds.), *Human factors in outer space production*. Boulder, Colorado: Westview Press.

Helmreich, R. L., Wilhelm, J., Tanner, T. A., Sieber, J. E., & Burgenbach, S. *A critical review of the Life Sciences Management at Ames Research Center for the Spacelab Mission Development Test III*. NASA Tech. Paper No. 1464, 1979.

Hersey, P., & Blanchard, K. *Management of organizational behavior: Utilizing human resources* (4th Ed.). Englewood Cliffs, New Jersey: Prentice-Hall, 1982.

Hollander, E. P. *Leadership dynamics: A practical guide to effective relationships*. Glencoe, Illinois: Free Press, 1978.

Hunter, E. J., & Nice, D. S. (Eds.). *Military families: Adaptation to change*. New York: Praeger, 1978.

Janis, I. L. Groupthink. *Psychology Today*, 1971, **5**(6), 43–46.

Jones, D. R., & Annes, C. A. The evolution and present status of mental health standards for selection of USAF candidates for space missions. *Aviation, Space, and Environmental Medicine*, 1983, **54**(8), 730–734.

Kanas, N. A., & Fedderson, W. E. *Behavioral, psychiatric, and sociological problems of long duration missions*. NASA Tech. Memorandum X-58067, 1971.

Katz, D., & Kahn, R. L. *The social psychology of organizations* (2nd ed.). New York: Wiley, 1978.

Kehoe, J. P., & Abbott, A. P. Suicide and attempted suicide in the Yukon territory. *Canadian Psychiatric Association Journal*, 1975, **20**(1), 15–23.

Kubis, J. F. Isolation, confinement, and group dynamics in long duration spaceflight. *Astronautica Acta*, 1972, **17**, 45–72.

Kubis, J. F., & McLaughlin, E. J. Psychological aspects of space flight. *Transactions of the New York Academy of Sciences*, 1967, **30**(2), 320–330.

Langer, E. L. Rethinking the role of thought in social interaction. In J. Harvey, W. Ickes, & R. Kidd (Eds.), *New directions in attribution research*. Hillsdale, New Jersey: Erlbaum, 1978.

Law, P. Personality problems in Antarctica. *Medical Journal of Australia*, 1960, **8**, 273–282.

Lebedev, V. I. Stages of psychological adaptation under altered conditions of existence. *So Voprosy Psikhologii*, 1980, **4**, 50–59.

Leonov, A. A., & Lebedev, V. I. *Psychological problems of interplanetary flight*. NASA Tech. Translation NASA TT F-16536, 1975.

McGuire, F., & Tolchin, S. Group adjustment at the South Pole. *Journal of Mental Science*, 1961, **107**, 954–960.

McNeal, S. R., & Bluth, B. J. Influential factors of negative effects in the isolated and confined environment. In *Space manufacturing 4, Proceedings of the 5th Princeton AIAA Conference* (pp. 435–442). New York: AIAA, 1981.

Myers, D. H., & Davies, P. The seasonal incidence of mania and its relationship to climactic variables. *Psychological Medicine*, 1978, **8**(3), 433–440.

Miller, J. G. Information input overload and psychopathology. *American Journal of Psychiatry*, 1960, **116**, 695–704.

Mostert. N. *Supership*. New York: Warner Books, 1975.

Mullin, C. S. Some psychological aspects of isolated antarctic living. *American Journal of Psychiatry*, 1960, **117**, 323–325.

Murphy, M. R. Analysis of eighty-four commercial aviation incidents: Implications for a resource management approach to crew training. In *Proceedings of the Annual Reliability and Maintainability Symposium*, 1980, pp. 298–307.

Nardini, J. E., Hermann, R. S., & Rasmussen, J. E. Navy psychiatric assessment program in the antarctic. *American Journal of Psychiatry*, 1962, **119**, 97–105.

Natani, K. Future directions for selecting personnel. In T. S. Cheston & D. L. Winter (Eds.), *Human factors in outer space production* (pp. 25–62). Boulder, Colorado: Westview Press, 1980.

Natani, K., & Shurley, J. T. Sociopsychological aspects of a winter vigil at south pole station. In E. K. E. Gunderson (Ed.), *Human adaptibility to antarctic conditions* (Vol. 22), Antarctic Research Series, 89–114. Washington, D.C.: American Geophysical Union, 1974.

Nelson, P. D. Psychological aspects of antarctic living. *Miliary Medicine*, 1965, **130**, 485–489.

Nelson, P. D. The indirect observation of groups under confinement and/or isolation. In J. E. Rasmussen (Ed.), *Man in isolation and confinement* (pp. 167–194). Chicago: Aldine, 1973.

Oberg, J. E. *Red star in orbit*. New York: Random House, 1981.

Parkin, M. Suicide and culture in Fairbanks. A comparison of three cultural groups in a small city of interior Alaska. *Psychiatry*, 1974, **37**(1), 60–67.

Pearlman, C. A., Jr. Separation reactions of married women. *American Journal of Psychiatry*, 1970, **126**, 946–950.

Perrow, C. *Complex organizations: A critical essay* (2nd ed.). Glenview, Illinois: Scott, Foresman, 1979.

Pope, F. E., & Rogers, T. A. Some psychiatric aspects of an Arctic survival experiment. *Journal of Nervous and Mental Disease*, 1968, **146**, 433–445.

Radloff, R. W. Naturalistic observations of isolated experimental groups in field settings. In J. E. Rasmussen (Ed.), *Man in isolation and confinement* (pp. 195–218). Chicago: Aldine, 1973.

Radloff, R., & Helmreich, R. *Groups under stress: Psychological research in Sealab II*. New York: Appleton-Century-Crofts, 1968.

Rohrer, J. H. Interpersonal relationships in isolated small groups. In B. E. Flaherty (Ed.), *Psychophysiological aspects of space flight*. New York: Columbia University Press, 1961.

Sells, S. B. A model for the social system for the multiman extended duration space ship. *Aerospace Medicine*, November, 1966, 1130–1135.

Sells, S. B. The taxonomy of man in enclosed space. In J. E. Rasmussen (Ed.), *Man in isolation and confinement* (pp. 281–304). Chicago: Aldine, 1973.

Sells, S. B., & Gunderson, E. K. E. A social system approach to long-duration missions. In Space Science Board–NASA, *Human factors in long duration space flight* (pp. 179–208). Washington, D.C.: National Academy of Sciences, 1972.

Serxner, J. L. Sixty days under the sea. *World Medicine*, January 14, 1968, 55–56.

Shears, L. M., & Gunderson, E. K. E. Stable attitude factors in natural isolated groups. *Journal of Social Psychology*, 1966, **70**, 199–204.

Sherif, M., Harvey, O., White, B., Hood, W., & Sherif, C. *Intergroup conflict and cooperation: The robbers' cave experience*. Norman, Oklahoma: Institute of Group Relations, University of Oklahoma. 1961.

Shurley, J. T., Natani, K., & Sengel, R. Ecopsychiatric aspects of a first human space colony. *Third Princeton/AIAA conference on Space Manufacturing Facilities*, Princeton, New Jersey: May 1977.

Sidowski, J. B., Wycoff, L. B., & Tabory, L. The influence of reinforcement and punishment in a minimal social situation. *Journal of Abnormal and Social Psychology*, 1956, **52**, 115–119.

Skinner, B. F. *Contingencies of reinforcement: A theoretical analysis*. New York: Appleton-Century-Crofts, 1969.

Sloan, A. W. *Man in extreme environments*. Springfield, Illinois: Thomas, 1979.

Smith, S. Studies of groups in confinement. In J. P. Zubeck (Ed.), *Sensory deprivation: Fifteen years of research* (pp. 374–403). New York: Appleton-Century-Crofts, 1969.

Smith, S., & Haythorn, W. W. Effects of compatibility, crowding, group size, and leadership seniority on stress, anxiety, hostility and annoyance in isolated groups. *Journal of Personality and Social Psychology*, 1972, **22**, 67–97.

Smith, W. M. Observations over the lifetime of a small isolated group: Structure, danger, boredom, and vision. *Psychological Reports*, 1966, **19**, 475–514.

Snyder, A. I. Periodic marital separation and physical illness. *American Journal of Orthopsychiatry*, 1978, **48**(4), 637–643.

Stockton, W. S., & Wilford, J. N. *Spaceliner*. New York: Times Books, 1981.

Taylor, A. J. W. Ability, stability, and social adjustment among Scott base personnel, Antarctica: A preliminary study. *Occupational Psychology*, 1969, **43**, 81–93.

Taylor, A. J. W. Some behavioural science in Antarctica. *New Zealand Family Physician*, 1980, **7**, 75–80.

Taylor, D. L., Altman, I., Wheeler, L., & Kushner, E. Personality factors related to response to social isolation and confinement. *Journal of Consulting and Clinical Psychology*, 1969, **33**(4), 411–419.

Taylor, D. A., Wheeler, L., Altman, I. Stress reactions in socially isolated groups. *Journal of Personality and Social Psychology*, 1968, **9**, 369–376.

Vinograd, S. (Ed.). *Studies of social group dynamics under isolated conditions.* Washington, D.C.: Sciences Communication Division, The George Washington University Medical Center, 1974.

Vroom, V. M., & Yetton, P. *Leadership and decision making.* Pittsburgh: University of Pittsburgh Press, 1973.

Weick, K. E. Organization design: Organizations as self-designing systems. *Organizational Dynamics,* Autumn, 1977, 31–46.

Weybrew, B. B. Impact of isolation upon personnel. *Journal of Occupational Medicine,* 1961, **3,** 290–294.

Weybrew, B. B. Psychological problems of prolonged submarine submergence. In N. M. Burns, R. M. Chambers, & E. Hendler (Eds.), *Unusual environments and human behavior—Physiological and psychological problems of man in space.* New York: Macmillan, 1963.

Weybrew, B. B., & Noddin, E. M. Psychiatric aspects of adaptation to long submarine missions. *Aviation, Space, and Environmental Medicine,* 1979, **50,** 575–580. (a)

Weybrew, B. B., & Noddin, E. M. The mental health of nuclear submariners in the United States Navy. *Military Medicine,* 1979, **144**(3), 188–191. (b)

Whelan, F. J. Situational depression in Alaska pipeline workers. "Walton's Syndrome." *American Journal of Psychiatry,* 1976, **133**(6), 719–720.

White, K. G., Taylor, A. J. W., & McCormick, I. A. A note on the chronometric analysis of cognitive ability: Antarctic effects. *New Zealand Journal of Psychology,* 1983, **17,** 36–40.

Whyte, W. F. Models for building and changing social organizations. *Human Organization,* 1967, **26,** 22–31.

Wolfe, T. *The right stuff.* New York: Farrar, Straus, Giroux, 1979.

Yanowitch, R. E. Crew behavior in accident causation. *Aviation, Space, and Environmental Medicine.* October, 1977, 918–921.

BALANCE THEORY,
THE JORDAN PARADIGM,
AND THE WIEST TETRAHEDRON

Chester A. Insko

DEPARTMENT OF PSYCHOLOGY
UNIVERSITY OF NORTH CAROLINA
CHAPEL HILL, NORTH CAROLINA

I. Introduction

Balance theory was originally formulated by Heider (1946, 1958), but has been improved and extended by Cartwright and Harary (1956), Runkel and

ADVANCES IN EXPERIMENTAL
SOCIAL PSYCHOLOGY, VOL. 18

Peizer (1968), and others. Insko (1981) summarizes many of these developments. This article continues this topic, with greater emphasis upon the quantitative applications—particularly Wiest's tetrahedron approach. Since an appreciation of the complexities inherent in this matter requires an understanding of the subjects' implicit and explicit contributions, we begin with a consideration of research in the Jordan paradigm. Research in the Jordan paradigm implies that any quantitative approach which attempts to model a single triad (or semicycle) will be at least partially inadequate. This research is concerned with subjects' reactions to hypothetical social situations and thus relates to a subject matter of little intrinsic interest. However, since variables can be easily manipulated in hypothetical situations, the Jordan paradigm does provide a convenient arena for theory development and testing.

II. The Jordan Paradigm

A. JORDAN (1953)

Jordan presented subjects with 64 different hypothetical triadic situations, for example, "I dislike O, I like X; O has no sort of bond or relationship with X" (p. 277), and asked them to rate the degree of pleasantness–unpleasantness of each situation. The 64 different situations were generated by combining the eight possible permutations of sentiment (L) and unit (U) relations (LLL, LLU, LUL, ULL, LUU, ULU, UUL, UUU) with the eight possible permutations of signs $(+++, +--, -+-, --+, ++-, +-+, -++, ---)$. Research tradition has followed Jordan's precedent of allowing the first sign to refer to the $p-o$ (I to other) relation, the second to the $p-x$ (I to object) relation, and the third to the $o-x$ (other to object) relation. Thus, in the LLL case, $-+-$ means that p dislikes o, likes x, and perceives that o dislikes x. According to the traditional conception of triadic balance the first four of the above permutations $(+++, +--, -+-, --+)$ are balanced and the last four $(++-, +-+, -++, ---)$ are imbalanced.

Mean pleasantness–unpleasantness ratings (on a scale in which low numbers indicate the most pleasantness) were as follows: 26.2 $(+++)$, 39.5 $(+--)$, 55.3 $(-+-)$, 62.4 $(--+)$, 57.0 $(++-)$, 58.2 $(+-+)$, 54.8 $(-++)$, 58.4 $(---)$. Comparing the first four with the last four triads does, indeed, indicate an overall mean difference in the predicted direction. However, this overall difference appears to be largely due to the first two triads' $(+++, +--)$ differing from the remaining six. The troublesome triads are the third and fourth ones $(-+-, --+)$. These are triads, for example, in which p dislikes o and has an opposite or disagreeing relation with x. Heider, of course, maintains that it is balanced to dislike someone with whom there is disagreement. Jordan's subjects, on the other hand, did not consider such a situation pleasant.

One problem with Jordan's experiment is that negative unit relations were operationalized as "has no sort of bond or relationship with." Cartwright and Harary (1956) pointed out that the negation of a positive unit relation should not be construed as a negative unit relation. When they reanalyzed Jordan's data without the situations involving negated-positive unit relations the overall difference between the first four and the second four triads increased somewhat. However, the basic pattern of the first two triads' differing from the other six remained. This can be seen by examining the data for the situations involving only sentiment relations: 22.1 $(+++)$, 33.8 $(+--)$, 64.2 $(-+-)$, 71.5 $(--+)$, 64.5 $(+-+)$, 67.1 $(+-+)$, 59.1 $(-++)$, 69.9 $(---)$. These data still indicate that subjects do not regard it as particularly pleasant to dislike someone with whom they disagree (third and fourth triads), but do regard it as more pleasant to like someone with whom they agree (first and second triads).

B. THE ZAJONC (1968) REVIEW:
    POSTULATION OF MULTIPLE EFFECTS

Following the publication of Jordan's study a large number of subsequent investigations were conducted—most of which were mainly concerned with sentiment relations. In 1968 Zajonc did an exhaustive review of these studies. He had the interesting idea of computing three indexes for each study: balance, attraction, and agreement. Each index is the ratio of some four of the triads to the remaining four triads. Thus, balance is the ratio of the "balanced" triads to the "imbalanced" triads; attraction is the ratio of the p likes o triads to the p dislikes o triads; and agreement is the ratio of the p and o agree about x triads to the p and o disagree about x triads.[1] Across all studies, Zajonc found that "The results are in favor of the agreement variable, with balance holding a close second, and attraction a decided third place" (p. 347). Zajonc (1968) concluded that "This rough summary is damaging to the balance principle" (p. 347).

In retrospect what is important about the Zajonc review is not the negative conclusion, but the three indexes. In computing these indexes Zajonc was implicitly postulating three effects. Recall the pattern of results obtained by Jordan, a pattern in which the first two triads were regarded as more pleaant than the remaining six. The first two triads are triads in which there are "balance," attraction, and agreement. Each of Zajonc's indexes included these two triads, along with two others, in the numerator. As is explained in more detail below,

[1]Rodrigues (1967) and Insko, Songer, and McGarvey (1974) refer to attraction effects as "positivity" effects.

Anderson (1977) has raised a question concerning the psychological meaningfulness of the three effects. To what extent is it meaningful to analyze a two-triad versus six-triad effect into three different effects? This is an issue to which we will return later. For now it can simply be noted in passing that from a phenomenological perspective it certainly appears that "balance," agreement, and attraction are evident in each of the eight triads.

C. FIVE REACTIONS TO ATTRACTION
   AND AGREEMENT EFFECTS

Most social psychologists have not questioned the psychological reality of attraction and agreement effects. They have, however, reacted to these effects in quite different ways. Five of these reactions follow.

First, some social psychologists have decided that balance theory is invalid. If it is more pleasant to agree than to disagree with someone, regardless of how we feel about that person, balance theory makes an erroneous prediction. This reaction is implicit in Zajonc's above quoted conclusion (1968, p. 347).

Second, consistent with another possible interpretation of Zajonc's discussion of balance theory, some social psychologists have concluded that "balance," attraction, and agreement are real, but psychologically distinct, effects. This is the point of view, for example, of Cacioppo and Petty (1981). Clearly it is possible to regard the "balance" effect as fundamentally different from the attraction and agreement effects. On the other hand, our goal is certainly to reduce apparent complexity to underlying simplicity. And, as is argued below, an emphasis upon implicit thoughts, "cognitive-responses," or semicycles enables one to do just that. Cacioppo and Petty (e.g., 1979) and Petty and Cacioppo (e.g., 1977) have been willing to postulate cognitive responses as an explanation for differing attitude change effects. Perhaps this is also possible for attraction and agreement effects.

Third, some individuals, most notably Newcomb (1968), have restricted the balance–imbalance distinction to just those triads in which p likes o. Thus, the $+++$ and $+--$ triads are balanced, and the $++-$ and $+-+$ triads are imbalanced. Newcomb describes the remaining four triads in which p dislikes o as "nonbalanced." Since this position abandons the multiplicative rule, the theoretical position is fundamentally altered.

While there is nothing sacrosanct about theoretical positions, it should be understood that the multiplicative rule has an interesting parallel with two-valued logic. Thus, abandoning the multiplicative rule changes balance theory from a logic theory to a non-logic theory. In response to Abelson and Rosenberg's (1958) widely quoted distinction between logic and "psycho-logic," Runkel and Peizer (1968) pointed out that if attention is restricted to just plus and minus signs, the distinction between balance theory and two-valued logic is "virtually" erased. Consider, for example, "similar" and "dissimilar" as the two values. In a two-valued world if a is dissimilar to b and b is similar to c, it follows logically that a is dissimilar to c. And this logical implication is, of course, also an implication of the multiplicative rule. For the other $(+-, ++, --)$ possibilities the fit between two-valued logic and a two-valued multiplicative rule is equally obvious. From this perspective it is of interest to explore the possibility that two-valued logic can account for attraction and agreement effects. One of the purposes of this article is to demonstrate that such is indeed possible.

Fourth, some social psychologists have criticized Jordan and other researchers for the use of pleasantness scales rather than some other more cognitive scale like consistency or expectancy. This was done initially by Insko (1967). More recently, Gutman and Knox (1972), Crockett (1974), and Willis and Burgess (1974) have made the same argument.

Gutman and Knox (1972) obtained data for pleasantness, tension, and consistency scales. Although no tests of significance for the comparison of scales were reported, the results descriptively indicate that the attraction and agreement effects were larger for the pleasantness and tension scales. Miller and Norman (1976) obtained similar results, with the appropriate test of significance. Gutman, Knox, and Storm (1974), however, reported data that do not appear to indicate any notable differences between pleasantness and consistency scales for children of various ages. For both scales the attraction effect appears larger than the agreement and "balance" effects. Crockett (1974) argued that the dimension expect–unexpect most nearly captures the meaning of balance. His data descriptively indicate larger attraction and agreement effects with a pleasantness scale than with an expectancy scale.

Insko and Adewole (1979) and Insko, Sedlak, and Lipsitz (1982) have in total reported four studies which examined five rating scales (pleasantness, harmony, expectancy, consistency, stability) and one study which examined four rating scales (pleasantness, harmony, expectancy, consistency). All five of the studies found that the affective scales (pleasantness and harmony) produced greater attraction and agreement effects than did the relatively more cognitive scales. In view of the considerable differences among the studies in the types of between-subject factors, the consistency of results is noteworthy. With adult subjects, at least, there does not seem to be much doubt that affective scales reveal greater attraction and agreement effects than do relatively more cognitive scales.

Such results seemingly imply, in agreement with the fourth reaction, that balance theory should, indeed, be restricted to generalizations regarding more purely cognitive ratings. Although such a conclusion may seem warranted, two further findings indicate that the situation is not that simple. First, despite the fact that attraction and agreement effects were always smaller on the cognitive scales, these effects were sometimes still present. For example, deviation from zero tests indicated that attraction and agreement effects were present for consistency ratings in three out of five of the Insko and Adewole (1979) and Insko *et al.* (1982) studies.[2] Second, in all five studies the ''balance'' effect was not greater with cognitive than with affective scales. Thus, although there may be some validity to the assertion that balance–imbalance is a purely cognitive reaction, the situation is, in fact, more complex than such a simple hypothesis suggests.[3]

Finally, we have the fifth reaction to attraction and agreement effects. This is an argument that the subjects' explicit or implicit assumptions, or concerns, create semicycles in addition to the experimentally supplied p–o–x semicycle. From this perspective the attraction and agreement effects are just as much balance effects as is the usual ''balance'' effect. This argument has a number of versions depending upon the assumptions or concerns that are postulated. To date four have been suggested. These are the assumption of p and o contact, the assumption of p and o similarity, p's concern with being right about x, and p's concern with being liked by o. These four different balance theory interpretations of attraction and agreement effects will be taken up in order.

D. BALANCE THEORY INTERPRETATIONS OF ATTRACTION
    AND AGREEMENT EFFECTS

1. The Assumption of p–o *Contact*

In 1969 Aderman suggested that the lack of preference for certain ''balanced'' triads may be due to the subjects' implicit assumption that they would interact with o at some future time.[4] Aderman specifically focused on the two ''balanced'' triads in which there is neither attraction nor agreement ($- + -$, $- - +$). Recall that these are the third and fourth triads in Jordan's list—the triads that subjects have not regarded as particularly pleasant. Aderman argued that assumed future contact is unpleasant because o is disliked and because o disagrees with p.

But why should future contact with a disliked and disagreeing o be unpleasant? Aderman intuited a balance theory implication without being explicit about it—a common occurrence among social psychologists. Future contact is a

---

[2]The two exceptions were studies containing assumed dissimilarity conditions which, as explained below, tend to reverse or lower attraction and agreement effects for cognitive scales.

[3]As is explained in detail below, it is assumed that ratings on affective scales primarily reflect semicycles in which the self-concept is one of the elements, while ratings on cognitive scales primarily reflect semicycles in which the self-concept is not one of the elements.

[4]Although not concerned with attraction and agreement effects, an even earlier study of contact is Morissette (1958).

positive unit relation, and the addition of this relation to the three experimentally supplied relations results in a total of three semicycles—one for each of the three orthogonal effects. Table I is a reproduction of Insko, Songer, and McGarvey's (1974) Table 1. In order to simplify the discussion, the direction of the relations is not indicated, and thus, consistent with graph theory terminology, what would otherwise be labeled a semicycle is referred to as a cycle. A cycle is simply a closed loop. In Table I, a straight line represents a sentiment relation and a curved line a unit relation. Also, a solid line represents a positive relation and a dashed line represents a negative relation. Consistent with the Aderman postulation of assumed future contact, the curved p–o line is always solid.

As is indicated in the first column of Table I, there are three different cycles. Cycle 1 is balanced when p likes the o with whom there is interaction, and is imbalanced when p dislikes the o with whom there is interaction. Cycle 1 thus predicts an attraction effect. Cycle 2 is balanced when p agrees with the o with whom there is interaction and is imbalanced when p disagrees with the o with whom there is interaction. Cycle 2 thus predicts an agreement effect. Cycle 3 includes the three-sentiment relations and thus reflects the usual "balance" effect. Hereafter, we will remove the quotation marks and refer to it as a three-sign balance effect. *All three cycles are in reality balance effects.*

The cells in Table I contain 1's if the cycle for the given row is balanced and 0's if the cycle for the given row is imbalanced. The bottom row of the table is a sum across the three rows above. This simple summation reveals an intriguing fact. It is only the first two triads for which all three cycles are balanced; for the remaining six triads there are in every case one balanced and two imbalanced cycles. Thus, on the assumption of future contact, balance theory can predict the now familiar pattern that was first obtained by Jordan.

Do subjects, in fact, tend to think about an o with whom there is contact and interaction? McGarvey (1974) interviewed a small sample of 18 subjects after each subject had rated the degree of pleasantness for each of the standard eight triads. He found that 13 of the 18 subjects (72%) reported assuming a situation in which there was p to o interaction or contact. More recently, Insko and Adewole (1979) repeated this procedure with 150 subjects and found that 136 (91%) reported assumed interaction or contact.

What all this suggests to an experimental social psychologist is the need for an explicit manipulation of assumed future contact. Just because subjects report assumed contact does not mean that such contact is causally important. An experimental study was first done by Aderman (1969) and then subsequently by Insko *et al.* (1974) and McGarvey (1974). In all of these studies ratings were done only on pleasantness scales. More recently Insko and Adewole (1979) have reported two studies in which ratings were done on five different rating scales (pleasantness, harmony, expectancy, consistency, stability). We will initially

TABLE I

A Graph Theory Representation of the p-o-x Triad Assuming p-o Contact[a]

	Three-sign balance[b]				Three-sign imbalance[b]			
	+++	+--	-+-	--+	++-	+-+	-++	---
Cycle 1	1	1	0	0	1	1	0	0
Cycle 2	1	1	0	0	0	0	1	1
Cycle 3	1	1	1	1	0	0	0	0
Sum	3	3	1	1	1	1	1	1

[a]From "Balance, positivity, and agreement in the Jordan Paradigm, A defense of balance theory" by C. A. Insko, E. Songer, and W. McGarvey, *Journal of Experimental Social Psychology*, 1974, **10**, p. 56.

[b]A solid line represents a positive relation; a dashed line, a negative relation; a curved line, a unit relation; and a straight line, a sentiment relation. An entry of 1 indicates that the cycle is balanced and an entry of 0 indicates that the cycle is imbalanced.

describe the studies using only pleasantness ratings and then describe the studies examining the generality of these results across various rating scales.

In order to facilitate analysis of the data, Insko *et al.* (1974) suggested that it would be helpful to conceptualize Heider's p-o-x triad from the perspective of a three-factor analysis of variance in which the factors are p likes or dislikes o, p likes or dislikes x, and o likes or dislikes x. From this perspective the attraction effect is the p-o main effect, the agreement effect is the p-x by o-x interaction, and the three-sign balance effect is the triple interaction. Each of the three effects is thus the difference between the mean of some four triads and the remaining four triads. (Recall that the Zajonc indexes were ratios and not differences.) All together there are seven possible effects: three main effects, three double interactions, and one triple interaction. Since in the typical design each subject rates all eight triads, the three above factors (p-o, p-x, o-x) are within-subject factors.

Following Aderman, Insko *et al.* (1974) used between-subject manipulation of type of contact. Contact was manipulated by instructing the subjects in a given condition to assume a certain type of contact with o or (in the standard condition) giving them no instructions at all. When instructions regarding contact were given, they were repeated for each of the eight triads. Counting the research in Insko *et al.* (1974) as one experiment and including the two experiments reported by McGarvey as well as one additional unpublished experiment, there are four experiments which have systematically investigated the four important contact conditions (with only pleasantness ratings). These conditions are contact, no contact, breaking contact, and standard.[5] In the contact condition subjects were instructed: "Assume: I and O have had personal contact in the past and will have personal contact in the future." In the no-contact condition the subjects were instructed: "Assume: I and O have not had personal contact in the past and will never have personal contact in the future." In the breaking-contact condition subjects were instructed, "Assume: I and O have had personal contact in the past but will not have personal contact in the future." And finally in the standard condition subjects were given no instructions regarding contact.

There are important differences among the four different experiments, largely relating to the additional between-subjects factors included in the designs. Some of these factors will be described below. For now, the important consideration relates to type of contact.

How should attraction, agreement, and three-sign balance be affected by type of assumed contact? First, consider attraction and agreement. Clearly these effects should be largest when subjects are instructed to assume contact. Furthermore, if it is true that some but not all subjects assume contact, the attraction and agreement effects should be next largest in the standard condition. After the standard condition should come the no-contact condition where the unit relation is null. Finally, what about the breaking-contact condition? This is, in many respects, the most interesting condition. If breaking contact is a negative unit relation, reversed attraction and agreement effects should occur; i.e., consistent with the multiplicative rule, when personal contact is broken, it should be more pleasant to dislike than to like o and to disagree with than to agree with o. Thus, the rank order of the algebraic values of the attraction and agreement effects predicted by the unit relation interpretation is future contact $>$ standard $>$ no contact $>$ breaking contact. Furthermore, the effects in the future contact and standard conditions should be positive (i.e., in the usual direction), the effects in the no-contact condition should be within error variance of zero, and the effects in the breaking-contact condition should be negative (i.e., the reverse of the usual direction).

[5]Aderman's (1969) research is not included in this summary because his experiment did not clearly differentiate the no-contact and breaking-contact conditions.

What are the results for the four experiments? First, consider the attraction effect. In all four experiments the predicted rank order (future contact > standard > no contact > breaking contact) was obtained. Furthermore, the predicted reversed attraction effect in the breaking-contact condition was significant in each of the four experiments. Finally, the predicted nonsignificant attraction effect in the no-contact condition was obtained in three of the four experiments. Except, then, for a significant attraction effect in the no-contact condition of one experiment, the results are in complete accord with the unit relation interpretation.

What about the agreement effect? The predicted rank order of conditions was only partially in accord with the unit relation interpretation. All four experiments found the same rank order: future contact = standard > no contact > breaking contact. In none of the experiments was the predicted superiority of the future-contact condition to the standard condition obtained. The predicted reversed agreement effect was obtained in three of the four experiments, but the predicted nonsignificance of the agreement effect in the no-contact condition was obtained only in one of the four experiments. In three of the four experiments a significant agreement effect occurred in the no-contact condition. Clearly the unit relation interpretation does not fit the agreement effect data nearly as well as it does the attraction effect data. Nonetheless, the unit relation interpretation does account for some of the agreement variance. It is particularly noteworthy that the predicted reversed agreement effect was obtained in three of the four experiments.

Finally, what about the three-sign balance effect? Since the unit relation is not part of the three-sign balance cycle (Cycle 3), variations in the nature of this unit relation should have no effect (according to the unit relation hypothesis). The obtained results, however, are not in accord with this expectation. All four experiments found that a larger three-sign balance effect occurred in the standard condition than in the other three contact conditions. Further, two of the four experiments found that breaking contact produced a smaller three-sign balance effect than did no contact and future contact. How are such results to be explained. Quite possibly by attentional shifts. In retrospect it seems quite reasonable that the statement of an explicit assumption regarding contact would direct attention to the attraction and agreement cycles (which include the unit relation) and thus away from the three-sign balance cycle (which does not include the unit relation). It is, furthermore, plausible to assume that the greatest attentional shift should occur in the somewhat more dramatic breaking-contact condition.

Postulated attentional shifts thus allow for post hoc interpretations of some of the unexpected findings. Overall, however, there are still unexplained results. Perhaps the most noteworthy unexplained results are those for the no-contact condition. In three of four experiments significant agreement effects were obtained in the no-contact condition, and in one of the four experiments a significant attraction effect was found in the no-contact condition.

To what extent can these results with pleasantness scales be generalized to other scales? Insko and Adewole (1979) reported two experiments including manipulations of contact and type of rating scales. Five types of rating scales (pleasantness, harmony, expectancy, consistency, stability) were used. The results indicated approximate comparability of the contact results across scales. Contact produced main effects on agreement in both experiments, and in neither experiment was the contact by scales interaction significant. Contact also produced main effects on attraction in both experiments. The contact by scales interaction was significant in the first experiment, but not in the second. The interaction in the first experiment was small relative to the contact main effect (F = 4.32 and 80.39, respectively), and need not concern us here. It appears to be generally the case that the contact manipulation has approximately equivalent effects across the five scales.

One troublesome aspect of the results relates to the previously described tendency for significant agreement and attraction effects to occur in no-contact conditions. Significant agreement and attraction effects occurred in the no-contact conditions of both of Insko and Adewole's experiments—particularly on the pleasantness and harmony scales. It appears as if assumed contact can account for some, but certainly not all, of the variance in agreement and attraction effects.

2. Psychological Meaningfulness of Attraction, Agreement, and Three-Sign Balance Effects

As previously indicated, Anderson (1977) has questioned the psychological meaningfulness of attraction, agreement, and three-sign balance effects. Thus, before proceeding with even further theoretical interpretations of attraction and agreement effects it is appropriate to consider this matter in some detail. The prior discussion of contact and the alternative patterns of results produced by the contact manipulation provide an appropriate context for understanding the issues in dispute. Although Anderson makes a number of points, present discussion will be limited to his questioning of the meaningfulness of the attraction, agreement, and three-sign balance effects. Anderson approaches this matter with an analysis of variance critique.

Anderson's analysis of variance critique focuses upon the three-factor design. His essential argument, however, can be more simply described with reference to a two-factor design. Consider a two-factor design in which each factor has two levels or conditions, thereby generating the familiar 2×2 table. A two-factor analysis of variance applied to such a table involves three contrasts—contrasts which are labeled a main effect for columns, a main effect for rows, and a row by column interaction. The main effect for columns compares the mean of the two cells in one column with the mean of the two cells in the other column. The main effect for rows compares the mean of the two cells in one row with the mean of the two cells in the other row. And finally, the row-by-column interaction compares the mean of the two cells in one diagonal with the mean of the two cells in the other diagonal. Thus, we have a set of orthogonal contrasts in which one particular half of the cells is always compared with the remaining half of the cells.

Analysis of variance is based on the so-called general linear model. This model assumes that any one dependent-variable assessment is composed of a number of additive components. For the above example there are five such components: a component for rows, a component for columns, a component for the row-by-column interaction, a component for the grand mean (the simple difference from zero), and a component for error. These components are assumed to be additive and independent.

Following Anderson's argument, suppose that some experiment produces results in which three of the cells are identical and one is different. Assuming a small enough within-cell variance, a standard analysis of variance of such results would reveal three significant effects: the main effect for rows, the main effect for columns, and the row-by-column interaction. (Typically the grand mean test is not done.) According to Anderson, forcing the analysis of variance contrasts on such results is "Procrustean." The "natural interpretation" of the results is as a difference between one cell and the other three cells. The basic problem here, according to Anderson, relates to the unjustified assumptions of additivity and independence, which looks at the three-versus-one difference as if it were composed of three independent and additive components.

Insofar as Anderson questions the appropriateness of the row, column, and row-by-column contrasts he raises an important issue which deserves explicit attention. On the other hand, questioning of the general linear model is another matter. There is nothing in the general linear model which requires that the particular contrasts followed by the standard analysis of variance always be utilized. One could, for example, use one of the three between-cell degrees of freedom to test the one- versus three-cell difference alluded to above. After that, the two other degrees of freedom could be utilized to make orthogonal comparisons among the three similar cells, although these contrasts would obviously be nonsignificant. We thus would still have a situation with five components, and the assumptions of additivity and independence would still hold. It is, of course, well known that the F test for any between-cell effect is based on the assumption that the between-cell component and the error component are independent.

Anderson has, however, rendered a service by questioning the universal appropriateness of the particular contrasts suggested by analysis of variance. As he points out, these contrasts may not be psychologically meaningful. Consider now the basic pattern of results first discovered by Jordan (1953). Jordan found that the first two triads $(+++, +--)$ were rated as more pleasant than the remaining six triads. Here we have a two-versus-six contrast. Insko *et al.* (1974), however, argued that this pattern of results could be regarded more meaningfully from the perspective of three of the analysis of variance contrasts: $p-o$ main effect (attraction effect), $p-x$ by $o-x$ interaction (agreement effect), and the triple interaction (three-sign balance effect). And, of course, consistent with the general linear model these effects are assumed to be additive and independent. [Actually it was Zajonc (1968) who first singled out these effects. It is somewhat ironic that in retrospect his contribution was more supportive of than harmful to balance theory.] The relevant question here concerns the psychological meaningfulness, or the theoretical appropriateness, of the three analysis of variance contrasts. The mere fact that a single two-versus-six contrast is simpler than the three analysis of variance contrasts does not necessarily imply that the analysis of variance contrasts are not psychologically meaningful or theoretically appropriate. Although Anderson does not specifically use the term ''parsimony,'' his argument is in fact an appeal to parsimony. Given a two-versus-six pattern, the simplest conceptualization is in terms of a single two-versus-six contrast and not as a main effect, double interaction, and triple interaction. This is certainly true. However, much more is known about the situation. It is known that alternative eight-cell patterns can be produced. Breaking contact, for example, produces a pattern in which the third and fourth triads (triads in which p dislikes and disagrees with o) are rated as most pleasant. From the perspective of a two-versus-six contrast the reason for such an alternative pattern would not be at all clear. The simplest interpretation of one data pattern may not be the simplest interpretation of a set of alternative data patterns. Unless it is used with an eye to all that is known, Occam's razor may cut bone and muscle as well as useless fat.

Now it may well be that subsequent developments will indicate that a cycles interpretation of the Jordan paradigm data is inadequate. The way to demonstrate this, however, is with direct consideration of this interpretation, and not with the assertion that a single contrast for one particular eight-cell pattern is more ''natural.'' Nonetheless, this does not mean that we disagree with the assertion that in some contexts the analysis of variance contrasts may be theoretically inappropriate. The appropriateness or inappropriateness of the contrast cannot be decided in general, but only through a detailed consideration of all that is known about a particular research problem.

3. The Assumption of p–o Similarity

Returning to various balance interpretations of attraction and agreement effects, Insko and Adewole (1979) tested the hypothesis that these effects are due to assumed p–o similarity. Examination of McGarvey's (1974) interview results indicated that in 8 out of 18 instances the subjects reported imagining o to be a specific acquaintance, usually a friend or a peer. This implies that some subjects, at least, implicitly conceptualized o as someone who was *similar*. They did not conceptualize o as a "man from Mars," a member of another culture or subculture, a resident of a mental institution, an elderly person, or a child. From a balance theory perspective, similarity is a unit relation just as is contact. Thus, if the curved lines in Table I are taken as an indication of similarity (rather than contact) there are cycles predicting agreement (p agrees with a similar o) and attraction (p likes a similar o).

As Insko and Adewole point out, it is interesting to note that social comparison theory takes an analogous position regarding agreement with similar others. As Festinger (1954) states the social comparison theory position, "a person who believes that Negroes are the intellectual equals of whites does not evaluate his opinions by comparison with the opinion of a person who belongs to some very anti-Negro group" (p. 121). Festinger does not indicate why this assumption is made. He appears to have intuited a balance implication without being explicit about it—as previously indicated, a rather common occurrence among social psychologists.

Insko and Adewole (1979) and also Insko et al. (1982) manipulated similarity by stating either an assumption of similarity ("O generally has interests and attitudes similar to yours") or an assumption of dissimilarity ("O generally has interests and attitudes dissimilar to yours"). Both experiments obtained the same results. The manipulation had the expected effects on both attraction and agreement, but only for the more cognitive scales (expectancy, consistency, stability). Only for the cognitive scales were the attraction and agreement effects larger in the similar than in the dissimilar conditions. Unlike the situation for contact, there was no effect on the affective scales (pleasantness and harmony). Agreement with similar and dissimilar others was equally pleasant, but not equally consistent.

Such results imply that the assumed similarity interpretation is even less adequate than the contact interpretation (where effects were obtained for all scales). It should also be noted that the results are not consistent with social comparison theory. Indeed, as Insko and Adewole point out, "the basic assumption of a drive for self-evaluation might be interpreted as implying a greater effect on the affective than on the cognitive scales—certainly not a lesser effect" (1979, p. 807).

An adequate interpretation of attraction and agreement effects must be able to account for two facts. First, as previously indicated, past research has made it clear that attraction and agreement effects are larger on affective than on cognitive scales. There is no obvious way in which the cycles in Table I (for either contact or similarity) can explain such scale differences. Second, consistent with Zajonc's (1968) summary of the early literature, subsequent studies (e.g., Insko & Adewole, 1979) have found that the agreement effect is descriptively larger than the attraction effect. It is also evident that there is no obvious way in which the contact and similarity interpretations can explain these results. Thus although contact and similarity may account for some of the attraction and agreement variance, there is still variance remaining to be explained.

4. The Being Right Interpretation

Insko *et al.* (1982) formulated what they refer to as the being right interpretation of the agreement effect. They began by speculating about the reason for the failure of similarity to alter the magnitude of the agreement effect on the affective scales. They argued that personal relevance, or benefit, flows from agreement regardless of whether o is similar or dissimilar. To the extent that this is true, the problem is to specify what it is about agreement that is more beneficial than is disagreement. One possible answer is that agreement implies that p is right about x and that disagreement implies that p is wrong about x.

To determine whether or not subjects have any explicit or implicit recognition of this matter, 51 subjects were asked to rate the eight $p-o-x$ triads and then state whether in any of these situations they considered o to be knowledgeable concerning x. Sixty-seven percent of the subjects responded affirmatively.

How can this implicit or explicit concern with being right be expressed in balance theory terms? If subjects assume that p is (+) right and that o is (+) right, the multiplicative rule predicts p to o agreement (+), since only with such agreement are all three relations positive. Figure 1a pictures the semicycle for this set of relations. Semicycles differ from cycles in that arrows, rather than straight lines, are used to specify relations. Such arrows have the advantage of indicating the direction of any particular relation. The "two-sided" arrow between p and o in Fig. 1 indicates that agreement is bidirectional. If p agrees with o, o agrees with p.

Assuming that information regarding o's knowledge of x affects the subject's assumption that o is right, the semicycle in Fig. 1a implies that one should be able to modify the agreement effect by manipulating o's assumed knowledge of x. The greater is o's assumed knowledge of x, the greater is the probability that o is right, and such an assumption is inconsistent with the further assumption that p is right about x when p and o disagree.

Given the semicycle pictured in Fig. 1a and the implicit assumption that p and o are both right, it is quite understandable that the agreement pattern for the

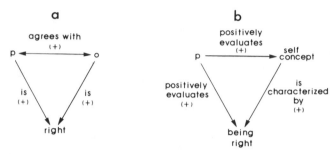

Fig. 1.　Two semicycles (a and b) predicting the agreement effect on the basis of knowledge-related considerations. From "A two-valued logic or two-valued balance resolution of the challenge of agreement and attraction effects in p–o–x triads, and a theoretical perspective on conformity and hedonism" by C. A. Insko, A. J. Sedlak, and A. Lipsitz, *European Journal of Social Psychology* 1982, **12**, p. 147.

p–o–x triads should be rated as relatively more consistent than the disagreement pattern. What about the expectancy and stability scales? There may be some reason to expect analogous effects on all of the cognitive scales, but the above argument applies most directly to the consistency scale. The stability scale may reflect some affective considerations, and the expectancy scale may relate more to past experience than to consistency.

What, however, is a possible theoretical basis for an agreement effect on the affective scales? A brief digression suggests a possible answer.

It seems apparent that pleasure and pain are self-related and cannot exist apart from persons (or organisms), while consistency need not be self-related and can exist apart from persons (e.g., between logical symbols). This implies that situations with personal relevance will produce an effect on affective scales. From a balance theory perspective such situations involve semicycles in which p's self-concept is one of the elements. Following Heider (1958) and Wiest (1965) it is traditional to assume that p has high self-regard or positively evaluates his/her self-concept. Indeed, as Wiest points out, since p has a positive unit relation with his/her self-concept, such positive evaluation is balanced.

Following Insko *et al.* (1982), assume that it is meaningful to conceive of the self-concept as an element, that p positively evalutes his/her self-concept, and that affect is a function of balance–imbalance in semicycles including the self-concept as an element. Assume further that it is possible to transform the relation, p is right, into the element, "being right." Transformation of relations to elements is a departure from traditional practice in balance theory, and will be discussed more fully below. For the present, note that the four assumptions enable the statement of a semicycle predicting an agreement effect on the affective scales: p positively evaluates ($+$) being right, p positively evalutes ($+$) his/her self-concept, the self-concept is characterized by ($+$) being right. The semicycle is pictured in Fig. 1b.

The semicycle in Fig. 1b predicts an agreement effect on the affective scales. But past research has repeatedly found that agreement effects are larger on affective than on cognitive scales. Why should this be? Stated differently, why should balance–imbalance in Fig. 1b have a greater impact than balance–imbalance in Fig. 1a? A possible answer to this question focuses on the fact that elements differ not only in sign but also in polarity of sign. The self-concept in Fig. 1b is a highly polarized positive element. Thus, balance (and consequent pleasure) should increase to the extent that the elements which are positively associated with the self-concept are themselves highly polarized in the positive direction. Thus, to the extent that being right is a highly valued element in the context of the hypothetical social situation, Fig. 1b should produce a greater effect on the affective scales than would Fig. 1a on the cognitive scales. The polarized evaluation of both the self-concept and being right need not be explicit but, on the contrary, may be overlearned and implicit.

Unfortunately, however, the Insko et al. (1982) results were not totally consistent with expectations. Their experiment included the usual within-subject ratings of the eight triads and two between-subject factors, rating scales (pleasantness, harmony, expectancy, consistency, stability), and assumed knowledge. The assumed knowledge factor had three levels: knowledgeable ("O is knowledgeable concerning X"), not knowledgeable ("O is not knowledgeable concerning X"), and standard (no stated assumption concerning knowledge of x). The results indicated that for all scales the agreement effect was largest in the knowledgeable condition, intermediate in the standard condition, and smallest in the not-knowledgeable condition. Since the assumed knowledge manipulation did not have a greater effect on the affective (pleasantness, harmony) scales than on the cognitive (expectancy, consistency, stability) scales, the results were only partially in agreement with expectations.

It is important to consider carefully what Insko et al. (1982) did and did not find. They did find that the assumed knowledge manipulation altered the agreement effect on the affective scales and, of course, also on the cognitive scales. Thus, the obtained results are consistent with Fig. 1a and b or with the being right interpretation of agreement effects. The effect of the assumed knowledge manipulation on the cognitive scales is a function of the semicycle in Fig. 1a and the effect of the assumed knowledge manipulation on the affective scales is a function of the self-relevant semicycle in Fib. 1b. The problem, however, is that agreement effects in standard conditions are typically larger on affective than cognitive scales, and the researchers did not find that the assumed knowledge manipulation altered the agreement effect to a greater extent on the affective than on the cognitive scales. Such results imply that the speculation regarding the high positive evaluation of being right is at least partially in error. Apparently the evaluation of being right is not sufficiently polarized to produce an overly large effect on the affective scales. Although the being right interpretation may explain some of the variance in the agreement effect, there is clearly still unexplained variance.

5.   The Being Liked Interpretation

The final interpretation of the agreement effect (and also the attraction effect) is the being liked interpretation proposed by Insko *et al.* (1982). This interpretation is also based on two semicycles. The first semicycle is pictured in Fig. 2a. This semicycle implies that agreement produces *o* to *p* liking and also, of course, that disagreement produces *o* to *p* disliking. To investigate this matter Insko *et al.* (1982) had 30 subjects examine each of the eight standard triads and rate for each of them the extent to which *o* would like or dislike *p*. Note that in the standard triads *p* to *o* sentiment is specified but *o* to *p* sentiment is not. The results indicated a large effect of both *p* to *o* liking and *p* and *o* agreement on *o* to *p* liking. Subjects anticipated a greater degree of *o* to *p* liking when *p* liked rather than disliked *o* and when *p* and *o* agreed rather than disagreed about *x*. The effect of *p* to *o* sentiment on *o* to *p* sentiment is an example of the reciprocated sentiment effect about which Heider (1958) was very explicit. Heider made a major point of the fact that the *p–o* dyad is balanced when *p* to *o* and *o* to *p* are of the same sign. On the other hand, Heider did not discuss the effect of agreement on *o* to *p* sentiment, but such an effect was clearly found. Figure 2a is, of course,

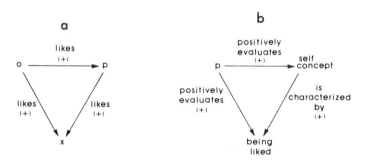

Fig. 2.   One semicycle (a) predicting the agreement–sentiment effect, and another semicycle (b) predicting an agreement effect on the basis of a concern with being liked. From ''A two-valued logic or two-valued balance resolution of the challenge of agreement and attraction effects in *p–o–x* triads, and a theoretical perspective on conformity and hedonism'' by C. A. Insko, A. J. Sedlak, and A. Lipsitz, *European Journal of Social Psychology*, 1982, **12**, p. 155.

an illustration of this agreement–sentiment effect. In this illustration p and o agree by both liking x, but they could, of course, also agree by both disliking x.

The semicycle in Fig. 2a implies that o likes p. But why should such liking be rated as consistent? Such ratings should occur if p has still further reason to suppose that o likes p. This may or may not be the case depending on whether there is further reason to suppose o to p liking—p and o contact or general presumed likableness, for example.

Even, however, if there were no further reason to assume o to p liking, there is still the possibility that the o to p liking implied by agreement would be rated as pleasant. Why is this? A relevant semicycle can be stated if the o to p liking relation can be transformed into the element "being liked." Given this transformation the semicycle is as follows: p positively evaluates being liked (or negatively evaluates being disliked), p positively evaluates his/her self-concept, the self is characterized by being liked (or being disliked). This semicycle is pictured in Fig. 2b. When there is agreement, the semicycle of Fig. 2a implies that the self is liked, and the resulting balance in the semicycle of Fig. 2b produces pleasant affect. On the other hand, when there is disagreement there is the corresponding implication that the self is disliked, and the resulting imbalance in the self-related semicycle produces unpleasant affect.

The above argument provides a rationale for an agreement effect on the affective scales. But why should the agreement effect be larger on the affective than on the cognitive scales? As previoulsy indicated, such a result has been found repeatedly. Paralleling the above discussion of the being right interpretation, balance (and consequent pleasure) should increase to the extent that the elements which are positively associated with the self-concept are themselves highly polarized in the positive direction. Thus, to the extent that being liked is a highly valued element in the context of the hypothetical social situation, semicycle (b) should produce a large effect on the affective scales. Further, there is additional reason to suppose that this effect of semicycle (b) on the affective scales is larger than the effect of semicycle (a) on the cognitive scales to the extent that there are no salient reasons to suppose that o likes p beyond the fact that p and o agree. Recall that it is the existence of additional reasons that o likes p which provides a basis for an effect on the cognitive scales.

The semicycle in Fig. 2b obviously parallels the semicycle in Fig. 1b. The statement of both semicycles assumes that it is meaningful to conceive of a self-concept, that the self-concept is positively evaluated, and that it is possible to transform a relation into an element. In Fig. 1 the relation "p is right" is transformed into the element "being right." In Fig. 2 the relation "o likes x" is transformed into the element "being liked."

The experiment designed to test the being liked interpretation included a four-level manipulation of scales (pleasantness, harmony, expectancy, consistency) and a manipulation of o to p sentiment which, in the nonstandard conditions, covaried either consistently or inconsistently with p and o's agreement about x. This agreement–sentiment manipulation included three levels: standard, agree–like, and disagree–like. In the standard condition there was no statement of o to p sentiment; in the agree–like condition there was a statement of o to p liking whenever there was agreement and o to p disliking whenever there was disagreement; and in the disagree–like condition there was a statement of o to p liking whenever there was disagreement and a statement of o to p disliking whenever there was agreement.

The results are consistent with expectations. The agreement–sentiment manipulation altered the agreement effect so that it was largest in the agree–like condition, intermediate in the standard condition, and smallest in the disagree–like condition. Furthermore, and of most importance, the agree–like manipulation interacted with the scales manipulation. As the means in Table II indicate, the tendency for the most agreement to occur in the agree–like condition and the least in the disagree–like condition was largely due to the affective scales (pleasantness and harmony).

These results are consistent with the being liked interpretation of agreement effects. According to this interpretation large agreement effects on affective scales are a function of the explicit or implicit inference that agreement produces o to p liking and disagreement produces o to p disliking, and the consistency–inconsistency of such sentiment with a positively evaluated self-concept. This is fairly straightforward and simple.

One potentially puzzling matter relates to the fact that being right does not appear as important as being liked in the context of hypothetical $p–o–x$ triads.

TABLE II

AGREEMENT–SENTIMENT BY SCALES INTERACTION MEANS FOR AGREEMENT[a,b]

	Pleasantness	Harmony	Expectancy	Consistency
Standard	1.06	1.64	.14	1.44
Agree–like	2.30	2.36	−.11	.90
Disagree–like	−1.41	−.80	−.16	.14

[a]From "A two-valued logic or two-valued balance resolution of the challenge of agreement and attraction effects in $p–o–x$ triads, and a theoretical perspective on conformity and hedonism" by C. A. Insko, A. J. Sedlak, and A. Lipsitz, *European Journal of Social Psychology,* 1982, **12,** p. 158.

[b]The entries are the means of the differences between the means of the four agreement and four disagreement triads. Ratings were done on a 7-point scale.

Why is this? Insko *et al.* (1982) point out that McGarvey's (1974) postexperimental interview with subjects who had just rated the eight triads revealed that the subjects who conceptualized specific situations tended to imagine interactions which had more of a social than a task atmosphere. The o's were friends or peers and the x's were such things as musical taste, a car, room decoration, or food. This obviously suggests that there may be more task-oriented situations in which being right is a more salient concern, and thus the being right interpretation is a more relevant account of agreement effects. On the other hand, it could be that for many people being liked is generally more highly valued than is being right.

6. Being Liked and the Attraction Effect

Can a concern with being liked also account for the attraction effect and, in particular, the finding that the attraction effect is larger on affective scales? Yes, most certainly. Again, there are two semicycles. The first semicycle relates p to o sentiment with o to p sentiment. Recall that Insko *et al.* (1982) found in their preliminary study that subjects expected more o to p liking when p liked o than when p disliked o. The second semicycle is again the semicycle in Fig. 2b. It includes the self-concept and being liked (or being disliked) as elements: p positively evaluates being liked, p positively evaluates his/her self-concept, the self-concept is characterized by being liked. Since the self-concept is an element in this semicycle, balance in the semicycle predicts positive affect. Thus, this semicycle predicts an attraction effect for the affective scales. Furthermore, on the assumption that the positive evaluation of being liked is highly polarized, the degree of balance (and consequent pleasure) for this semicycle would be relatively large.

Evidence consistent with the being liked interpretation of attraction effect comes from an experiment by Insko and Adewole (1979). This experiment included the usual five scales (pleasantness, harmony, expectancy, consistency, stability) and a two-level manipulation of reciprocated sentiment (reciprocation and standard). In the reciprocation level or condition, o to p sentiment was always the same as p to o sentiment, and in the standard condition there was no mention of o to p sentiment. As the means in Table III indicate, the attraction effect was greater in the reciprocation condition than in the standard condition only with the affective scales. These results are totally consistent with the being liked interpretation of attraction effects.

7. Why Are Agreement Effects Larger Than
Attraction Effects?

Consistent with Zajonc's (1968) review of the early literature it has been repeatedly found that agreement effects are larger than attraction effects. Note

TABLE III

RECIPROCATION BY SCALES INTERACTION MEANS FOR ATTRACTION[a,b]

	Pleasantness	Harmony	Expectancy	Consistency	Stability
Standard	.82	.52	.15	.39	−.08
Reciprocation	1.76	1.94	.04	−.30	−.22

[a]From "The role of assumed reciprocation of sentiment and assumed similarity in the production of attraction and agreement effects in $p-o-x$ triads" by C. A. Insko and A. Adewole, *Journal of Personality and Social Psychology*, 1979, **37**, p. 796.

[b]The entries are the means of the differences between the means of the four p likes o and the four p dislikes o triads. Ratings were done on a 7-point scale. The entries in Table 3 of Insko and Adewole (1979, p. 796) are the means of differences between sums and also include data for $q-o-x$ triads.

that the means in the standard condition of Table II are generally larger than the means in the standard condition in Table III. Why is this the case? One possible answer is that the concern with being right increases the magnitude of the agreement effect beyond that of the attraction effect. While the being liked interpretation applies to both agreement and attraction effects, the being right interpretation applies only to the agreement effect. Thus, the agreement effect may be larger than the attraction effect because of the additional concern with being right.

The above argument obviously assumes that the agreement effect is explained both by the being liked and the being right interpretations. Such an assumption, however, raises a question concerning the extent to which the contact and similarity interpretations are also relevant to the agreement effect (and the attraction effect). This is a question for future research. Currently it is not clear just how essential the contact interpretation is. On the other hand, it is probably safe to conclude that the similarity interpretation is of minimal, if any, importance. Recall that a manipulation of similarity alters the agreement and attraction effects only when they are measured with cognitive scales, and that agreement and attraction effects for cognitive scales are typically of relatively small magnitude.

8. Transformation of Relations to Elements

The being liked interpretation of both agreement and attraction effects and the being right interpretation of agreement effects all involve the transformation of relations to elements. For the being liked interpretation, the o to p sentiment relation is transformed into the element, being liked; and for the being right interpretation the relation p is right is transformed into the element being right. To what extent is such transformation justified? Some reassurance can be obtained from the obvious fact that in our language verbs are routinely transformed into nouns, and that the use of alternative representations for different purposes is common in artificial intelligence (Hunt, 1975; Raphael, 1976). There are really two problems. The first is to determine what exactly is meant by an element (or a noun). The second is to determine the cause or reason for the transformation. Unfortunately, we do not have definitive solutions for either problem.

With regard to the first problem it has become common to observe that a noun, or element, is clearly more than a "person, place or thing." What, then, is a noun? There appears to be no consensus among linguists regarding the appropriate conceptualization of nouns (cf. Lyons, 1966; Sporta, 1966). Quite plausibly, there is a developmental change from semicycles in which the elements are concrete objects to semicycles in which the elements may be abstract concepts. Brown (1958, p. 247), in fact, found that children aged 3–5 used nouns that were typically names of things, and argued that perhaps such a concrete conception of nouns stays with us as adults even though it retains only a "probabilistic truth."

The second problem is to determine the cause or reason for the element-to-relation transformation. This is a matter of more than passing interest because of the above assumption that o to p liking is transformed into the element, being liked, while other relations, for example p positively evaluates being liked and p positively evelutes his/her self-concept, remain relations. Perhaps these relations are not transformed into elements because such transformations would not create semicycles in which degree of balance could be determined. This suggests that the tendency toward balance, or consistency, may be one possible cause of the relation-to-element transformation. Given such a tendency it may or may not be helpful to transform relations into elements.

Another possible determinant of the relation-to-element transformation may be the extent to which p merely assumes (or experiences) the relation or actively attends to the relation. Attending to the relation o likes p, for example, may transform it into the element, liking or being liked.

9. Pleasantness and Balance

In addition to assuming that relations may be transformed into elements, the being right and being liked interpretations also assume that affect is a function of balance–imbalance in semicycles that include the self-concept as an element. The essential idea here is that hedonic affect is self-related. If the self is not involved either directly or vicariously there can be no affect, although there may be consistency. Given that the self is an element in the semicycle, balance implies pleasant affect and imbalance implies unpleasant affect. The parallel between hedonism and balance can be easily seen by examining the four possible semicycles or bands: the self (+) positively associated (+) with reward (+), the self (+) positively associated (+) with cost (−), the self (+) negatively associated (−) with reward (+), and the self (+) negatively associated (−) with cost (−). The first and last of these possibilities are both balanced and hedonic. Thus, we have the interesting theoretical possibility of a balance theory account of hedonistic tendencies.

But to what extent does this theoretical account fit the previously obtained results in the Jordan paradigm? The most obvious problem is that there appear to be semicycles which do not include the self-concept as an element and yet are rated as more pleasant when they are balanced than when they are imbalanced. Three examples are the contact semicycle for attraction, the contact semicycle for agreement, and the three-sign balance semicycle.

Consider first the two contact semicycles. Recall that Insko and Adewole (1979) found that a manipulation of contact increased attraction and agreement for both affective and cognitive scales. Since neither the semicycle relating contact and p to o attraction nor the semicycle relating contact and p and o agreement includes the self-concept as an element, how is the result for the affective scales to be explained? The results indicate that assumed contact did not generally increase pleasantness ratings across all eight triads. Rather, assumed contact increased the pleasantness difference between the p likes o and p dislikes o triads (attraction effect) and also the difference between the p and o agree and p and o disagree triads (agreement effect). Closer examination of the data indicates that this increase in the magnitude of the attraction and agreement effects is primarily due to the low ratings of the two triads in which there is both p to o dislike and p and o disagreement (cf. Table 3 in Insko et al., 1974, p. 61). To the extent that contact under these circumstances took on an assumed confrontational atmosphere with the potential for verbal abuse, it is quite understandable that the relevant triads would be perceived as suggesting inconsistency in self-relevant semicycles and thus unpleasantness. The fact that contact alone was not sufficient to evoke assumed o to p liking and associated pleasantness suggests that information regarding p and o contact has little or no impact when presented in the context of information regarding p to o liking–disliking and p and o agreement–disagreement. Despite initial hopefulness that assumed contact was a very important variable or process in the Jordan paradigm, the total pattern of results suggests that assumed contact in fact plays a somewhat minor role. Semicycles including the contact relation (see Table I) do, of course, explain the fact that a manipulation of contact alters the attraction and agreement effects on the cognitive scales.

The argument for the three-sign balance semicycle is somewhat more complex. Recall that previous research has repeatedly found that the three-sign balance effect occurs with both affective and cognitive scales. Since this semicycle does not include the self-concept as an element, how is the effect with affective scales to be explained? This semicycle is balanced both when p likes an o with whom there is agreement and also when p dislikes an o with whom there is disagreement. The first of these two types of three-sign balance includes the two triads which Jordan (1953) found to be most pleasant. Recall that Jordan found that the triad in which p likes o and agrees with o in liking x, and the triad in which p likes o and agrees with o in disliking x, were rated relatively more pleasant than the remaining six triads. Thus, judging from Jordan's data the only problem is to account for the pleasantness of the three-sign balance triads in which p likes an o with whom there is agreement. Since, however, these triads involve both attraction and agreement this can be done easily. First, note that both the agreement and the p to o liking imply that o likes p and that the positive evaluation of being liked balances a semicycle including the self-concept as an element (see Fig. 2b). Second, note that agreement implies that p is right about x, and that being right also balances a semicycle including the self-concept (see Fig. 1b). Third, there is the additional possibility that the consistency of p to o liking and p to o agreement reinforces the validity of both the p to o judgment and the p to x judgment. Agreeing with someone who is liked and liking someone with whom there is agreement may create a sense of being right about both orientations, and being right is consistent with a positively evaluated self-concept.

What, however, about the other type of three-sign balanced triad? These are the triads in which p dislikes an o with whom there is disagreement. Is it really ture that these triads do not differ in pleasantness from the three-sign imbalanced triads? As previously indicated Jordan (1953) did not find such a difference. This is also true of other investigators (e.g., Aderman, 1969). On the other hand, Insko *et al.* (1974), and Rodrigues (1967) did find descriptively small differences. Perhaps the effect is not real. On the other hand, it may be that in some as yet not clearly specified circumstances the effect does occur. Perhaps the pleasantness of such three-sign balanced triads may be weakly suggested by the consistency of p to o disliking and p to o disagreement. Such a consistency may possibly create a sense of being right about both orientations, and being right is consistent with a positively evaluated self-concept. Note, however, that the detection of such a subtle matter may only occur if subjects pay close attention to each triad and are willing to be good phenomenologists. This is a matter for further study.

10. The Problem of Long- and Short-Term Self-Esteem

A crucial assumption in the balance account of affective ratings or, more generally, of hedonistic tendencies is that p has high self-esteem. Given that p has high self-esteem, it is both balanced and hedonic for p to receive positive outcomes and to avoid or escape negative outcomes. The meaning of this parallel between self-consistency and hedonism is captured in everyday language by references to rational economic decisions or, more generally, to rational economics. However, such a parallel obviously depends upon positive self-evaluation or high self-esteem.

Recognition of the crucial role of self-esteem suggests that the balance account of hedonistic tendencies might be tested by examining individuals with low self-esteem. There is a problem, however, in that it is by no means clear what balance theory does and does not predict for such individuals. One possible prediction is that such individuals should be less concerned with maximizing outcomes. Or, more specifically, such individuals might not regard agreement as pleasant and with sufficiently negative self-esteem would even regard disagreement as pleasant. Closer examination of the problem, however, suggests that it is necessary to distinguish between long- and short-term self-esteem.

It is no surprise that most people tend to rate themselves toward the high-positive ends of most evaluative scales. Unpublished data for ratings by University of North Carolina students, for example, revealed a mean of 5.38 (on a 7-point scale) across a variety of self-descriptive scales (ambitious–lazy, quarrelsome–agreeable, unattractive–attractive, warm–cold, etc.). What, however, about the occasional subjects who rate themselves toward the neutral portion of self-evaluative scales? Do such persons have long-term, low self-esteem, or are their low ratings a reflection of more or less recent events relating to problems with the opposite sex, examination scores, financial problems, and so on? Sometimes very real events can indeed produce low self-esteem—but low self-esteem that is only short-term. The self-*concept* can be partially regarded, analogously to an attitude structure (Rosenberg, 1960), as a set of consistent relations between a positively evaluated self and various attitudes, values, abilities, accomplishments, possessions, friends, group memberships, and so on. Thus, some negative occurrence, such as a divorce, theoretically produces inconsistency and implies the possibility that the self at the "center" of the structure is negative. For many people, however, such a consistency producing, domino effect throughout the structure does not occur. Rather, with the passage of time there is a tendency to believe that having a divorce is perfectly acceptable, due to factors beyond one's own control, and so on. Such alteration, of course, also produces a consistent self-concept. However, during the period of temporarily lowered self-esteem the individual may be motivated to seek social support and find agreement particularly pleasant. The reason for such behavior is that social agreement provides evidence that the self is of overall value in spite of the recent negative occurrence. Thus, for individuals with high, long-term self-esteem, balance theory could be interpreted as predicting that the lower the short-term self-esteem, the greater the tendency to maximize outcomes.

Of course, there may be instances in which the negative events have sufficient strength or number that the individual decides that he or she is, in fact, genuinely worthless; i.e., that the self is negative. Such individuals with low, long-term self-esteem should indeed find social support inconsistent. If such individuals are consistent they should abuse themselves, commit acts that they know will lead to punishment, or commit suicide. Clearly, however, such matters are poorly understood.

Generally what is being advocated is that for those individuals with high self-esteem, both short- and long-term, there should be more of a tendency to maximize outcomes than for those individuals with low self-esteem, both short- and long-term. Complications arise, however, when short- and long-term self-esteem are not consistent. The individuals who should be most highly motivated to maximize outcomes are those with high, long-term but low, short-term self-esteem. The reason for this prediction is that it is such individuals who are suffering the most inconsistency and thus are in most need of social support and positive outcomes to convince them that they are worthy persons.

Although not elaborated in terms of a self-concept structure, Heise (1977, 1979) makes a parallel distinction between enduring feelings, which he refers to as fundamental sentiments, and temporary feelings, which he refers to as transient sentiments. For Heise, "Fundamental sentiments are the relatively stable components of feelings, reflected in substantial test–retest correlations found for attitude measurement 20 and 30 years apart" (1977, p. 164). On the other hand, "Transient feelings are influenced by perceiving events" and they "are manifest at any particular moment and therefore are directly measurable by psychometric instruments like semantic differential scales" (1977, p. 164). As stated by Heise, his "basic premise is that people operate so as to confirm the fundamental sentiments about self and others that are evoked by definitions of situations" (1977, p. 164). And it is interesting that Heise's equations make predictions that parallel the above discussion of the differential effects of long- and short-term self-esteem. It is also interesting that his equations make the symmetrical prediction that the strongest motivation toward negative outcomes should occur for those individuals with low fundamental sentiment but high transient sentiment.

11. The Implicitness–Explicitness
of Balance Inferences

A final matter bearing on the balance theory account of attraction and agreement effects relates to the implicitness–explicitness of balance inferences. Although balance inferences may, of course, be quite explicit, most of them are undoubtedly implicit. For many social situations the relevant balance processes are highly overpracticed and thus may occur more or less "automatically" without explicit attention to all of the relations in the relevant semicycle or semicycles. Thus, the above theoretical account of the agreement effect, for example, does not assume that the subject explicitly goes through a complex reasoning process. Insko *et al.* (1982) make this point.

The subject . . . does not say to himself/herself "let's see, since I agree with *o* that implies that o likes me and that is nice since transforming liking into being liked is consistent with the positive evaluation of myself which is, of course, another one of my sentiments.'' On the other hand, . . . if the right questions are asked of a careful phenomenologist he would agree that one of the reasons why agreement is pleasant is that agreement makes him feel good about himself, and that he feels good about himself because of the implication he is liked or is right, or both. (p. 163)

Insko et al. go on to point out that the recognition of the implicitness of balancing processes clarifies an issue raised by Cacioppo and Petty (1981). Cacioppo and Petty found that a manipulation of the time given subjects to rate $p-o-x$ triads (10 versus 30 seconds) had no effect on the attraction and agreement effects, but did have an effect on the three-sign balance effect. The three-sign balance effect was only significant with the longer time interval. Cacioppo and Petty thus argued that balance processes require time and that attraction and agreement effects therefore cannot be balance effects. But this argument fails to recognize that balance inferences undoubtedly differ in the extent to which they are practiced, automatic, and implicit. The fact that it takes someone 30 seconds to follow a logical argument does not mean that more immediate reactions cannot also be logical—particularly if these reactions have occurred many times before. And this is clearly the case for self-relevant attraction and agreement reactions.

E. APPLICATION TO CONFORMITY

There is an obvious parallel between the being liked and the being right interpretations of agreement effects and Deutsch and Gerard's (1955) widely referenced concepts of normative and informational social influence. Deutsch and Gerard define normative social influence as ''influence to conform to the positive expectations of another'' and informational social influence as ''influence to accept information from another as *evidence* about reality'' (p. 629). Such similarity suggests the interesting possibility of exploring the extent to which conformity in an Asch-type (1956) situation can be at least partially explained by the concerns with being liked and being right. This was, in fact, done in some research by Insko, Drenan, Solomon, Smith, and Wade (1983). In applying the being liked and being right interpretations to "objective" judgments in an Asch-type situation it is, of course, necessary to replace the $p-x$ and $o-x$ sentiment relations with a $p-o$ agreement–disagreement unit relation.

In view of both the importance of conformity in social psychology and the prominence of Deutsch and Gerard's (1955) research, one would have thought that there would be a sizable amount of evidence bearing on interpersonal and informational sources of social influence. After reviewing this evidence, however, Insko et al. (1983), in fact, concluded that the relevant data are largely circumstantial. This point can be most simply illustrated by discussing Duetsch and Gerard's well-known experiment.

Deutsch and Gerard found more conformity with public than with private responding in an Asch-type, line-judgment experiment. There are, however, three problems with this result as evidence for the concern with being liked. First, Deutsch and Gerard's experiment confounded publicness of responding with degree of contact between subjects. Their experiment, in fact, involved the comparison of orally reported responses in a face-to-face situation with switch-operated responses in a situation in which subjects were separated by partitions. Second, in addition to providing a plausible manipulation of the concern with being liked, public responding possibly also increases objective self-awareness, and objective self-awareness may in itself increase conformity. There are two experiments indicating that objective self-awareness increases conformity (Duval, 1976; Wicklund & Duval, 1971) and one experiment failing to find such an effect (McCormick, 1977, described in Wicklund & Frey, 1980). Third, it is not clear whether public responding increases the salience of the concern with being liked or alternatively the salience of the concern with being judged correct. While the latter concern may, in some sense, fall under the rubric of normative social influence, it clearly is different from the concern with being liked.

What about informational social influence, or the concern with being right? Deutsch and Gerard (1955) interpreted the occurrence of conformity in their private situation as evidence for informational social influence. The implicit argument is seemingly one of elimination. Once normative social influence is eliminated, what else is left except for informational social influence? Actually, there are a number of possibilities; conformity may occur, for example, in order not to be different from similar peers. It is interesting to note, however, that some commentators, for example, Allen (1965) and Aronson (1980), have expressed skepticism regarding the actual occurrence of conformity with objective stimuli (like those used by Deutsch and Gerard) and private responding. Perhaps part of the reason for the skepticism relates to the fact that none of the relevant experiments has created a private response condition in which the subjects felt that the experimenter would not learn of their judgments.

The Insko *et al.* (1983) experiment utilized a face-to-face (or side-by-side) situation like that used by Asch (1956). The judgments, however, related not to lengths of lines but to colors. On each trial the confederates and the single subject were presented with three colors and asked to judge whether the middle color was more like the color on the left or the color on the right. On 10 critical trials the confederates selected a color opposite to the one selected by a large majority (between 89 and 65%) of pretest subjects. The experiment included two independent variables. The first of these, determined–undetermined, was intended as a manipulation of the concern with being right. In the determined condition subjects were told that spectrometric readings had been used to determine whether, in fact, the middle color was more like the color on the left or the color on the right. They were furthermore told that if they wished, after the experiment was over, they could compare their judgments with the correct answers. On the other hand, in the undetermined condition subjects were told that since spectrometric readings could not be taken with mixed wave lengths, there was no way to specify whether the middle color was more like the color on the left or the color on the right. Although it is not intuitively clear whether more conformity should occur in the determined or undetermined condition, it is clear that from the perspective of the concern with being right, more conformity should occur in the determined condition.

The second factor in the experiment was a manipulation of private versus public responding. As determined by a rigged card draw, subjects made their judgments either orally and in writing or just in writing. Subjects were, furthermore, told not to write their names on their response slips and, when leaving the room, to drop them in a box filled with other unsigned response slips. Such a procedure, of course, guaranteed total privacy of response in the private condition. Note also that the private–public manipulation was not confounded with degree of contact between subjects and confederates.

In addition to the confounding of the private–public manipulations with contact, two further problems with Deutsch and Gerard's evidence for the being liked interpretation are, as previously indicated, that public responding may increase objective self-awareness and that it is not clear whether public responding increases the concern for evaluation in the sense of being liked or in the sense of being judged correct. Insko et al. (1983) attempted to handle the first of these problems with the addition of a camera-control condition. In this condition the subjects responded privately, but a video camera was aimed at the group. If objective self-awareness increases conformity with color judgments, there should be more influence in the camera-control condition than in the private condition. The second problem is addressed by the private–public by determined–undetermined interaction. If public responding increases concern for evaluation in the sense of being judged correct, the private–public difference should be larger in the determined condition where there is, in fact, the possibility of being judged correct or incorrect.

The results of the experiment indicated two main effects and no interaction. There was more conformity with determined than with undetermined responding and more conformity with public than with private responding. Furthermore, the camera-control condition did not differ from the private condition. Such results provide convincing evidence that the being liked and being right interpretations of the agreement effect can also be applied to a nonhypothetical conformity situation.

It should be noted that there are undoubtedly many differences between the phenomenologies of subjects who are in an Asch-type situation and the phenomenologies of subjects who are considering a hypothetical triad in the Jordan paradigm. Thus, balance theory certainly does not require that the interpretation of the agreement effect be the same as the interpretation of conformity effects. On the other hand, the results of the Insko *et al.* (1983) experiment do provide interesting evidence for the generality of the semicycles that appear to be operating in the Jordan paradigm.

F.   RELATION TO KELMAN'S TYPOLOGY

Finally, discussion of the Jordan paradigm will be concluded by briefly noting an intriguing parallel with Kelman's (1961) functional theory of social influence. Kelman argues that an understanding of social influence requires that we adequately conceptualize the underlying motivational functions. As is well known, Kelman distinguishes among three types of social influence: identification, compliance, and internalization. Identification occurs when an individual adopts an other's opinion because of the relationship with that person. Compliance occurs when an individual accepts influence from an other because of potential rewards and punishments controlled by that person. And internalization occurs when an individual accepts influence because the advocated opinion is congruent with his or her value system.

One of the interesting things about Kelman's typology is the partial similarity to the above description of semicycles that appears to be operating in the Jordan paradigm. Identification parallels the $p-o-x$ semicycle, compliance parallels the two semicycles descriptive of the concern with being liked, and internalization parallels the two semicycles descriptive of the concern with being right.

III.   The Wiest Tetrahedron

A.   INTRODUCTION

Now that a case has been made for the role of implicit semicycles in the explanation of attraction and agreement effects, the reader is in a better position to understand the research on the quantification of balance theory. Even though the concern is with quantification, there is still the problem of the subject's assuming or supplying semicycles that go beyond the experimentally presented semicycle.

B. WIEST (1965)

One of the truly significant developments in the history of balance theory occurred when Wiest (1965) had the idea of conceptualizing Heider's p–o–x triad as a cube. One dimension of the cube consists of the negative to positive values of the p to o sentiment relation, one the negative to positive values of the p to x sentiment relation, and one the negative to positive values of the o to x sentiment relation. Each of the three dimensions in the cube thus represents different quantitative values of one of the three triadic relations. Following Cartwright and Harary's (1956) multiplicative rule, four of the corners of the cube represent balance in the p–o–x semicycle, and four represent imbalance in the p–o–x semicycle. When Wiest connected the four balanced corners of the cube with straight lines, a tetrahedron (a three-sided pyramid) was formed inside the cube. Figure 3 is Wellens and Thistlethwaite's (1971a,b) representation of Wiest's cube and tetrahedron. In this figure Z represents the p to o relation, X represents the p to x relation, and Y represents the o to x relation.

The tetrahedron thus represents a simple linear extrapolation from polarized balance in the p–o–x triad. Wiest assumed that any particular triad that lies either within the tetrahedron or on the surface of the tetrahedron is balanced. He argued, however, that most triads, or their point representations, tend to drift away from the center and toward the surface of the tetrahedron. Why is this? One possible reason, as Wiest points out, is Osgood and Tannenbaum's (1955) assumed tendency toward maximum polarization of sentiments or attitudes. According to Osgood and Tannenbaum, attitudes have a tendency to drift toward simpler, extreme judgments and away from more difficult, discriminating judgments. If this is really true for all three attitudes in the triad (p–o, p–x, o–x),

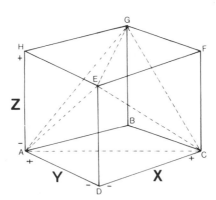

Fig. 3.   Wiest's three-dimensional space as defined by the three relations (or dimensions) p–x (X), o–x (Y), and p–o (Z). From "An analysis of two quantitative theories of cognitive balance" by A. R. Wellens and D. L. Thistlethwaite, *Psychological Review*, 1971, **78**, p. 142.

however, the triads should move to the corners of the tetrahedron and not just generally to the surfaces. Of course, the tendency may occur to a greater extent for p's attitude toward o and x than for p's assumed attitude of o toward x. But is this assumption really valid for all attitudes? Osgood and Tannenbaum's assumption of movement toward maximum polarization appears most reasonable for attitudes that are characterized by ambivalence (cf. Kaplan, 1972). As Tashakkori and Insko (1979) point out, an ambivalent attitude is imbalanced and thus should be unstable. In this case there should indeed be movement toward polarization. No special assumed tendency is required. In the case of attitudes not characterized by ambivalence, however, balance theory provides no apparent basis for an assumed movement toward polarity.

How did Wiest test his tetrahedron model? His approach was correlational. He observed that if the tetrahedron is "sliced" at some point on any one of the three dimensions, the boundaries of the tetrahedron describe a scatter plot for the correlation between the two remaining dimensions. The nature of the scatter plot, and thus the expected correlation, varies as a function of the point at which the slice is made. Note in Fig. 3 that if the X dimension is sliced, or set at one of the more negative values, the expected correlation between Z and Y is negative. With negative values of X, positive values of Z are associated with negative values of Y. On the other hand, as the X dimension is set at increasingly positive values the expected correlations between Z and Y become increasingly positive. Thus, Wiest was able to generate the prediction that the algebraic value of the correlation between Z and Y should increase as the values of X become algebraically greater. Wiest confirmed this prediction with sociometric ratings of fifth-, sixth-, and seventh-grade children. Of course, in such a situation the triad is a $p-o-q$ triad rather than a $p-o-x$ triad. Wiest's data indicate that the correlations between p's liking of o and o's perceived liking of q were smallest for the least liked q and largest for the most liked q.

C. WELLENS AND THISTLETHWAITE'S GENERALIZED TETRAHEDRON FORMULATION

Although Wiest's correlational interpretation of the tetrahedron is certainly interesting, it is clear that he did not achieve the goal of predicting one value of a dimension given specified values for the two remaining dimensions. Wellens and Thistlethwaite (1971a,b) achieved this end with their generalized tetrahedron formulation. If two values for X and Y are specified on the "bottom" of the cube in Fig. 1 and this point is projected into the cube parallel to the Z dimension, the projection will intersect the tetrahedron at its lower boundary and then emerge from its upper boundary. The predicted value on the upper boundary (Z_u) is given by the formula

$$Z_u = k - |X - Y|$$

where X and Y are the values for the two specified dimensions and k is a constant representing the highest possible scale value on the negative-to-positive scale. For the lower boundary (Z_L) a somewhat different formula is required

$$Z_L = |X + Y| - k$$

Illustrative predictions for these two formulas are given in Table IV. It is, of course, arbitrary whether the dependent variable Z relates to the $p-o$, $p-x$, or $o-x$ relations, but in Table IV it is assumed that Z relates to the $p-o$ relation. It is also assumed that the measurements are done on a 5-point, minus-to-plus scale so that $k = 2$.

It is important to note three things regarding the values in Table IV. First, observe that when either the $p-x$ or $o-x$ values are polarized (at ±2) the predicted values for $p-o$ are the same for both upper and lower boundary formulas. This is a reflection of the fact that the two boundaries of the tetrahedron have come together at one edge. Second, observe that when neither the $p-x$ nor $o-x$ values are polarized the predicted $p-o$ values are either more positive or less negative for the upper than for the lower boundary formula. Generally it is the case that in the more ambiguous, less polarized cases the upper boundary formula predicts a more positive value. Third, observe that the predicted values are all 2's in the same-sign diagonal for the upper boundary formula, while this is not the case for the lower boundary formula. The same-sign diagonal is of interest because it specifies the instances in which p and o are in perfect agreement regarding x ($-2/-2$, $-1/-1$, $0/0$, $+1/+1$, $+2/+2$). In these instances the

TABLE IV

PREDICTIONS OF THE UPPER AND LOWER BOUNDARY FORMULAS WHEN $k = 2$[a]

	Upper boundary $o-x$						Lower boundary $o-x$					
$p-x$	-2	-1	0	$+1$	$+2$	M	-2	-1	0	$+1$	$+2$	M
$+2$	-2	-1	0	1	2	$.0$	-2	-1	0	1	2	$.0$
$+1$	-1	0	1	2	1	$.6$	-1	-2	-1	0	1	$-.6$
0	0	1	2	1	0	$.8$	0	-1	-2	-1	0	$-.8$
-1	1	2	1	0	-1	$.6$	1	0	-1	-2	-1	$-.6$
-2	2	1	0	-1	-2	$.0$	2	1	0	-1	-2	$.0$
M	$.0$	$.6$	$.8$	$.6$	$.0$		$.0$	$-.6$	$-.8$	$-.6$	$.0$	

[a]From "Interpersonal attraction and the polarity of similar attitudes: A test of three balance models" by A. Tashakkori and C. A. Insko, *Journal of Personality and Social Psychology*, 1979, **37**, p. 2264.

upper boundary formula always predicts the maximum amount of attraction, 2, while the lower boundary formula only predicts maximum attraction when p and o are both extremely positive or extremely negative about x.

In order to predict a single value for Z, Wellens and Thistlethwaite developed their generalized tetrahedron formulation

$$Z = aZ_u + bZ_L$$

where a and b are weights for the range limits. It appears implicit in Wellens and Thistlethwaite's formulation that $a + b = 1$, thus assuring that Z is an average of the upper and lower boundary predictions. As Wellens and Thistlewaite point out, the values for a and b vary according to the assumptions that are made regarding the distribution of points between the upper and lower boundaries. Consideration of these assumptions takes us to the equal- and unequal-weights models.

D. THE EQUAL- AND UNEQUAL-WEIGHTS MODELS

Wiest assumed that the points drift toward the surface of the tetrahedron. If it is also assumed that the points drift equally toward the two boundaries we have a further basis for Wellens and Thistlethwaite's equal-weights model. In this model a and b are both assigned values of .5, and the predicted Z is a simple average of the predictions for the upper and lower boundary formulas. Other distributions of points are, of course, possible, and it is important to note that any distribution with a mean at the center of the tetrahedron would provide a basis for the equal-weights model.

To the extent that the distribution of points is skewed, one boundary should be weighted more heavily than the other. In their role-playing experiments with a $p-o$ dependent variable, Wellens and Thistlethwaite found that their data were fit best by a model in which the upper boundary weight, a, was .75, and the lower boundary weight, b, was .25. Such assignment of weights produces Wellens and Thistlethwaite's unequal-weights model.

Illustrative predictions with $k = 2$ for the equal- and unequal-weights models are given in Table V. As would be expected from the multiplicative rule, both models predict strong interactions and no, or weak, main effects. One interesting difference between the models is the obvious curvilinear trend in the 0 column and row of the unequal-weights model, and the complete lack of trends in the 0 column and row of the equal-weights model. Note that in the 0 row the predicted values for the unequal-weights model peak in the 0 column. The unequal-weights model also predicts weak curvilinear trends in the ± 1 columns and rows. In the $+1$ row the predicted values peak in the $+1$ column. Other similarities and differences between the two models are discussed below.

CHESTER A. INSKO

TABLE V

PREDICTIONS OF THE EQUAL-WEIGHTS AND UNEQUAL-WEIGHTS
TETRAHEDRON MODELS WHEN $k = 2$[a,b]

	Equal weights $o-x$						Unequal weights $o-x$					
$p-x$	-2	-1	0	$+1$	$+2$	M	-2	-1	0	$+1$	$+2$	M
$+2$	-2	-1	0	1	2	.0	-2	-1.0	.0	1.0	2	.0
$+1$	-1	-1	0	1	1	.0	-1	$-.5$	.5	1.5	1	.3
0	0	0	0	0	0	.0	0	.5	1.0	.5	0	.4
-1	1	1	0	-1	-1	.0	1	1.5	.5	$-.5$	-1	.3
-2	2	1	0	-1	-2	.0	2	1.0	.0	-1.0	-2	.0
M	.0	.0	.0	.0	.0		.0	.3	.4	.3	.0	

[a]From "Interpersonal attraction and the polarity of similar attitudes: A test of three balance models" by A. Tashakkori and C. A. Insko, *Journal of Personality and Social Psychology*, 1979, 37, p. 2265.
[b]For equal weights, $a = .5$ and $b = .5$. For unequal weights, $a = .75$ and $b = .25$.

Wellens and Thistlethwaite used a role-playing procedure in which subjects provided data for each of the 25 cells created by 5 × 5 design. In the Wellens and Thistlethwaite (1971a) experiment the dependent variable was the $p-o$ relation, and x was specified as a "resolution about recent student demonstrations occurring on the West Coast." Subjects were asked to role play each of the five scale positions on the $p-x$ relation in combination with each of the five scale positions on the $o-x$ relation and estimate their feelings on the $p-o$ relation. The results revealed a strong interaction and, of most interest, the peaks predicted by the unequal-weights model.

In the Wellens and Thistlethwaite (1971b) experiments the dependent variables were the $p-o$ relation, the $p-x$ relation, or the $o-x$ relation. There were thus three experiments. In each experiment the subjects were asked to role play each of the five levels of one relation in combination with each of the five levels of the other relation. The results for the experiment with the $p-o$ relation as a dependent variable replicated the findings of Wellens and Thistlethwaite (1971a); i.e., there was a strong interaction and also the occurrence of the peaks predicted by the unequal-weights model. The experiments with $p-x$ and $o-x$ as dependent variables likewise revealed strong interactions. However, the peaks predicted by the unequal-weights model did not occur. These results thus provide more support for the equal-weights model when the dependent variable relates either to attitudes or person perception, but more support for the unequal-weights model when the dependent variable relates to interpersonal attraction.

E. TASHAKKORI AND INSKO (1979)

Tashakkori and Insko (1979) did not use a role-playing methodology as had Wellens and Thistlethwaite, but a variation of the Byrne (1969, 1971) anonymous stranger technique. The dependent variable was the p–o relation, interpersonal attraction. A PDP-11 computer was used to provide each subject with information regarding an anonymous stranger's attitude on five different issues. For four of the five issues the subject's attitude (p–x relation) was -2, 0, or $+2$, and for four of the issues the other's attitude (o–x relation) was -2, 0, or $+2$. One of the five issues for the p–x relation, and a different one of the five issues for the o–x relation, always deviated 1 unit from the remaining four issues. This means that in the $-2/-2$ cell, for example, only three of the five issues in fact involved both p–x and o–x relations of -2. For one of the issues the p–x relation was -1 and the o–x relation was -2, and for one of the issues the p–x relation was -2 and the o–x relation was -1.[6] Such a departure from completely uniform pairings was used in an attempt to create verisimilitude and to prevent subjects in cells with identical p–x and o–x relations from thinking that they were judging themselves, a problem noticed during pilot testing. Unlike the Wellens and Thistlethwaite research, each subject provided data for only one cell of the 3 × 3 design.

Since the equal- and unequal-weights models give predictions for one and not five issues, it was decided simply to generate the prediction for each of the issues separately and then average across issues. These predictions for each cell of the design are given in Table VI.

One of the main purposes of the Tashakkori and Insko (1979) experiment was to demonstrate the superiority of a balance theory approach over the approach followed by Byrne (1969, 1971). Byrne has reported a sizable amount of experimental evidence suggesting that preacquaintance attraction is a linear function of the proportion of similar attitudes. Similarity is defined by Byrne as "any response on the same side of the neutral point as the subject's response, and dissimilarity as any response on the opposite side of the neutral point" (1971, p. 75). As Byrne is aware, such a definition of similarity ignores both the polarity of p and o's attitudes and the discrepancy between p and o's attitudes (for a given side of the scale). Polarity refers to the extent to which the two attitudes deviate from the neutral point, and discrepancy (for a given side of the scale) refers to the extent to which the same-sign attitudes deviate from each other. For same-sign attitudes (attitudes which Byrne defines as similar) polarity is $|X + Y|$ and discrepancy is $|X - Y|$. It is interesting to note that the first of these two

---

[6]For cells in which the p–x or o–x value was 0, the direction of deviation was random across subjects.

TABLE VI

<small>MEAN PREDICTED ATTRACTION IN EACH CELL OF THE DESIGN BASED ON THE EQUAL-WEIGHTS
TETRAHEDRON AND THE UNEQUAL-WEIGHTS TETRAHEDRON[a,b]</small>

	Equal weights $o-x$				Unequal weights $o-x$			
$p-x$	-2	0	$+2$	M	-2	0	$+2$	M
$+2$	-1.61	$-.01$	1.60	$-.01$	-1.61	$.09$	1.60	$.04$
0	$-.01$	$.00$	$.01$	$.00$	$.09$	$.80$	$.11$	$.45$
-2	1.61	$.02$	-1.64	$.00$	1.61	$.13$	-1.64	$.06$
M	$.00$	$.00$	$.00$		$.05$	$.45$	$.05$	

[a]From "Interpersonal attraction and the polarity of similar attitudes: A test of three balance models" by A. Tashakkori and C. A. Insko, *Journal of Personality and Social Psychology,* 1979, **37**, p. 2267.

[b]The slight variations from symmetry in these values are due to minor variations in the number of items per subject and to random variation in the feedback patterns. Note also that the marginals reflect the greater number of subjects in the 0 conditions.

expressions occurs in the lower boundary formula and the second in the upper boundary formula.

As a result of some research done by Nelson (1965), Byrne did expand his formula for predicting attraction so as to include the discrepancy between the subject's and the other's attitude (for a given side of the scale) as well as the proportion of attitudes on the same side of the scale. Nelson found that a small discrepancy produced more attraction than did a large discrepancy. According to Byrne, "If a subject is strongly committed to racial integration, for example, he not only prefers integrationists to segregationists, he prefers those strongly in favor (like himself) to those mildly in favor of integration" (1971, p. 77). This expansion of the formula, however, still did not take into account the polarity of the attitudes. Byrne's formula predicts, for example, that two people mildly in favor of integration should be just as attracted as two people strongly in favor of integration.

Concern with the possible effect of polarity (the difference between $+3/+3$ agreement and $+1/+1$ agreement, for example) leads fairly directly to concern with 0/0 agreement, or attraction between two people who agree in having a neutral attitude. Since Byrne, however, uses 6-point scales to manipulate the $p-x$ and $o-x$ relations, the issue of agreement between two people with neutral attitudes does not arise. On the other hand, it is interesting that Byrne uses 7-point scales (with middle-neutral points) to measure the $p-o$ relation. Following Byrne's definition of similarity it is clear that the use of scales with neutral points for the $p-x$ and $o-x$ relations would leave 0/0 agreement undefined as either

TABLE VII

Mean Liking, $p-o^{a,b}$

| | Liking $o-x$ | | | |
$p-x$	-2	0	$+2$	M
$+2$	$-.64$	.14	1.43	.27
0	.21	.64	.04	.38
-2	1.64	$-.18$	$-.86$	.11
M	.36	.31	.16	

[a]From ''The role of assumed reciprocation of sentiment and assumed similarity in the production of attraction and agreement effects in $p-o-x$ triads'' by C. A. Insko and A. Adewole, *Journal of Personality and Social Psychology,* 1979, **37,** p. 2271.
[b]The marginals reflect the greater number of subjects in the 0 conditions.

similar or dissimilar. Thus, to the extent that Byrne wishes to account for the attraction resulting from agreement between two people with neutral attitudes, some revision of his formulation appears necessary.

From the perspective of the generalized tetrahedron formulation, Byrne's approach suffers from the lack of a polarity term. Note the variation along the same-sign diagonal for the lower boundary formula in Table IV. Predicted attraction is least in the 0/0 cell and most in the two most polarized cells, $-2/-2$ and $+2/+2$. On the other hand, the upper boundary formula, which does not include a polarity term, does not predict any variation along the same-sign diagonal.

For the Tashakkori and Insko (1979) experiment the predicted values are, as previously indicated, given in Table VI. Note that for both the equal- and unequal-weights models the values along the same-sign diagonal decrease in the 0/0 cell. It is also apparent that the decrease is larger for the equal- than the unequal-weights model. The reason for this, of course, is that the lower boundary formula (with its polarity term) has a greater weight in the equal-weights model.

Tashakkori and Insko's (1979) mean liking scores in each cell of the design are presented in Table VII.[7] These scores can be compared with the predicted values of the equal- and unequal-weights models in Table VI. As previously

[7]Measurements were done with 7-point scales in which end point cautions were used to discourage the use of the end points. Thus, from a functional perspective, the scales consisted of 5 points.

indicated, both of these models predict variation along the same-sign diagonal so that there is less liking in the 0/0 cell than in the −2/−2 and +2/+2 cells. This prediction was confirmed.

Some of the written comments regarding o for the subjects in the 0/0 cell are particularly interesting. Here are two examples: "a Freshman [who] didn't seem to be extremely well-informed, close to myself"; "[a person who] is not very well acquainted with current events, just like me." These are subjects who recognized that o was similar on the five issues, but yet were not attracted to that person. Thus, if similarity is defined in terms of objective similarity on the manipulated issues we have a clear indication of a breakdown of the similarity–attraction relationship—a breakdown that can be predicted by balance theory but that is not included in Byrne's formulation.

As predicted by both of the models the liking assessment revealed a significant interaction. Note that across the +2 row the liking scores increase, and that across the −2 row the liking scores decrease. A trend analysis revealed both a linear-by-linear interaction and a quadratic-by-quadratic interaction. The quadratic-by-quadratic interaction results from the curvilinear trends in the 0 column and 0 row, and the lack of such trends in the remaining columns and rows. The quadratic, or curvilinear, trends agree with the unequal-weights model and also with the results obtained by Wellens and Thistlethwaite—although they did not do a trend analysis on their data.

One other result that favors the unequal-weights model is the significant difference between the regression weights for the upper and lower boundary formulas. When rescaled so as to sum to 1 these weights were .70 and .30—not greatly different from Wellens and Thistlethwaite's "unequal weights" of .75 and .25.

These results, then, provide relatively more support for the unequal-weights than for the equal-weights model. There is, however, one result that provides a potential problem for a conclusion regarding the superiority of the unequal-weights model. This is the fact that correlations between predicted and obtained results for the unequal-weights model (.51) and the equal-weights model (.48) do not differ significantly. Does this mean that there is no basis for concluding in favor of the unequal-weights model? No, not necessarily. A major problem with the use of correlations to test the relative adequacy of theoretical models is that correlations are greatly affected by the rank-order similarity of predicted and obtained results. This assertion can be simply illustrated by the fact that the correlation between the numbers 1 to 10 and the square of these numbers is .88. Birnbaum (1973, 1974) has explicitly questioned the assumption that a superior model will necessarily correlate higher with obtained results and presents hypothetical data to illustrate his point. He advocates the use of analysis of variance and visual inspection of graphically displayed results—an approach not unlike the present one of examining trends and/or special contrasts among subsets of the cells. In addition, of course, there is the possibility of comparing the two tetrahendron models by testing the inequality of boundary weights. Despite the superiority of the unequal-weights to the equal-weights model, it is apparent that even the unequal-weights model does not provide a totally adequate fit for the data. Comparison of the predicted values in Table VI with the obtained results in Table VII points to one salient problem. This is the failure of the obtained results to produce as much disliking in the different-sign corner cells as liking in the same-sign corner cells. According to the theoretical values in Table VI, the absolute values of these opposite- and same-sign corner cells should be approximately the same. What accounts for the failure of the subjects to indicate as much $p-o$ disliking as $p-o$ liking? There is nothing in the $p-o-x$ triad, or semicycle, that predicts such a result. However, as was argued in connection with the research on the Jordan paradigm, it is quite likely that the subjects are implicitly (or explicitly) influenced by other concerns. One set of possibilities parallels the being liked interpretation of agreement effects illustrated in Fig. 2. In the same-sign corner cells p and o both like (or both dislike) x, thereby creating a balanced semicycle when o is assumed to like p. Figure 2a is the same as the $p-o-x$ semicycle except for the direction of the relation between p and o. Thus, in the same-sign corner cells in which p and o agree about x, it is implied both that p likes o and that o is assumed to like p. Furthermore, the p to o liking and o to p assumed liking themselves create a balanced semicycle, or dyad. Finally, if it can be assumed that the $o-p$ liking relation can be transformed into the element "being liked," the semicycle in Fig. 2b can be stated. According to this semicycle it is balanced for a positively evaluated self-concept $(+)$ to be characterized by $(+)$ being liked $(+)$. It is therefore apparent that there is nothing in the same-sign corner cells to contradict the simple implication of the $p-o-x$ semicycle that polarized agreement about x should produce p to o liking.

The situation for the opposite-sign corner cells, however, is more complex. When p and o disagree about x, it is implied both that p dislikes o and that o dislikes (or is assumed to dislike) p. Furthermore, such mutual dislike itself creates a balanced $p-o$ semicycle; p dislikes an o who is assumed to dislike p. Again, assuming that o to p sentiment can be transformed into an element, we have the possibility of a further semicycle. In this case, however, the semicycle is imbalanced; p's positively evaluated self-concept $(+)$ is characterized by $(+)$ being disliked $(-)$. Imbalance in this self-relevant semicycle should theoretically create a reluctance to assume that p dislikes o because p dislikes o implies that o dislikes p, and o dislikes p provides a crucial element in the self-relevant semicycle.

The basic argument for the opposite-sign corner cells is really quite simple. Theoretically the subjects were reluctant to dislike o, since such dislike implied that o disliked p and such reciprocal dislike threatened positive evaluation of the self-concept. A crucial link in this argument is the assumption that the subjects indeed were more willing to assume polarized o to p liking in the same-sign corner cells than they were willing to assume polarized o to p disliking in the opposite-sign corner cells. An assessment of reciprocal o to p liking, in fact, confirmed this assumption.

In general, these results indicate the superiority of the tetrahedron approach over the Byrne (1969, 1971) formulation, provide relatively more support for the unequal-weights than the equal-weights model, and finally, indicate that the situation is sufficiently complex to involve more than the one $p-o-x$ semicycle which was explicitly modeled.

F. TASHAKKORI AND INSKO (1981)

Tashakkori and Insko (1981) conducted two experiments, the first of which, like the Tashakkori and Insko (1979) experiment, involved a $p-o$ (interpersonal attraction) dependent variable. Tashakkori and Insko (1981) used a somewhat simpler pattern of item feedback in which only one of the five items deviated from the row and column values for $p-x$ and $o-x$ and, of even more importance, had five-level manipulations of $p-x$ and $o-x$ that included the ± 1 values. The predicted values of the equal-weights and unequal-weights models (for the particular pattern of item feedback) are given in Table VIII.

The main reason for including the ± 1 values for the $p-x$ and $o-x$ factors, or relations, was to enable a more complete specification of the predictions of the two models. Tashakkori and Insko (1981) systematically explored this matter by using the theoretical values in Table VIII to calculate the predicted variance in

TABLE VIII

MEAN PREDICTED LIKING ($p-o$) IN EACH CELL OF THE DESIGN BASED ON THE EQUAL-WEIGHTS ($a = .5$, $b = .5$) AND UNEQUAL-WEIGHTS ($a = .75$, $b = .25$) TETRAHEDRON MODELS ($k = 2$)[a]

	Equal weights $o-x$						Unequal weights $o-x$					
$p-x$	-2	-1	0	$+1$	$+2$	M	-2	-1	0	$+1$	$+2$	M
$+2$	-1.80	-1.00	.00	1.00	1.80	.00	-1.80	-1.00	.00	1.00	1.80	.00
$+1$	-1.00	$-.90$	.00	.90	1.00	.00	$-.90$	$-.45$	.50	1.35	1.10	.32
0	.00	.00	.00	.00	.00	.00	.10	.50	.90	.50	.10	.42
-1	1.00	.90	.00	-0.90	-1.00	.00	1.10	1.35	.50	$-.45$	$-.90$	.32
-2	1.80	1.00	.00	-1.00	-1.80	.00	1.80	1.00	.00	-1.00	-1.80	.00
M	.00	.00	.00	.00	.00	.00	.06	.29	.38	.28	.06	.21

[a]From "Interpersonal attraction and person perception: Two tests of three balance models" by A. Tashakkori and C. A. Insko, *Journal of Experimental Social Psychology*, 1981, **17**, p. 270.

each of the trend components of the overall interaction for each model. There are 16 such components—one for each of the 16 degrees of freedom for the overall interaction. The predicted variances for each trend component are given in Table IX. As the values in Table IX indicate, both models predict a large linear-by-linear (1×1) component, and much smaller linear-by-cubic (1×3), cubic-by-linear (3×1), and cubic-by-cubic (3×3) components. The cubic trends can be seen in the predicted values in Table VIII. Note that the predictions for the equal-weights model in the $+1$ row are -1.00, $-.90$, 0.00, $.90$, and 1.00. These values contain both linear and cubic components of trend variance. A cubic trend involves two inflection points (e.g., decrease, increase, decrease). However, the small, large, large, small pattern of change provides a basis for expecting significant cubic variance once the linear component is removed. Across the $+2$ row $(-1.80, -1.00, 0.00, 1.00, 1.80)$ the cubic component is smaller and the linear component is larger; across the 0 row $(0.00, 0.00, 0.00, 0.00, 0.00)$ there is no variance of any kind; and across the -1 and -2 rows the trends are opposite in sign to those in the $+1$ and $+2$ rows.

TABLE IX

PREDICTED VARIANCE IN THE INTERACTION BY THE TWO
MODELS FOR EACH OF THE SIXTEEN TREND COMPONENTS[a]

Component[b]	Equal weights	Unequal weights
1×1	46.85	46.85
1×2		
1×3	.46	.46
1×4		
2×1		
2×2		.62
2×3		
2×4		
3×1	.46	.46
3×2		
3×3	.63	.63
3×4		
4×1		
4×2		.01
4×3		
4×4		.07

[a]From "Interpersonal attraction and person perception: Two tests of three balance models" by A. Tashakkori and C. A. Insko, *Journal of Experimental Social Psychology,* 1981, **17,** p. 271.
[b]The numbers 1, 2, 3, and 4 refer to the linear, quadratic, cubic, and quartic components, respectively. The first number is for $p–x$ and the second for $o–x$.

Aside from two higher order trend components of trivial magnitudes, the only difference between the two models relates to the quadratic by quadratic (2 × 2) component. As the values in Table VIII indicate, the unequal-weights model predicts a curvilinear trend across the 0 row (0.10, 0.50, 0.90, 0.50, 0.10). There are also curvilinear trends across the +1 row (−0.90, −0.45, 0.50, 1.35, 1.10), and the −1 row (1.10, 1.35, 0.50, −0.45, −0.90). Note that for these two latter trends the peaks occur not in the center but in the +1/+1 and −1/−1 cells, respectively.

The obtained mean liking scores for the p to o relation are given in Table X. A trend analysis of the significant interaction revealed three effects: linear by linear, quadratic by quadratic, and cubic by cubic. The linear-by-cubic and cubic-by-linear components are not significant, but since these components each constitute less than 1% of the total predicted variance in the interaction the failure is not too surprising. From the standpoint of differentiating the two models, the most interesting result is the significant quadratic-by-quadratic interaction. Note the curvilinear trend in the 0 row, the peak at the +1/+1 cell in the + row, and the peak at the −1/−1 cell in the −1 row.

A further result consistent with the unequal-weights model is a significant difference between the two boundary weights. When rescaled so as to sum to 1, they were again found to be .70 and .30—reasonably close to Wellens and Thistlethwaite's weights of .75 and .25.

It is also interesting that, as in the Tashakkori and Insko (1979) experiment, the values along the same-sign diagonal (1.90, 1.50, .70, 1.70, 1.80) increase on either side of the 0/0 cell. It is apparent that five out of five similar attitudes are not always the same as five out of five similar attitudes. These data make it clear that similarity of nonpolarized attitudes, and in particular of neutral at-

TABLE X

MEAN LIKING, p–o^a

p–x	Liking o–x					
	−2	−1	0	+1	+2	M
+2	−1.20	−.80	−.60	.70	1.80	−.02
+1	−.20	−.10	.20	1.70	.60	.44
0	−.30	.00	.70	.70	.00	.22
−1	1.00	1.50	−.10	−.40	−.30	.34
−2	1.90	1.10	−.10	−.10	−1.60	.24
M	.24	.34	.02	.52	.10	.24

[a] From "Interpersonal attraction and person perception: Two tests of three balance models" by A. Tashakkori and C. A. Insko, *Journal of Experimental Social Psychology*, 1981, **17**, p. 275.

titudes, does not result in markedly high attraction. Such results are consistent with the findings of Wetzel and Insko (1982) that similarity to ideal is a more major determiner of attraction than is similarity to self. Their procedure involved the manipulation of the two types of similarity through the use of content free dimensions. But are neutral attitudes really "un-ideal" attitudes? In view of the Tashakkori and Insko (1981) subjects' tendency to give unflattering characterizations of the neutral other on a postexperimental questionnaire ("boring," "unimaginative," "wishy-washy," "uninformed," "apathetic"), it indeed appears that neutral attitudes are not regarded as ideal. Similarly unflattering characterizations of the neutral other were obtained in the 1979 experiment.

In one respect the 1981 experiment did obtain dfferent results from those of the 1979 experiment. This is in the correlations between predicted and obtained liking scores. In the 1981 experiment these correlations were .64 and .65 for the equal- and unequal-weights models. In the 1979 experiment the analogous correlations were .48 and .51, respectively. How can this difference be explained? One possibility is that the 1979 experiment contained a greater proportion of subjects in either the 0 column or row. However, the correlations for the comparable corner cells still differ between experiments (.79 for both models in the 1979 experiment and .93 for both models in the 1981 experiment). Another possibility relates to the somewhat more complex pattern of item feedback in the 1979 experiment. In the 1979 experiment two of the items deviated from the remaining three, while in the 1981 experiment one item deviated from the remaining four. It may be that the more complex pattern produced more uncertainty and thus reduced the accuracy of prediction. This whole matter of combining predictions from different items obviously is not well understood and needs to be studied further.

Although the data for the 1981 experiment are in many respects in good agreement with the unequal-weights model, it is again apparent that the means in the opposite-sign corner cells are not as polarized in the negative direction as the means in the same-sign corner cells are polarized in the positive direction (see Table X). Similar results were obtained in the 1979 experiment (see Table VII). Also in agreement with the 1979 experiment, an assessment of reciprocal o to p liking in the 1981 experiment revealed a greater reluctance to assume reciprocal disliking in the opposite-sign corner cells than to assume reciprocal liking in the same-sign corner cells.

The theoretical argument developed to account for the above pattern of results is based on the inconsistency of being disliked and having a positive self-concept. Consistent with this position, Tashakkori and Insko (1981) argued that the avoidance of mutual dislike was, in fact, responsible for the appearance of relatively greater support for the unequal- than the equal-weights model. As previously pointed out, one important difference between the upper and lower boundary predictions is that when neither $p-x$ nor $o-x$ is polarized the upper boundary predictions are either more positive or less negative than are the lower boundary predictions (see Table IV). Thus, when subjects avoided mutual dislike they were shifting away from the generally negative lower boundary toward the generally positive upper boundary. This argument implies that the appearance of support for the unequal-weights model as applied to the $p-o-x$ semicycle was, in fact, due to the operation of semicycles that were not being modeled. Possibly, then, the equal-weights model would be most appropriate for the $p-o-x$ semicycle—if that semicycle could be studied in isolation from other relevant ones.

The approach taken by Tashakkori and Insko (1981) to this problem was to do an experiment in which the o to p relation was manipulated along with the p to x relation. The dependent variable was the o to x relation. This approach certainly does not isolate the $p-o-x$ semicycle from all other semicycles. However, since the o to p relation was manipulated, Tashakkori and Insko (1981) argued that there was less opportunity for the subject to avoid being disliked and thus less basis for inequality in the boundary weights. They thus predicted that the equal-weights model would provide a better fit for the data than would the unequal-weights model. This prediction was not totally without precedent since Wellens and Thistlethwaite (1971b) found that with both $o-x$ and $p-x$ dependent variables "the results were best described by an equal-weights version of the Wiest's tetrahedron model" (p. 82). In both of these experiments there was a manipulation of the p to o, rather than o to p, relation; but the close psychological connection between these two relations may reduce the importance of the difference.

After subjects completed the first Tashakkori and Insko (1981) experiment they were asked to return a few days later for a further study. They were also asked to sign a consent form giving the experimenter permission to present some of their attitudes to other subjects. Thus, when subjects did return 3–6 days later, it was plausible for the experimenter to inform them that five of their attitudes had, in fact, been presented to another subject (just as some prior o's attitudes had previously been presented to them). Accordingly, subjects were shown the other subject's supposed liking judgment of them and asked to judge this subject's attitude on each of the five issues. Thus, there were five-level manipulations of $p-x$ and $o-p$ with an $o-x$ dependent variable. In order to prevent subjects from receiving any of the items used in the first experiment, they were assigned to a different level of the $p-x$ factor in the second experiment. Except for this constraint, subjects were randomly assigned to conditions.

Cell means for each subject's mean $o-x$ judgment are presented in Table XI. A trend analysis of the significant interaction revealed the expected linear-by-linear and cubic-by-cubic effects. In view of the nonsignificant quadratic-by-quadratic effects these results are consistent with the equal-weights model. Also consistent with the equal-weights model is the nonsignificance of the difference between boundary weights.

TABLE XI

Mean Perception of o's Attitude, $o-x^a$

$p-x$	$o-p$					M
	-2	-1	0	$+1$	$+2$	
$+2$	$-.36$	$.26$	$.24$	$.95$	1.52	$.50$
$+1$	$-.38$	$.02$	$.18$	$.62$	$.80$	$.24$
0	$-.24$	$.34$	$.10$	$.32$	$.49$	$.19$
-1	$.34$	$.76$	$.08$	$-.52$	$-.78$	$-.02$
-2	1.00	$.00$	$-.59$	$-.56$	-1.46	$-.32$
M	$.07$	$.28$	$.00$	$.12$	$.09$	$.11$

[a] From "Interpersonal attraction and person perception: Two tests of three balance models" by A. Tashakkori and C. A. Insko, *Journal of Experimental Social Psychology*, 1981, 17, p. 282.

Tashakkori and Insko (1981) predicted that the data would be in greater agreement with the equal- than the unequal-weights model, and the obtained results are consistent with this expectation. One result, however, is not consistent with either of the models. This is a significant main effect for $p-x$ such that large values of $p-x$ are associated with large values of $o-x$. The marginal means are in Table XI. The means indicate that subjects tended to perceive the other as having attitudes in agreement with their own.

How can such an agreement tendency be explained? Recall that research in the Jordan paradigm has revealed evidence for four types of balance explanations for the agreement effect. These are assumed contact, assumed similarity, concern with being right, and concern with being liked. Two of these explanations, assumed contact and concern with being liked, are not obviously applicable to the present data. The subjects did not have, nor did they anticipate having, contact with the other. Also, since the o to p relation was manipulated there was less opportunity for the subjects to avoid being disliked. This leaves assumed similarity and concern with being right as possible explanations. Perhaps the subjects recognized the similarity between themselves and the other who had been in the same role, and this led to balancing agreement. Or perhaps the subjects attributed attitudes to the other in agreement with their own in order to provide some assurance of being right. The latter of these two possibilities is perhaps more plausible, but this, again, is a matter for future research.

G. PSYCHOLOGICAL MEANING OF THE UPPER
     AND LOWER BOUNDARIES

Up to this point the upper and lower boundaries have been treated mainly as mathematical abstractions. Perhaps, however, it is worth speculating about the possible psychological meaning of these boundaries.

Recall that when either of the two dimensions of the tetrahedron is extremely polarized there is no difference between the upper and lower boundary predictions (see Table IV). For the nonpolarized levels, however, the upper boundary predictions are less negative, or more positive, than the lower boundary predictions. This implies that when neither relation is polarized, different but equally consistent reactions are possible. One can regard the jar as either half full or half empty, one can "look on the bright side" or "look on the dark side," one can be optimistic or pessimistic. Thus, in the nonpolarized instances (when the boundaries are distinct) upper boundary reactions are "sunny" reactions and lower boundary reactions are "dark" reactions.

IV. The Logic and Non-Logic of Thought and Feelings

Since Runkel and Peizer's (1968) important article it has been clear that if balance theory is restricted to just positive and negative relations the distinction between the multiplicative rule and two-valued logic is "virtually" erased.[8] And it seems intuitively compelling that thought and feeling are at least to some degree logical. But is thought totally logical? Common sense suggests not. This is a matter that was confronted by McGuire (1960) when he set out to incorporate logic in a theory of attitude change. McGuire focused on two problems. The first problem is that hedonistic considerations may distort logical inferences. The second problem is that logic is two-valued while human thought is capable of many-valued distinctions. McGuire's solution to the first problem was to postulate a separate "wishful thinking" tendency which was assumed to distort logical inferences. His solution to the second problem was to combine logic and probability theory into a "probabilogical" approach. This probabilogical approach was developed further by Wyer and Goldberg (1970) and by Wyer (1974).

Since balance theory is also basically a logic theory, it is interesting to point out, by way of summary, how the two problems confronted by McGuire are solved. With regard to the hedonistic tendency, the solution flows from a recog-

---

[8]As previously indicated, Runkel and Peizer (1968) pointed this out as a reaction against Abelson and Rosenberg's (1958) widely quoted distinction between logic and "psycho-logic." It is interesting to note that Abelson (1983) has more recently critiqued balance theory because of its historical dependence on the "weak . . . linkage drawn between configurations of stimulus elements and configurations of cognitive elements" (p. 41), and Harary (1983) has replied that the basis of balance theory is really boolean algebra; i.e., that aspect of formal logic which relates to the algebra of classes. In view of the continuing confusion perhaps it would be preferable if some label other than "balance" were used to refer to all two-valued implications of the multiplicative rule. Possibly we should refer to "two-valued logic," and also the "linear-extrapolation beyond two-valued logic."

nition that the balancing of semicycles in which a positive self-concept is one of the elements results in hedonic advantage. Since the balancing of self-related semicycles is just as logical as the balancing of non-self-related semicycles it is not really necessary to postulate a separate wishful thinking tendency. With regard to the many valued characteristic of human thought, the solution flows from simple linear extrapolation. Consider initially the polar extremes for the three plus-to-minus relations in some triad or semicycle. These polar extremes are the pure exemplars of the two-valued signs. Following the multiplicative rule and two-valued logic, four of these extremes are balanced and four are imbalanced. Represented spatially, four of the eight corners of the cube are balanced and four are imbalanced. The problem is how to generalize beyond the pure signs to the quantitative values. This is done by connecting the corners with straight lines, i.e., through simple linear extrapolation. Although such an approach has not been developed for semicycles with other than three relations, for three-relations semicycles the approach appears simpler and more elegant than is the combining of two-valued logic and probability theory.[9] Whether or not the linear extrapolation approach will enable superior predictions is a matter for future research and theoretical development. For now, it is sufficient to note that the small amount of existing research has provided an impressive degree of support for the linear extrapolation beyond logic.

REFERENCES

Abelson, R. P. Whatever became of consistency theory? *Personality and Social Psychology Bulletin*, 1983, **9**, 37–54.
Abelson, R. P., & Rosenberg, M. J. Symbolic psycho-logic: A model of attitude cognition. *Behavioral Science*, 1958, **3**, 1–13.
Aderman, D. Effects of anticipating future interaction on the preference for balanced states. *Journal of Personality and Social Psychology*, 1969, **11**, 214–219.
Allen, V. L. Situational factors in conformity. In L. Berkowitz (Ed.), *Advances in Experimental Social Psychology* (Vol. 2). New York, Academic Press, 1965.
Anderson, N. H. Some problems in using analysis of variance in balance theory. *Journal of Personality and Social Psychology*, 1977, **35**, 140–158.
Aronson, E. *The Social Animal* (3rd Ed.). San Francisco, Freeman, 1980.

[9]With two-element semicycles, for example p likes o and perceives that o likes p, connection of the $-3/-3$ and $+3/+3$ points with a straight line leads to the prediction that the p to o and o to p relations are the same. With a four-element semicycle, for example p likes o, and perceives that o likes q and that q likes r, it is less apparent how to proceed. One possibility, however, is to use tetrahedrons sharing a common relation. Thus, the first tetrahedron would relate to the $p-o-q$ semicycle and the second the $p-q-r$ semicycle. A tetrahedron for the first semicycle would predict the p to q relation, and given that relation the tetrahedron for the second semicycle could predict the p to r relation.

Asch, S. E. Studies of independence and conformity: I. A minority of one against a unanimous majority. Psychological Monographs, 1956, 70(9) (Whole No. 416).

Birnbaum, M. H. The devil rides again: Correlation as an index of fit. Psychological Bulletin, 1973, 79, 239–242.

Birnbaum, M. H. Reply to the devil's advocate: Don't confound model testing and measurement. Psychological Bulletin, 1974, 81, 854–859.

Brown, R. Words and things. Glencoe, Illinois: Free Press, 1958.

Byrne, D. Attitudes and attraction. In L. Berkowitz (Ed.), Advances in experimental social psychology (Vol. 4). New York: Academic Press, 1969.

Byrne, D. The attraction paradigm. New York: Academic Press, 1971.

Cacioppo, J. T., & Petty, R. E. The effects of message repetition and position on cognitive response, recall, and persuasion. Journal of Personality and Social Psychology, 1979, 37, 97–109.

Cacioppo, J. T., & Petty, R. E. Effects of extent of thought on the pleasantness ratings of p–o–x triads: Evidence for three judgmental tendencies in evaluating social situations. Journal of Personality and Social Psychology, 1981, 40, 1002–1009.

Cartwright, D., & Harary, D. Structural balance: A generalization of Heider's theory. Psychological Review, 1956, 63, 277–293.

Crockett, W. H. Balance, agreement and subjective evaluations of the p–o–x triads. Journal of Personality and Social Psychology, 1974, 29, 102–110.

Deutsch, M., & Gerard, H. B. A study of normative and informational social influences upon individual judgment. Journal of Abnormal and Social Psychology, 1955, 51, 629–636.

Duval, S. Conformity on a visual task as a function of personal novelty on attitudinal dimensions and being reminded of the object status of self. Journal of Experimental Social Psychology, 1976, 12, 87–98.

Festinger, L. A theory of social comparison processes. Human Relations, 1954, 1, 117–140.

Fillenbaum, S. Mind your p's and q's: The role of content and context in some uses of and, or, and if. In C. H. Bauer (Ed.), The psychology of learning and motivation (Vol. 11). New York: Academic Press, 1977.

Gutman, G. M., & Knox, R. E. Balance, agreement, and consistency ratings of hypothetical social situations. Journal of Personality and Social Psychology 1972, 24, 351–357.

Gutman, G. M., Knox, R. E., & Storm, T. G. Developmental study of balance agreement, and attraction effects in the ratings of hypothetical social situations. Journal of Personality and Social Psychology, 1974, 29, 201–211.

Harary, R. Consistency theory is alive and well. Personality and Social Psychology, 1983, 9, 60–64.

Heider, F. Attitudes and cognitive organization. Journal of Psychology, 1946, 21, 107–112.

Heider, F. The psychology of interpersonal relations. New York: Wiley, 1958.

Heise, D. R. Social action as the control of affect. Behavioral Science, 1977, 22, 163–176.

Heise, D. R. Understanding events. Cambridge: Cambridge University Press, 1979.

Henle, M. On the relation between logic and thinking. Psychological Review, 1962, 69, 366–378.

Hunt, E. B. Artificial intelligence. New York: Academic Press, 1975.

Insko, C. A. Theories of attitude change. New York: Appleton-Century-Crofts, 1967.

Insko, C. A. Balance theory and phenomenology. In R. Petty, T. Ostrom, & T. Brock (Eds.), Cognitive responses in persuasion. Hillsdale, New Jersey: Erlbaum, 1981.

Insko, C. A., & Adewole, A. The role of assumed reciprocation of sentiment and assumed similarity in the production of attraction and agreement effects in p–o–x triads. Journal of Personality and Social Psychology, 1979 37, 790–808.

Insko, C. A., Drenan, S., Solomon, M. R., Smith, R., & Wade, T. J. Conformity as a function of the consistency of positive self-evaluation with being liked and being right. Journal of Experimental Social Psychology 1983, 19, 341–358.

Insko, C. A., Sedlak, A. J., & Lipsitz, A. A two-valued logic or two-valued balance resolution of the challenge of agreement and attraction effects in p–o–x triads, and a theoretical perspective on conformity and hedonism. *European Journal of Social Psychology,* 1982, **12,** 143–167.

Insko, C. A., Songer, E., & McGarvey, W. Balance, positivity, and agreement in the Jordan paradigm. A defense of balance theory. *Journal of Experimental Social Psychology,* 1974, **10,** 53–83.

Johnson-Laird, P. N. Models of deduction. In R. J. Falmagne (Ed.), *Reasoning: Representation and process.* Hillsdale, New Jersey: Erlbaum, 1975.

Jordan, N. Behavioral forces that are a function of attitude and of cognitive organization. *Human Relations,* 1953, **6,** 273–287.

Kaplan, K. J. On the ambivalence–indifference problem in attitude theory and measurement. *Psychological Bulletin,* 1972, **77,** 361–372.

Kelman, H. C. Process of opinion change. *Public Opinion Quarterly,* 1961, **25,** 57–58.

Lyons, J. Towards a "notional" theory of the "parts of speech." *Journal of Linguistics,* 1966, **2,** 209–236.

McCormick, T. F. *The development of attitudes and the mediation of self-focused attention.* Unpublished doctoral dissertation, University of Texas at Austin, 1977.

McGarvey, W. E. *Beyond three-sign balance: Balance theory predictions for more than three bands in the Jordan paradigm.* Unpublished doctoral dissertation, University of North Carolina, 1974.

McGuire, W. J. A syllogistic analysis of cognitive relationships. In C. I. Hovland and M. J. Rosenberg (Eds.), *Attitude organization and change.* New Haven: Yale University Press, 1960.

Miller, C. E., & Norman, R. M. Balance agreement and attraction in hypothetical social situations. *Journal of Experimental Social Psychology,* 1976, **12,** 109–119.

Morrissette, J. An experimental study of the theory of structural balance. *Human Relations,* 1958, **11,** 239–254.

Nelson, D. *The effect of differential magnitude of reinforcement on interpersonal attraction.* Unpublished doctoral dissertation, University of Texas, 1965.

Newcomb, T. M. Interpersonal balance. In R. P. Abelson, E. Aronson, W. J. McGuire, T. M. Newcomb, M. J. Rosenberg, & P. H. Tannenbaum (Eds.), *Theories of cognitive consistency: A sourcebook.* Chicago: Rand McNally, 1968.

Osgood, C. E., & Tannenbaum, P. H. The principle of congruity in the prediction of attitude change. *Psychological Review,* 1955, **62,** 42–55.

Petty, R. E., & Cacioppo, J. T. Forewarning, cognitive responding, and resistance to persuasion. *Journal of Personality and Social Psychology,* 1977, **35,** 645–655.

Raphael, B. *The thinking computer: Mind inside matter.* San Francisco: Freeman, 1976.

Rodrigues, A. The effects of balance, positivity and agreement in triadic social relations. *Journal of Personality and Social Psychology,* 1967, **5,** 472–476.

Rosenberg, M. J. An analysis of affective–cognitive consistency. In C. I. Hovland & M. J. Rosenberg (Eds.), *Attitude organization and change.* New Haven: Yale University Press, 1960.

Runkel, P. J., & Peizer, D. B. The two-valued orientation of current equilibrium theory. *Behavioral Science* 1968, **13,** 56–65.

Sporta, S. Phoneme distribution and language universals. In J. H. Greenberg (Ed.), *Universals of language.* Cambridge, Massachusetts: MIT Press, 1966.

Tashakkori, A., & Insko, C. A. Interpersonal attraction and the polarity of similar attitudes: A test of three balance models. *Journal of Personality and Social Psychology,* 1979, **37,** 2262–2277.

Tashakkori, A., & Insko, C. A. Interpersonal attraction and person perception: Two tests of three balance models. *Journal of Experimental Social Psychology,* 1981, **17,** 266–285.

Wellens, A. R., & Thistlethwaite, D. L. An analysis of two quantitative theories of cognitive balance. *Psychological Review,* 1971, **78,** 141–150.(a)

Wellens, A. R., & Thistlethwaite, D. L. Comparison of three theories of cognitive balance. *Journal of Personality and Social Psychology,* 1971, **20,** 89–92.(b)

Wetzel, C. G., & Insko, C. A. The similarity–attraction relationship: Is it an ideal one? *Journal of Experimental Social Psychology* 1982, **18,** 253–276.

Wicklund, R. A., & Duval, S. Opinion change and performance facilitation as a result of objective self-awareness. *Journal of Experimental Social Psychology,* 1971, **7,** 319–342.

Wicklund, R. A., & Frey, N. Self-awareness theory: When the self makes a difference. In D. M. Wegner & R. R. Vallaher (Eds.), *The self in social psychology.* New York: Oxford University Press, 1980.

Wiest, N. M. A quantitative extension of Heider's theory of cognitive balance applied to interpersonal perception and self-esteem. *Psychological Monographs,* 1965, **79**(14) (Whole No. 607).

Willis, R. H., & Burgess, T. D. G., II. Cognitive and affective balance in sociometric dyads. *Journal of Personality and Social Psychology,* 1974, **29,** 145–152.

Wyer, R. S. *Cognitive organization and change: An information-processing approach.* Hillsdale, New Jersey: Erlbaum, 1974.

Wyer, R. S., & Goldberg, L. A. A probabilistic analysis of the relationships between beliefs and attitudes. *Psychological Review,* 1970, **77,** 100–120.

Zajonc, R. B. Cognitive theories in social psychology. In G. Lindzey &. E. Aronson, (Eds.), *The handbook of social psychology* (Vol. 1). Reading, Massachusetts: Addison-Wesley, 1968.

THE SOCIAL RELATIONS MODEL

David A. Kenny

DEPARTMENT OF PSYCHOLOGY
UNIVERSITY OF CONNECTICUT
STORRS, CONNECTICUT

Lawrence La Voie

DEPARTMENT OF PSYCHOLOGY
UNIVERSITY OF MIAMI
CORAL GABLES, FLORIDA

I. Introduction 142
   A. Model 142
   B. Relation to Kelley's Covariation Principle 145
II. Design 149
III. Illustrations 153
   A. Role of the Perceiver and the Perceived 154
   B. Individual Differences in Nonverbal Communication 156
   C. Reciprocity of Attraction 157
   D. Social Development 160
   E. Interpersonal Perception 161
   F. Self–Other Differences 162
IV. Statistical Analysis 163
   A. Estimation 163
   B. Multivariate Generalization 165
   C. Fixed Effects 166
   D. Significance Testing 167
V. Design of Experiments 167
VI. Group Effects 170
VII. Relation to Other Procedures 171
VIII. Limitations 173
   A. Theoretical Limitations 173
   B. Practical Issues 175
IX. Conclusion 176
   References 178

ADVANCES IN EXPERIMENTAL
SOCIAL PSYCHOLOGY, VOL. 18

Copyright © 1984 by Academic Press, Inc.
All rights of reproduction in any form reserved.
ISBN 0-12-015218-5

I. Introduction

The study of two-person social interaction is a cornerstone of social psychology. Person perception, interpersonal attraction, bargaining, nonverbal communication, aggression, prosocial behavior, and persuasion can all be viewed from a dyadic perspective. This focus on dyads is justified ecologically since 73% of naturally formed groups are dyads (James, 1953).

Within social psychology, there are two major orientations to the study of dyads. In the first approach, one member of the dyad is called the subject and provides the measures on the dependent variable. The other member's behavior is controlled by the experimenter through the use of either confederates or of prepared stimulus materials. The second approach is the observational approach in which there are no manipulations. In this approach, the behavior of both persons in the dyad is observed. We present in this chapter a third approach that is a blend of the manipulational and observational approaches. It is manipulational because the researcher controls with whom each person interacts. It is observational since the behavior of both persons is observed. Each person in the dyad serves as both subject and stimulus.

The study of two-person interaction requires an understanding of the full complexity that is involved. For instance, consider two persons, Peter and Paul, interacting. The behavior of Peter is a function of Peter himself, of his partner Paul, and of the relationship that Peter has with Paul. These three effects may be denoted as actor, partner, and relationship effects, respectively. The model that describes the dyad using these components is called the Social Relations Model (Kenny, 1981). Let us discuss each component of the model in more detail.

A. MODEL

The *actor effect* is perhaps the easiest of the three effects to understand. How much Peter talks, how much he likes others, and how much he trusts others in general are all presumably a function of Peter's personality, skill, and character. The actor effect refers to Peter's average level of behavior in the presence of a variety of other partners (Paul, Henry, Mary, and so on).

The *partner effect* refers to the amount of behavior that a person consistently elicits from others. Certain persons engender speech, attraction, and trust regardless of the person with whom they are interacting. Thus, the partner effect refers to the average level of behavioral response that Paul elicits from others. The average reaction to a given person is the partner effect for that person.[1]

---

[1]For certain variables there might be a question about what is the actor effect and what is the

The whole need not be the sum of its parts. The behavior of Peter toward Paul may not be totally explained by a knowledge of how Peter relates, on the average, to others and what response Paul elicits from others, on the average. Peter and Paul have formed a unique relationship and that relationship alters in some way Peter's response to Paul. Peter has made a *unique adjustment* to Paul and the unique adjustment will be referred to as the *relationship effect*. This relationship effect is directional. That is, the unique adjustment made by Peter toward Paul need not be exactly the same as Paul's adjustment toward Peter. For instance, Paul may be attracted to Peter but the attraction may not be reciprocated. The coordination of these adjustments will be discussed later.

Like any model we must allow for random variation or noise. How Peter relates to Paul will change over time. Thus, the final term in the Social Relations Model is *instability* or error.

In equation form the model for the behavior of person i with partner j at occasion k is

$$X_{ijk} = \mu + \alpha_i + \beta_j + \gamma_{ij} + \epsilon_{ijk}$$

The terms are μ, constant term across actors and partners; α_i, actor effect for person i; β_j, partner effect for person j; γ_{ij}, relationship effect for i with j; and ϵ_{ijk}, instability or error. Again, we should note that the model is dyadic. Scores are taken from both persons in an interaction. Since our interest is in the population of persons and relationships and not the particular ones sampled, each term is considered to be a random variable.

The Social Relations Model's five components of constant, actor, partner, relationship, and instability effects are relatively easy to understand. If there is a component that is confusing, it is the relationship component. We will therefore reexplain that component. One should realize that the relationship effect is an interaction component. That is, it represents the extent to which A's behavior toward B cannot be explained by A's actor effect or by B's partner effect. The "main effects" of actor and partner are controlled and the remaining systematic variance is due to relationship. Another way to understand the relationship component is to view it as the different or distinct way in which A reacts to B as opposed to how A reacts to C, D, and so on. Warner, Kenny, and Stoto (1979) refer to it as the unique adjustment that A makes to B. It represents the extent to which A trusts, speaks to, likes, and smiles at B more than others, controlling for B's partner effect.

---

partner effect. For instance, for attraction, could we not consider the object of affection to be the actor? We will designate the actor to be the one from whom we obtain the data point. Thus, for attraction the actor is the rater. The actor is the responder and the partner is the stimulus. For some variables, the dyad yields only a single observation and X_{ijk} equals X_{jik}, e.g., length of interaction or productivity. For such variables the actor–partner distinction collapses and they are indistinguishable.

By conducting a Social Relations analysis we understand the sources of variation in social data. Variance can be partitioned into actor, partner, relationship, and instability. Once we know the partitioning of the variance, we can better understand the process. If there is no partner variance, then a person does not consistently affect the behavior of others. For instance, La Voie (1981) found that children aged 5 and 7 did show actor, but not any partner, effects for a measure of vocal activity, rate of utterances. We can conclude, based on the result of actor but not partner effects, that vocal activity in this case is largely due to individual stylistic differences rather than due to the influence of the partner.

Social behavior is likely to be interdependent. The response of person i to j may be correlated with the response of j to i. That correlation can be diagrammed as follows:

$$X_{ijk} = \mu + \alpha_i + \beta_j + \gamma_{ij} + \epsilon_{ijk}$$
$$X_{jik} = \mu + \alpha_j + \beta_i + \gamma_{ji} + \epsilon_{jik}$$

Interdependence between social behaviors can be due to three separate correlations represented by the lines connecting the two equations. They are the actor–partner correlation (α with β), relationship correlation (γ), and occasion correlation (ϵ). The actor–partner correlation is the simplest of the three correlations to understand. Are persons who are trusting trustworthy? Do persons who smile, make others smile? This correlation refers to persons and not to the relationship because it is a measure of association between individual level effects of actor and partner.

The correlation between the relationship effects measures the correlation of the γ's. It is a correlation computed across dyads with the earlier mentioned actor–partner correlation partialed out. This correlation can be used to assess reciprocal and compensatory processes in dyadic interaction. It measures the extent to which the persons' relationship effects are coordinated. The relationship correlation may be larger when both persons are measured at the same time than when measured at different times. If the same-time correlations are larger than the different-time correlations, it would indicate an occasion correlation. These three correlations have been called rho$_1$, rho$_2$, and rho$_3$ by Warner *et al.* (1979).

For instance, the actor–partner correlation for the variable dominance would measure the extent to which persons who are dominant tend to elicit dominance or submissiveness from their partners. The relationship correlation measures the correlation of the relative dominance in the dyad. Thus, if A dominates B more than he or she dominates others and more than others dominate B, how does B respond? The occasion correlation measures the extent to which the coordination of dominance in the relationship is unstable. For instance, if A was dominant and B submissive on one occasion and the pattern reversed on the next occasion, the occasion correlation would be high. In this article we present an overview of the Social Relations Model. In Section I,B we compare it to something that social psychologists already know: Kelley's cube. Then in Section II, we consider various designs that can be used to estimate the model's parameters. Section III deals with actual and potential applications of the model to various problems in social psychology. In Section IV we discuss statistical aspects of the model. We then turn our attention (Section V) to the role of the model in manipulational research. Finally, we elaborate how the model analyzes group level effects (Section VI), its relation to other methods (Section VII), and the model's limitations (Section VIII).

B. RELATION TO KELLEY'S COVARIATION PRINCIPLE

One way to understand the components of the Social Relations Model is to relate them to Kelley's (1967) Covariation Principle. Kelley is concerned with how an observer explains person–entity relationships. For instance, the statement "Peter laughs at Paul's joke," could be explained in a number of different ways. Kelley posits that observers use three pieces of information in explaining such statements. They are consistency, distinctiveness, and consensus. *Consistency* refers to the stability of the actor–entity relationship across time and situations. Does Peter always laugh at Paul's jokes? *Distinctiveness* refers to whether the actor tends to relate only to the particular entity. Does Peter laugh at only Paul's jokes? *Consensus* refers to whether other actors relate to the entity in the same way. Does everyone laugh at Paul's jokes? According to Kelley, observers use this information in explaining social behavior.

The Covariation Principle is related to the Social Relations Model as follows: If someone observes a behavior that is extreme, then, given the Social Relations Model, either the actor, partner, relationship, or instability component must be extreme. If consistency is low, then the explanation for the extremity is instability and is not due to the actor, the partner, or the relationship. To make an attribution to these components, there must be consistency.

There are four possible combinations of distinctiveness (high and low) and consensus (high and low) which are presented in Table I. The entry in each cell of the table refers to the inference that an observer would make given the row and column headings as well as high consistency. For instance, given high consensus (everyone laughs at Paul) and high distinctiveness (Peter laughs at only Paul), we infer a partner effect: Paul elicits laughter. Given low consensus (no one else laughs at Paul) and low distinctiveness (Peter laughs at everyone's jokes), we infer an actor effect: Peter is a laugher. Given low consensus and high dis-

TABLE I

ATTRIBUTION TO COMPONENTS OF THE SOCIAL
RELATIONS MODEL GIVEN HIGH CONSISTENCY AND
VARIOUS COMBINATIONS OF CONSENSUS AND
DISTINCTIVENESS

Consensus	Distinctiveness	
	High	Low
High	Partner	Actor or partner
Low	Relationship	Actor

tinctiveness, we infer a relationship effect: Peter's reaction to Paul is unique. Finally, the combination of high consensus and low distinctiveness can be explained by either an actor or partner effect. McArthur (1972) presented subjects with different pieces of information and she has basically found this pattern of results.

While Kelley's Covariation Principle provides a useful guide for predicting subjects' attributions, the Social Relations Model is a formal model of dyadic social behavior. Moreover, Kelley's model is essentially an *idealized* model of attribution whereas the Social Relations Model is a purely *descriptive* model of social behavior. We can view Kelley's model as a statement of how the lay social psychologist ought to explain social behavior, whereas the Social Relations Model represents a description of social behavior for the social psychologist.

A major advantage of the Social Relations Model over the Covariation Principle is its quantitative nature. Kelley's model is qualitative in that Peter either laughs or does not. To appreciate this advantage we will consider an example. Consider four persons: Matt, Mark, Luke, and John. We ask each to state how much they trust each of the others. Say, for example, that Matt is trusted by almost everyone and John is distrusted by almost everyone, i.e., there are only partner effects. We would then expect the result in Table II. For this table as well as the next three, we will use a 10-point scale with a mean of 5. Thus, Matt is trusted consistently more than the others while John is distrusted by everyone.

Table III presumes a different result. Here, Mark trusts more than the others and John trusts less, i.e., there are only actor effects. In Table IV, it is assumed that Matt and Mark trust each other and that Luke and John also trust each other; i.e., there are only relationship effects. Also in Table IV, Matt and John distrust each other and Mark and Luke distrust each other. While these patterns of results are easily discernible individually, their combined effects are quite difficult to comprehend. Table V presents the combined effects present in Tables II, III, and

TABLE II

Model with Only Partner Effects

Actor	Partner			
	Matt	Mark	Luke	John
Matt	—	5	5	3
Mark	7	—	5	3
Luke	7	5	—	3
John	7	5	5	—

TABLE III

Model with Only Actor Effects

Actor	Partner			
	Matt	Mark	Luke	John
Matt	—	5	5	5
Mark	7	—	7	7
Luke	5	5	—	5
John	3	3	3	—

TABLE IV

Model with Only Relationship Effects

Actor	Partner			
	Matt	Mark	Luke	John
Matt	—	6	5	4
Mark	6	—	4	5
Luke	5	4	—	6
John	4	5	6	—

TABLE V

Model with Actor, Partner, and Relationship Effects

Actor	Partner			
	Matt	Mark	Luke	John
Matt	—	6	5	2
Mark	10	—	6	5
Luke	7	4	—	4
John	4	3	4	—

TABLE VI

Reference	Data description	Study design	Data analysis
T. J. Berndt (1981)	See reference	Round robin	D. A. Kenny & T. J. Berndt (unpublished)
J. A. Burleson (1982)	See reference	Round robin	J. A. Burleson (1982)
T. J. Curry & R. M. Emerson (1970)	See reference	Dyad–round robin	D. A. Kenny & L. La Voie (unpublished)
S. Duncan & D. W. Fiske	See reference	Checkerboard	D. A. Kenny & L. La Voie (unpublished)
P. Goldenthal (1981)	See reference	Half block	D. A. Kenny (unpublished)
R. Hastie, S. Penrod, & N. Pennington (1983)	See reference	Round robin	D. A. Kenny & R. B. Polley (unpublished)
D. A. Kenny & N. Bernstein (unpublished)	None available	Checkerboard; subjects: opposite-sex undergraduates in a get-acquainted session	D. A. Kenny & N. Bernstein (unpublished)
D. A. Kenny & C. A. Lowe (unpublished)	None available	Two sets of roommates with ratings of roommates set aside resulting in a checkerboard; residential setting	D. A. Kenny & C. A. Lowe (unpublished)
J. F. Lanzetta & R. E. Kleck (1970)	See reference	Round robin	D. A. Kenny (unpublished)
R. G. Lord, J. S. Phillips, & M. C. Rush (1980)	See reference	Round robin	D. A. Kenny, R. Lord, & S. A. Garg (1983)
L. C. Miller, J. M. Berg, & R. L. Archer (1983)	See reference	Round robin	D. A. Kenny & L. C. Miller (unpublished)
B. M. Montgomery (1983)	See reference	Round robin	B. M. Montgomery (1983)
R. B. Polley (1979)	See reference	Round robin	R. B. Polley (1979)
R. M. Sabatelli, R. Buck, & A. Dreyer (1982)	See reference	Dyad with two half blocks	D. A. Kenny (unpublished)
R. M. Warner & D. B. Sugarman (1983)	See reference	Round robin	R. M. Warner & D. B. Sugarman (1983)
B. E. Whitley, J. W. Schofield, & H. N. Snyder (1984)	See reference	Block–round robin	B. E. Whitley, J. W. Schofield, & H. N. Snyder (1984)
T. L. Wright, L. J. Ingraham, & D. R. Blackmer (1984)	See reference	Round robin	T. L. Wright, L. J. Ingraham, & D. R. Blackmer (1984)

IV. Thus, it has actor, partner, and relationship effects. It is a jumbled and confusing picture and its meaning is difficult to see. Comprehension of the table requires not a simple set of rules of thumb such as those given by Kelley but a quantitative representation given by the Social Relations Model.

A summary of pertinent studies referred to repeatedly throughout the article is presented in Table VI.

II. Design

The unconfounding of actor, partner, relationship, and instability effects requires specific designs that are somewhat infrequently employed in social psychology. The conventional dyadic design in which each person interacts with only one person cannot be used to estimate the Social Relations parameters. The parameters of the Social Relations Model can only be estimated for designs in which persons interact with multiple partners. This is not to say that a simple dyadic design tells us nothing about social interaction. Rather, we cannot learn anything about the Social Relations Model from that design. We consider six alternative designs that can be used to estimate the Social Relations parameters in this section.

The Social Relations Model was originally proposed as a model for the round robin design (Warner, Kenny, & Stoto, 1979). A round robin design consists of a set of persons each of whom is paired with the other persons. Measurements are taken from both members of the dyad. The design is pictorially represented in Table VII. An "×" implies that a measurement is taken while a "—" implies that the observation is missing. The design has been used in social psychology to study interpersonal attraction (Newcomb, 1979), person perception (Campbell, Miller, Lubetsky, & O'Connell, 1964), nonverbal behavior (Lanzetta, & Kleck, 1970), intergroup relations (Brewer & Campbell, 1976), social interaction and self-concept (Manis, 1955), and small groups (Lord, Phillips, & Rush, 1980). A key feature of the design is that the self-measures, as indicated by the descending diagonal, are missing. Even if such observations are present they still are set aside for subsequent analysis. (See Section III,F on self-measures.) To estimate all the variances and correlation effects there must be at least four persons.[2] More precise estimation is possible by increasing the number of persons in the design or by replicating the design. For instance, Lord et al. (1980) employed the minimum of four persons per group but had a total of 24 groups. Such a replicated round robin design has two important advantages over a single large round robin with many subjects. First, for the replicated design, the

---

[2]Three persons could be used if relationship coordination effects are assumed to be zero.

TABLE VII

SIX DIFFERENT DESIGNS[a]

| Round robin (N = 4) | | | | | | Checkerboard (N = 4) | | | | |
| | Partner | | | | | | Partner | | | |
Actor	1	2	3	4		Actor	1	2	3	4
1	—	×	×	×		1	—	×	—	×
2	×	—	×	×		2	×	—	×	—
3	×	×	—	×		3	—	×	—	×
4	×	×	×	—		4	×	—	×	—

| Circle (N = 5) | | | | | | Block (N = 6) | | | | | | |
| | Partner | | | | | | Partner | | | | | |
Actor	1	2	3	4	5	Actor	1	2	3	4	5	6
1	—	×	—	—	×	1	—	—	—	×	×	×
2	×	—	×	—	—	2	—	—	—	×	×	×
3	—	×	—	×	—	3	—	—	—	×	×	×
4	—	—	×	—	×	4	×	×	×	—	—	—
5	×	—	—	×	—	5	×	×	×	—	—	—
						6	×	×	×	—	—	—

| Dyad–block (N = 8) | | | | | | | | | Block–round robin (N = 8) | | | | | | | | |
| | Partner | | | | | | | | | Partner | | | | | | | |
Actor	1	2	3	4	5	6	7	8	Actor	1	2	3	4	5	6	7	8
1	—	×	—	—	×	×	×	×	1	—	×	×	×	×	×	×	×
2	×	—	—	—	×	×	×	×	2	×	—	×	×	×	×	×	×
3	—	—	—	×	×	×	×	×	3	×	×	—	×	×	×	×	×
4	—	—	×	—	×	×	×	×	4	×	×	×	—	×	×	×	×
5	×	×	×	×	—	×	—	—	5	×	×	×	×	—	×	×	×
6	×	×	×	×	×	—	—	—	6	×	×	×	×	×	—	×	×
7	×	×	×	×	—	—	—	×	7	×	×	×	×	×	×	—	×
8	×	×	×	×	—	—	×	—	8	×	×	×	×	×	×	×	—

[a]An "×" indicates an observation is made and a "—" indicates the observation is missing.

subjects need only interact with a small number of subjects, whereas the single large design can make excessive demands on the subject's time. Also, a replicated design with small N per round robin has nearly equal the degrees of freedom for the individual level effects (actor and partner) and the relationship effects, whereas the degrees of freedom of the single large round robin are mostly for the relationship effect.

The second design in Table VII is a checkerboard design. Note that the patterning of "×" and "—" is as in a checkerboard. This design is much simpler than a full round robin ($N = 4$) since a subject need only interact with two other subjects. It represents not only a saving of subject time, but also of experimenter time since scheduling problems are considerably reduced. The design is relatively easy to implement. First, person 1 interacts with person 2, and person 3 interacts with person 4. Then persons 1 and 4, and 2 and 3 interact. Since there are only two interactions for each person, order effects can be more easily controlled than in a round robin design.

As is the case for the round robin design, multiple replications of the design are used to obtain precise estimates. La Voie (1981) shows how the checkerboard design can provide full information concerning actor, partner, and relationship variances as well as estimates of the correlation of effects. Although the checkerboard design contains fewer dyads than does the round robin design, the components of the Social Relations Model can be estimated with little loss of information.

The checkerboard design has been used by Duncan and Fiske (1977) to study social interaction, Andersen and Bem (1981) to study sex role stereotypes, and La Voie (1981) to study social development. We expect that much of the future work employing the Social Relations Model will employ this design as opposed to the round robin design.

The third design in Table VII is a circle design. Person 1 interacts with 2 and so on. The last person interacts with person 1. If we were to draw links between the interacting pairs of persons, we would have a circle. Preliminary work indicates the variances and correlations of the Social Relations Model can be estimated for this design. To our knowledge this design has not been employed in social psychological work. The design is related to the generations design (Insko, Thibaut, Moehle, Wilson, Diamond, Gilmore, Solomon, & Lipsitz, 1980). This design involves the systematic replacement of persons as an analog of generational succession. Thus, four persons are in the first group. In the second group, three persons remain, one leaves, and that one is replaced by a new member. The generations design is a circle design with a group size of two and the last person does not interact with the first. Thus, the circle is broken and we have a chain.[3]

The fourth design is the block design. Persons are broken up into two groups or blocks. Subjects rate or interact with only those in the other groups. This design has been used in studies of nonverbal communication (DePaulo &

[3]The reader has probably noted already that many of these designs are quite similar to communication networks studied by Bavelas (1948). A wheel with many spokes is the most common design used in social psychology. The hub of the wheel is the single confederate who interacts with each subject.

Rosenthal, 1979) and bargaining (Flint, 1970). The variances and the correlations of the Social Relations Model can be estimated from the design. Actually the previously discussed checkerboard design is a special version of the block design. Note that persons 1 and 3 of the checkerboard design can be considered to be in one group and 2 and 4 in the other.

As can be seen in Table VII the block design consists of two sets of observations: the upper right rectangle and the lower left rectangle. Sometimes only one set of observations is available and we have the *half-block* design. This happens when persons 1–4 rate persons 5–8.

The block design is particularly useful for studying asymmetric dyads. In an asymmetric dyad persons can be distinguished by their roles, e.g., mother–child, teacher–student, or patient–therapist. In a symmetric dyad, persons are not distinguishable, e.g., roommates or friends. For asymmetric dyads, e.g., teacher–student, one of the half-blocks would be student data and the other half teacher data. We can then allow actor, partner, and relationship variance to vary across roles.

The final two designs in Table VII are mixtures of two designs. The first is a mixture of the block and dyadic designs. The purpose of this design is to study special dyads, such as roommates or spouses, within the Social Relations Model. We call the dyad "special" because those dyads may be qualitatively different from the other dyads. One then begins with a set of special dyads. In the dyad–block design, one of the dyad members of each special dyad is randomly designated as A and the other as B. Then each A person interacts with all the B's and each B person with all the A's. We also have the interactions between members of special dyads. We can then evaluate not only whether special dyads differ in level from nonspecial dyads, but we can also investigate the following hypotheses: (1) special dyads have similar (or dissimilar) actor effects; (2) special dyads have similar (or dissimilar) partner effects; (3) special dyads differentially respond to other people in similar (or dissimilar) ways; and (4) others differentially respond to the members of special dyads in similar (or dissimilar) ways. We can also test hypotheses about how the interactions of special dyads differ from ordinary dyads. Quite clearly we can learn much about special dyads from this design. The design has been used by Moskowitz (1983) to study the consistency of personality traits, and her special dyads were friends.

The last design in Table VII is a block–round robin design. In one sense the design is a round robin. All eight persons interact with each other. However, the eight persons can be divided into types, for example, male and female. Thus, there are four quadrants: (1) male–actor, male–partner; (2) female–actor, female–partner; (3) male–actor, female–partner; and (4) female–actor, male–partner. Quadrants 1 and 2 can be analyzed as round robins, and quadrants 3 and 4 as blocks. We can then compute the Social Relations parameters for each quadrant. We can also determine whether a person reacts to others in the same way regardless of their sex. Whitley, Schofield, and Snyder (1984) have used this design to study peer preferences of black and white children. Moreover, using a block–round robin design, Miller, Caul, and Mirsky (1967) studied communication between feral and socially isolated monkeys. The block–round robin design seems especially appropriate for the study of ingroup–outgroup relationships.

Regardless of the pattern of interactions that is used, there is an additional design consideration. Data can be gathered with no social interaction, in dyads, or in groups.

For studies requiring no interaction as in the case of person perception, it is normally relatively simple to have each person serve both as a subject and as a stimulus person. For example, each subject produces a photograph, written material, videotape, or recording. Then the subjects judge some or all of the stimulus materials from the others subjects according to one of the designs presented in Table VII or some combination of those designs. While not common, this type of procedure has been used in nonverbal sensitivity studies (De Paulo & Rosenthal, 1979; Lanzetta & Kleck, 1970; Sabatelli, Buck, & Dreyer, 1982). To use subjects as stimulus persons would most likely require two experimental sessions: one to produce stimulus materials and a second to gather data. In no-interaction studies it seems reasonable that there should be no reciprocity or compensation. That is, relationship effects should be uncorrelated. If we assume that the correlation is zero, then a round robin design with only three subjects can be used to estimate parameters.

Studies of attraction, communication, and bargaining generally require dyadic interaction. If it is possible to have each subject interact with two or more others, the designs in Table VII may be used. Experimental variables can be studied by providing the subjects with information before the interaction. For instance, subjects could be instructed to cooperate or to compete.

It is also possible to study dyadic interactions in group contexts. For instance, Lord *et al.* (1980) had groups of four subjects perform a set of tasks and then make dyadic ratings. In a group design the dyads may not be independent. That is, A may like B because C likes B. Such nonindependence does violate assumptions of the Social Relations Model, a topic we return to in Section VIII.

III. Illustrations

In Section III we apply the Social Relations Model to six different areas of social psychology.

1. Role of the perceiver and the perceived.
2. Individual differences in nonverbal communication.
3. Reciprocity of attraction.
4. Social development.
5. Interpersonal perception.
6. Self–other differences.

For the first three topics, we present the results of analyses of multiple data sets. For the last three topics, the discussion merely states the hypothetical utility of the model. Table VI provides an overview of the 17 different data sets. Virtually all of the results that we report in this section have not been previously published.

A. ROLE OF THE PERCEIVER AND THE PERCEIVED

One principle of person perception is that perceiver contributes almost as much to the perception as the person being perceived. Some have even argued that to predict the perception by person A of person B it may be more important to know who the perceiver is than the perceived. For example, Bourne (1977) states that "(G)lobal, trait-descriptive judgments of an individual's personality . . . are largely dependent upon the particular perspective of the individual who produces them" (p. 871). Dornbusch, Hastorf, Richardson, Muzzy, and Vreeland (1965) are often cited as supporting the conclusion that there is more consensus within a rater across ratees than there is between raters within a ratee. However, their study concerned not the rating of traits but, rather, the selection of traits. That is, each subject was asked to describe another person and not to rate the persons on a set of rating scales.

One way of quantifying the relative role of the perceiver and the perceived is to compare the actor variance with the partner variance from the Social Relations Model. For rating data the actor effect would measure the tendency of perceivers to see the other persons in general as being high or low in the scale. The partner effect measures the degree to which there is consensus about the perceived person.

In Table VIII, six different studies are very briefly described that attempted to measure various aspects of persons. The studies involve over 750 persons and they include quite a heterogeneous set of traits. Some of the traits are rather subjective (e.g, friendliness), while others are less so (e.g., ability).

In Table IX, we have the variance partitioning for the six studies. For five of six studies there is more partner variance than actor variance. Recall that actor variance is rater variance and partner variance is ratee variance. In four of the studies there is at least twice as much partner variance as actor variance. There is

TABLE VIII

DESCRIPTION OF STUDIES OF PERCEPTIONS

Study	Groups	Persons per group	Setting	Subjects	Variables
R. B. Polley, 1979	10[a]	12	Self-analytic group	College students	Friendliness, task orientation, dominance
R. G. Lord, J. S. Phillips, & M. C. Rush, 1980	24	4	Work group	College students	Ten measures of leadership
R. Hastie, S. Penrod, & N. Pennington, 1983	41	9	Mock jury trial	Adult jurors	Persuasiveness, openminded-ness
R. M. Warner & D. B. Sugarman, 1983	1	20	No interaction	College students	Physical attractiveness
B. M. Montgomery, 1983	9	6	Discussion group	College students	Openness
B. E. Whitley, J. W. Schofield, & R. N. Snyder, 1984	9	18	Classroom	6th grade children	Academic ability

[a]Five groups, measured at two points in time.

TABLE IX

VARIANCE PARTITIONING OF STUDIES OF PERCEPTIONS

	Percentage variance		
Study	Actor/rater	Partner/ratee	Relationship/error
R. B. Polley, 1979	.09	.51	.41
R. G. Lord, J. S. Phillips, & M. C. Rush, 1980	.32	.25	.41
R. Hastie, S. Penrod, & N. Pennington, 1983	.19	.24	.57
R. M. Warner & D. B. Sugarman, 1983	.15	.42	.44
B. M. Montgomery, 1983	.09	.53	.38
B. E. Whitley, J. W. Schofield, & A. N. Snyder, 1984, unpublished results	.17	.51	.32
Average	.17	.41	.42

much stronger consensus in the ratings of persons than most of us would have guessed.

It can be argued that the studies in Tables VIII and IX are not representative of the typical studies of personality ratings. First, two of the studies use traits that have consensually agreed upon objective (but not necessarily valid) criteria (physical attractiveness and academic ability). Also, the traits were studied in contexts where variance should be maximal. For instance, Montgomery (1983) had her subjects discussing sensitive topics, and so it is not that surprising that peers would agree about who was open and who was not open. Finally, in Polley's study (1979), subjects were encouraged in the group to evaluate each other on the three dimensions. Thus, consensus could result from the discussion process and not the perceptual process.

Even though we must view the results in Table IX with some caution, they do highlight the fact that there is consensus in the rating of personality. Consensus does not necessarily mean that the ratings are indeed valid, but consensus does indicate that the ratings are not purely idiosyncratic constructions of a single perceiver.

For three of the six studies the largest component is error or relationship effects. Only Montgomery (1983) had temporal replications and was therefore able to distinguish error and relationship effects. She found no evidence for relationship effects, which is not surprising since her subjects were initially strangers.

B. INDIVIDUAL DIFFERENCES IN NONVERBAL COMMUNICATION

There are two skills in nonverbal communication. One can be a skilled sender of nonverbal messages and one can be a skilled receiver. If we measure the accuracy of receiver A in decoding sender B, then sender variance corresponds to partner variance in the Social Relations Model and receiver variance to actor variance. At issue is the relative magnitude of sender and receiver variance. In terms of research interest, there is much more study of receiver variance than sender variance. There has been an extraordinary focus on what factors make persons better receivers. There is relatively little research on what makes persons better senders.

In Table X are the descriptions of three studies from which the Social Relations variance partitioning can be accomplished. The studies are fairly hetereogeneous in the use of materials but homogeneous in terms of setting. The Lanzetta and Kleck (1970) study used a paradigm in which receiver's had to judge from a videotape whether someone was shocked or not. The Goldenthal (1981) study had senders pose one of six emotions while being videotaped. The emotions were happiness, surprise, sadness, anger, disgust, and fear. The receivers then viewed the videotape and judged which emotion was posed. The Sabatelli et al. (1982) study had senders view emotionally charged slides. They were secretly videotaped and the receivers had to judge the type of emotional response that was appropriate for the slide.

The striking result, contained in the columns on the right-hand side of Table X, is the small amount of receiver or actor variance and the large amount of sender or partner variance. Although small, the receiver variance for two of the studies is statistically reliable, while for the other study the sample size is only 12. Thus, it would be a mistake to conclude that there is no receiver variance but correct to view it as quite small when compared to sender variance.

The results should not be overinterpreted. The number of studies is small and the experimental setting may dampen motivational factors. All subjects were probably trying to be good receivers, while in the two of the studies subjects were not even aware that they were sending. Moreover, the process may be multiplicative in nature and not additive. However, the analysis strikingly points to the critical importance of sender effects.

C. RECIPROCITY OF ATTRACTION

Mutual likes and dislikes are supposedly a fundamental fact of social life. Surprisingly, as recently as 1979 Newcomb found the evidence for this principle to be rather weak. Kenny and Nasby (1980) and Kenny and La Voie (1982) have applied the Social Relations Model to the measurement of reciprocity of attraction. They demonstrate that reciprocity is appropriately measured by the relationship level correlation, that is the correlation between γ_{ij} and γ_{ji}.

In Table XI are 19 different dyadic or relationship reciprocity correlations from 10 different studies. The studies involved over 1000 persons, most of whom

TABLE X

VARIANCE PARTITIONING OF NONVERBAL ACCURACY[a]

Study	Subjects	Task	Percentage variance		
			Actor/ receiving	Partner/ sending	Error/ relationship
J. F. Lanzetta & R. E. Kleck, 1970	12 male college students	S: Shocked 10 times, not shocked 10 times R: Judge when S is shocked	.00	.49	.51
P. Goldenthal, 1981	Female college students, 39 S's, 58 R's	S: Pose one of six emotions R: Judge which emotion is posed	.02	.44	.54
R. M. Sabatelli, R. Buck, & A. Dreyer, 1982	48 married couples	S: React to 15 emotionally charged slides R: Judge reaction as one of 5 types	.05	.35	.59

[a]S, Sender; R, receiver.

TABLE XI

RESULTS OF STUDIES OF RECIPROCITY

Study	Dyadic reciprocity	Population	Groups	Subjects per group
Short-term acquaintance				
B. M. Montgomery, 1983	.18	College students	9	6
S. Duncan & D. W. Fiske, 1977	.13	Professional students	22	4
D. A. Kenny & N. Bernstein, unpublished	.10	College students	30	4
J. A. Burleson, 1982	.26	College students	21	8
Long-term acquaintance				
T. S. Curry & R. M. Emerson, 1970		College students	6	8
Week 1	.19			
Week 8	.52			
T. L. Wright, L. J. Ingraham, & D. R. Blackmer, 1984	.74	Graduate students	4	9
R. E. Miller, W. F. Caul, & I. A. Mirsky, 1983	.53	Sorority members	1	45
B. E. Whitley, J. W. Schofield, & H. N. Snyder, 1984[a]		6th Graders	9	18
BB	.58			
WW	.76			
BW	.55			
FF	.59			
MM	.49			
FM	.12			
J. A. Burleson, 1982	.49	College students/band members	10	18
D. A. Kenny & C. A. Lowe, unpublished	.60	College students	18	4
T. J. Berndt, 1981		Grade schoolers		
Kindergarten	.05		7	8
2nd grade	.23		4	11
4th grade	.50		4	9

[a] B, black; W, white; F, female; M, male.

were college students. The designs used are round robin, checkerboard, and block–round robin. We have grouped the correlations by length of acquaintance. The top four correlations are from studies in which persons have known each other for less than 1 hour. These are close encounters of the briefest kind. For these four studies the degree of reciprocity is quite low. Ironically, the largest correlation is for the Burleson study (1982), which had only 2-minute interactions. However, The Burleson study is the only short-term acquaintance study with multiple replications and so error and relationship effects can be distinguished, which tends to raise dyadic correlations.

The remaining 15 correlations are from long-term acquaintance studies. With few exceptions the correlations are quite healthy. Thus, reciprocity clearly emerges in extended relationships. One exception involves the Curry and Emerson (1970) study. For that study, the persons were only acquainted for a week and so we can view it as a short-acquaintance study. The Berndt (1981) data set also shows low levels of reciprocity for young children. One explanation of these low correlations is that young children are only superficially acquainted. Alternatively, it may be that the measures were not sensitive enough at that age. Finally, Whitley *et al.* (1984) show low levels of reciprocity for opposite sex dyads in sixth grade. Schofield and Sagar (1977) have shown that interactions between the sexes for these children were very infrequent, and so we can view oposite sex dyads as being relatively unacquainted. Acquaintance and reciprocity would appear to be strongly related.

D. SOCIAL DEVELOPMENT

The Social Relations Model is ideally suited for the study of social development. The distinction provided between the individual and the relationship is relevant for such areas as the study of the emergence of social interaction, social skills, and the development of social relationships. For example, the distinction between peer acceptance (an individual level variable), and friendship (a dyadic variable), is central to the study of peer social relations (Masters & Furman, 1981).

Perhaps one of the most perplexing problems in social development has been that of distinguishing social interaction due to the relationship between persons from the social behaviors of individuals (Burgess, 1981; Hinde, 1981). This conceptual problem is central to the study of emerging social relationships between toddlers. For example, the study of early social interaction has concentrated on either the developing social competence of *individuals* or *relationship* processes such as responsiveness. At the level of the individuals, social competence of young children is well documented (e.g., Hay, Pederson, & Nash, 1982; Mueller & Brenner, 1977). At the level of the relationship, responsiveness between partners has been found (Berndt, 1981; Newcomb & Brady, 1982). The articulation of behavior into the actor, partner, and the relationship provides a quantitative approach for distinguishing social relations from individual social behavior for the study of emerging social interaction. For instance, there is individual level process, i.e., how sociable are young children toward peers. In addition, there is the relationship between persons. Perhaps one criterion of peer social interaction might be that of relationship variance. Relationship effects provide compelling evidence that children are engaging in social interaction. In addition, the relationship correlation can be estimated and could be included as another criterion for peer relations.

The study of established social relationships of peers also requires methods for distinguishing the relationship from individual responses (Smollar & Youniss, 1982). For example, for the study of social relationships, popularity or peer acceptance refers to the individual and friendship refers to the relationship. We can illustrate the application of this new strategy as follows. Masters and Furman (1981) examined the behavioral correlates of popularity and friendship. They proposed that the determinants of friendship were different from those of popularity. Popularity and friendship scores were derived from a round robin set of peer ratings. Given the Social Relations Model, their measures of popularity and friendship are confounded. A Social Relations analysis would unconfound these effects. In the model, popularity would be defined as a partner effect, and friendship would refer to the relationship level.

Studies of social skills have raised similar concerns as to the distinction between process at the individual and at the relationship levels (Conger & Keane, 1981; Wanlass & Prinz, 1982). The partner effect refers to peer acceptance while the relationship effect refers to friendship, or specific liking of a partner. One can also define friendship as the reciprocated liking of partners.

Perhaps the most important contribution of the Social Relations Model to the study of social development is that the separation of social behavior for the individual and the relationship should influence the level of intervention. Clinicians advocate working with the individual target child, the peer group, and the dyad. All three strategies have merit. What is required is an understanding of the most effective level of intervention. For instance, based on the results for peer acceptance, popularity of target children will probably be most affected by working with the peer group and the target child, particularly for older children. On the other hand, La Voie (1981) reports that structuring and directing skills are largely due to the individual and not the relationship. The implication of this finding is that structuring, social leadership, and other social initiation skills may perhaps be effectively taught through an individual level intervention (e.g., Furman, Rahe, & Hartup, 1979). Skills necessary to maintain friendship, however, may require intervention at the level of the relationship. It is important to the understanding of peer relations to examine at what level an intervention might be most effective. The conventional social skills criteria of peer acceptance may not capture possible effects for the relationship, only for the partner.

E. INTERPERSONAL PERCEPTION

Tagiuri, Bruner, and Blake (1958) have distinguished three major aspects of social perception: mutuality, congruence, and accuracy. Let us consider each in terms of attraction and perceived attraction. Mutuality refers to reciprocity of attraction. If Mary likes Jane, does Jane like Mary? Congruence concerns perceived reciprocity. If Mary likes Jane, does she think Jane likes her? Accuracy refers to the veridicality of perceptions. If Jane thinks Mary likes her, does Mary like her? Mutuality, congruence, and accuracy are obviously crucial to any meaningful theory of social perception. McLeod and Chaffee (1973) have systematically reviewed the three aspects and have pointed out that numerous theorists have given different names to them. Furthermore, the three aspects, while conceptually independent, need not be so empirically. If there is both mutuality and congruence, then accuracy must follow.

The Social Relations Model can be used to measure mutuality, congruence, and accuracy at both the individual and dyadic level. For congruence and accuracy there are two individual level correlations—one for actors and another for partners. Kenny (1981) describes the measurement of these three processes. He finds congruence of interpersonal attraction at both the individual and dyadic levels. However, mutuality and accuracy emerge at only the dyadic level.

The three aspects could be studied for other variables besides attraction. For instance, willingness to disclose, type of impression made, and trust could also be studied.

F. SELF–OTHER DIFFERENCES

A major topic in social psychology is the relationship between processes governing self-perception versus other perception. One important question is whether there are differences between the two or whether they each are governed by one general process. The Social Relations Model permits a number of empirical tests that compare self–other data.

Consider the study of Lanzetta and Kleck (1970). They had subjects predict when someone else was being shocked from a videotape of that person's facial expressions. Subjects were also shown videotapes of their own facial expressions. The dependent measure is the accuracy of the judgments. It is reasonable to ask whether persons are more accurate self-perceivers than other perceivers. This would be a hypothesis of *level*. For rating data, tests of level would assess whether subjects are modest (self-ratings lower than other ratings) or vain (self-ratings higher than other ratings). For the Lanzetta and Kleck study, persons are slightly more accurate at perceiving self than others. Thus, the level of accuracy is higher for self than other.

We can also test whether self-measures are more *variable* than other perceptions. In a sense, we can evaluate whether persons who have different relationships with others have different "relationships" with themselves. For the

Lanzetta and Kleck study persons are more variable in self-accuracy than in other accuracy.

We can also *relate* self-ratings with actor and partner effects. For the Lanzetta and Kleck study the correlation of partner with self-measures would assess the extent to which persons who are accurately perceived by others are accurately perceived by self. The correlation of actor with self-measures would assess the extent to which accurate perceivers of others are accurate perceivers of self. Since there is no actor variance in the Lanzetta and Kleck study (see Table X), we can only discuss the correlation of self-accuracy with the partner effect. There is a modest correlation of .33 between the two. Thus, if others are accurate at perceiving you, you are somewhat more accurate at perceiving yourself.

With self-measures, we can then test hypotheses concerning (1) the levels of self–other data, (2) the variability, and (3) the extent to which self-measures contain actor and partner effects.

The Social Relations Model gives us a thorough understanding of how self- and other measures differ. Moreover, since the same persons are used as both self and other, the two populations are necessarily equivalent, a fact not true in most self–other studies.

IV. Statistical Analysis

Although the Social Relations Model makes intuitive sense and although the designs are not difficult to understand, the statistical analysis is not correspondingly straightforward. It involves new procedures and computer programs that are a mixture of analysis of variance and structural modeling techniques. These methods are described in Kenny (1981), Kenny and La Voie (1982), La Voie (1981), and Warner *et al.* (1979). Here we provide only a brief introduction to the statistical analysis.

A. ESTIMATION

Perhaps the most important aspect concerning the estimation procedure is to understand what it is that is being estimated. Unlike typical analysis of variance models, the effects themselves are not of key interest. That is, we are not really concerned with how large is person A's actor effect relative to person B's. Rather, the focus is on how much of the *variance* is due to actor. We wish to know how different two randomly chosen actors are from each other and not how different any two particular actors are from each other. Thus, the focus is not on the means themselves but rather on variance partitioning. Moreover, we are also interested in the correlation of effects. For instance, are large actor effects associated with large partner effects?

These variances and correlations cannot be estimated in the usual way. That is, one cannot estimate each person's actor effect and then compute the variance of those effects to estimate the actor variance. Such a variance would be inflated since it would not only estimate the actor variance, but also contain the relationship and instability variance. We must then estimate variances and correlations of components that we do not perfectly measure. Estimation of the variances and correlations is then indirect. We can directly estimate linear combinations of unknown variances. That is, the variance of estimated actor effects equals the unknown actor variance plus the relationship and instability variance. If we have enough estimates of the unknown quantities, they can be estimated by solving a set of simultaneous linear equations. A relatively simple example can illustrate how this is done. For the checkerboard design in Table VII, let us consider four of the eight scores: X_{12}, X_{14}, X_{32}, and X_{34}. In terms of the Social Relations Model, ignoring instability, these scores are given by

$$X_{12} = \mu + \alpha_1 + \beta_2 + \gamma_{12}$$
$$X_{14} = \mu + \alpha_1 + \beta_4 + \gamma_{14}$$
$$X_{32} = \mu + \alpha_3 + \beta_2 + \gamma_{32}$$
$$X_{34} = \mu + \alpha_3 + \beta_4 + \gamma_{34}$$

Let us designate persons 1 and 3 as "rows" and persons 2 and 4 as "columns." We are then arranging the four numbers as follows:

$$
\begin{array}{cc}
X_{12} & X_{14} \\
X_{32} & X_{34}
\end{array}
$$

For this example we seek to determine estimates of σ_α^2, α_β^2, and σ_γ^2.

Using what we know from analysis of variance, let us estimate the row, column, and interaction effects. The difference between the "row" means is

$$\frac{X_{12} + X_{14}}{2} - \frac{X_{32} + X_{34}}{2} = \alpha_1 - \alpha_3 + \frac{\gamma_{12} + \gamma_{14} - \gamma_{32} - \gamma_{34}}{2}$$

The difference in "column" means is

$$\frac{X_{12} + X_{32}}{2} - \frac{X_{14} + X_{34}}{2} = \beta_2 - \beta_4 + \frac{\gamma_{12} - \gamma_{14} + \gamma_{32} - \gamma_{34}}{2}$$

The estimate of row by column interaction is

$$X_{12} - X_{14} - X_{32} + X_{34} = \gamma_{12} - \gamma_{14} - \gamma_{32} + \gamma_{34}$$

Let us denote the above three expressions as A, B, and C, respectively. If we square C we have

$$C^2 = \gamma_{12}^2 + \gamma_{14}^2 + \gamma_{32}^2 + \gamma_{34}^2 + 2\gamma_{12}\gamma_{34} + 2\gamma_{14}\gamma_{32} - 2\gamma_{12}\gamma_{14}$$
$$- 2\gamma_{12}\gamma_{32} - 2\gamma_{34}\gamma_{14} - 2\gamma_{34}\gamma_{32}$$

So far we have done only simple high school algebra. Now we need to do some statistics. We need to determine the *expected value* of C^2. The expected value tells us what C^2 estimates. The expected value of the squared terms (e.g., γ_{12}^2) is σ_γ^2. The product terms have an expected value of zero if we assume that the interaction effects are independent. Thus, the expected value of C^2 or $E(C^2)$ equals $4\sigma_\gamma^2$. We can in a similar fashion show that $E(A^2) = 2\sigma_\alpha^2 + \sigma_\gamma^2$ and that $E(B^2) = 2\sigma_\beta^2 + \sigma_\gamma^2$. Thus, A^2, B^2, and C^2 estimate a linear combination of three unknown parameters: σ_α^2, σ_β^2, and σ_γ^2. We can solve for each by

$$\hat{\sigma}_\gamma^2 = (C^2/4)$$
$$\hat{\sigma}_\alpha^2 = (4A^2 - C^2)/8$$
$$\hat{\sigma}_\beta^2 = (4B^2 - C^2)/8$$

The "hat" means that the variance component is estimated. Since A^2, B^2, and C^2 can be computed from the data, we can then estimate the unknown variance components.

In general, variance components are estimated in the following manner. First, a series of means squared or mean cross-products is computed. Each of these will estimate a linear combination of the unknown parameters. Using the algebra of expectations (Hays, 1963) the exact form of the linear combination can be determined. Thus, the expected value of the known mean squares and cross-products equals the unknown variance and covariance components times a coefficient matrix. Given sufficient information, one can solve for the unknown parameters. The major difficulty is determining which mean squares or cross-products to compute and then to determine their expected value.

B. MULTIVARIATE GENERALIZATION

As discussed so far in this article the Social Relations Model is univariate. A single variable is analyzed and its variance is partitioned and the correlation of effects is measured. A procedure has been developed for estimating the covariation between two variables (Kenny, 1981).

Let us consider the two variables of liking and smiling. There are four different individual level correlations.

1. Are likers smilers (actor–actor correlation)?
2. Do likers elicit smiling behavior (actor–partner correlation)?
3. Are persons who are liked smilers (partner–actor correlation)?
4. Do persons who are liked elicit smiling (partner–partner correlation)?

Moreover, there are two correlations at the dyadic level:

1. If A likes B, does A smile at B (intrapersonal–dyadic correlation)?
2. If A likes B, does B smile at A (interpersonal–dyadic correlation)?

We call the first *intrapersonal* since responses of the same person are correlated. The second is called *interpersonal* since the responses of different persons are correlated. There are also two correlations between the instability components:

1. If A likes B more at one occasion, does A smile at B more at that occasion (intrapersonal–occasion correlation)?
2. If A likes B more at one occasion, does B smile at A more at that occasion (interpersonal–occasion correlation)?

This multivariate generalization reemphasizes the different levels of analysis. For every measured variable there are two theoretical variables at the individual level: actor and partner. At the dyadic level there are also two variables: the relationship effect of A with B and the relationship effect of B with A. For multiple variables we can compute separate correlations matrices (or more generally covariance matrices), one at the individual level and the other at the dyadic level. These matrices can then serve as input for any multivariate procedure, e.g., multiple regression, factor analysis, or structural equation modeling (path analysis).

The multivariate generalization allows for the handling of variables that are essentially individual level variables, e.g., age of subject, internal–external locus of control, or dogmatism. Such variables can be thought to have the following Social Relations structure: they contain only an actor effect. We can correlate these individual level variables with actor and partner effects of other variables. Since these variables do not change with the partner, they cannot correlate with the relationship effects.[4]

C. FIXED EFFECTS

Certain variables in the analysis may be fixed variables. For instance, sex of subject and experimental manipulations are normally considered to be fixed variables; that is, we seek to generalize only to the levels of the variable studied. For random effects variables we seek to generalize to the population and not to the specific units studied. The estimation procedure must be modified for fixed variables for three different cases.

First, we may seek to estimate the effects of such fixed variables on random

---

[4]For special dyads, it is possible to correlate the relationship effects with individual difference variables when the dyad–block design is employed.

variables. For instance, we seek to estimate the effect of some experimental manipulation on a dependent measure. This can be readily accomplished. Second, we may seek to perform a Social Relations analysis (i.e., partition the variance of a fixed variable into actor, partner, and interaction) on the fixed variable. This, too, is relatively simple. What is not so simple is to perform a Social Relations analysis on a random variable that is affected by a fixed variable. At present, the algebra for such computations is only developed for the checkerboard design (La Voie, 1981). It is not yet fully developed for the round robin design.

D. SIGNIFICANCE TESTING

There are two different strategies for significance testing. They are the jackknife and treating the "group" as the unit of analysis. The jackknife procedure, which was developed by Tukey (e.g., Mosteller & Tukey, 1978), is an ingenious procedure for performing significance testing when no clear standard approach is available. This procedure involves setting aside part of the data and computing the statistic for which a standard error is needed. Possibly one-tenth of the data are set aside. The statistic is estimated 10 times with a different one-tenth set aside. These estimates are not independent since they share 80% of the entire data set. Fortunately, Tukey has provided a method to correct for nonindependence. The corrected statistics are called *pseudovalues* and their mean is computed. One then evaluates whether the mean of the pseudovalues is significantly different from zero by a one-sample *t* test. To apply the jackknife to the designs that we have presented, one must leave out or omit one subject. If there are multiple groups, the jackknife standard errors can be pooled in the same way as variances are pooled for a *t* test. For instance, Kenny and Nasby (1980) used this pooled jackknife error term.

An alternative and simpler significance testing strategy is available if a replicated design is used. For instance, let us assume that there are 32 round robins with five persons in each round robin. One estimates the relevant parameter for each group (i.e., for each of the 32 round robins). Then one evaluates whether the mean of that parameter across groups is significantly different from zero by a one-sample *t* test. We call this the group error term. One can test whether the pooled jackknife error term is homogeneous with the group error term, and if so the two error terms can be pooled. If the jackknife error term is substantially smaller than the group error term, then the group error term should be used.

V. Design of Experiments

Before we consider the design of experiments in terms of the Social Relations Model, we should discuss how experiments are typically done in social psychology. Only a few confederates or stimulus persons are used in most experiments. Some characteristic or some behavior of these persons is manipulated. Thus, the subjects are exposed to a few persons whose behavior is experimentally varied. While this type of design answers many important questions about social behavior, it provides only a limited view. First, data are taken only from the subjects and not the stimulus persons. The studies are one-sided, and so reciprocity or compensation effects are impossible to measure. Second, since a small number (usually one) of the confederates or stimulus persons is used, results cannot be generalized beyond the particular confederates used. Third, variance cannot be uniquely partitioned into actor, partner, and interaction effects. We can know whether the subjects changed their behavior because of the manipulation, but we cannot understand the general sources that bring about variation in the responses.

To apply the Social Relations Model in an experimental context, each subject in the study must serve as both partner and actor; to use experimenters' terms, they must serve as both stimulus persons and subjects. In certain cases this may not be practical or even possible, but in other cases it may require only a little extra work which may reap great rewards.

The spirit of the Social Relations Model is that the subject in the experiment serves both as a provider of data and as a stimulus person or partner for the subjects. Using subjects twice has been recommended by Tagiuri (1969). For certain types of experiments the complex nature of the manipulations may preclude using each person as a subject and as a stimulus person. However, for some areas of research it may be relatively easy to have subjects serve as stimulus persons, while for others we might have to be quite creative and inventive.

Assuming that subjects can serve as stimulus persons, there are a series of possible patterns by which the treatment can be delivered. They are presented in Table XII. We use the checkerboard design to illustrate the patterns, but they can be extended to other designs. The letters A and B refer to two levels of an independent variable. The first type of manipulation in the table is an individual level manipulation. We call it an individual level manipulation because a person is in the same experimental condition across all interactions. As depicted in Table XII, persons 1 and 2 are in condition A and 3 and 4 in B. For instance, a set or expectation given to actors could be varied. Alternatively, characteristics of partner could be varied. For instance, in a non-face-to-face study, the attractiveness of a partner could be manipulated by a photograph. It should be noted that a partner manipulation may show not only partner effects but also actor effects. As Snyder, Tanke, and Berscheid (1977) have shown, changing the attractiveness of a person changes not only the expectations of the perceiver but also the behavior of the supposedly attractive other. Thus, changing expectations about the partner may alter the partner's behavior.

If an individual level manipulation is employed, we can adapt the basic

TABLE XII

POSSIBLE PATTERNS OF MANIPULATIONS[a]

Individual level

| | | Partner | | |
Actor	1	2	3	4
1	—	A	—	A
2	A	—	A	—
3	—	B	—	B
4	B	—	B	—

Dyad level

| Symmetric manipulation | | | | | Asymmetric manipulation | | | |
| | | Partner | | | | | Partner | | |
Actor	1	2	3	4	Actor	1	2	3	4
1	—	A	—	B	1	—	B	—	A
2	A	—	B	—	2	A	—	B	—
3	—	B	—	A	3	—	A	—	B
4	B	—	A	—	4	B	—	A	—

Group level

| | | Partner | | | | | Partner | | |
Actor	1	2	3	4	Actor	5	6	7	8
1	—	A	—	A	5	—	B	—	B
2	A	—	A	—	6	B	—	B	—
3	—	A	—	A	7	—	B	—	B
4	A	—	A	—	8	B	—	B	—

[a]Illustrated for the checkerboard design where A and B represent two levels of a given manipulation.

model that Kraemer and Jacklin (1979) suggest for the analysis of dyadic data. For instance, assume that certain persons were given either high or low expectancies. Kraemer and Jacklin (1979) distinguish three different effects: (1) the main effect of expectancy on the person's own behavior, (2) the main effect of expectancy on the partner's behavior, and (3) the interaction of own expectancy with the expectancy of the partner. La Voie (1981) has shown how these effects can be estimated by the checkerboard design.

The middle two manipulations presented in Table XII are dyadic in nature. In one case both members receive the same treatment (dyadic–symmetric), and in the other the members receive different treatments (dyadic–asymmetric). An example of the former is having both members exhibit competitive or cooperative orientations, and an example of the latter design is having one member be a leader and the second a follower. It is probably desirable for both dyadic designs to run the same dyad in the opposite direction. These would be counterbalanced asymmetric and symmetric designs. That is, competitive dyads are rerun under a cooperative orientation.

The final pattern of manipulation in Table XII is a group level manipulation. Here the whole group is given the manipulation. For instance, Hastie, Penrod, and Pennington (1983) had jurors operate under different decision roles. This type of design could be used to test whether the Social Relations parameters vary as a function of the manipulation. It is possible to employ a group level manipulation in a within design. That is, each person would interact with their partner in both conditions A and B. This design would be identical to a counterbalanced dyadic–symmetric design.

Although we can present four different types of design plans for embedding the testing and estimation of experimental effects within a Social Relations analysis, we do not have much experience in this area. La Voie (1981) has shown that the checkerboard design can be useful for individual level manipulations. Group level manipulations would seem to present no difficult analysis problems. Finally, designs with counterbalanced dyadic asymmetric manipulations can be analyzed by a multivariate analysis.[5] Nonetheless, work in this area is still very preliminary. We do not yet have a sufficient track record to judge the utility of these designs.

It seems advisable to us not to assign haphazardly dyads to various experimental treatments. Some systematic assignment plan, such as those in Table XII, is necessary for a Social Relations analysis to be undertaken.

VI. Group Effects

We have concentrated on actor, partner, relationship, and instability effects. There is, however, one other term in the model. It is the constant term. It represents the average level of response across actors and partners. If the design is replicated by having multiple groups, each design will have its own mean. If the subjects interact in dyads, as opposed to groups, then the estimate of the constant term (i.e., the mean) should be relatively homogeneous across groups. The variability of the mean for groups should be explained by the variance in actor, partner, and interaction effects.

---

[5]This is accomplished by treating all the A observations as one variable and all the B observations as the second variable. The relationship correlation has meaning only in the correlation between A and B and not within.

When the design is not dyadic, but a group study, the constant term may reflect not only individual and dyadic processes but also group level processes. For instance, in the study of interpersonal attraction by Kenny and Nasby (1980) the mean for attraction in six groups varied considerably more than would be expected given individual and dyadic processes. For some groups members generally liked one another, whereas for other groups the level of attraction was not as high. There is, then, variance at the group level. As was pointed out by Willis to us, such group level variance can be interpreted as evidence for a norm. Interestingly, in the reanalysis of the data from Lord *et al.* (1980), there was only very weak evidence for group level effects in ratings of leadership. Groups do not differ much in the level of leadership. Thus, there may be group norms for attraction but not for leadership.

If there is variance for a given variable at the group level, it may be that the variable shares variance with other variables at the group level. For instance, we can speculate that groups with high levels of trust have high levels of interpersonal attraction. There are, then, four different levels of correlations: group, dyad, person, and occasion. Given X_{ijkm} and Y_{ijkm} where m refers to group we have

$$X_{ijkm} = \mu_m + \alpha_{im} + \beta_{jm} + \gamma_{ijm} + \epsilon_{ijkm}$$
$$Y_{ijkm} = \mu_m' + \alpha_{im}' + \beta_{jm}' + \gamma_{ijm}' + \epsilon_{ijkm}'$$

There are five correlations at one of the four levels. They are (1) group level (μ_m with μ_m'), (2) dyad level (γ_{ijm} with γ_{ijm}'), (3) individual level (α_{im} and β_{im} with α_{im}' and β_{im}'), and (4) occasion level (ϵ_{ijkm} with ϵ_{ijkm}').

Kenny and La Voie (1984) have proposed a model for group level effects that is related to the Social Relations Model. They are concerned with group data structures in which each individual in the group provides one data point. Each person's response is assumed to be a combination of an individual component and a group component. One way of reexpressing the model of Kenny and La Voie (1984) into the Social Relations Model is as follows:

$$X_{ik} = \mu_m + \alpha_{im} + \epsilon_{im}$$

where the subscript m refers to group. The model is like the Social Relations Model, but the partner and relationship effects have been omitted. Thus, the model of Kenny and La Voie places severe restrictions on the Social Relations Model, but the data structure they study is also much more restricted.

VII. Relation to Other Procedures

The Social Relations Model presented in this article, while unique, is very closely related to the work of others. Cronbach (1955) was perhaps the first to propose a components model for interpersonal data. According to Cronbach an actor's rating of a partner on a trait is a function of a constant, an actor effect, a trait effect, and an actor by trait interaction. (Cronbach calls an actor a judge and a partner a target.) The Social Relations Model essentially reverses trait and partner. As pointed out in Kenny (1981), Cronbach's model examines individual differences between actors given a set of partners and traits, whereas the Social Relations Model examines a single trait for a set of actor and partners.

Jackson (1972) has modified Cronbach's model in the following fashion. An actor responds to a series of items. The actor has a threshold for responding to the items as well as a sensitivity. Jackson's threshold term is similar to the actor effect of the Social Relations Model. The sensitivity term is a constant for each actor that multiplies the item effect. The model in equation form is

$$X_{ij} = \mu + \alpha_i + k_i\beta_j + \epsilon_{ij}$$

where k_i is the sensitivity parameter. Jackson (Reed & Jackson, 1975) has applied his model to the interpersonal domain by replacing items with partners. His notion of threshold and sensitivity should be incorporated within a modified version of the Social Relations Model.

Models developed for sociometric data are clearly related to the Social Relations Model since sociometric data typically have a round robin structure with all group members stating whether they like or dislike everyone else in the group. White, Boorman, and Breiger (1976) have developed methods to analyze sociometric data. They focus on discovering cliques or networks within groups. Holland and Leinhardt (1981) have developed a model with actor, partner, and reciprocity parameters for dichotomous responses. Such a model is essentially a discrete version of the Social Relations Model. The work by Holland and Leinhardt has been extended by Feinberg and Wasserman (1981) and Wong (1983).

Finally, a number of researchers have analyzed round robin data structures by multidimensional scaling. For instance, Jones and Young (1972) analyzed the ratings over time of a group of persons by multidimensional scaling. The classical multidimensional scaling model presumes that the matrix is symmetric, i.e., that $X_{ij} = X_{ji}$. Recent work in multidimensional scaling (e.g., Harshman, 1978) has extended the model to allow for asymmetric data structures. Multidimensional scaling has the advantage that the relevant dimensions can be uncovered as opposed to presumed.

The Social Relations Model intensively compares many different dyads. An alternative approach is to intensively study a few dyads over time. Sequential analysis (Bakeman & Dabbs, 1976; Gottman & Notarius, 1978) is a very different way of studying dyadic processes.

VIII. Limitations

The Social Relations Model, while flexible and intuitively appealing, has a number of limitations that need to be carefully considered both in planning future research studies and in interpreting the results of studies. We can divide these limitations into theoretical and practical considerations. Theoretical limitations concern the assumptions of the model. Practical considerations concern issues in the actual implementation of the design and analysis.

A. THEORETICAL LIMITATIONS

The Social Relations Model has built into it a series of assumptions about the nature of two-person relationships. The major assumptions are as follows.

1. Social interactions are exclusively dyadic.
2. Persons are randomly sampled from some population.
3. There are no order effects.
4. The effects combine additively and relationships are linear.

We now consider these assumptions in greater detail.

The interaction between persons is presumed to be solely a function of the persons in the interaction. There are no extradyadic effects. Persons are presumed not to influence the interactions of the dyads that they are not a member of. When persons are in groups, the truth of this assumption is quite unlikely. We would expect persons to communicate with each other and influence each other's perception of third parties. For instance, A and B discuss person C. In terms of the model, A and B's relationship effects with C are correlated. If this correlation is strong enough, the partner effect will be biased. For instance, if people in a group communicate about person A and they come to a consensus about A's standing on the trait, then A will have a spurious partner effect. These extradyadic effects may also bias the actor effects. Their presence can seriously distort the estimates of variance of the components.

There is no fool-proof way to control for extradyadic effects. [Holland & Leinhardt (1981) have argued that triadic and higher level effects are weak for sociometric data.] If one can limit their presumed effects, they can be tested and controlled. For instance, for the Curry and Emerson study (see Table VI), the eight persons are actually four sets of roommates. Let us presume that the extradyadic effects are limited to roommates. That is, roommates communicate with each other about the other six persons. It turns out that the relationship effects of pairs of roommates are correlated. After 1 week the correlation is .21, and it is .27 after 8 weeks. While not very large, these correlations do provide evidence of extradyadic effects.

Although extradyadic effects are a serious problem, the problem can be solved if we limit the scope of extradyadic effects. Moreover, most other methods totally ignore the problem.

Another limitation is the assumption that persons are randomly sampled from some population. Normally social psychologists are rather cavalier about random sampling. We hardly ever even attempt to sample randomly. However, the Social Relations Model centers on variance and its estimation. If persons are nonrandomly sampled, the variance components could be seriously distorted. For instance, if persons in the group are married couples, then the actor and partner variance will be underestimated since couples should have similiar effects. Thus, the use of intact groups violates the assumption of random sampling. This problem was especially apparent in the analysis of data from the Kenny and Lowe Study (D. A. Kenny and C. A. Lowe, unpublished). The subjects were two pairs of roommates. When analyzed as a round robin very anomalous results occurred. The similarity of the roommates and their high level of attraction distorted the results.

The Social Relations Model represents an essentially static view of interpersonal behavior. However, it requires multiple interactions with different partners that are necessarily sequentially ordered. The model as stated ignores any order effects caused by repeated interactions. Normally order effects are conceived as constant effects added to scores. (More complex order effects are discussed in the next paragraph.) For instance, with repeated interactions persons may increase their rate of self-disclosure. We know of no general strategy for controlling for these type of order effects for the round robin design. It would seem that some type of modified Latin square approach could solve the problem, but this solution has yet to be developed. La Voie (1981) has shown that the checkerboard design can allow for order effects.

More problematic than a simple order effect are the subtle order effects, such as a contrast effect and a context effect. In a *contrast effect* one's response reverses across repeated interactions. For instance, in the Kenny and Bernstein study persons interacted with two opposite sex partners (D. A. Kenny and N. Bernstein, unpublished). There was some evidence that subjects compared the two persons with whom they interacted. They rated one high and the other low. This contrasting of the two partners artificially depresses actor effects. A *context effect* is a subtle, distorting effect that can occur when the order of partners is counterbalanced. It presumes that persons rate their first partner near the midpoint of the scale. Then all subsequent interactions are rated in that context. For instance, for peer ratings if the first partner is high on the scale, he or she is rated near the midpoint and the remaining partners tend to be rated below the midpoint. The first partner, then, anchors the rating scale. A context effect can produce spurious actor effects.

The model as stated presumes that the actor, partner, and relationship effects are additive. The effects may combine in a multiplicative manner as was discussed for Jackson's model of inferential accuracy. There is an empirically based method for determining nonadditivity (Tukey, 1949), but this method would need to be adapted. Researchers need to consider whether an additive formulation is reasonable.

Also, the dyadic correlation is assumed to be linear. However, there is good reason to believe that the reciprocity correlation might be nonlinear. Cappella (1981) discusses the two sides of reciprocity. If A likes B does B like A? (This can be called *positive reciprocity*.) Also if A dislikes B, does B dislike A? (This can be called *negative reciprocity*.) It would seem likely that positive reciprocity would be stronger than negative reciprocity. This would result in a nonlinearity that cannot as yet be measured.

B. PRACTICAL ISSUES

From our own point of view the practical limitations are more serious obstacles to actual use of the Social Relations Model in social psychology than the theoretical issues. The first major problem is the implementation of the design. Without exception researchers who have conducted studies using one of the designs in Table VII have been presented with all sorts of scheduling, coordination, and data management problems. The scheduling problem is to some degree offset by running all the subjects in one session, but this limits the length of interactions. Coordination is absolutely essential, since the pairing of persons must be done by some plan and not done haphazardly. Care must be taken not only in assigning persons to conditions, but also to partners.

The presence of missing data is especially troublesome for the Social Relations designs. The loss of one data point means that all the subject's data must be thrown out. For checkerboard design all the data for the group of four are unanalyzable if one data point is missing. If the number of missing data is small the mode could be used, but the effects of this strategy are not well understood. It may be possible to adapt the procedures developed by Wong (1982) to solve some missing data problems.

The complete Social Relations Model separates error and relationship effects. In order to accomplish this there must be more than one observation for each dyad (Warner *et al.*, 1979). Most researchers obtain multiple replications temporally. They measure the same dyad over time. Such an approach presumes no change over time in the model's parameters. For instance, La Voie (1981) analyzed interactions between pairs of children that were separated over a time period of 6 months. He found that for most variables the mean was larger at the second point in time. This change in the mean artificially inflates the error variance and deflates other variances. Besides temporal replications one can use multiple measures of the same variable. Burleson (1982) took this approach in his study of interpersonal attraction. Again, it must be assumed that the means of the measures are equal. Regardless of the source of replications, procedures are needed to test assumptions about the stability of parameters across replications, and new procedures are needed that make less restrictive assumptions about the replications.

Most studies contain only a single replication for each dyad. For these studies error and relationship effects are confounded. That is, we cannot separate what is relationship variance and what is noise. It is likely that the dyadic level correlation will be seriously attenuated when there is a single replication. This is not a problem when measuring robust correlations such as reciprocity of attraction, but it is a major difficulty in measuring smaller dyadic correlations.

A Social Relations analysis cannot be done using the standard computer packages. Fortunately, computer programs have been written for both the round robin, checkerboard, and block designs. They are called SOREMO (Kenny, 1983b) for the round robin design, CHECKERS (La Voie, 1983) for the checkerboard design, and BLOCKO (Kenny, 1983a) for the block design. All programs are multivariate and results are averaged across multiple replications of the design.

IX. Conclusion

The Social Relations Model represents one method of studying two-person relationships. It attempts to separate the effects of persons and dyad. The model hearkens back to social psychology as practiced in the 1940s and 1950s. Then social psychology was interactive and largely nonexperimental. In the mid-1950s the field was shaken by Cronbach's (and others) critique of measures of accuracy in person perception. Their analyses showed that dyadic data were composed of various components, and dyadic scores required more complex analysis than those conventionally employed. Unfortunately, the field responded by becoming more experimental and largely abandoning dyadic interaction. The work of Ickes (1982) and Duncan and Fiske (1977) as well as others indicates that the study of social interaction is showing a resurgence.

In discussing the model with our colleagues three major questions or dis-agreements have arisen. They concern (1) the labeling of the components, (2) the social psychological versus the statistical validity of the components, and (3) the failure to include a situational component.

Our labeling of the three major components of the model as actor, partner, and relationship effects has proved controversial. Some colleagues have told us that calling actor and partner *individual* level effects seems to imply that social behavior takes place within individuals. Others have objected to use of the term relationship, since it can embody situational as well as other nondyadic compo-nents. We prefer to use our terms since they embody the notion that social behavior occurs at multiple levels. Less controversial terms like row, column, and interaction effects do not communicate the notion of different levels of generalization. It should be emphasized that the analysis only apportions vari-ance (as well as covariance). It does not necessarily pinpoint the social-psycho-logical process that generates that variance. That is, environmental factors might well determine actor variance and personality factors could be determining the relationship variance. Our use of the terms actor, partner, and relationship are meant only to provide an initial hypothesis for location of the processes that generate the variance.

As with any statistical model that partitions variance, we should question whether the variance partitioning is truly meaningful or only a statistical exer-cise. The utility of the model will be proved not by a statistical theorem but by its ability to help us understand social behavior. We hope that the illustrations section of this article shows some utility of the model. Although we are confi-dent, we must admit the verdict is still out. Most probable is that the verdict will be mixed. In the area of interpersonal attraction, we believe the model has provided us with new insights (e.g., Kenny & La Voie, 1982; Kenny & Nasby, 1980). In other areas the model might well be unworkable.

Perhaps the most glaring omission in the model is that it does not include situation. Most recent definitions of social psychology emphasize the role of situational factors on social behavior. Actually, the model does contain a situa-tional component, the partner. For some unknown reason, most social psychol-ogists view situation as asocial. It seems sensible to us that the person with whom one is interacting is a very powerful situational force. Person-as-situation is not commonly recognized in social psychology. The partner in the interaction may be one important situational component. Other situational factors can be studied by the procedures discussed in Section V.

The Social Relations Model has three potential contributions to the study of dyads. First, it provides a purely methodological–statistical solution to the analy-sis of dyadic data. The difficulties of dyadic data analysis pointed out by Cron-bach and others in the 1950s remained virtually unexamined for nearly 25 years. The Social Relations Model represents a new approach to the analysis of dyadic data structures. For instance, peer ratings are commonly used to assess persons in groups. Kane and Lawler (1978) noted a number of methodological issues concerning the use of peer ratings. Many of these issues are resolved by applying the Social Relations Model to the peer rating data (Kenny, Lord, & Garg, 1983).

Second, the model can provide social psychology with better procedures to resolve theoretical issues of the discipline. For instance, one issue is the degree of reciprocity and compensation in dyadic interaction. Cappella (1981) has reviewed research concerning the reciprocity or compensation of gaze, speech, distance, and self-disclosure. He concluded that both reciprocity and compensation occur. Since these processes are directly measured by the Social Relations Model, the model should prove useful in this area of research. We have already noted the utility of the model for questions of person perception, social development, self–other processes, and reciprocity of attraction.

Third, the model is useful because it looks at social behavior as simultaneously operating at multiple levels. A single score is viewed as a function of four different levels of analysis: (1) the person (α and β), (2) the dyad (γ), (3) the occasion (ϵ), and (4) the group (μ). Processes can be simultaneously studied at all four levels. Very different principles operate at these different levels, and only by simultaneously examining social behavior at different levels can we fully appreciate the complexity and simplicity of social life.

ACKNOWLEDGMENTS

This research was supported in part by Grant BNS-8210137 from the National Science Foundation and by the MacArthur Foundation during D.A.K.'s sabbatical at the Center for Advanced Study in the Behavioral Sciences. Charles Judd, Phoebe Ellsworth, and Jeffrey Berman have provided a number of important suggestions. We also thank those researchers listed in Table VI who provided us with data to analyze. Finally, Rebecca Warner, Judith Harackiewicz, Lynn Gale, and Richard Polley assisted us in the computer programming, and Robyn Ireland and Rosemary Martin provided us with clerical assistance.

REFERENCES

Andersen, S. M., & Bem, S. L. Sex typing and androgyny in dyadic in interaction: Individual differences in responsiveness to physical attraction. *Journal of Personality and Social Psychology,* 1981, **41,** 74–86.

Bakeman, R., & Dabbs, Jr., J. M. Social interaction observed: Some approaches to the analysis of behavior streams. *Personality and Social Psychology Bulletin,* 1976, **2,** 335–345.

Bavelas, A. A. Mathematical models for group structures. *Applied Anthropology,* 1948, **7,** 16–30.

Berndt, T. J. The effects of friendship on prosocial intentions and behavior. *Child Development,* 1981, **52,** 636–643.

Bourne, E. Can we describe an individual's personality? Agreement on stereotype versus individual attributes. *Journal of Personality and Social Psychology*, 1977, **35**, 863–872.

Brewer, M. B., & Campbell, D. T. *Ethnocentrism and intergroup attitudes: East African evidence*. Beverly Hills, CA: Sage, 1976.

Burgess, R. L. Relationships in marriage and family. In S. Duck & R. Gilmour (Eds.), *Personal relationships Vol. 1, Studying personal relationships*. New York: Academic Press, 1981.

Burleson, J. A. *Reciprocity of interpersonal attraction within acquainted versus unacquainted small groups*. Unpublished doctoral dissertation, University of Texas, 1982.

Campbell, D. T., Miller, N., Lubetsky, J., & O'Connell, E. J. Varieties of projection in trait attribution. *Psychological Monographs*, 1964, **78**, (entire issue 592).

Cappella, J. N. Mutual influence in expressive behavior: Adult–adult and infant–adult dyadic interaction. *Psychological Bulletin*, 1981, **89**, 101–132.

Conger, J. C., & Keane, S. P. Social skills intervention in the treatment of isolated or withdrawn children. *Developmental Psychology*, 1981, **90**, 478–495.

Cronbach, L. H. Processes affecting scores on ''understanding of others'' and ''assumed similarity.'' *Psychological Bulletin*, 1955, **12**, 177–193.

Curry, T. J., & Emerson, R. M. Balance theory: A theory of interpersonal attraction? *Sociometry*, 1970, **33**, 216–238.

DePaulo, B. M., & Rosenthal, R. Telling lies. *Journal of Personality and Social Psychology*, 1979, **37**, 1713–1722.

Dornbusch, S. M., Hastorf, A. H., Richardson, S. A., Muzzy, R. E., & Vreeland, R. S. The perceiver and the perceived: Their relative influence on the categories of interpersonal cognition. *Journal of Personality and Social Psychology*, 1965, **5**, 434–440.

Duncan, S., & Fiske, D. W. *Face to face interaction: Research, methods, and theory*. Hillsdale, New Jersey: Erlbaum, 1977.

Feinberg, S. E., & Wasserman, S. S. Categorical data analysis of data of single sociometric relations. In S. Leinhardt (Ed.), *Sociological methodology 1981*. San Francisco: Jossey-Bass, 1981.

Flint, R. A. *The relative importance of structure and individual differences in determining behavior in two person games*. Unpublished doctoral dissertation, University of New Mexico, 1970.

Furman, W., Rahe, D. F., & Hartup, W. W. Rehabilitation of socially withdrawn preschool children through mixed-age and same-age socialization. *Child Development*, 1979, **50**, 915–922.

Goldenthal, P. *Nonverbal portrayal of emotional states: Acting and social skill*. Unpublished doctoral dissertation. University of Connecticut, 1981.

Gottman, J. M., & Notarius, C. Sequential analysis of observational data using Markov chains. In T. R. Kratochwill (Ed.), *Single subject research*. New York: Academic Press, 1978.

Harshman, R. *Models for analysis of asymmetrical relationships among N objects or stimuli*. Paper presented at Psychometric and Mathematical Psychology Meeting, McMaster University, 1978.

Hastie, R., Penrod, S., & Pennington, N. *Inside the jury*. Cambridge, Massachusetts: Harvard University Press, 1983.

Hay, D. F., Pederson, J., & Nash, A. Dyadic interaction in the first year of life. In K. H. Rubin & H. S. Ross (Eds.), *Peer relationships and social skills in childhood*. New York: Springer-Verlag, 1982.

Hays, W. L. *Statistics for psychologists*. New York: Holt, Rinehart & Winston, 1963.

Hinde, R. A. The bases of a science of interpersonal relationships. In S. Duck & R. Gilmour (Eds.), *Personal relationships, Vol. 1, Studying personal relationships*. New York: Academic Press, 1981.

Holland, P. W., & Leinhardt, S. An exponential family of probability distributions for directed graphs. *Journal of American Statistical Association*, 1981, **76**, 33–50.

Ickes, W. A basic paradigm for the study of personality, roles, and social behavior. In W. Ickes & E. S. Knowles (Eds.), *Personality, roles and social behavior*. New York: Springer-Verlag, 1982.

Insko, C. A., Thibaut, J. W., Moehle, D., Wilson, M., Diamond, W. D., Gilmore, R., Solomon, M. R., & Lipsitz, A. Social evolution and the emergence of leadership. *Journal of Personality and Social Psychology*, 1980, **39**, 431–448.

Jackson, D. N. A model for inferential accuracy. *The Canadian Psychologist*, 1972, **13**, 185–194.

James, J. The distribution of free-forming small group size. *American Sociological Review*, 1953, **18**, 569–570.

Jones, L. E., & Young, F. W. Structure of a social environment: Longitudinal individual differences scaling of an intact group. *Journal of Personality and Social Psychology*, 1972, **24**, 108–121.

Kane, J. S., & Lawler, E. E. Methods of peer assessment. *Psychological Bulletin*, 1978, **85**, 555–586.

Kelley, H. H. Attribution theory in social psychology. In D. Levine (Ed.), *Nebraska symposium on motivation* (Vol. 15). Lincoln, Nebraska: University of Nebraska Press, 1967.

Kenny, D. A. Interpersonal perception: A multivariate round robin analysis. In M. B. Brewer & B. E. Collins (Eds.), *Knowing and validating in the social sciences: A tribute to Donald T. Campbell*. San Francisco: Jossey-Bass. 1981.

Kenny, D. A., *BLOCKO: A FORTRAN program for block data structures*. Unpublished manuscript, University of Connecticut. 1983. (a)

Kenny, D. A. SOREMO: A FORTRAN program for round robin data structures. Unpublished manuscript, University of Connecticut, 1983. (b)

Kenny, D. A., & La Voie, L. Reciprocity of attraction: A confirmed hypothesis. *Social Psychology Quarterly*, 1982, **45**, 54–58.

Kenny, D. A., & La Voie, L. Separating individual and group effects. *Journal of Personality and Social Psychology*, 1984, in press.

Kenny, D. A., Lord. R., & Garg, S. A. *Social relations analysis of peer ratings*. Unpublished manuscript, University of Connecticut, 1983.

Kenny, D. A., & Nasby, W. Splitting the reciprocity correlation. *Journal of Personality and Social Psychology*, 1980, **38**, 249–256.

Kraemer, H. C., & Jacklin, C. N. Statistical analysis of dyadic social behavior. *Psychological Bulletin*, 1979, **86**, 217–224.

Lanzetta, J. F., & Kleck, R. E. The encoding and decoding of nonverbal affects in humans. *Journal of Personality of Social Psychology*, 1970, **16**, 12–19.

La Voie, L. *The analysis of social interaction: Individual and interactive effects in same- and mixed-aged dyads*. Unpublished doctoral dissertation, University of Connecticut, 1981.

La Voie, L. *CHECKERS: A FORTRAN computer program for checkerboard data structures*. Unpublished manuscript, University of Miami, 1983.

Lord, R. G., Phillips, J. S., & Rush, M. C. Effects of sex on perceptions of emergent leadership, influence, and social power. *Journal of Applied Psychology*, 1980, **65**, 176–182.

Manis, M. Social interaction and the self concept. *Journal of Abnormal and Social Psychology*, 1955, **51**, 362–370.

Masters, J. L., & Furman, W. Popularity, individual friendship selection, and specific peer preference. *Developmental Psychology*, 1981, **17**, 344–350.

McArthur, L. A. The how and what of why: Some determinants and consequences of casual attributions. *Journal of Personality and Social Psychology*, 1972, **22**, 171–193.

McLeod, J. M., & Chaffee, S. H. Interpersonal approaches to communication research. *American Behavioral Scientist*, 1973, **16**, 467–500.

Miller, L. C., Berg, J. M., & Archer, R. L. Openers: Individuals who elicit intimate self-disclosure. *Journal of Personality and Social Psychology,* 1983, **44,** 1234–1244.

Miller, R. E., Caul. W. F., & Mirsky, I. A. Communication of affects between feral and socially isolated monkeys. *Journal of Personality and Social Psychology,* 1967, **3,** 231–239.

Montgomery, B. M. *An interactionist approach to small group research, analyzing peer assessments.* Unpublished manuscript, University of Connecticut, 1983.

Moskowitz, D. S. *Cross-situational generality of dominance and friendliness.* Unpublished manuscript, McGill University, 1983.

Mosteller, F., & Tukey, J. W. *Data analysis and regression.* Reading, Massachusetts: Addison-Wesley, 1977.

Mueller, E., & Brenner, J. The origins of social skills and interaction among play-group toddlers. *Child Development,* 1977, **48,** 854–851.

Newcomb, A. F., & Brady, J. E. Mutuality in boys' friendship relations. *Child Development,* 1982, **53,** 392–395.

Newcomb, T. M. Reciprocity of attraction: A nonconfirmation of a plausible hypothesis. *Social Psychology Quarterly,* 1979, **42,** 299–306.

Polley, R. B. *Both sides of the mirror: Small groups and subjectivity.* Unpublished doctoral dissertation, Harvard University, 1979.

Reed, P. L., & Jackson, D. N. Clinical judgment of psychopathology: A model for inferential accuracy. *Journal of Abnormal Psychology,* 1975, **84,** 475–482.

Sabatelli, R. M., Buck, R., & Dreyer, A. Nonverbal communication accuracy in married couples: Relationship with marital complaints. *Journal of Personality and Social Psychology,* 1982, **43,** 1088–1097.

Schofield, J. W., & Sagar, H. A. Peer interaction in a desegregated middle school. *Sociometry,* 1977, **40,** 130–138.

Smollar, J., & Youniss, J. Social development through friendship. In K. H. Rubin & H. S. Ross (Eds.), *Peer relationships and social skills in childhood.* New York: Springer-Verlag, 1982.

Snyder, M. L., Tanke, E. D., & Berscheid, E. Social perception and interpersonal behavior: On the self-fulfilling nature of social stereotypes. *Journal of Personality and Social Psychology,* 1977, **35,** 656–666.

Tagiuri, R. Person perception. In G. Lindzey & E. Aronson (Eds.), *The handbook of social psychology* (Vol. 3). Reading, Massachusetts: Addison-Wesley, 1969.

Tagiuri, R., Bruner, J. S., & Blake, R. R. On the relation between feelings and perception of feelings among members of small groups. In E. Maccoby *et al., Readings in Social Psychology,* New York: Holt, Rinehart & Winston, 1958.

Tukey, J. W. One degree of freedom for nonadditivity. *Biometrics,* 1949, **5,** 232–242.

Wanlass, R. L., & Prinz, R. J. Methodological issues in conceptualizing and treating childhood social isolation. *Psychological Bulletin,* 1982, **92,** 39–55.

Warner, R. M., Kenny, D. A., & Stoto, M. A new round robin analysis of variance for social interaction data. *Journal of Personality and Social Psychology,* 1979, **37,** 1742–1757.

Warner, R. M., & Sugarman, D. B. *Physical attractiveness and familarity: A multivariate round robin analysis.* Paper presented at 1983 EPA meeting, 1983.

White, H., Boorman, S., & Breiger, R. Social structure from multiple networks: I. Blockmodels of roles and positions. *American Journal of Sociology,* 1976, **81,** 730–780.

Whitley, B. E., Schofield, J. W., & Snyder, H. N. Peer preferences in a desegregated school: A round robin analysis. *Journal of Personality and Social Psychology,* 1984, **46,** 799–810.

Wong, G. Round robin analysis of variance via maximum likelihood. *Journal of the American Statistical Association,* 1982, **77,** 714–724.

182 DAVID A. KENNY AND LAWRENCE LA VOIE

Wong, G. *Bayesian models for directed graphs*. Unpublished manuscript, Memorial Sloan-Kettering Cancer Center, 1983.
Wright, T. L., Ingraham, L. J., & Blackmer, D. R. The simultaneous study of individual differences and relationship effects in attraction. *Journal of Personality and Social Psychology,* 1984, in press.

COALITION BARGAINING

S. S. Komorita

DEPARTMENT OF PSYCHOLOGY
UNIVERSITY OF ILLINOIS
CHAMPAIGN, ILLINOIS

ADVANCES IN EXPERIMENTAL
SOCIAL PSYCHOLOGY, VOL. 18

I. Introduction

William Gamson (1964) reviewed theory and research in coalition formation for the first volume of *Advances in Experimental Social Psychology,* in one of the most frequently cited articles in the area of coalition formation. Since then, a variety of new theories has been proposed, and there have been several additional reviews of the coalition literature (Chertkoff, 1970; Stryker, 1972; Burhans, 1973; Murnighan, 1978; Miller & Crandall, 1980). Gamson's (1964) article had a significant influence on theory and research because he introduced the reader to some important ideas and concepts from other disciplines, especially from economics and mathematical game theory. Another reason is that Gamson proposed several theories of coalition formation that investigators could contrast and subject to empirical test. The predictions of two of the theories, in particular, were contrasted by a large number of investigators: Minimum resource theory (Gamson, 1961a) and minimum power theory (Gamson, 1964). These theories will be described and evaluated in Sections III,A,1–2.

Webster defines *coalition* as a combination or union; a temporary alliance of factions, parties, etc. for some specific purpose. Although an alliance refers to any association entered into for mutual benefit, and a coalition implies a temporary alliance, we shall use the two terms synonymously. This general definition of coalition implies that any social group or organization is a coalition, and that a coalition forms for the same reasons that a group forms. This is one reason why Shaw (1981), in his textbook *Group Dynamics,* introduced the topic of coalition formation in a chapter on "Group Formation and Development." According to Cartwright and Zander (1968), groups form because "a collection of individuals can accomplish some purpose (or do so at a level of efficiency) not otherwise possible, or people expect to derive satisfaction from associating together" (p. 54). Since there are many types of groups and many reasons (purposes, motives) for forming a group, to narrow the scope of the problem, several theorists have proposed more restrictive definitions of coalition formation.

According to Thibaut and Kelley (1959), a coalition is "two or more persons who act jointly to affect the outcomes of one or more other persons" (p. 205). For Gamson (1964), a coalition is "the joint use of resources to determine the outcome of a decision in a mixed-motive situation involving more than two units'' (p. 85). "A resource is some weight controlled by the participants such that some critical quantity of these weights is necessary and sufficient to determine the decision'' (p. 82). The term "mixed-motive situation" was first introduced by Schelling (1960) and refers to a situation in which there is a conflict between cooperative and competitive tendencies. In a coalition situation the participants must cooperate in the joint use of resources but must also bargain competitively over the distribution of the outcome (rewards for cooperation).

The definition proposed by Gamson is appropriate for situations in which resources are involved, but, as we shall see, there are many coalition situations in which resources are not involved. Accordingly, for the purpose of this article, we shall adopt the definition proposed by Thibaut and Kelley, with the stipulation that "acting jointly" includes the act of reaching agreement on the distribution (division) of the outcome.

C. TYPES OF COALITION THEORIES

Coalition formation is of interest to a variety of social scientists (e.g., economists, political scientists, sociologists, psychologists), and, not surprisingly, many types of theories have been proposed. In general, these theories can be classified according to their assumptions regarding the motives for forming coalitions. The assumptions about the motives that determine coalition preferences are summarized in the following sections.

1. Maximize Control over Others

The purpose of forming coalitions to maximize control of others is assumed by Caplow's (1959, 1968) theory, which assumes that (1) members of a triad differ in strength, (2) a stronger member can control a weaker member, and (3) each member seeks control over the others. Caplow assumes that the primary motive to form a coalition is to control (dominate) other members, and the motive to maximize external rewards that can be obtained by coalition formation is ignored. Thus, his theory does not yield predictions about the distribution of rewards among the coalition members.

2. Maximize Status in the Group

The purpose of forming coalitions to maximize group status was first proposed by Hoffman, Festinger, and Lawrence (1954) and later formalized by Laing and Morrison (1973). Based on social comparison theory (Festinger, 1954), Hoffman et al. assume that members of a group are motivated to evaluate their relative status in a group and strive to maximize status. In their coalition experiment, those who were behind in points, as hypothesized, united against the leader. Chertkoff (1975), in his review of sequential effects in coalition formation, claims that a union against the leader may represent an attempt to achieve status (Hoffman *et al.*; Emerson, 1964; Anderson, 1967), but since status is determined by payoffs during the game, it is difficult to separate trying to win from trying to achieve status.

3. Minimize Conflict

Several theories assume that coalition preferences are based on minimizing conflict among the members. Gamson's (1964) "anti-competitive theory," for example, assumes that "coalitions will form along the path of least resistance in bargaining"—one in which "an agreement can be reached on an equal basis, with a minimum of haggling, unpleasantness, and subsequent resentment" (p. 91). As evidence to support his theory, Gamson (1964) cites the results of studies by Vinacke (1959) and by Bond and Vinacke (1961), in which female subjects were found to prefer and form coalitions for equal shares of the reward, and behaved less competitively than males.

In a political situation, several related theories have been proposed that assume that coalition preferences are based on minimizing ideological conflict. Assuming a unidimensional continuum (e.g., a liberal–conservative dimension), if the participants are ordered from left to right on the continuum, these theories predict that persons will prefer coalition partners who are adjacent to their position on the continuum. Hence, these theories predict that coalitions that "minimize the range" of positions (Leiserson, 1970), "minimize policy differences" (DeSwaan, 1973), or "minimize conflict of interest" (Axelrod, 1970) are most likely to form. The results of an experiment by Miller (1979), under the assumption of "single-peaked preference functions," provide partial support for these conceptualizations.

4. Maximize Similarity of Attitudes and Values

This class of theories is based on Heider's (1958) balance principle, and assumes that coalition choice is based on similarity of attitudes and values. Support for this approach has been reported by Mazur (1968), Lawler and Youngs (1975), and Webster and Smith (1978). However, Crosbie and Kullberg (1973) found that resources were more important than the balance principle of predicting coalition behavior. The balance principle is very similar to minimum range theories, e.g., both imply that "The enemy of my enemy is my friend (coalition partner)." Thus, support for one class of theories implies support for the other, and vice versa.

5. Maximize Multiple (Unknown, Unspecified) Motives

This category includes Gamson's (1964) "utter confusion theory" which assumes that coalition formation "is best understood as an essentially random choice process" (p. 92). As evidence to support this theory, Gamson cites instances in which many factors may produce results that are random or unpredictable, e.g., who yells first and loudest, bewilderment and lack of understanding, or spatial arrangement of players around a table.

Many of these extraneous factors cited by Gamson can be easily controlled and isolated. However, a more important implication is his suggestion that some subjects may be motivated by factors other than maximizing reward, such as altruism and sympathy for the weak players. This problem of multiple motives in the typical coalition experiment was critically reviewed by Stryker (1972), who suggested that it would be extremely valuable to extend coalition theories to situations in which "rewards are internal to the triadic relationship, rather than emanating from outside" (p. 373). Stryker's recommendation is quite compelling. In many real-life situations, rewards are indeed internal to the relationship, and such an approach would greatly extend the generality of coalition research. However, such an approach would involve multiple (unspecified) motives among the participants, and would be highly intractable. Some members may be motivated to achieve the goals of the group, some may be motivated to maximize control or status, while others may be motivated by similarity of attitudes and values. Thus, such an approach would represent an attempt to develop a general theory of coalition formation, which is really a theory of why groups (or subgroups) form. We shall not pursue this approach, however, and shall restrict our review to theories belonging to the next category of motives.

6. Maximize Share of External Reward

The final class of theories assumes that all participants are motivated to maximize some specified, quantitative (divisible) commodity, such as money or points. These assumptions restrict the generality of these theories, but they are the most theoretically advanced. Theories based on reward maximization can be classified into two main types. *Normative theories* are based on axioms of "rational" (intelligent) behavior and attempt to prescribe behavior that will yield maximal reward for each of the participants. *Descriptive theories,* in contrast, attempt to predict how individuals are likely to behave, whether rational or not. Normative theories have been proposed by economists and game theorists, while descriptive theories have been proposed by social psychologists. For obvious reasons, we shall focus our attention on descriptive theories. For a review of normative theories, the interested reader is referred to Luce and Raiffa (1957) and to Rapoport (1970).

D. SCOPE OF REVIEW

In the subsequent sections of this article, we shall restrict our review to theories based on reward maximization. The main reason for this restriction is that the vast majority of experimental studies have attempted to test one or more of these theories. Predictions can be logically and clearly derived from their assumptions, and, more importantly, they are readily amenable to experimental test. This is one of the main reasons for the greater progress in developing and testing this class of theories.

In addition, no attempt will be made to present an exhaustive review of the coalition literature. Instead, we shall attempt to integrate and organize the literature by comparing and evaluating a limited set of coalitions theories. For reviews of the earlier coalition literature, the reader is referred to the excellent reviews by Chertkoff (1970) and by Stryker (1972), and for a more recent and comprehensive review of the literature, the reader is referred to Murnighan (1978).

II. Classification of Coalition Situations

A. SIMPLE VS MULTIVALUED GAMES

Coalition situations vary widely and they can be classified in a number of ways. Since we shall restrict our review to theories based on maximizing reward, we shall first classify coalition situations on the basis of the characteristic function of a game (cf. Luce & Raiffa, 1957; Rapoport, 1970). The *characteristic function* of a game is a rule that specifies a value (prize, reward) for each possible coalition. In a *simple game,* the characteristic function has only two values, one value for all winning coalitions and another value for all losing coalitions. Consider the following four-person simple game, sometimes called an *apex game*:[1]

> *Losing Coalitions:* $v(A) = v(B) = v(C) = v(D) = 0$
> $v(BC) = v(BD) = v(CD) = 0$
> *Winning Coalitions:* $v(AB) = v(AC) = v(AD) = 100$
> $v(ABC) = v(ABD) = v(ACD) = v(BCD) = 100$
> and $v(ABCD) = 100$

where A, B, C, and D denote the four players, and $v(\ )$ denotes the value (prize, reward) for the coalition in parentheses. Note that all coalitions have one of two

---

[1]In an apex game (Horowitz, 1973), there is a single "strong" (apex) player and $N - 1$ "weak" (base) players. Two types of minimal-winning coalitions are possible: An apex coalition consisting of the apex player and one of the base players, and the base coalition consisting of the $N - 1$ base players.

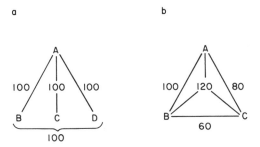

Fig. 1.   Example of four-person simple (apex) game, a, and three-person multivalued (quota) game, b.

values: 0 for all losing coalitions and 100 for all winning coalitions (a two-valued characteristic function). Also note that only one of the winning coalitions (BCD) excludes player A, whereas three coalitions exclude each of the others. Hence, player A has an advantage (bargaining strength) over the other three players.

The main implication of this example is that in a simple game there is little incentive to form large coalitions. Since the value of all winning coalitions is the same, forming a large coalition means that the value or prize must be divided among a larger number of coalition members. Consequently, all theories predict that minimal-winning coalitions are likely to form in simple games. A *minimal-winning coalition* (MWC) is defined as a winning coalition that becomes a losing coalition if any single member is deleted. For example, the ABC coalition is not a minimal-winning coalition because it would still be a winning coalition if either player B or C were deleted. The MWCs in this game are AB, AC, AD, and BCD. Hereafter, we shall only consider MWCs because all theories predict that only MWCs are likely to form, and non-minimal-winning coalitions rarely form. Figure 1a illustrates the structure of this game and shows the four MWCs.

In contrast to simple games, in a *multivalued game* various possible coalitions are assigned many different values, and winning and losing coalitions are not defined. Consider the three-person multivalued game shown in Fig. 1b. This game is called a *quota game* and is defined as follows.[2]

$$v(A) = v(B) = v(C) = 0$$
$$v(AB) = 100 \qquad v(AC) = 80 \qquad v(BC) = 60$$
$$\text{and } v(ABC) = 120$$

---

[2]A quota game is one in which there is a vector of weights associated with the players such that for any pair of players i and j, $v(ij) = q_i + q_j$. The weights (q_i and q_j) are called the quota values of the players, and the value of each coalition is equal to the sum of the quota values of the players in the coalition. In the three-person game of Fig. 1b, the quota values of players A, B, and C are 60, 40, and 20, respectively.

One of the main implications of this example is that, unlike a simple game, there may be an incentive to form larger coalitions. Note that the value of the *grand coalition*, the coalition of all players (ABC), is much larger than any of the two-person coalitions. This type of game is called a *superadditive game*, a game in which the value of any coalition is at least as large as the sum of the values of any disjoint (nonoverlapping) subsets of the coalition. For example, if we let $v(ABC) = 0$, the game would not be superadditive, and there would be no incentive to form the ABC coalition.[3] Also note that player A has an advantage over the other players but for a different reason than in a simple game. Player A has greater bargaining strength because the coalitions that include him/her have greater values (120, 100, 80) than the coalitions that include the other players.

B. GAMES WITH RESOURCE WEIGHTS

The vast majority of coalition experiments conducted by social psychologists have been restricted to simple games. In such experiments *resources* or *weights* have been assigned to the players to manipulate their power (bargaining strength). In Vinacke and Arkoff's (1957) three-person "pachisi-board game," for example, the weights consist of numbers on three "counters" that are randomly assigned to the subjects. The object of the game is to move one's counter on spaces around a board (as in a Monopoly game), and whoever moves his/her counter around the board first wins a prize of 100 points. The experimenter rolls a single die and the number of spaces each player moves his/her counter is equal to the product of his/her weight and the value of the die. Subjects are informed that at any time during the game any player may form an alliance with any other player. To form an alliance they must agree on how they will divide the prize if they win. If an alliance forms, the two players combine (sum) their weights, as well as their accumulated spaces on the board.

Another commonly used game is Gamson's (1961b) "political convention" paradigm in which resource weights consist of votes and a majority of the votes is necessary to form a winning coalition. For example, a frequently used distribution of resources is 5(4–3–2), where the first number denotes the number of votes required to win, and the numbers in parentheses denote the resource weights (votes) of the three players.[4] Henceforth, we shall assume, without loss

[3]In the three-person case, a superadditive game must satisfy the following two conditions: $v(ijk) \geq v(ij) + v(k)$, and $v(ij) \geq v(i) + v(j)$, for any pair of players i and j. These conditions are satisfied in the quota game of Fig. 1b. In a nonsuperadditive game, at least one of these conditions is violated, e.g., if we let $v(ABC) = 0$, the game would be nonsuperadditive because the first condition is not satisfied.

[4]This type of game is called a *weighted majority game*, a game in which each player is assigned a weight and a majority of the weights is necessary to form a winning coalition. Henceforth, we shall denote such games as follows: $Q(v_1 - v_2 \ldots -v_n)$, in which v_i denotes the weights of the n players, and Q denotes the combined weights required to form a winning coalition.

of generality, that in simple games the value (prize) for all winning coalitions is 100, and the value of all losing coalitions is zero. If we label the players by capital letters (A, B, C) in descending order of their resource weights, this game is defined as follows:

$$v(A) = v(B) = v(C) = 0$$
$$v(AB) = v(AC) = v(BC) = 100$$
$$\text{and } v(ABC) = 0$$

Now consider the Vinacke–Arkoff paradigm when the weights (numbers on counters) of players A, B, and C are 4, 3, and 2, respectively. In contrast to Gamson's paradigm, in the Vinacke–Arkoff paradigm, player A can win alone if player B and C do not form a coalition, and this game is defined as follows:

$$v(B) = v(C) = 0$$
$$v(A) = 0 \text{ (if BC forms)}; \quad v(A) = 100 \text{ (if no coalition forms)}$$
$$v(AB) = v(AC) = v(BC) = 100$$
$$\text{and} \quad v(ABC) = 0$$

In characteristic function form, it can be seen that Gamson and Vinacke–Arkoff paradigms are not the same. The Vinacke–Arkoff paradigm is much more complex, especially for player A, because player A has more options (form a coalition with B or C, or attempt to inhibit the formation of any coalition). In Gamson's paradigm, in contrast, player A's only options are to form a coalition with B or C. Thus, it is plausible that the BC coalition is more likely to occur in the Vinacke–Arkoff paradigm, especially in the early trials, than in Gamson's paradigm.

The main implication of these examples is that various experimental paradigms can be transformed to their characteristic functions, and can be easily interpreted and compared. For example, Gamson's paradigm is a symmetric game in which all players are equal in power (bargaining advantage). If resource weights were not assigned in 5(4–3–2), and subjects were simply informed that any two-person coalition (AB, AC, BC) is a winning coalition, the game would be trivial: the three coalitions should be equally likely and the prize should be divided equally (50–50). When resource weights are used, however, there is considerable evidence to indicate that the BC coalition occurs much more frequently than the AB and AC coalitions, and the prize is not divided equally (at least on the early trials).

This discrepancy between power (based on the characteristic function of the game) and the results of coalition experiments suggest that resource weights have qualitatively different functions. In Section II,C two basic functions of resource weights will be proposed, one based on power and the other based on equity norms. We shall then show that various theories of coalition formation can be differentiated and evaluated on the basis of their assumptions regarding the role (function) of resource weights.

1. The Concept of Power

We have used the terms "power" and "bargaining strength" without explicitly defining these concepts. Some writers make a distinction between the two concepts (Schelling, 1960; Stevens, 1963; Komorita, 1977). However, since most definitions of power imply that one has bargaining strength if one has power, we shall use the two terms synonymously. Social power has been defined in a variety of ways, and various approaches to the study of power have been proposed (cf. review by Schopler, 1965). For the purpose of this article, we shall adopt the definition proposed by Thibaut and Kelley (1959) because their conceptualization is particularly relevant and appropriate for bargaining situations.

According to Thibaut and Kelley (1959), when two individuals interact (bargain) with one another, each compares and evaluates his/her outcome in the relationship with the best possible outcome each can expect in alternative relationships. An individual's maximum outcome expected in alternative relationships is called his/her *comparison level for alternatives* (CLalt). If outcomes in the relationship exceed the individual's respective CLalts, they are likely to remain in the relationship, but if the outcome for one of the parties is less than his/her CLalt, he/she is likely to terminate the relationship and seek rewards in alternative relationships.

The main implication of this conceptualization is that the party with better alternatives (CLalt) can threaten to leave the relationship, at less cost than for the party with the smaller CLalt, and thus has greater bargaining strength. Moreover, one party's power over another is limited by the other's CLalt: Demands for concessions beyond the other's CLalt are likely to induce the other to seek alternative relationships. There is considerable empirical support for this conceptualization of bargaining strength (Thibaut & Faucheux, 1965; Thibaut & Gruder, 1969; Komorita & Kravitz, 1979; Komorita, Lapworth, & Tumonis, 1981), and one of the promising theories of coalition formation, the bargaining theory (Komorita & Chertkoff, 1973), is based on this conceptualization.

2. Justice Norms in Coalition Bargaining

In addition to the effects of power, another important factor in coalition bargaining is the effects of justice norms: that which an individual believes to be a fair or reasonable distribution of rewards in a relationship. Like the concept of power, the concept of "justice" is very elusive and ambiguous, and for the purpose of this article we shall restrict our presentation to those norms that are particularly relevant in coalition bargaining.

Of particular relevance for simple games with resource weights are Homans' (1961) concept of "distributive justice" and Adams' (1963) equity theory. Both theories assume that one's share of the reward (output) in a relationship should be directly proportional to one's resource (contribution, input). If the proportional relation between input and output is violated, there will be feelings of injustice/inequity, and attempts will be made to restore distributive justice/equity. In a coalition situation, such attempts to restore equity may involve demands for an equitable share through bargaining, or the choice of alternative coalition partners who may provide an equitable share. The predictions of some theories of coalition formation, as we shall see, are based on justice norms, while other theories completely ignore such norms.

3. The Functions of Resource Weights in Simple Games

The previous discussion of power and justice norms suggests that in simple games resource weights may serve two basic functions. On the one hand, resource weights serve a *strategic function* in that they affect the pattern of minimal-winning coalitions and determine the alternative coalitions available to the players. On the other hand, resource weights also serve a *normative function* by providing a standard or frame of reference for a fair or equitable division of the reward in a coalition.

To illustrate the two functions of resource weights, consider two of the games used in a study by Murnighan, Komorita, and Szwajkowski (1977): 9(8–3–3–3) and 15(8–7–7–7). The minimal-winning coalitions are identical in the two games: AB, AC, AD, and BCD. According to the strategic function of resource weights, player A's bargaining strength should be equal in the two games. Since the number and size of winning coalitions that include each player are the same in the two games, there should be no difference in coalition outcomes. Murnighan *et al.* found that the two games did not differ significantly in the frequencies of the various coalitions: The two-person coalitions occurred in 86% of the cases, while the BCD coalition occurred in 14% of the cases. However, the mean share of the reward for player A in the two games did differ significantly: Player A's mean share was 72.7 in the 8–3 coalition and 62.9 in the 8–7 coalition. This difference in player A's mean payoff can be attributed to the normative function of resource weights: Player A presumably could justify and demand a larger share in the 8–3 coalition than in the 8–7 coalition because the resource weight of the weaker player was much smaller in 8–3 than in 8–7.

These results suggest that the strategic function (pattern of winning coalitions) determines which coalitions are likely to form, while the normative function determines the nature of payoff splits among the coalition members. If this hypothesis is valid, then any theory that ignores one or the other function of resource weights is not likely to yield accurate predictions of coalition outcomes (Komorita & Nagao, 1983). In Section III,B we shall provide some evidence for the validity of this hypothesis.

III. Coalition Formation in Simple Games

As we indicated earlier, we shall restrict our article to theories that are based on maximizing some specified, divisible reward, such as money or points. Among the theories that are based on reward maximization, some theories only predict how the reward will be divided and do not yield predictions about which coalitions are likely to form. Since both response measures are of interest to social psychologists, we shall further restrict our review to theories that predict both of these measures. Thus, the predictions of the following five theories will be contrasted and evaluated: (1) minimum resource theory (Gamson, 1961a), (2) minimum power theory (Gamson, 1964), (3) bargaining theory (Komorita & Chertkoff, 1973), (4) weighted probability model (Komorita, 1974), and (5) equal excess model (Komorita, 1979).

A. COALITION THEORIES IN SIMPLE GAMES

For the case of simple games, we shall contrast the five theories when resource weights are assigned and when they are not. When resource weights are assigned, we shall use the following four-person game: 9(8–3–3–3). In this game the MWCs are AB, AC, AD, and BCD. The MWCs are identical to the apex game shown in Fig. 1a (discussed in Section II,A), in which resource weights are not assigned. Thus, in terms of their characteristic functions, the two games are identical. We shall contrast the predictions of the five theories for these two games, and, as we shall see, they make markedly different predictions in these games.

1. Minimum Resource Theory

a. Games with Resource Weights.   The basic assumption of Gamson's (1961a) minimum resource theory is that all participants will expect and demand a share of the reward that is directly proportional to the amount of resources that each contributes to the coalition. Gamson called this proportionality rule the "parity norm" and stated that the norm is simply an application of Homan's

(1961) distributive justice in a coalition situation. Gamson also stated that ''Players may be able to gain a larger than proportional share by skillful bargaining. However, this will involve a violation of the parity norm; such a victimization of the other players will be regarded as wrong and will not occur'' (1964, p. 88).

In the game 9(8–3–3–3), the parity norm prescribes that the payoff split in the 8–3 coalition should be $\frac{8}{11}$ and $\frac{3}{11}$ for the ''strong'' (8) and ''weak'' (3) player, respectively. We shall hereafter refer to such predictions as follows: AC (73–27), where the letters denote the coalition and the numbers in parentheses denote the payoff share of 100 points for the first and second members of the coalition, respectively. In the 3–3–3 coalition, the parity norm prescribes BCD (33–33–33). Since the BCD coalition maximizes the shares for all three members of the coalition, minimum resource theory predicts that BCD should be most likely.

This example illustrates one of the main implications of the theory, and why it is called minimum resource theory. It always predicts that the winning coalition that minimizes the sum of resources of the coalition members is most likely to form. In 9(8–3–3–3), for example, the 3–3–3 coalition is just large enough (9 votes) to form a winning coalition, and is the ''cheapest winning'' coalition. As another example, in the game 5(4–3–2), the 3–2 coalition is cheapest winning and is predicted to be most likely. Since this principle frequently implies that the strong player (4) will be excluded, Gamson (1964) proposed the hypothesis that ''Strength is weakness.'' We shall examine the validity of this paradoxical hypothesis in Section III,B,3.

b. Games without Resource Weights. In some experiments, resource weights are not used to manipulate the power of the players, but instead subjects are simply given a list specifying which coalitions are winning and which ones are losing. In the apex game shown in Fig. 1a, for example, subjects are informed that (1) players A, B, C, and D alone are losing coalitions; (2) BC, BD, and CD are losing coalitions; (3) AB, AC, and AD are winning coalitions; and (4) ABC, ABD, ACD, BCD, and ABCD are winning coalitions.

In games in which resource weights are not assigned, as in the apex game, no predictions can be derived from minimum resource theory. Its predictions are based entirely on the parity norm, which, in turn, is based on resource weights. This restriction severely limits the generality of the theory. More importantly, this reliance on resource weights implies that minimum resource theory is based entirely on the normative function of resource weights and completely ignores their strategic function. We shall examine the implications of this hypothesis in Section (III,B) when we compare and evaluate the relative validity of this theory.

2. Minimum Power Theory

a. Games with Resource Weights. Gamson's (1964) minimum power theory is based on an extension of Shapley and Shubik's (1954) index of pivotal power. The concept of pivotal power is based on the idea that when a player is added to a losing coalition, in some cases the new coalition remains a losing coalition, but in other cases, the addition of the player transforms the losing coalition to a winning one. In such instances the player is said to be pivotal (or decisive). Thus, the more often a player can transform a losing coalition into a winning one, the greater the player's pivotal power. Shapley and Shubik's index of pivotal power assumes that the sequences in which winning coalitions are formed are all equally likely. Hence, instances of pivotal power are counted over all possible permutations of the players, and "a player's *pivotal power* is the proportion of times his resources can change a losing coalition into a winning one. It is given by the index P/N where N is the total number of permutations among the players and P is the number of permutations in which his resources are pivotal" (Gamson, 1964, p. 90).

In 9(8–3–3–3), the number of players (N) is 4, and, therefore, there are 24 possible sequences (permutations) in which a winning coalition can be formed. For example, in the sequence BCAD, player A is pivotal because neither B alone nor BC (when C is added to B) are winning coalitions. However, when A is added to BC, player A converts a losing coalition into a winning one. The number of permutations in which players A, B, C, and D are pivotal are 12, 4, 4, and 4, respectively. Dividing these values by 24 yields the pivotal power indexes.

The pivotal power indexes by themselves do not yield predictions about coalition outcomes. Consequently, Gamson (1964) proposed that the players will expect and demand a share of the reward that is proportional to pivotal power, rather than to resources. Thus, in 9(8–3–3–3), minimum power theory predicts a 75–25 split in the 8–3 coalition, and 33–33–33 in the BCD (proportional to pivotal power of 12–4–4–4). Since BCD maximizes the shares of all three members, the theory predicts BCD should be most likely. As in the case of minimum resource theory, minimum power theory always predicts that the winning coalition that minimizes the sum of pivotal power indexes of the members is most likely to form.

b. Games without Resource Weights. In deriving predictions for minimum power theory in 9(8–3–3–3), the magnitude of resource weights was not involved. The derivations were based only on the number of instances in which each player was pivotal. This means that the predictions of minimum power theory are based only on the pattern of MWCs. If the pattern of MWCs are the same in two games, the pivotal power indexes and the predictions of minimum power theory are also the same. We indicated earlier that the MWCs in 9(8–3–3–3) are the same as in the apex game (shown in Fig. 1a), in which resource weights are not assigned. Hence, minimum power theory makes the same predictions in the two games: BCD should be most frequent for a 33–33–33 split. This invariance of predictions over games with the same pattern of MWCs indicates that minimum power theory ignores the normative function of resource weights, and is based entirely on the strategic function.

3.   Weighted Probability Model

a.   Games with Resource Weights.   The basic assumption of the weighted probability model (Komorita, 1974) is that because of the logistic problem of communicating offers, large coalitions are more difficult to form than small ones. As the number of potential coalition members increases, difficulty in achieving reciprocity of choices and in achieving unanimous agreement on reward division increases. Moreover, the number of potential defectors from the coalition also increases with coalition size. Thus, a large coalition is not only more difficult to form but may be more difficult to maintain. These assumptions are consistent with the inverse relation between group size and the cohesiveness of a group reported by Cartwright and Zander (1968).

The unique feature of the model is that it yields an exact probability prediction for each coalition. The probability of coalition j (P_j) is given by Eq. (1),

$$P_j = w_j / \Sigma w_j \qquad (1)$$

in which $w_j = 1/(n_j - 1)$; n_j denotes the number of players in coalition j; and the summation is over all possible MWCs.

For the game 9(8-3-3-3), the w_j values for MWCs of AB, AC, AD, and BCD, are 1/1, 1/1, 1/1, and 1/2, respectively, and $\Sigma w_j = 7/2$. Substituting these values in Eq. (1), the probabilities of the MWCs are 2/7, 2/7, 2/7, and 1/7, respectively. Thus, unlike minimum resource and minimum power theories, which predict that the "weak-union" (BCD) is most likely to form, the weighted probability model predicts that the "strong-weak alliances" (AB, AC, or AD) are most likely to form.

To derive predictions of reward division among the coalition members, the model assumes that each member's share of the reward will be directly proportional to the probability of being included in the winning coalition, given by Eq. (2):

$$P_i = \Sigma P_j \qquad (i \in j) \qquad (2)$$

where P_i denotes the probability that player i will be included in the winning coalition, and the summation is over the MWCs that include player i.

For 9(8-3-3-3), player A is included in AB, AC, and AD, with probabilities (P_j) of 2/7 each; hence, $P_A = 6/7$. The remaining players (B, C, and D) are each included in two MWCs, one with player A with probability 2/7, and the other in BCD with probability 1/7. Hence, $P_B = P_C = P_D = 3/7$. Direct proportionality with respect to these probabilities of inclusion yields predicted payoff splits of 67-33 in AB, AC, and AD, and 33-33-33 in BCD.

b.   Games without Resource Weights.   Like minimum power theory, the predictions of the weighted probability model are not based on the magnitude of resource weights, and are based on the sizes (n_j) of MWCs in the game. Hence, its predictions are based entirely on the strategic function of resource weights and the model ignores their normative function. Like minimum power theory, this means that its predictions are invariant for all games that differ in resource weights but have the same pattern of MWCs. Since the MWCs in the apex game without resource weights (Fig. 1a) are the same as in 9(8–3–3–3), the weighted probability model makes the same predictions for the two games: AB(67–33), AC(67–33), and AD(67–33), each with probability 2/7, and BCD (33–33–33), with probability 1/7.

4. Bargaining Theory

a. Games with Resource Weights. The basic assumption of the bargaining theory (Komorita & Chertkoff, 1973) is that in a given coalition, those who are "strong" (above average) in resources are likely to expect and demand a share of the reward that is based on the parity norm, whereas those who are "weak" (below average) are likely to expect and demand equality. This means that each member of a potential coalition will appeal to that norm of justice that maximizes his/her share of the reward. In an iterated (multitrial) experiment, the theory makes differential predictions on the initial trial and at the asymptote. Thus, unlike the previous static theories, the bargaining theory is a dynamic theory and predicts changes in the players' expectations and outcomes over trials of an iterated (multitrial) game.

In a one-trial game, or on the first trial of an iterated game, the bargaining theory predicts that the most likely coalition is one in which E^1_{ij} is maximized for all members i of coalition j, where E^1_{ij} is defined as the "split-the-difference" (mean) of expectations based on the parity norm and the equality norm. In 9(8–3–3–3), for example, if players A and B begin negotiations, the theory predicts that A will demand parity (73–27 division), whereas B will demand equality (50–50 division). Then E^1_{AB} will be the mean of the two expectations: shares of 61 and 39, respectively. In the BCD coalition, parity and equality are the same; thus, the theory predicts 33–33–33 in BCD. Since the two-person coalitions mutually maximize the expectations of the players, they are predicted to be most likely for a 61–39 division.

In an iterated game, it is assumed that players who have been excluded on the previous trial will make large concessions (lower their expectations), and make attractive offers to members of the winning coalition, so as to induce one or more members to defect from the winning coalition. For individual i of the winning coalition j, temptation to defect is defined by Eq. (3):

$$T_{ij} = (Emax_{ik} - O_{ij})/Emax_{ik} \qquad (j \neq k) \qquad (3)$$

in which $Emax_{ik}$ denotes individual i's maximum expectation *in alternative coalitions* (j ≠ k), and O_{ij} denotes individual i's share of the reward in coalition j on the previous trial. In 9(8–3–3–3), suppose the AB coalition formed on trial 1 for a 61–39 division, as predicted by the theory. In negotiations on the next trial, player A's $Emax_{ik}$ will be 73, A's maximum expectation in AC or AD, based on parity. Hence, T_{ij} for player A will be $(73 - 61)/73 = .16$. Player B, in contrast, will not be tempted to defect: B's share of 39 in AB exceeds his/her $Emax_{ik}$ of 33 in BCD. Hence, the theory predicts that player A's level of aspiration will increase over trials of the game, as a function of the attractive offers received from players C and D, whereas the levels of aspiration of B, C, and D are expected to decrease over trials.

At the asymptote (after an indefinite number of trials), it is assumed that expectations in coalition j will converge to a solution (E_{ij}^{∞}) that is proportional to the member's $Emax_{ik}$, given by Eq. (4)

$$E_{ij}^{\infty} = Emax_{ik}/\Sigma\ Emax_{ik} \qquad (j \neq k) \qquad (4)$$

in which the summation is over the members of coalition j. In 9(8–3–3–3), E_{ij}^{∞} in the AB (or AC, AD) coalition will be 69–31, based on player A's $Emax_{ik}$ of 73 in AC and AD, and player B's $Emax_{ik}$ of 33 in BCD. In the BCD coalition, each member's $Emax_{ik}$ will be the same: expectation of 50 (based on equality) in the two-person coalition with player A. Hence, E_{ij}^{∞} in BCD will be 33–33–33.

Although the asymptotic expectations of players B, C, and D are greater in the BCD coalition (33 each) than in the coalition with player A (31), the theory predicts that at the asymptote the most likely coalition is one in which the sum of temptation to defect from the coalition (ΣT_{ij}) is minimized. If we substitute the asymptotic values (E_{ij}^{∞}) for O_{ij} in Eq. (3), it can be shown that $\Sigma T_{ij} = .11$ in AB, AC, and AD, while $\Sigma T_{ij} = 1.00$ in BCD. These ΣT_{ij} values imply that if the BCD coalition forms for a division of 33–33–33, each member will be highly tempted to defect to join player A for a maximum expectation of 50 (equal shares). Thus, the coalition is not likely to be stable. In contrast, if AB (or AC, AD) forms for a 60–31 division, there will be less temptation to defect than in BCD, and one of these coalitions is predicted to be more likely (stable). Thus, the bargaining theory predicts that after an indefinite number of trials, the AB, AC, and AD coalitions are most likely to form (are most stable), with a reward division of 69–31.

    b. Games without Resource Weights. The bargaining theory, in its original form, yields predictions only when resources are assigned. Hence, Komorita and Tumonis (1980) proposed an extension of the theory so as to yield predictions when resources are not assigned. As in the original theory, expectations are based on two norms of justice, where one of the norms is equality. In the apex game (Fig. 1a), for example, if players A and B are negotiating the division of reward, player A is expected to demand a share in AB that is proportional to equal shares in alternative coalitions, denoted the *proportionality norm.* According to the proportionality norm, player A's alternative is 50 (equal shares in AC or AD), while B's alternative is 33 (equal shares in BCD). Proportionality with respect to these expectations in alternative coalitions yields shares of 60 and 40 for A and B, respectively. As in the original theory, a split-the-difference solution between the two norms (equality and proportionality) is predicted on trial 1 (or in a one-trial game): a 55–45 division in AB, AC, or AD. In the BCD coalition, equality and proportionality yield the same expectations; hence, a division of 33–33–33 is predicted in BCD. Since the AB, AC, and AD coalitions mutually maximize the expectations of the players, the two-person coalitions are predicted to be most likely on trial 1 for a 55–45 division. In summary, the extension of the theory proposed by Komorita and Tumonis simply substitutes the proportionality norm for the parity norm.

At the asymptote, expectations are predicted to converge to a solution that is proportional to each member's maximum expectation in alternative coalitions ($Emax_{ik}$). The $Emax_{ik}$ values for player A in AB, AC, and AD are 60 (based on the proportionality norm), while they are 33 for B, C, and D (based on equality or proportionality) in BCD. Proportionality with respect to these $Emax_{ik}$ values yields predicted divisions of 64–36 in AB, AC, and AD and 33–33–33 in BCD. If we substitute these predicted values in Eq. (3), it can be shown that the sum of temptation to defect (ΣT_{ij}) is minimized in the two-person coalitions. Hence, after an indefinite number of trials, they are predicted to be most likely (stable) for a 64–36 division.

With regard to the functions of resource weights, unlike the previous theories, the bargaining theory is based on both functions. When resource weights are assigned, the trial 1 and asymptotic predictions are based on both functions because maximum expectations in alternative coalitions depend on both norms of reward division, as well as the pattern of MWCs.

5. Equal Excess Model

a. *Games without Resource Weights.* Since the equal excess model (Komorita, 1979) was proposed for games in which resource weights are not assigned, we shall first describe the model for this case. Consider the apex game of Fig. 1a. In the prenegotiation phase of coalition formation (prior to negotiations), the model assumes that each player will prefer and attempt to form the coalition that maximizes initial expectation, given by Eq. (5):

$$E_{iS}^0 = v(S)/s, \tag{5}$$

in which E_{iS}^0 denotes the initial expectation of individual i in coalition S; $v(S)$ denotes the value of coalition S; and s denotes the number of players in S. For player A, expectations in AB, AC, and AD are 50 (100/2), and player A will be indifferent between these coalitions. For players B, C, and D, however, expectations in coalitions with A are 50, but only 33 (100/3) in the BCD coalition.

Hence, they are expected to prefer the two-person coalition and are expected to send offers to player A.

According to the equal excess model, expectations are predicted to change over successive rounds of bargaining, and like the bargaining theory, it is a dynamic model. If a coalition forms after a given round, it is assumed that the coalition that jointly maximizes the expectations of the members is most likely to form. The most likely reward division on round r is specified by the equal excess norm, given by Eq. (6):

$$E_{iS}^r = \max E_{iT}^{r-1} + (1/s)[v(S) - \Sigma \max E_{iT}^{r-1}] \quad (S \neq T) \quad (6)$$

in which $\max E_{iT}^{r-1}$ denotes the maximum expectation of member i in alternative coalitions on round $r - 1$; s denotes the number of persons in coalition S; $v(S)$ denotes the value of coalition S; and the summation is over the members of coalition S.

To derive predictions on round 1, expectations on round 0 (E_{iS}^0) are substituted in Eq. (6). For the AB coalition, the initial expectations in alternative coalitions are 50 and 33.3 for A and B, respectively. Substituting these values in Eq. (6), we have

$$E_{A(AB)}^1 = 50 + (\tfrac{1}{2})[100 - (50 + 33)] = 58.3 \quad (7a)$$

$$E_{B(AB)}^1 = 33 + (\tfrac{1}{2})[100 - (50 + 33)] = 41.7 \quad (7b)$$

The expectations on round 1 in the AC and AD coalitions are the same as in AB, and the expectations in BCD are 33–33–33 (because B, C, and D's expectations in alternative coalitions are the same). Since expectations in the two-person coalitions (58.3–41.7) are greater than expectations in BCD, if a coalition forms on round 1, the model predicts that AB, AC, or AD will be most likely.

Equation (6) specifies that each member should receive his/her best alternative ($\max E_{iT}$) and the excess, $v(S) - \Sigma \max E_{iT}$, should be divided equally among the coalition members. This norm of "equal shares of the excess" is a special case of the Nash (1950, 1953) solution to the general bargaining problem, and is consistent with the predictions of Aumann and Maschler's (1964) bargaining set, a normative theory of N-person cooperative games.

For subsequent rounds of bargaining, expectations on the previous round ($r - 1$) are substituted in Eq. (6). Table I shows the predictions of the model for successive iterations of Eq. (6). Expectations in the non-minimal-winning coalition are not included because they are uniformly less than in the MWCs. It can be seen that the expectations of player A increase over rounds while the expectations of B, C, and D decrease over rounds of bargaining. This means that player A's share in AB, AC, or AD should be smaller if an agreement is reached in the early rounds than in later rounds of bargaining. Also note that expectations are mutually maximized in the two-person coalitions, except at the asymptote. At the asymptote, the model predicts that expectations will converge to an equilibrium

TABLE I

PREDICTIONS OF EQUAL EXCESS MODEL FOR FOUR-PERSON APEX GAME[a]

Coalitions	Expectations over rounds of bargaining						
	0	1	2	...	5	...	Asymptote
AB, AC, AD	50–50	58–42	63–27	...	66–34	...	67–33
BCD	33–33–33	33–33–33	33–33–33	...	33–33–33	...	33–33–33

[a]The four-person apex game is the game depicted in Fig. 1a and defined in Section II,A. Expectations in non-minimal-winning coalitions are not included because they are uniformly less than expectations in MWCs.

solution in which the expectations of all players will be equal to their expectations in alternative coalitions; hence, none of the players will be tempted to defect. The main implication of these predicted values is that the two-person coalitions should be most likely in the early rounds, but their probability should decrease with successive rounds of bargaining.

The motivational basis of these predicted changes in expectations is that player A will be initially indifferent between the AB, AC, and AD coalitions, but B, C, and D will each prefer a coalition with A. Thus, player A will receive many offers, and these offers are expected to increase his/her level of aspiration. Conversely, B, C, and D will receive few offers, thus lowering their level of aspiration. The predicted relation between bargaining duration (rounds) and coalition outcomes is consistent with the results of a computer simulation study conducted by Friend, Laing, and Morrison (1977). When bargaining persistence was low, they found large differences in the frequencies of various coalitions, but when bargaining persistence was high, the frequencies were closer to equal likelihood. Similar effects of bargaining persistence and duration have been reported by Vinacke (1962).

The concept of rounds (r) of bargaining is an important parameter of the model, and in its original formulation, a round of bargaining was defined as "a sequential process in which each bargainer makes an offer or counteroffer, and each person accepts or rejects offers that were received" (Komorita, 1979, p. 370). The main weakness of the model is that it does not specify the exact round on which a coalition (agreement) is likely to occur. However, it is assumed that situational factors affect the round on which an agreement is likely. In particular, three classes of variables are assumed to affect bargaining persistence (duration).

1. *Competitiveness of the players:* If the bargainers are highly motivated to maximize reward, an agreement is predicted to be likely on late rounds of bargaining, e.g., large stakes are assumed to increase bargaining persistence.

2. *Familiarity and experience with coalition games:* Naive bargainers are expected to reach an agreement on early rounds, while sophisticated (experienced) bargainers are expected to reach agreement on late rounds.
3. *Restrictions on communication and information:* Procedures and paradigms that restrict communication and information among the bargainers are predicted to inhibit changes in expectations over rounds of bargaining.

Based on these assumptions about the effects of situational variables, Komorita (1979) hypothesized that the round 1 values would yield the most accurate predictions if the bargainers were naive and had little experience with the structure of coalition games (such as undergraduate students drawn from the subject pool), if small monetary incentives (or points) were involved, and if communication and information among the bargainers were restricted in any way. However, the asymptotic values are recommended if the bargainers were paid volunteers who were playing for relatively large stakes, if they were provided considerable practice and training in the strategies of coalition games, and if communication and information were not restricted, as in face-to-face bargaining. In Section IV we shall examine the results of an experiment that attempted to test these hypotheses.

   b. Games with Resource Weights. Unlike the other four theories, when resource weights are used to manipulate the power of the players, no direct predictions can be derived from the equal excess model. Accordingly, Komorita (1979) suggested that the trial 1 assumptions of the bargaining theory might be adopted as an extension of the model. In games with resource weights, we shall therefore assume that on the first round of bargaining (E_{iS}^1), the bargainers split the difference between the parity and equality norms. For example, in the game $9(8-3-3-3)$, this extension of the model yields predictions on round 1 that are identical to those of the bargaining theory on trial 1. These round 1 estimates are then substituted in Eq. (6), and successive iterations of Eq. (6) yield predictions on subsequent rounds of bargaining. It can be shown that the asymptotic predictions in $9(8-3-3-3)$ are identical to those in the apex game, where resources are not assigned (shown in Table I). Thus, in resource games the equal excess model makes the same predictions as the bargaining theory for naive bargainers (round 1/trial 1), but makes different predictions for sophisticated bargainers (asymptotic predictions).

   In summary, the equal excess model was proposed for games in which resource weights are not assigned, but has been extended to resource weight games. In resource weight games, the model is based on both the normative and strategic functions of resource weights: On round 1 its predictions are based on both functions but at the asymptote its predictions are based entirely on the strategic function. To the extent that the model is valid, this suggests that naive bargainers attend to the normative function of resource weights, while sophisticated bargainers attend to their strategic function. In Section IV we shall present other evidence to support this hypothesis.

B. EVALUATION OF THEORIES IN SIMPLE GAMES

1. Contrasts in 9(8–3–3–3) and in Apex Game

Table II summarizes the predictions of the five theories in 9(8–3–3–3) and the apex game. The entries E^1 and E^∞ for bargaining and equal excess theories denote predictions on trial 1/round 1 and at the asymptote, respectively. The last row of Table II shows the results of the two games, pooled over several experiments. Since the subjects in all of these experiments were naive, we shall use the round 1 and trial 1 estimates of the equal excess and bargaining theories to evaluate their predictions.

With regard to the frequencies of coalition formation, both minimum resource and minimum power theories predict that the BCD coalition should be most frequent. However, the two-person coalitions (AB, AC, and AD) occurred

TABLE II

PREDICTED COALITION AND PAYOFFS IN APEX COALITION[a]

| | Games | | Predicted |
Theories	9(8–3–3–3)	Apex	coalition
Minimum resource	73–27	[b]	Base
Minimum power	75–25	75–25	Base
Weighted probability	67–33	67–33	Apex
Bargaining			
E^1	61–39	55–45	Apex
E^∞	69–31	64–36	Apex
Equal excess			
E^1	64–36	58–42	Apex
E^∞	67–33	67–33	Apex
Observed results[c]	67–33 (.83)	58–42 (.87)	

[a]Apex coalition refers to AB, AC, and AD; base coalition refers to BCD. All theories predict an equal split (33–33–33) in the base coalition.

[b]No predictions can be derived from minimum resource theory when resource weights are not assigned.

[c]Values in parentheses denote proportion of occurrence of the apex coalition. Data are based on pooled results of studies by Chertkoff (1970), Komorita and Tumonis (1980), Kravitz (1981), and Murnighan, Komorita, and Szwajkowski (1977).

in 83 and 87% of the cases (shown in parentheses). Thus, the frequency data do not support the predictions of these two theories. The main reason these theories are inaccurate is that they overestimate the share of the reward for the strong player (A). In 9(8–3–3–3), minimum resource and minimum power theories predict shares of 73 and 75, respectively, whereas the observed mean share was 67.

The other three theories correctly predict that the two-person coalitions should be most frequent. Moreover, the predicted payoff shares of these theories are more accurate than minimum resource and minimum power theories. These data, however, do not seem to provide a sensitive test of the latter three theories. The weighted probability model accurately predicts that the probability of the two-person coalitions should be .83 (6/7), but it is relatively inaccurate in predicting the mean share of the strong player (A) in the apex game (67 vs 58). The round 1 predictions of the equal excess model (E^1) are fairly accurate in both games. The trial 1 predictions of the bargaining theory (E^1) underestimate player A's share in both games, but the observed payoff shares are well within the bounds (E^1 to E^∞) predicted by the bargaining theory. These contrasts suggest an important difference between the three theories. On the one hand, the weighted probability model makes an exact (point) prediction of both coalition frequencies and the payoff splits. Hence, this model is highly vulnerable to rejection. On the other hand, bargaining and equal excess theories both predict a range of outcomes (E^1 to E^∞), and therefore, they are less vulnerable to rejection.

There are other important differences between these theories, and we shall examine such differences, as well as similarities, in Section IV,A. In this context, note that the asymptotic predicted shares of the equal excess model (E^∞) are identical to the predicted shares of the weighted probability model. In simple games (excluding veto games), both theories predict that the payoff shares should be an equilibrium solution in which none of the players will be tempted to defect from the coalition. This is consistent with our hypothesis that the predictions of the weighted probability model and the asymptotic prediction of the equal excess model are based entirely on the strategic function of resource weights. This hypothesis, in turn, suggests that the predictions of the weighted probability model may be restricted to sophisticated bargainers.

2. Contrasts Illustrating the Functions of Resource Weights

a. Theories Based on the Strategic Function.   Table III shows the predictions of the five theories in three games selected to illustrate the functions of resource weights. Consider the predictions of minimum power theory and weighted probability model in games 50(40–30–20) and 50(49–49–1). The fact that they make identical predictions in the two games illustrates that their predic-

S. S. KOMORITA

TABLE III

Predictions of Theories in Three Simple Games[a]

	Simple games		
Theories	50(40–30–20)	50(49–49–1)	50(49–7...7–1)[b]
Minimum resource	30–20 (60–40)	49–1 (98–2)	49–1 (98–2)[c]
Minimum power	Any (50–50)	Any (50–50)	X...X (12.5 each)[d]
Weighted probability	Any (50–50)	Any (50–50)	49–X (87.5–12.5)[d]
Bargaining			
Trial 1	30–20 (55–45)	49–1 (74–26)	49–1 (74–26)
Asymptote	30–20 (50–50)	49–1 (50–50)	49–1 (87.5–12.5)
Equal excess			
Round 1	30–20 (55–45)	49–1 (74–26)	49–1 (74–26)
Asymptote	30–20 (50–50)	49–1 (50–50)	49–1 (87.5–12.5)

[a]Values in parentheses denote payoff predictions.
[b]Denotes nine-person game, where (7...7) denotes that there are seven players each with seven resource units.
[c]Minimum resource predicts that either the 49–1 coalition or the 7...7–1 coalition are likely to form.
[d]X denotes one of the weaker players (7 or 1).

tions are based exclusively on the strategic function of resource weights. In both of these games the MWCs are the same (AB, AC, and BC), and the predictions of both of these theories are invariant over games in which the pattern of MWCs are the same. Thus, they ignore the magnitude of resource weights and ignore the normative function of resource weights. There are no data for game 50(49–49–1), but there is considerable evidence to refute their predictions in 50(40–30–20). This game is equivalent to the game 5(4–3–2), discussed earlier. The BC coalition occurs more frequently than AB or AC in this game, and player B achieves a larger share of the reward than player C. We shall examine the predictions of the five theories in this game in greater detail in Section III,B,3.

    b.   Theory Based on the Normative Function.   Consider the predictions of minimum resource theory in game 50(49–49–1) and in the nine-person game 50(49–7 . . . 7–1), where 7 . . . 7 denotes that there are 7 players each with 7 resource units. The MWCs are markedly different in the two games. In 50(49–49–1) the three players are strategically equivalent because they are included in the same number of MWCs. In 50(49–7 . . . 7–1), in contrast, player A has a tremendous advantage because he/she is included in eight MWCs, while the others are included in only two, 49–X and (7 . . . 7–1). Yet, minimum resource theory predicts that the reward division in the 49–1 coalition should be the same (98–2) in the two games. Thus, minimum resource theory ignores the players' strategic positions in the game (pattern of MWCs), and its predictions are based entirely on the normative function (parity norm).

A striking example of this hypothesis is its predictions in 50(49–49–1). Minimum resource theory predicts that the AC and BC coalitions are most likely for a reward division of 98–2. But why should player C accept a share of 2 units in AC or BC? Player C is *strategically* equal to A and B (A and B need C as much as C needs A or B), and this is the reason minimum power and weighted probability theories predict a 50–50 division in AB, AC, and BC.

    c. Theories Based on Both Functions. Finally, to illustrate the fact that bargaining theory and equal excess model are based on both functions of resource weights, consider their predictions in 50(49–49–1) and in 50(49–7 . . . 7–1). On trial 1, the bargaining theory makes the same predictions in the two games, and predicts a split the difference between parity and equality. Similarly, the round 1 predictions of the equal excess model are also the same in the two games because it incorporates the trial 1 assumptions of the bargaining theory in resource weight games.

    At the asymptote, the predictions of both theories are markedly different from their trial/round 1 predictions in the two games: 49–1 (50–50) in the three-person game and 49–1 (87.5–12.5) in the nine-person game. Thus, unlike minimum resource theory, which makes identical payoff predictions in the two games, the payoff predictions of the bargaining and equal excess theories are markedly different in the two games. Their asymptotic predictions are based on the strategic function and coincide with the payoff predictions of the weighted probability model. Unlike the weighted probability model, however, these two theories are also based on the normative function because they predict that certain coalitions are more likely than others, e.g., in 50(40–30–20), they predict that 30–20 is more likely than the others, whereas the weighted probability model predicts that the three coalitions are equally likely.

3. Contrasts in 5(4–3–2)

    Support for minimum resource theory is based primarily on three-person games. Several types of resource distributions have been used in three-person games, but most experiments have been based on the game 5(4–3–2), where A > B > C, and (B + C) > A. In the vast majority of experiments using this game, the BC coalition has been found to occur most frequently, thus supporting the predictions of minimum resource, bargaining, and equal excess theories (cf. reviews by Chertkoff, 1970; Stryker, 1972; Murnighan, 1978). The payoff shares for players B and C are generally between parity (60–40) and equality

(50–50), and Table III shows that the payoff predictions of bargaining and equal excess theories are more accurate than those of minimum resource theory. These results, of course, are clearly inconsistent with the predictions of minimum power theory and the weighted probability model.

Since player A, the "strong" player, is typically excluded in 5(4–3–2), Gamson (1964) proposed the principle that "strength is weakness." However, this paradoxical principle seems to operate only in games in which the strategic function of resource weights is irrelevant, i.e., when the players are all equal in power. In 5(4–3–2), for example, the three players are included in the same number of winning coalitions. Since they are equal in power, the normative function of resource weights is likely to be much more salient than the strategic function, at least for naive, inexperienced subjects. In the game 9(8–3–3–3), in contrast, the strong player (8) has strategic power because he/she is included in three MWCs, while the weaker players are included in only two. As we have seen, the strong player is included in the winning coalition in the vast majority of cases (see Table II), and strength is certainly not weakness in this game.

Kelley and Arrowood (1960), moreover, hypothesized that the BC coalition occurs more frequently in 5(4–3–2) because the strong player (A) may not have learned that power, based on resource weights, is really illusory. Hence, to test this hypothesis, they replicated this game for a large number of trials. As hypothesized, they found that the BC coalition was most frequent in the early trials, but the frequencies of the three coalitions did not differ significantly on later trials. Similar results have been obtained in a study by Chertkoff and Braden (1974).

These results suggest that "strength is weakness" because the strong player in 5(4–3–2) makes demands based on the parity norm, and such tough demands induce the weaker players to coalesce. Exclusion from the winning coalition presumably leads to concessions by the strong player, and on later trials the strong player is able to tempt one of the others to defect from the BC coalition. The main implication of these observations is that strength is weakness only in games in which all players are equal in strategic power, and only when the players are naive and unfamiliar with the structure of coalition games (Komorita & Moore, 1976; Murnighan, 1978).

More importantly, these observations suggest that the normative function of resource weights may be more salient for naive, inexperienced bargainers, while the strategic function may be more salient for sophisticated, experienced bargainers. This hypothesis is consistent with the changes in expectations predicted by the bargaining and equal excess theories from trial/round 1 to the asymptotic level. Thus, Komorita and Kravitz (1983) have hypothesized that the predictions of minimum resource theory may be limited to naive bargainers, while the predictions of minimum power theory and the weighted probability model may be restricted to sophisticated bargainers.

TABLE IV

PREDICTIONS OF THEORIES IN VETO GAME, 6(4–3–1–1)[a]

	Minimum resource	Minimum power	Weighted probability	Bargaining theory[b]	Observed values[c]
Coalition	ACD	ACD	AB	AB	AB (.69)
Division	67–17–17	78–11–11	60–40	54–46	72–28

[a]Predictions of equal excess model are not shown because its predictions are identical to those of bargaining theory, both on trial/round 1 and at the asymptote.

[b]In the study by Michener et al. all groups played each game once. Hence, the trial 1 predictions of bargaining theory are shown. At the asymptote both bargaining theory and equal excess model predict AB (100–0).

[c]Value in parenthesis denotes proportion of occurrence of AB coalition. The ACD coalition occurred in 19% of cases and non-MWCs occurred in 12% of cases. Data from Michener et al. (1976).

4. Contrasts in Veto Games

The contrasts that we have presented thus far suggest that the predictions of minimum power theory are clearly inadequate; minimum resource theory and the weighted probability model are accurate in some games but inaccurate in others; and bargaining and equal excess theories seem to be the most accurate. We shall now contrast these theories in a class of games called veto games, which present problems for all five theories.

A *veto game* is a simple game in which one of the players, the veto player, is included in all winning coalitions. Consider the four-person veto game, 6(4–3–1–1), used in a study by Michener, Fleishman, and Vaske (1976). Player A is the veto player, and the MWCs are AB and ACD. Michener et al. used eight veto games and eight nonveto games and contrasted the predictions of minimum resource, minimum power, and bargaining theory.[5] Their results showed that the predictions of bargaining theory were clearly more accurate in nonveto games. In veto games, however, bargaining theory was more accurate in predicting coalition frequencies (AB vs ACD), but was less accurate than minimum power theory in predicting the mean payoff share of the veto player.

For illustrative purposes, we shall contrast the five theories in only one of the 16 games used by Michener et al. Table IV shows the predictions of the five theories in 6(4–3–1–1). The AB coalition occurred in 69% of the cases, ACD occurred in 19%, and non-MWCs (e.g., ABCD) occurred in 12% of the cases. The frequencies of coalitions thus support the predictions of weighted proba-

[5]Strictly speaking, minimum resource theory should not be included in these contrasts because Gamson (1961a) explicitly specifies that minimum resource theory is not applicable in veto games.

bility, bargaining, and equal excess theories. Since all groups played each of the 16 games once, Michener *et al.* used the trial 1 predictions of the bargaining theory. For the same reason, the round 1 predictions of the equal excess model are shown in Table IV. At the asymptote, both of these theories predict AB (100–0) and ACD (100–0–0).

The mean payoffs were AB (72–28) and ACD (84–8–8), and thus, weighted probability, bargaining, and equal excess theories grossly underestimate the veto player's share. Although minimum power theory predicts that ACD should be more frequent than AB, its payoff prediction in AB is 70–30 and is more accurate than the predictions of the other theories. All of the other theories underestimate the veto player's share, and this discrepancy also occurred in the other veto games used by Michener *et al.* Thus, none of the five theories can fully account for these data on veto games.

Another problem for all five theories is to explain the results of veto games reported by Murnighan and Roth (1980). In their study, resource weights were not used, and subjects were informed that one of the players had a ''left shoe'' while all of the others had a ''right shoe.'' Their task was to find a matching pair of shoes (left plus right), and to reach agreement on the division of the reward for the appropriate match. Hence, the MWCs in this game are AX_i, where A denotes the veto player (monopolist), and X_i denotes one of the $N - 1$ nonveto players.

Three variables were manipulated in their study: (1) group size (three to seven), (2) communication (allowing vs not allowing messages to be sent among all players), and (3) trials of veto games (1–10). Murnighan and Roth found significant effects for all three variables. The mean share of the veto player increased with group size and over trials of the game, and was greater when no communication was permitted among the players.

The significant main effects of these variables provide some provocative contrasts among the theories. Minimum resource theory, of course, is not included because it does not yield predictions when resource weights are not assigned. First, the significant effect of communication is implied by the weighted probability model. It assumes that restrictions on communication channels make it difficult for the weak (nonveto) players to coordinate their efforts, e.g., reach an implicit agreement not to outbid each other. The other three theories cannot account for the effect of communication availability on the veto player's share of the payoff.

Second, the increase in the veto player's payoff over trials is predicted by bargaining and equal excess theories. Both theories predict that the expectations of the veto player should increase over trials/rounds. The other two theories are static theories and do not predict changes in expectations over trials.

Finally, the effects of group size are predicted by minimum power theory and weighted probability model, but are inconsistent with the predictions of bargaining and equal excess theories. Table V shows the predictions of the four

TABLE V

PREDICTED SHARE OF VETO PLAYER AS A FUNCTION OF GROUP SIZE[a]

	Group size				
	3	4	5	6	7
Minimum power	80.0	90.0	94.1	96.1	97.3
Weighted probability	66.7	75.0	80.0	83.3	85.7
Bargaining					
Trial 1	75.0	75.0	75.0	75.0	75.0
Asymptote	100	100	100	100	100
Observed[b]	62.8	78.8	77.5	78.7	87.1

[a]Predictions of equal excess model are not shown because its predictions are identical to those of bargaining theory, both on trial/round 1 and at the asymptote. Minimum resource theory does not yield predictions when resource weights are not assigned.
[b]Data from Murnighan and Roth (1980).

theories as a function of group size, and the mean shares of the veto player reported by Murnighan and Roth (1980). It can be seen that bargaining and equal excess theories make identical predictions that are constant across group size, while the shares predicted by the minimum power and weighted probability theories increase with group size. Of the latter two theories, minimum power theory overestimates the veto player's share, while the weighted probability model provides a fairly accurate estimate of the observed values.[6]

In summary, none of the theories can account for all of the data on veto games. In resource weight games, as in 6(4–3–1–1) used by Michener *et al.*, minimum power theory provided a reasonable estimate of the payoff data, but it failed to predict the most likely coalition. The other four theories underestimated the veto player's share of the reward. This underestimation of the veto player's share was also found in a study by Murnighan and Szwajkowski (1979) in several veto games with resource weights. This underestimation in resource weight veto games suggests an interaction between the salience of the two functions of resource weights and the distribution of MWCs in the game. When all players are included in the same number of MWCs (equal in strategic power), as in 5(4–3–2), the players may attend to differences in resource weights, and the normative function may dominate the strategic function. In contrast, when there is an

[6]For the games used by Murnighan and Roth (1980), the predictions of weighted probability model are identical to those predicted by the Shapley–Roth *value* (Roth, 1977a,b; Shapley, 1953). For their data, Murnighan and Roth concluded that the predictions of weighted probability and Shapley–Roth value were most accurate.

extreme imbalance of strategic power, as in a veto game, the players may attend to inclusion in MWCs, and the strategic function may dominate the normative function.

In nonresource veto games, as in the games used by Murnighan and Roth (1980), the weighted probability model seems to be most accurate, but it is only adequate at best. Although the model can account for the effects of communication and of group size, it fails to explain the increase in the veto player's payoff share over trials. The other theories, in their present form, are clearly inadequate in veto games.

5. Summary Evaluation of Theories in Simple Games

Of the five theories described and evaluated in simple games, two of the theories, minimum resource and minimum power theories, seem to be less adequate than the other three. One of the main weaknesses of minimum resource theory is that it is based entirely on the normative function of resource weights, and consequently, when resources are not assigned, no predictions can be derived. This is a serious weakness because it severely restricts the generality of the theory. Moreover, when resources are assigned, its validity seems to be limited to three-person games with naive subjects. In larger groups, as in game 9(8–3–3–3), its predictions are extremely inaccurate.

Minimum power theory is based entirely on the strategic function of resource weights and predictions can be derived for both games with and without resource assignment. Its main weakness is that it is inaccurate in all types of games. It generally overestimates the payoff share of the "strong" player in a game, and thus predicts that the weaker players will coalesce against the strong player. For example, the results of game 9(8–3–3–3) do not support this prediction. This does not imply that the concept of pivotal power is invalid, but suggests that Gamson's (1964) hypothesis that rewards will be divided in direct proportion to pivotal power may be invalid. It is plausbile that some other transformation of pivotal power to reward division may yield more accurate predictions. It is also plausible that indexes of pivotal power based only on MWC sequences may yield more accurate predictions.[7]

[7]In 9(8–3–3–3), pivotal power is based on all possible sequences of forming winning coalitions. But since non-MWCs rarely form, the following six non-MWC sequences might be deleted in assessing pivotal power: BCAD, BDAC, CBAD, DBAC, and DCAB. If pivotal power is assessed on the remaining 18 MWC sequences, the pivotal power indexes are 6/18 for player A and 4/18 for each of the others. Director proportionality with respect to these indexes yields payoff predictions of 60–40 for the two-person coalitions and 33 each in BCD. Since the three weaker players prefer a coalition with player A, the two-person coalitions are predicted to be most likely and this modified minimum power theory yields more accurate predictions.

Of the remaining three theories, all three yield predictions with and without resource weights, and make remarkably similar predictions. Thus, it will be difficult to differentiate their predictive accuracy in simple games. One reason for the similarity in their predictions is that all three theories assume that a player's bargaining strength is based on the alternative coalitions that are available to the player. These alternative coalitions are assumed to be used as threats against the other members of a potential coalition. In this sense, all three theories are based on Thibaut and Kelley's (1959) concept of CLalt. The weighted probability model assumes that a player's bargaining strength is a function of the number and size of alternative coalitions: the larger the number and the smaller the size, the greater the bargaining strength. Bargaining and equal excess theories, in contrast, assume that the quality (magnitude) of a player's alternative coalitions is the most important factor, and ignore the number of alternatives. It does not matter how many alternatives are available to the player, as long as the player has one good alternative.

There are several other important differences between these theories. First, in resource games the weighted probability model is based entirely on the strategic function, while bargaining and equal excess theories are based on both functions of resource weights. Second, the weighted probability model is a static theory and makes precise predictions; the other two, in contrast, are dynamic theories and are less precise (predict a range of outcomes). Hence, the weighted probability model is highly vulnerable to rejection while the other two are less vulnerable.

The main advantage of bargaining and equal excess theories, compared to the weighted probability model, is that they are more general and applicable in a wider range of situations. However, this advantage is gained, at least in part, at the expense of predictive precision. In the veto game, 6(4−3−1−1), for example, the trial/round 1 predictions of the two theories grossly underestimate the veto player's share of the reward (see Table IV), but the observed mean is within the range predicted by the two theories (100−0 at the asymptote).

In the AB coalition in this game, the equal excess model predicts 54−46, 75−25, 84−16, and 100−0 on rounds 1, 2, 3, and at the asymptote, respectively. Table IV shows that the round 2 prediction yields the most accurate estimate of the observed data (72−28). However, Komorita (1979) hypothesized that the round 1 prediction would be most accurate, and there is considerable evidence to support this hypothesis, at least in nonveto games. It is plausible, therefore, that the most accurate estimate of payoffs may depend on many situational factors, including the type of game (veto vs nonveto). The concept of rounds of bargaining was originally conceptualized as a parameter of the equal excess model, but no precise (operational) way of deriving predictions was proposed, other than the use of the round 1 estimate. To eliminate this ambiguity of the equal excess model, we shall present a one-parameter extension of this model in Section IV,C.

Since the bargaining theory also predicts a range of outcomes, it suffers from the same problem as the equal excess model. However, the problem for the bargaining theory is more serious because it only provides two estimates of payoffs: on trial 1 and at the asymptote. In veto games this range is so large that it is almost useless as a predictive model. For this and other reasons, it is plausible that the bargaining theory is not applicable in veto games.

IV.   Coalition Formation in Multivalued Games

The vast majority of experiments in coalition formation have been restricted to simple games. This is unfortunate because multivalued games are applicable in a wider range of real-life situations than simple games. In a simple game the value (reward) for all winning coalitions is constant, whereas in multivalued games the values of various possible coalitions may differ, depending on the size and composition of the coalition. Because of their greater generality and applicability, coalition experiments using multivalued games have become increasingly common. Yet, it is only in recent years that attempts have been made to develop theories that predict both coalition likelihood and the reward division in multivalued games.[8]

A.   COALITION THEORIES IN MULTIVALUED GAMES

In multivalued games, resources are rarely assigned and the power of a player is based on the values of the coalitions that include the player. Accordingly, we shall restrict our review to cases where resources are not assigned. This restriction, of course, automatically excludes minimum resource theory because predictions cannot be derived when resources are not assigned. Of the remaining four theories, the equal excess model was specifically formulated for multivalued games. The other three, however, were proposed for simple games and additional assumptions are required to yield predictions in multivalued games. Komorita and Tumonis (1980) proposed and tested extensions of bargaining theory and weighted probability in multivalued games. The proposed extension of the bargaining theory was quite successful, but the extension of the weighted

[8]There are several normative theories that can be used to predict reward division in multivalued games, but none of them yields predictions of coalition likelihood. Hence, we shall not include these theories in this article.

probability model was less than successful. Although other tests of the weighted probability model will be necessary before a final evaluation can be made, to simplify the presentation we shall not include the extension of this model in this article.

The fifth and final theory, minimum power theory, is based on the concept of pivotal power (Shapley & Shubik, 1954). Pivotal power, in turn, is based on the Shapley value (Shapley, 1953), and the logical extension of minimum power theory to the case of multivalued games is the Shapley value. However, the Shapley value only predicts the average (expected) payoffs for the N-players and does not yield predictions of coalition likelihood. Hence, we shall propose an extension of the Shapley value, called the Shapley-w, that yields predictions of coalition likelihood in multivalued games.

In accordance with these selection criteria, we shall illustrate the predictions of the equal excess model, the Shapley-w, and the extension of the bargaining theory in three types of three-person multivalued games. The three types of games are defined in Table VI, and hereafter will be denoted Games I, II, and III. Games I and II are quota games, nonsuperadditive and superadditive, respectively. Game I is nonsuperadditive because the value of the grand coalition (ABC) is zero (see Footnote 3 on superadditive games). Note that Game II is the same as the game shown in Fig. 1b, except that $v(ABC)$ is 150 rather than 120. In both games the quota values of players A, B, and C are 60, 40, and 20, respectively (see Footnote 1 on quota games).

Game III is sometimes called a "pure bargaining game" (Rapoport, 1970) because the grand coalition is expected to form, and the main purpose of using the game is to predict the shares negotiated by the three players. For theoretical purposes, the one-person values are treated as payoffs for the one-person coali-

TABLE VI

THREE TYPES OF THREE-PERSON MULTIVALUED GAMES[a]

Game type	Values of coalitions						
	$v(A)$	$v(B)$	$v(C)$	$v(AB)$	$v(AC)$	$v(BC)$	$v(ABC)$
I	0	0	0	100	80	60	0
II	0	0	0	100	80	60	150
III[b]	60	40	20	0	0	0	150

[a]Games I and II are variants of a quota game, a game in which there are weights (q_i) such that $v(ij) = q_i + q_j$, for all pairs of players i and j. The quota values of players A, B, and C are 60, 40, and 20, respectively.

[b]Game III is sometimes called a "pure bargaining game." For theoretical purposes, values for players A, B, and C are treated as values of one-person coalitions; also, values of $v(ij)$ are treated as $v(i) + v(j)$, instead of zero, as shown in the table.

TABLE VII

PAYOFF PREDICTIONS OF EQUAL EXCESS MODEL IN GAME I[a]

	Expectations over rounds of bargaining[b]					
Coalition	0	1	2	3	. . .	6
AB	50–50	55–45	57.5–42.5	59–41	. . .	60–40
AC	40–40	50–30	55–25	57.5–22.5	. . .	60–20
BC	30–30	35–25	37.5–22.5	39–21	. . .	40–20

[a]A, B, and C denote the three players: $v(AB) = 100$, $v(AC) = 80$, $v(BC) = 60$, and $v(ABC) = 0$.

[b]First and second numbers denote expected shares of the first and second members of each coalition, e.g., on round 1 in the AB coalition, the expectations of players A and B are 55 and 45, respectively. Predicted payoffs are invariant after round 6 and converge to the asymptotic values of 60, 40, and 20 for players A, B, and C, respectively.

tions. Hence, unanimous agreement is required to form the grand coalition, and if one player is dissatisfied with his/her share and refuses to join ABC, all must take his/her one-person value. Note that the one-person values are the quota values in Games I and II.

1. The Equal Excess Model in Multivalued Games

a. Predictions in Game I. The predictions of the equal excess model in Game I are straightforward. It was designed for this situation. The initial expectations of the players, based on Eq. (5), are AB (50–50), AC (40–40), and BC (30–30). Substituting these values of E_{iS}^0 in Eq. (6), the round 1 predictions (E_{iS}^1) are as follows: AB (55–45), AC (50–30), and BC (35–25). Since the AB coalition maximizes the expectations of players A and B, the model predicts that if a coalition forms on round 1, the AB coalition is most likely for a 55–45 reward division. Successive iterations of Eq. (6) (substituting expectations on previous rounds) yield predicted values on subsequent rounds of bargaining. Table VII shows the predictions of the model on various rounds of bargaining. Note that at the asymptote (E_{iS}^∞), the expectations of the three players converge to an equilibrium state (the quota values) in which none of the players will be tempted to defect from any coalition.[9] The main implication of such predicted changes in expectations is that the AB coalition is predicted to be most likely if an agreement occurs (coalition forms) in the early rounds, but its likelihood should decrease with successive rounds of bargaining.

[9]The asymptotic (quota) values can be computed easily by solving three simultaneous linear equations ($A + B = 100$; $A + C = 80$; and $B + C = 60$).

As in the case of simple games, it is assumed that situational factors will affect the round on which an agreement is most likely. In particular, if subjects are naive bargainers (e.g., undergraduate students) and are bargaining for small incentives, the round 1 values are hypothesized to be most accurate. However, if subjects are experienced bargainers and are bargaining for relatively large stakes, the asymptotic values are hypothesized to provide the most accurate estimate.

b. Predictions in Game II. In Game II the expectations in the two-person coalitions are the same as in Game I, shown in Table VII. Initial expectations in the grand coalition are 50–50–50 [based on Eq. (5)]. Players A and B will be indifferent between the AB and ABC coalitions, but player C will prefer the grand coalition. In its original form (Komorita, 1979), it was assumed that each player would use initial expectations (E_{iS}^0) in the two-person coalitions to justify their demands on round 1 in ABC. However, bargaining in the grand coalition is a unique situation in which no player can threaten to defect to an alternative coalition that does not include one of the players who is being threatened. For example, player A cannot threaten B and C with the AB or AC coalitions because these alternative coalitions include B and C. It is plausible, however, that two players will threaten the third (e.g., A and B might threaten C with the AB coalition). For these reasons, a slight revision of the original model will be proposed here, and it will be assumed that the round 1 expectations in the two-person coalitions (E_{iS}^1) will be used to justify each player's demands in the grand coalition.

Based on this revision of the model, if we substitute the round 1 expectations in the two-person coalitions in Eq. (6), the round 1 expectations in the grand coalition are 62–52–37, and the asymptotic expectations are 70–50–30. Since these expectations (on all rounds) are greater than the expectations in the two-person coalitions (see Table VII), the model predicts that the grand coalition is most likely to form.

c. Predictions in Game III. The equal excess model predicts that the players will receive their respective alternatives, the one-person values, and the excess, $v(ABC) - \Sigma v(i)$, will be divided equally among the three players. Substituting $v(i)$ for $\max E_{iT}^{r+1}$ in Eq. (6), the predicted reward division in the grand coalition is 70–50–30. If we substitute these round 1 values in Eq. (6), the predicted values are invariant because the excess, $v(ABC) - \Sigma E_{i(ABC)}^1$, is zero. Thus, in Game III the model predicts no change in expectations over rounds of bargaining $(E^1 = E^\infty)$.

2. The Bargaining Theory in Multivalued Games

a. Predictions in Game I. The bargaining theory was originally proposed for simple games. For multivalued games, Komorita and Tumonis (1980) proposed an extension of the theory in which a proportionality norm is substituted for the parity norm. As in the original theory, each player is predicted to demand a share of the reward based on the equality or proportionality norm, whichever yields the larger share. In Game I, the equality norm prescribes AB(50–50), AC(40–40), and BC(30–30). Since the AB coalition maximizes the expectations of players A and B, they are expected to reciprocate offers to each other. Player B is predicted to demand an equal share in AB, while player A is predicted to demand a share that is proportional to their expectations in alternative coalitions: 40 for A in AC and 30 for B in BC. Proportionality with respect to these alternative expectations yields a 57–43 division. On trial 1, the splitting the difference between the demands of the two players (equality and proportionality) yields predicted shares of 53.5–46.5. Similarly, the trial 1 predicted shares are 45–35 in AC and 32–28 in BC. Since the AB coalition maximizes the expectations of players A and B, this coalition is predicted to be most likely for a 53.5–46.5 split.

At the asymptote, payoff shares are predicted to converge to a solution that is proportional to each member's maximum expectation in alternative coalitions, denoted Emax. Player A's Emax in AB is 50, based on proportionality in AC, while player B's Emax in AB is 33.3, based on proportionality in BC. Proportionality with respect to these Emax values yields an asymptotic solution of 60–40 in AB. It can be shown that temptation to defect is minimal in AB and maximal in BC. Hence, at the asymptote the AB coalition is predicted to be most likely for a 60–40 split.

　　b.　Predictions in Game II. In superadditive games, such as Game II, some additional assumptions are necessary to derive predictions from the bargaining theory. There are several possible extensions (variants) of the theory, but we shall describe only one of them. It will be assumed that expectations in the two-person coalitions will be used to justify demands in the grand coalition, and in particular, each player will demand his/her respective Emax values in the two-person coalitions. The Emax values of players A, B, and C are 57 (proportionality in AB), 50 (equality in AB), and 40 (equality in AC), respectively. Proportionality with respect to these Emax values yields values of 58–51–41, and a split-the-difference between proportionality and equality yields trial 1 predicted values of 54–50.5–45.5. Since these values are greater than those in the two-person coalitions, the grand coalition is predicted to be most likely on trial 1. At the asymptote, it will be assumed that payoffs will converge to a solution that is proportional to the players' respective Emax values: 58–51–41. It can be shown that temptation to defect is minimal in the grand coalition; hence, ABC is predicted to be most likely at the asymptote.

　　c.　Predictions in Game III. As in Game II, there are several possible extensions of the bargaining theory, but we shall assume the extension of the theory described earlier. For the coalition values in Game III, it will be assumed that $v(i)$, the one-person values, will be used to justify demands in the grand coalition. Proportionality with respect to these values yields shares of 75–50–25. On trial 1, the split the difference between equality and proportionality yields a solution of 62.5–50–37.5. At the asymptote, it will be assumed that payoffs will converge to expectations based on proportionality, a 75–50–25 split. Since these shares are greater than each person's alternative (one-person value), the grand coalition is predicted to be most likely, both on trial 1 and at the asymptote.

3. The Shapley-w Model

The Shapley value (1953) is a normative theory and is restricted to superadditive games (Games II and III). Moreover, like other normative theories, it does not yield predictions of coalition likelihood. Many variants (extensions) of the Shapley value have been proposed. These include pivotal power (Shapley & Shubik, 1954), minimum power (Gamson, 1964), and Roth's (1977a,b) extension of the Shapley value for risk-averse and risk-neutral players. We shall propose still another variant of the Shapley value, denoted Shapley-w, and we shall show that this extension is a special case of Adams' (1963) equity theory and Homans' (1961) concept of distributive justice.

The Shapley value assumes that the power of player i is a function of what player i contributes to a coalition when player i is added (the increment in the value of the coalition). Based on this idea, we shall propose that the contribution or "worth" of player i to coalition S is equal to the difference between the value of coalition S, including player i, and the value of the coalition if player i defects from coalition S (excluding player i).

The "worth" of player i to coalition S, denoted w_{iS}, is given by Eq. (8):

$$w_{iS} = v(S) - v(S - \text{``i''}),\tag{8}$$

in which $v(S - \text{``i''})$ denotes the value of coalition S when player i is deleted. The Shapley value of player i is the average (unweighted mean) of such increments over all possible subsets of the players. As an extension of the Shapley value, we shall assume that the members of coalition S will agree to a division that is proportional to their respective w_{iS} values. To simplify the presentation, we shall first illustrate the predictions of the Shapley-w model in Game III, and then illustrate its predictions in the other two games (I and II).

   a. Predictions in Game III.   In Game III the choice of each player is between their respective single-person value, $v(i)$, and their expected share in the grand coalition (G). In accordance with Roth's (1977b) analyses of the Shapley value, we shall assume that $v(ij) = v(i) + v(j)$. This means that $v(S - \text{``i''})$ in Eq. (8) represents the sum of the values of the remaining players in G. For example, the "worth" of player A in the grand coalition is equal to $v(G) - [v(B) + v(C)]$. Thus, the w_i values in Game III are given in Eqs. 9a,b,c.

$$w_A = v(G) - [v(B) + v(C)] = 150 - (40 + 20) = 90\tag{9a}$$

$$w_B = v(G) - [v(A) + v(C)] = 150 - (60 + 20) = 70 \qquad (9b)$$

$$w_C = v(G) - [v(A) + v(B)] = 150 - (60 + 40) = 50 \qquad (9c)$$

Suppose each player demands w_i, what each contributes to G (what each thinks he/she is "worth"). Since the sum of the w_i values exceeds the value of the grand coalition by 60 points ($210 - 150$), one or more players must concede from w_i. If we assume that the players *concede equally* (20 points each) from their respective w_i values, the predicted values are identical to the asymptotic solution of the equal excess model (70–50–30).

In contrast, the Shapley-w assumes that the players *concede proportionally* from the w_i values, and it can be shown that this assumption corresponds to the following model view given in Eq. (10)

$$\theta(w_i) = (w_i/\Sigma w_j)v(S) \qquad (10)$$

in which $\theta(w_i)$ denotes Shapley-w for player i, w_i denotes the "worth" of player i, $v(S)$ denotes the value of the grand coalition, and the summation is over all players ($j = 1, 2, 3, \ldots, n$). Based on Eq. (10), the predicted shares in Game III are 64–50–36.

The intriguing feature of the Shapley-w model is that the w_i values can be interpreted as "inputs" in Adams' (1963) equity theory and Homans' (1961) "distributive justice" formulation. Both theories assume that an individual's "output" (share of the reward) should be directly proportional to his/her respective input (contribution or worth). Equation 10 shows that Shapley-w is simply a special case of these theories in a coalition bargaining situation.

   b. Predictions in Game I.   When the value of the grand coalition is zero, as in Game I, we shall assume that

$$w_{iS} = v(S) - [\Sigma v(T)/t] \qquad (11)$$

where T denotes the alternative coalitions of the other members of coalition S that do not include player i; $v(T)$ and t denote the value and number of persons in coalition T, respectively; and the summation is over the remaining members of coalition S.

   In the three-person nonsuperadditive case, as in Game I, each coalition consists of two persons and each member in S has only one alternative coalition. Hence, Eq. (11) can be reduced to the following form

$$w_{iS} = v(ij) - [v(jk)/2] \qquad (12)$$

in which i and j denote the two players in coalition ij, and $v(jk)$ denotes the value of the alternative coalition of player j. In the AB coalition, for example, we have

$$w_A = v(AB) - [v(BC)/2] = 100 - 30 = 70 \qquad (13a)$$

$$w_B = v(AB) - [v(AC)/2] = 100 - 40 = 60 \qquad (13b)$$

Substituting these values of w_i in Eq. (10) (proportional shares), the predicted shares in the AB coalition are (54–46) for A and B, respectively.

Similarly, the w values are 50 and 30, respectively, for players A and C in the AC coalition, and 40 and 20, respectively, for players B and C in the BC coalition. Substituting these values in Eq. (10) yields predicted shares of (50–30) for A and C in AC, and (40–20) for B and C in BC, respectively. Since the AB coalition mutually maximizes the expectations of players A and B, the Shapley-w model predicts that the AB coalition is most likely to form for shares of (54–46) for A and B, respectively.

c. Predictions in Game II. In Game II the choice of each player is based on expectations in the two-person and three-person coalitions. Note that the alternative coalitions specified in Eq. (11) cannot include player i. Hence, such alternative coalitions cannot be based on the grand coalition because it includes player i. This means that expectations in the two-person coalitions in Game II are the same as in Game I: AB(54–46), AC(50–30), and BC(40–20).

In the grand coalition, $w_A = v(G) - v(BC) = 90$, $w_B = v(G) - v(AC) = 70$, and $w_C = v(G) - v(AB) = 50$. These values are identical to the w values for Game III. Thus, the predicted shares in G are the same as in Game III: (64–50–36) for A, B, and C, respectively. Since expectations in G are greater than in the two-person coalitions for all three players, this coalition is predicted to be most likely to occur.

4. Summary of Predictions

Table VIII summarizes the predictions of the three theories in the three types of games. All three theories predict that the AB coalition is most likely to form in Game I, and that the grand coalition is most likely to form in Games II and III. Moreover, the payoff predictions of the three theories are also remarkably similar. The main difference is that Shapley-w yields a single-point prediction, while bargaining and equal excess theories predict a range of payoffs (E^1 to E^∞), depending on whether subjects are naive or experienced bargainers. This difference suggests that the validity of these theories might be differentiated by contrasting their predictions for naive and experienced subjects.

B. EVALUATION OF THEORIES IN MULTIVALUED GAMES

1. Evaluation of Theories in Game-Type I

To evaluate the predictions of the three theories in game-type I, we shall use data from a study by Komorita and Kravitz (1981) in which subjects were given

TABLE VIII

Summary of Payoff Predictions in Games I, II, and III[a]

Theories[b]	Game I	Game II	Game III
Equal excess			
E^1	55–45	62–52–37	70–50–30
E^∞	60–40	70–50–30	70–50–30
Bargaining			
E^1	54–46	54–51–45	63–50–37
E^∞	60–40	58–51–41	75–50–25
Shapley-w	54–46	64–50–36	64–50–36

[a]In Game I, $v(ABC) = 0$ and all three theories predict that the AB coalition is most likely to form. Hence, entries for Game I denote the predicted payoff shares of players A and B, respectively. In Games II and III, $v(ABC) = 150$ and all three theories predict that the grand coalition is most likely to form. Hence, entries denote the predicted payoff shares of players A, B, and C, respectively.

[b]E^1 and E^∞ denote the trial/round 1 and asymptotic payoff predictions of bargaining and equal excess theories.

prior experience with coalition games. Three levels of prior experience were used. In the maximal experience condition subjects played three sets of games: (1) four practice games in which they were given "training" on tactics and strategies of maximizing payoffs, (2) four additional games played for points, denoted game G, and (3) four trials of a test game. In the intermediate condition, subjects played the four games denoted G, and then played four trials of the test game. In the minimal experience condition, subjects were given one practice trial and then played four trials of the test game.

In the test game, the values of the AB, AC, and BC coalitions were 400, 300, and 200, respectively (quota values of 250, 150, and 50 for players A, B, and C, respectively). Table IX shows the mean proportion of occurrence and the mean payoff shares in each coalition in the four test games. The AB coalition occurred most frequently and BC occurred least frequently, as predicted by the three theories. In the AB coalition (1) the equal excess model predicts that the payoff shares should be 225–175 on round 1 and 250–150 (the quota values) at the asymptote, (2) the bargaining theory predicts shares of 220–180 on trial 1 and 255–145 at the asymptote, and (3) the Shapley-w predicts shares of 218–182.

We shall first evaluate the predictions of the bargaining theory and the equal excess model. Table IX shows that the mean shares of player A increase with increasing experience while player B's mean shares decrease with experience. This pattern of changes in payoffs is predicted by both theories. In the intermedi-

TABLE IX

MEAN PROPORTION OF OCCURRENCE AND MEAN PAYOFF SHARES IN EACH
COALITION IN GAME-TYPE I[a]

Experience	Possible coalitions		
conditions[b]	AB	AC	BC
Minimal	.66 (209–191)	.32 (205–95)	.02 (100–100)
Intermediate	.59 (220–180)	.39 (210–90)	.02 (158–42)
Maximal	.50 (237–163)	.41 (227–73)	.09 (162–38)
Combined	.58 (221–179)	.38 (215–85)	.04 (152–48)

[a]Data from Komorita and Kravitz (1981) for three-person test game in which values
of AB, AC, and BC coalitions were 400, 300, and 200, respectively. Data have been
pooled over two incentive conditions (money vs prizes) and are based on 14 triads in each
condition.

[b]Conditions represent subjects' degree of prior experience (familiarity) with coalition games.

ate and maximal prior experience conditions, the mean shares of the players are
well within the range of payoffs predicted by both theories. However, in the
minimal experience condition, both theories overestimate player A's share in AB
(209) and in AC (205), and underestimate the shares of players B and C. The
main implication of these comparisons is that both theories provide reasonably
accurate predictions in games of this type, but it would be desirable to provide
more precise predictions of coalition outcomes.

With regard to the validity of the Shapley-w, the main weakness of the
model is that it cannot account for the differences in the players' payoffs as a
function of prior experience. In the AB coalition, for example, its predictions
(218–182) are very accurate for the intermediate condition (220–180). However,
it overestimates player A's share in the minimal experience condition and underestimates A's share in the maximal condition. Thus, Shapley-w in game-type I
may be restricted to bargainers who have a moderate level of experience.

In addition to these data, the results of studies by Kahan and Rapoport
(1974), Miller (1980), and Komorita and Tumonis (1980) provide partial support
for all three theories in game-type I. Indeed, Miller has hypothesized the principle that in games of this type, the coalition with the largest value per person is
most likely to form. This principle is predicted by all three theories, and the
results of all three studies support this prediction.

2. *Evaluation of Theories in Game-Type II*

In illustrating the predictions of the theories in game-type II, the value of the
grand coalition $v(ABC)$ was much larger than the values of any subset coalition

(see Table VI). Hence, we assumed that the grand coalition would form and contrasted the theories in terms of the predicted payoff shares in the grand coalition. Suppose, however, that $v(ABC)$ is allowed to vary in value. At the lower limit of zero, we have game-type I that we considered in the previous section. At the upper limit when $v(ABC) = \infty$, the values of the two-person coalitions become virtually irrelevant because threats to form them lose credibility. We shall postpone a consideration of this hypothesis to Section IV,B,3.

The most interesting and critical comparison of theories involves intermediate values of the grand coalition, especially when $v(ABC) = \max v(ij)$, where $\max v(ij)$ denotes the largest two-person value. All three theories predict that the probability of the grand coalition, $p(ABC)$, is a direct function of its value, relative to the value of $\max v(ij)$. When $v(ABC) = \max v(ij)$, the three theories predict that $p(ABC) = 0$. For larger values, $p(ABC)$ is predicted to increase monotonically with its value. However, as a function of $v(ABC)$, no precise probability prediction can be derived from these models.

To evaluate the three theories we shall contrast their predictions with the results of a study by Medlin (1976), in which the value of the grand coalition was systematically varied. As predicted by all three theories, Medlin found that the likelihood of the grand coalition varied directly with the value of the grand coalition, relative to the value of the two-person coalition with the largest value (or with the sum of the quota values of the three players). To evaluate the payoff predictions of the various theories, we shall restrict ourselves to only one of the conditions of Medlin's study: the condition in which $v(ABC)$ was maximal and the grand coalition occurred with high frequency. For this condition, Table X shows the predicted and observed payoff shares in the grand coalition for the five games used by Medlin. Table X also shows values of *RMSE,* a goodness-of-fit index (square root of mean of squared deviations between predicted and observed values). Values of *RMSE* were calculated from the mean payoffs reported by Medlin, and are not based on individual triad data; hence, no statistical tests were performed on the differences between these *RMSE* values.

The mean values of *RMSE* indicate that the Shapley-*w* model yields the best fit and the equal excess model is a close second. The main reason bargaining theory yields a poor fit is because it underestimates player A's share in the grand coalition, especially in game 5. For the five games in Medlin's study, the predictions of bargaining theory are more egalitarian than the predictions of the other two models. However, this is not always the case and depends on the value of the grand coalition as we shall see in Section IV,B,3.

3. Evaluation of Theories in Game-Type III

To evaluate the theories in game-type III (the pure bargaining game), we shall present a subset of the data from a study by Komorita and Kravitz (1979).

TABLE X

Predicted and Observed Payoff Shares in Game-Type II[a]

Theories[b]	Type II games					Mean RMSE[c]
	1	2	3	4	5	
Equal excess	65–40–35	61–45–19	57–50–43	67–47–27	77–43– 9	3.70
Bargaining	52–45–43	49–43–32	53–50–47	54–47–39	55–44–31	6.97
Shapley-w	62–41–37	59–44–21	56–50–44	64–47–29	76–43–11	2.36
Observed[d]	60–47–33	58–45–21	53–49–47	62–47–31	73–47–10	
	(.87)	(.62)	(.87)	(1.0)	(.50)	

[a]All three theories predict that the grand coalition is most likely to form; hence, entries denote the predicted shares of players A, B, and C, respectively, in the grand coalition.

[b]Predictions of bargaining theory and equal excess model are asymptotic values because subjects were relatively experienced bargainers and played for nontrivial stakes.

[c]RMSE denotes root mean square error, a goodness-of-fit index. Mean RMSE are weighted means, weighted by frequency of occurrence of the grand coalition.

[d]Data are from Medlin (1976). The five games in his study differed in $v(ABC)$ and the distribution of quota values. Values in parentheses denote proportion of occurrence of the grand coalition.

In all conditions of their study there was a single "strong" bargainer whose single-person alternative, $v(i)$, was greater than the alternatives of the weaker bargainers. Three variables were manipulated: (1) the number of bargainers (two, three, and four), (2) the size of the alternatives of the strong bargainer relative to those of the weaker bargainers, and (3) the size of the prize to be divided (negotiated) among the bargainers. Three norms of reward division were contrasted: equal excess, proportionality (assumed by the bargaining theory), and the equality norm. The grand coalition occurred in over 96% of the cases, and the equal excess norm was found to be most accurate in predicting the mean payoff splits in the grand coalition.

To simplify the presentation, and to conform to game-type III of Table VI, we shall restrict ourselves to the triad (one strong and two weak players), and to the case where $v(A) = 24$ and $v(B) = v(C) = 6$. When two players have identical alternatives (single-player coalitions), all theories predict the same payoffs for the two players. Hence, to simplify the presentation, we shall evaluate the theories in terms of the *proportional share* of $v(ABC)$ predicted for the single strong player (A).

Table XI shows the predicted and observed proportional shares of the strong player for the five values of $v(ABC)$ used by Komorita and Kravitz. The round 1 and asymptotic values of the equal excess model are not differentiated because they are identical for this type of game. The last column of Table XI shows values of RMSE, calculated from the mean values of player A's share only;

S. S. KOMORITA

TABLE XI

Predicted and Observed Proportional Shares of the "Strong" Player (A)
in the Grand Coalition in Game-Type III[a]

Theories[b]	Prize values					RMSE
	42	60	84	144	288	
Equal excess	.62	.53	.48	.42	.38	.062
Bargaining						
E^1	.58	.58	.58	.58	.58	.150
E^∞	.67	.67	.67	.67	.67	.229
Shapley-w	.56	.44	.40	.37	.35	.038
Observed[c]	.52	.47	.41	.40	.39	

[a]Predictions are based on $v(A) = 24$ and $v(B) = v(C) = 6$, and prize values denote $v(ABC)$. Since all theories predict equal shares for the two weak players (B and C), they are not shown; they can be derived by subtracting the strong player's proportional share from 1.0 and dividing by two. RMSE values are based on deviations of means for the strong player only.

[b]For the equal excess model, $E^1 = E^\infty$ in this game (predictions are invariant over rounds of bargaining).

[c]Data are from Komorita and Kravitz (1979). A significant main effect of prize value was obtained, indicating that mean proportional shares decreased significantly with increasing prize values.

hence, these values should be treated as very rough estimates of fit. Nonetheless, it can be seen that the predictions of bargaining theory are grossly inaccurate, while the Shapley-w and equal excess models provide reasonably accurate predictions of the data. Note that the observed proportional shares decrease with increasing prize value, but the predictions of the bargaining theory, both on trial 1 and at the asymptote, are invariant over prize value. The predictions of Shapley-w and equal excess models, in contrast, decrease with prize value. This decrease in the proportional shares of the strong player as a function of prize value was found in all of the other conditions of the study by Komorita and Kravitz. Hence, these results suggest that the proposed extension of the bargaining theory may not be applicable in game-type III.

4. Summary Evaluation of Theories in Multivalued Games

In multivalued games, the predictions of the bargaining theory were shown to be reasonably accurate in game-type I, but were clearly inadequate in game-types II and III. Although the extension of the theory proposed here does not seem to be a promising general theory for multivalued games, other variants of the theory may yield more accurate predictions. Similarly, the Shapley-w model yielded the most accurate predictions in game-types II and III, but its predictions were less accurate in game-type I.

The equal excess model seems to be more promising as a general theory of coalition formation, not only for multivalued games, but for simple games as well. It is one of the most accurate theories in simple games, and it provides reasonably accurate predictions in all three types of multivalued games. As we indicated earlier, its main weakness is that its predictions are not precise, and consequently, in Section IV,C we shall propose an extension of this model that yields more precise predictions.

C. AN EXTENSION OF THE EQUAL EXCESS MODEL

The equal excess model assumes that the competitive motivation of subjects and familiarity and experience with coalition games will affect the round on which an agreement is likely to occur. One of the main weaknesses of the model is that it does not yield precise predictions, and does not specify the exact round on which an agreement is likely to occur. Moreover, the results of the study by Komorita and Kravitz (1981) indicate that there is no one-to-one correspondence between observed changes in payoff splits over rounds (or trials) of bargaining and the changes in expectations predicted by the model. Since it would be desirable to specify more precisely the role of such situational factors on coalition behavior, we shall propose an extension of the model that incorporates such factors as a parameter of the model.

1. Extension of the Model in Game-Type III

In game-type III (see Table VI and Section IV,A,1,c), each player has a single-person alternative; the two-person coalitions have no value, and the problem is to predict how the three players will divide the prize in the grand coalition. For game-type III the idea of "equal excess," as a norm of reward division, can be expressed as in Eq. (14)

$$S_i = A_i + (1/n)(V - \Sigma A_i) \tag{14}$$

in which V denotes the value of the reward to be divided among the n bargainers, S_i denotes the share of V for individual i, and A_i denotes the alternative of individual i (the consequence to i if an agreement cannot be reached among the n bargainers). The equal excess norm specifies that each person should receive his/her alternative (A_i) and that the excess $(V - \Sigma A_i)$ should be divided equally among the bargainers.

To incorporate situational factors in such bargaining situations, a one-parameter extension of the model is proposed in Eq. (15)

$$S_i = wA_i + (1/n)(V - w \Sigma A_i) \qquad (15)$$

in which S_i denotes the estimated share of V for individual i, and w denotes a parameter to be estimated.

The w parameter represents the salience or importance of the bargainers' alternatives: (1) if $w = 0$, $S_i = V/n$ (equality), and alternatives (A_i) are ignored; (2) if $w = 1$, we have the original model [Eq. (14)], and (3) it can be shown that if $w = V/\Sigma A_j$, $S_i = V(A_i/\Sigma A_j)$, and the bargainer's shares of V are directly proportional to their alternatives (proportionality norm).

Another interpretation of the w parameter is in terms of the variance of S_i and A_i. Assuming that $V = \Sigma S_i$ (bargainers should not accept shares that sum to less than V), it can be shown that:

$$S_i - \bar{S} = w(A_i - \bar{A}) \qquad (16)$$

where $\bar{S}$ and $\bar{A}$ denote the means of S_i and A_i. If we square, sum, and divide by n on each side of Eq. (16), we have:

$$\text{Variance of } S_i = w^2(\text{Variance of } A_i) \qquad (17)$$

Equation (17) shows that if $w = 0$, the variance of $S_i = 0$ (all share equally); if $w = 1$, the variance of S_i = variance of A_i. This is a severe constraint on the variance of S_i and there is no a priori reason to assume that the variance of S_i must match the distribution and variance of A_i. The w parameter relaxes this assumption, and if no constraints are placed on the w parameter, a wide range of S_i values are possible.

Assuming that all bargainers are motivated exclusively to maximize their shares of the reward, it is reasonable to impose the following constraints: (1) $\Sigma S_i = V$ (group rationality: bargainers should not accept shares that sum to less than V), and (2) $S_i \geq A_i$ (individual rationality: no bargainer should accept a share less than his/her alternative). Thus, given these constraints, it can be shown that w must be positive in value ($w > 0$). Indeed, it can be shown that the equal excess model is a special case of the Nash (1950, 1953) solution to the general bargaining problem. Nash has shown that given certain axioms of "rational" choice, his solution is unique and maximizes the sum of the products of the bargainer's utility increments.

It can also be shown that the proposed extension [Eq. (15)] is a special case of Harris' (1976) linear equity formula [Eq. (8), p. 204], and Harris has shown that this formula has certain mathematical properties desirable in any equity formulation. Studies by Harris (1980) and Harris and Joyce (1980) indicate greater support for the linear formula than for Adams' (1963) ratio (proportionality) formula. Furthermore, Birnbaum (1978, 1980) provides considerable evidence to suggest that for a variety of perceptual tasks, "the basic operation by which subjects compare two stimuli is best represented by subtraction" (1978, p. 34), where the operation of subtraction refers to the judgment of the difference between two stimuli rather than the judgment of their ratio. Birnbaum (1980) also argues that subjects are likely to use subtraction whenever subjective values of the stimuli constitute an interval scale and ratios are therefore not meaningful: "Differences between points always have a well-defined zero point ($x - y = 0$ if $x = y$) even when the original scale is only an interval scale" (1980, p. 327). Finally, the results of a recent study by Mellers (1982) refute not only the proportionality assumption of equity theory, but Harris's (1976) linear model as well. Although her data are not inconsistent with Birnbaum's (1978) subtraction hypothesis, her data indicate that the validity of the linear model may depend on the distribution of input values in the group.

One of the main advantages of this extension is that it provides a mechanism to examine situational factors that may affect bargaining outcomes. For example, in the tests of the model by Komorita and Kravitz (1979) and by Komorita et al. (1981), male undergraduates bargained in a face-to-face situation, and strong pressures toward equality were observed. However, Psathas and Stryker (1965) have argued that face-to-face bargaining inhibits the competitive tendencies of subjects. Thus, the observed tendencies toward the equality norm might be attributed to face-to-face bargaining, and if subjects had been asked to bargain by written notes, pressures toward equal splits might have been minimal. To the extent that this hypothesis is valid, the proposed extension of the model can accomoodate such situational differences, and the w parameter provides a quantitative measure (index) of such differences.

2. Extension of Model to Game-Types I and II

The one-parameter extension of the model to game-types I and II is based on a revision of Eq. (6) (Section III,A,5), and is given in Eq. (18),

$$E_{iS} = w \max E_{iT} + (1/s) [v(S) - w \sum \max E_{iT}] \qquad (18)$$

in which E_{iS} denotes the estimated share of player i in coalition S, $\max E_{iT}$ denotes player i's maximum expectation in alternative coalitions, $v(S)$ denotes the value of coalition S, w denotes a parameter to be estimated, and the summation is over s, the number of members of S.

It can be seen that the r parameter of Eq. (6) is replaced by the w parameter in Eq. (18). If $w = 0$, the alternatives ($\max E_{iT}$) of the bargainers are ignored and $E_{iS} = v(S)/s$. This case corresponds to $r = 0$ of the original model [Eq. (6)], where expectations are based on equal shares of the prize, $v(S)$. If $w = 1$, we have the original model but without the superscript r. This case corresponds to the asymptotic predictions of the original model. Thus, as an extension of the model, we shall specify that $0 \leq w \leq 1$.

The main implication of this extension of the model is that an exact estimate of expectations E_{iS} can be obtained. Although this precision is gained at the expense of transforming a dynamic model into a static one, we believe the benefits from this trade-off exceed the costs, especially at this stage of theoretical development in coalition research.

There is increasing evidence to suggest that many situational factors affect coalition outcomes. As a direct extension of the original model, it is assumed that familiarity and experience with the structure of coalition games affect the w parameter. This hypothesis has been supported by the results of a study by Komorita and Karvitz (1981), and suggest that w is smaller for naive bargainers than for experienced bargainers. Indeed, the results of a study by Kahan and Rapoport (1974) suggest that for highly trained bargainers, w approaches 1.0.

Other situational factors are also hypothesized to affect the w parameter. For example, face-to-face bargaining is expected to yield lower estimates of w than bargaining by means of written offers. This hypothesis is supported by the results of experiments by Komorita and Kravitz (1979) and is consistent with hypotheses proposed by Psathas and Stryker (1965). Thus, one of the main advantages of the proposed extension is that the w parameter provides a quantitative index to assess the effects of a variety of situational variables on coalition behavior.

To illustrate this extension of the model, consider the apex game when group size is varied (see Fig. 1a for $N = 4$). An apex game is a simple game in which there is a single "strong" player and $N - 1$ "weak" players, and two types of winning coalitions are possible: a "strong–weak alliance" and a coalition of the $N - 1$ weak players. Since the model predicts that the strong–weak alliance is most likely to form, and since there is considerable support for this prediction (see Table II), we shall restrict ourselves to payoff predictions in this coalition.

The equal excess model, as well as bargaining theory and weighted probability model, predict that the payoff share of the strong player should increase as group size (number of weak players) increases. The psychological basis of this prediction for bargaining and equal excess theories is that as the number of weak players increases, the share of the prize for members of the weak union decreases. Hence, when bargaining with the strong player in the strong–weak alliance, their bargaining strength is weakened because their alternative (expected share in weak union) is smaller. The weighted probability model, in contrast, predicts a larger share for the strong player because the weak union is more difficult to form as group size increases. Hence, the threat of the weak union is reduced and the strong player is not expected to concede as much.

Figure 2 shows the expected payoff shares of the strong player in the strong–weak alliance as a function of group size. For group size of 4, the game is identical to the one shown in Fig. 1a. The lower limit (share of 50) denotes the initial expectations (E_{iS}^0) and the upper limit denotes the asymptotic predictions

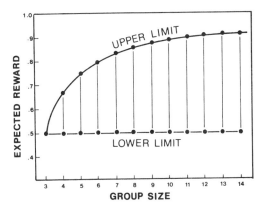

Fig. 2.   Expected share of the "strong" player in an apex game as a function of group size (adapted from Horowitz, 1973).

(E^{∞}_{is}) of the equal excess model. The upper limit is also predicted by the weighted probability model. On round 1 the equal excess model predicts a share that is midway between the lower and upper limits, and on successive rounds it bisects the remaining distance to the upper limit. The predictions of the bargaining theory are very similar to those of the equal excess model, except that it predicts two values (trial 1 and asymptote). Its trial 1 predictions are very similar to the round 1 values of the equal excess model, and its asymptotic values almost coincide with the asymptotic values of the equal excess model.[10]

In its present form, the equal excess model assumes that the round 1 values yield the best estimate of the strong player's share in the strong–weak alliance if subjects are naive and are playing for small incentives; the asymptotic values yield the best estimate for sophisticated bargainers playing for large incentives. The purpose of the one-parameter extension of the model is to yield a point prediction within the range of the lower and upper limits. Under the constraints that $0 \leq w \leq 1$, when $w = 0$ the lower limit is predicted, and when $w = 1$, the upper limit is predicted. Estimates of the w parameter can be obtained for various types of bargaining paradigms and for various types of subject populations. Thus, it would be possible to determine how various situational factors affect the w parameter, and the proposed extension provides a quantitative index to assess the effects of a variety of situational factors on coalition behavior.

[10]Values of the lower limit are predicted by the kernel theory (Davis & Maschler, 1965), and values of the upper limit are predicted by the main simple solution (von Neumann & Morgenstern, 1947) and by the competitive bargaining set (Horowitz, 1973). A fourth theory, Aumann and Maschler's bargaining set (1964), predicts payoffs ranging from the lower limit to the upper limit, and thus makes predictions that are very similar to the equal excess model. However, all four of these theories are normative (axiomatic) theories and do not yield predictions about the likelihood of various coalitions.

To illustrate this application of the w parameter, consider the results of experiments conducted by Selten and Schuster (1968) and by Horowitz and Rapoport (1974). In both studies a five-person apex game was used ($N = 5$ in Fig. 2). There were many important differences in the conditions of the two experiments, but we shall focus on only two—amount of practice and training given to subjects and the nature of the bargaining procedure. In Selten and Schuster's study the five players bargained in a face-to-face situation and were given minimal training and practice before the game. In Horowitz and Rapoport's study, the five players bargained by means of a computer-interactive system and were given 3 hours of practice and "coaching" prior to the test trials. According to the equal excess model, the strong player should achieve a larger mean share in Horowitz and Rapoport's study than in Selten and Schuster's study because of greater familiarity and experience. Similarly, according to Psathas and Stryker (1965), face-to-face interaction should inhibit the competitive tendencies of subjects; consequently, the strong player's share should be larger in Horowitz and Rapoport's study than in Selten and Schuster's study. Thus, both of these situational factors should yield a larger value of w in Horowitz and Rapoport's study than in Selten and Schuster's study.

The results of this contrast clearly support this hypothesis. In Selten and Schuster's study, the mean proportional share of the strong person was .61 ($w = .44$), while in Horowitz and Rapoport's study, it was .72 ($w = .88$). Without this extension of the model, the round 1 values ($w = .50$) would be predicted for the Selten–Schuster study, and the asymptotic values ($w = 1.0$) would be predicted for the Horowitz and Rapoport study. The gain in accuracy in this example is relatively small, but in other cases the gain may be much larger.

V.   Situational Factors in Coalition Bargaining

A.   EFFECTS OF BARGAINING RULES

We indicated earlier that coalition situations vary widely, and we then classified coalition games in terms of their characteristic function. Although we briefly described the experimental paradigms proposed by Vinacke and Arkoff (1957) and by Gamson (1961b), there are many other types of paradigms that have been proposed. There are reasons to believe that the validity of a given theory may depend on the particular paradigm used to test the theory, and in this section we shall briefly review some evidence to support this hypothesis. Gamson (1964), for example, in reviewing the coalition literature, concluded that each of the theories he reviewed had some empirical support, depending on the conditions under which it was tested. Thus, it is plausible that the validity of some theories may be unique to a given situation, while others may be valid in a variety of situations.

1. Differences in Experimental Paradigms

We shall first consider various constraints that may be imposed on communication among the bargainers, e.g., how are offers made and accepted/rejected (face to face or by written notes)? Are offers made simultaneously by all players, or is the order sequential? If sequential, who is allowed to make the first offer? Are offers binding or nonbinding? If nonbinding, how does a coalition form? It can be seen that the bargaining rules in a coalition experiment can vary enormously. Unfortunately, there are few systematic studies on the effects of such rules on coalition outcomes.

In Gamson's (1961b) convention paradigm, all players are first asked to indicate with whom they wish to form a coalition by showing a colored card (identifying each of the players). If two players reciprocate choices they are taken to another room to negotiate the division of rewards in a face-to-face situation. If they reach an agreement and it is a winning coalition the game terminates; if not, the procedure is repeated. To form a three-person coalition, an initial pair must reach an agreement, reciprocate choices with the third person to be added, and then reach an agreement among the three players. Thus, the formation of an n-person coalition may require $n - 1$ stages, with reciprocity and agreement required at each stage. Obviously, Gamson's procedure clearly inhibits the formation of large coalitions.

For this reason, S. Komorita and D. Meek (1972, unpublished results) proposed a paradigm in which reciprocity is not required and a large coalition could be formed in a single stage. In their procedure all players are allowed to send a written offer to form a single coalition. If the proposed coalition involves n players, a player is allowed to send $n - 1$ offers, one to each member of the proposed coalition. However, to form this coalition all members must accept the proposal. In a subsequent study by Komorita and Meek (1978), Gamson's procedure was compared with the Komorita–Meek procedure in three games varying in group size. One of the games was 9(8–4–3–2), which is very similar to 9(8–3–3–3) described earlier. Minimum resource theory predicts that the (4–3–2) coalition should be most frequent, while bargaining theory predicts that the (8–2) coalition should be most frequent. It was hypothesized that (4–3–2) should occur more frequently with Komorita and Meek's procedure, but the opposite effect was found. With Gamson's paradigm, (4–3–2) was the most frequent coalition ($p = .31$) while with the Komorita–Meek paradigm, it was the least frequent coalition ($p = .15$). To explain this unexpected result, it was hypothesized that Gamson's procedure allows face-to-face bargaining among members of (4–3–2), and in these sessions some groups not only negotiated the division of rewards, but also planned a strategy for future trials of the game. In particular, many groups made a commitment to reciprocate choices on the next trial of the game, and the greater frequency of (4–3–2) with Gamson's procedure may be unique to a situation in which the same game is iterated over trials.

These results suggest that face-to-face bargaining in a multiple-game experiment provides the opportunity to discuss strategies over the entire set of games and may thus yield unintended confounding effects. Moreover, Psathas and Stryker (1965) claim that face-to-face bargaining inhibits the competitive tendencies of subjects, and all theories assume that the players are motivated to maximize reward. They also state that another important weakness of face-to-face bargaining is that the effects of extraneous factors such as verbal assertiveness, personality, and physical appearance are not controlled. Although face-to-face bargaining may be a realistic representation of many real-world bargaining situations, for research purposes there are many limitations in allowing subjects to bargain freely and openly.

Another paradigm that has been used frequently is the computer-interactive program developed by Kahan and Helwig (1971). In this paradigm the players are separated and all bargaining is conducted through the computer-interactive system. In one of the earliest studies using this paradigm, the possibility of making secret vs no-secret (public) offers was contrasted (Kahan & Rapoport, 1974), but no significant effect of this manipulation was obtained. In another study, however, Horowitz and Rapoport (1974) varied the order in which the players were allowed to send offers. Using an apex game (as in the game of Fig. 1a), they found that if the strong (apex) player was allowed to make the first offer, his/her mean payoff share in the apex coalition (strong–weak alliance) was greater than his/her mean payoff in a condition where he/she was the last player to make an offer. Thus, the player who is allowed to make the first offer seems to have an advantage.

Another unique feature of the computer-interactive paradigm used by Rapoport and associates is that prior to playing the test games, subjects are provided 3 hours of practice and training on tactics and strategies of maximizing payoffs. Thus, the results of their experiments are more representative of experienced (sophisticated) bargainers, whereas the vast majority of coalition experiments reflect the behavior of relatively naive bargainers. This is another important factor that affects coalition outcomes.

2. Other Possible Effects of Procedural Differences

There are other procedural variables that may have significant effects on coalition outcomes. For example, in almost all experiments subjects are asked to play multiple games in an experimental session, and are asked to maximize payoffs over all games in the session. There is some evidence to suggest that social norms regarding a "fair" share for various positions in the game develop over trials (Rapoport & Kahan, 1976; Murnighan & Roth, 1980). There is also some evidence to suggest that coalition outcomes in a one-trial game may differ from outcomes in a multiple-trial game (Komorita, Lange, & Hamilton, 1983). This possibility was first hypothesized by Caplow (1959) in his distinction between "episodic vs terminal" coalition situations. For example, in a multiple-trial experiment, if subjects are rotated over positions in the game and if they realize that each will be assigned to advantageous positions an equal number of trials, there is the danger that a norm may develop to negotiate an equal split of the prize. This hypothesis would be consistent with Gamson's (1964) anticompetitive motive. However, in a one-trial game it would not be possible to develop such a norm. The main implication of these observations is that we know very little about the effects of such procedural variables, and how they might differentially affect the validity and generality of coalition theories.

Finally, in addition to differences in procedure, different investigators have also used a variety of "scenarios" in which subjects have been asked to role play an individual in a given real-life situation. In Gamson's (1961b) paradigm, for example, they are asked to role play a political candidate seeking to form a coalition with the majority of votes; in Chertkoff and Braden's (1974) paradigm, they are asked to role play stockholders at a corporate meeting who seek to gain control of the decision-making process; and in Komorita and Kravitz's (1981) paradigm, subjects are asked to role play businessmen considering a partnership (or corporate merger) so as to maximize profit. Fortunately, such differences in the "scenarios" presented to subjects do not seem to have significant effects on coalition outcomes.

B. CHARACTERISTICS OF SUBJECTS

1. Bargaining Experience

The equal excess model predicts a range of payoffs among the coalition members (E^1 to E^∞), depending on the players' familiarity and experience with the structure of coalition games. The results of the study by Komorita and Kravitz (1981) provide considerable evidence to support this prediction. Thus, for the procedure used by Rapoport and his associates, the asymptotic predictions of the model should be more accurate than the round 1 values. For example, in the study by Kahan and Rapoport (1974), three-person quota games were used (game-type I), and they report that payoffs became less egalitarian and approached the quota solution over trials of coalition games. Since the quota values coincide with the asymptotic values of the equal excess model, their results are consistent with the changes in expectations predicted by the model. More importantly, these results suggest that the results of many coalition experiments may be restricted to naive bargainers and may not generalize to experienced, sophisticated bargainers.

There are many other studies that have examined changes in coalition outcomes over trials of coalition games, but the results are not consistent. Some studies report no significant change in outcomes (e.g., Murnighan, Komorita, & Szwajkowski, 1977) while others report a significant change (e.g., Kahan & Rapoport, 1974). In general, simple games based on resource weights seem to evoke little variation in coalition outcomes, while multivalued games (with no resources) seem to evoke much larger changes in outcomes over trials. This interaction with type of game suggests that subjects in resource weight games may not readily learn the power structure of coalition games because of the conflict between the normative and strategic functions of resource weights.

2. Motivational Orientation of Subjects

A critical assumption made by almost all theories of coalition formation is that the players are motivated to maximize reward. To the extent that other motives operate in the experimental situation, there will be discrepancies between the predictions of the theories and the results of the experiment. Stryker (1972), in a critique of coalition studies, hypothesized that in most coalition studies, subjects attempt to define the situation as "a game requiring justice and fairness since one is being handed an advantage rather than earning it" (p. 376). In addition, he questions whether "the motivational assumptions made by investigators are warranted. . . .It seems clear that the award of points would not suffice to motivate players strongly to win, and the theories being examined assume such competitive motivation" (p. 355). Stryker's criticism is quite compelling, and several attempts have been made to test his hypothesis.

In a study by Komorita and Brinberg (1977), Stryker's hypothesis was tested by imposing different costs to play each position in the game, rather than assigning subjects randomly to each position. In one of the experimental conditions, players who were assigned large resource weights were required to pay more than those who were assigned smaller resource weights. In a control condition no costs were imposed. The "pay-to-play" manipulation was hypothesized to increase the salience of parity (equity) norms, and thus enhance the accuracy of minimum resource and bargaining theories, while the control condition was hypothesized to enhance the accuracy of the weighted probability model. Both hypotheses were supported and thus support Stryker's claim that deviations from the parity norm (toward equality) can be explained by the fact that subjects in the typical coalition experiment are randomly assigned to positions, and players with an advantage have not really earned it.

In addition to assignment of positions in the game, another important factor that affects motivational orientation is the size of incentives to bargain competitively. The equal excess model assumes that such incentives should affect the round on which an agreement is likely. If the incentives are negligible, as in most experiments, the round 1 values are assumed to provide the most accurate estimate of payoffs; if the incentives are much larger, relative to the value of time required to reach agreement, the asymptotic values are assumed to yield the best estimate. However, in two studies by Komorita and Kravitz (1978, 1981), no significant difference in coalition outcomes was obtained. In one study (1978), subjects played for points vs money, with a maximum of $2; in the second study (1981), subjects played for prizes worth up to a maximum of $2 vs money averaging $5 per player. It can be argued that these incentives are relatively small, and coalition outcomes may differ significantly if larger amounts of money (e.g., hundreds of dollars) were to be used.

3. Sex of Subjects

Studies by Vinacke (1959), Bond and Vinacke (1961), and Uesugi and Vinacke (1963) indicate that female subjects are less competitive (more accommodative) than male subjects. To the extent that females are less motivated to maximize payoffs and more concerned with reaching a mutually acceptable agreement, the predictions of most coalition theories should be less accurate for female than for male subjects. And, indeed, this hypothesis was supported in a study by Komorita and Moore (1976). For male groups of subjects, they found that the coalition that *maximizes resources* occurred least frequently ($p = .07$), as predicted by minimum resource and bargaining theories. However, for female groups the maximum resource coalition occurred almost as frequently ($p = .32$) as the minimum resource coalition ($p = .38$). They also analyzed the offers (demands) made by female and male subjects, and found a significant interaction between sex and power position (resources) in the game: When in the "strong" position, males made greater demands than females, but when in the "weak" position, females made greater demands than males. Thus, it is plausible that the equality norm may be more salient for females, whereas the parity norm may be more salient for males. One of the main theoretical implications of these results is that the motivational orientations of subjects—whether they are based on individual differences or manipulated by the experimenter—are likely to affect the validity of various theories of coalition formation.

VI. Summary and Conclusions

A. SUMMARY EVALUATION OF THEORIES

Of the descriptive theories presented and evaluated in this article, the equal excess model seems to be the most promising general theory of coalition bargaining, especially with the one-parameter extension of the model described in Section IV. In simple games its predictions are as accurate or more accurate than any of the other theories, and it yields reasonably accurate predictions in all three types of multivalued games considered in this article.

The bargaining theory is also a promising general theory. In simple games its predictions are as accurate as the equal excess model, but in superadditive multivalued games (game-types II and III), its predictions are less accurate than those of the equal excess model. As we indicated earlier, however, we only considered one of several possible extensions of this theory for multivalued games, and it is possible that other variants may yield more accurate predictions in superadditive games.

The Shapley-w model also seems to be a promising theory, especially in superadditive games. It is an important theory because it is a special case of equity theory (Adams, 1963; Homans, 1961) and integrates the effects of equity and power in multivalued games. Moreover, it is applicable in simple games and yields predictions that are very similar to the initial trial (round) predictions of bargaining theory and the equal excess model. Its major weakness is that it cannot account for changes in payoffs as a function of prior experience, and its predictions may be restricted to bargainers who have an intermediate level of sophistication.

The remaining theories seem to be limited in generality. In simple games the predictions of the weighted probability model are as accurate as those of bargaining and equal excess theories. However, an attempt to extend the theory to multivalued games was not successful, and it is plausible that its validity is restricted to simple games. Minimum resource theory is further limited in generality. It is not applicable in multivalued games, and in simple games in which resource weights are not assigned, no predictions can be derived. In resource weight games its validity may be restricted to three-person groups and to naive subjects. Finally, minimum power theory seems to be inaccurate in all types of games, and Gamson's (1964) assumption that players will agree to a solution that is proportional to pivotal power seems questionable. However, a revised theory based on computing pivotal power indexes based only on MWCs may yield more accurate predictions (see Footnote 7).

B. DIRECTIONS FOR FUTURE THEORY AND RESEARCH

1. Extending the Generality of Theories

a. Limitations of Theories. In the introduction to this article we classified coalition theories in terms of their motivational bases, and we restricted the scope of our review to theories that are based on maximizing some quantitative (divisible) external reward. Consequently, the theories reviewed in this article are restricted in generality. In addition, the vast majority of studies that have tested one or more of these theories have used college students as subjects who played for trivial incentives. It would be desirable to use other types of subjects and more valuable incentives.

b. *General and Middle-Range Theories.* Since it would be desirable to extend the generality of coalition theories, it would be tempting to formulate theories that include a variety of motives. However, we indicated earlier that such theories are likely to be highly intractable, and few attempts have been made to develop them. Such an attempt would be equivalent to the development of a general theory of group formation.

For this reason, many investigators have adopted the strategy of developing "middle-range" theories (Merton, 1957). Middle-range theories, as the term implies, are neither general nor specific. Theories of political coalitions (e.g., Riker, 1967) would fall in this category. From the perspective of developing middle-range theories, there is actually an enormous number of investigators who are involved in developing such theories. Consider theory and research on the friendship patterns of children, on marriage and divorce, on organizing a labor union, on collective action and group decision making, and on international alliances. All of these research areas involve attempts to develop middle-range theories of coalition formation, and we see that coalition formation is a very pervasive phenomenon. What is needed are studies that bridge the gap between such middle-range theories and specific theories. In particular, it would be desirable to determine if the predictions of theories at one level are consistent with the predictions of theories at another level. If they are found to be consistent, it would increase our confidence in the validity and generality of the theories; if they are found to be inconsistent, it would pose an interesting problem for research.

Probably the most promising attempts to develop a general theory are those based on an "exchange approach" (Blau, 1964; Homans, 1961; Thibaut & Kelley, 1959) (for a review and critique of this approach, the reader is referred to Chadwick-Jones, 1976; Heath, 1976). Of particular relevance are the theoretical ideas and principles proposed by Thibaut and Kelley (1959) and Kelley and Thibaut (1978). For example, the basic assumptions of bargaining and equal excess theories are based on their concept of CLalt. Their ideas have proven to be of enormous heuristic value. One example of this exchange approach is an intriguing study by Miller (1979), who tested the "minimum range" theory of political coalitions (see Section I,C,3) with an experimental paradigm. Using three-person groups, Miller assigned different payoff values to various legislative proposals, based on ideological positions on a "left–middle–right" scale (e.g., liberal–moderate–conservative). Subjects were instructed that a majority coalition would determine which proposal would be adopted. He found that players with adjacent positions (left–middle and middle–right) were more likely to coalesce, thus supporting minimum-range theory.

Since Miller's paradigm transforms "ideological distance" to payoff values, it is obviously an oversimplification of a complex real-life situation. Yet, it can be argued that any experimental paradigm that attempts to simulate some aspect of the real world is an oversimplification, and all experiments involve a compromise between maximizing external and internal validity (Campbell & Stanley, 1963). Thus, in an experiment based on an exchange approach, the underlying question posed in the study is as follows: "If these payoff values represent the utilities (motives) of the bargainers, how are they likely to behave, and what is the likely outcome?" As we have argued elsewhere (Davis, Laughlin, & Komorita, 1976, p. 517)

> This research strategy is based on the assumption that insights into the nature of behavior in complex social situations depends, partly at least, on the discovery of principles underlying behavior in simple (artificial, idealized) social situations. This approach is consistent with the arguments made by Guyer and Rapoport (1972, p. 410) when they state that, ". . . the fundamental laws of physics were developed in terms of the behavior of ideal objects moving through frictionless space."

2. Toward a Theory of Coalition Process

We have argued elsewhere (Komorita & Chertoff, 1973; Komorita & Kravitz, 1983) that at the present stage of theory and research in coalition bargaining, what is needed is a theory that predicts and explains not only coalition outcomes but also the process variables that mediate the stages in which these outcomes are reached. Although bargaining and equal excess theories make implicit assumptions about process, they specify neither the exact nature of changes in expectations of the bargainers nor the conditions under which such changes can be expected. They merely specify the initial state and the asymptotic state, and are ambiguous about the intermediate processes of changing expectations.

Several attempts have been made to examine coalition process, but none of them, with one exception, has attempted to develop a process theory. One of the first attempts to study coalition process was a study by Psathas and Stryker (1965) in which a simulation (role playing) paradigm was employed. They found that the larger the offer received by a player, the more likely he/she was to send a counteroffer to that player (to reciprocate the offer), and reciprocal counteroffers made to a potential coalition partner were larger than offers sent to another player (nonreciprocal offers). Another important attempt to examine process variables is the set of studies conducted by Rapoport and his associates (Kahan & Rapoport, 1974; Horowitz & Rapoport, 1974; Rapoport & Kahan, 1976). These studies were designed to test several normative theories, and although the bargaining set (Aumann & Maschler, 1964) was found to be most accurate in predicting the final payoff shares, it was less than successful in predicting the processes of coalition formation. Two other attempts have been made to examine coalition process (e.g., Chertkoff & Braden, 1974; Komorita & Moore, 1976), but neither of these studies led to the development of a process theory.

The most systematic attempt to develop a process model of coalition formation is the work of Laing and Morrison (1973) and Friend *et al.* (1977). However, their model is restricted to three-person "sequential games of status," in which each player seeks to maximize the rank of his total score in relation to the rank of the other two players (as in a pinochle game). Nonetheless, their model provides a valuable heuristic to develop a more general process model of coalition formation.

More recently, Komorita, Lange, and Hamilton (1983) simulated one of the players in a three-person quota game. Subjects were scheduled in groups of six and were led to believe that they had been divided into two triads. In actuality, they were divided into three pairs and each pair played with a simulated player (computer program). They found that the minimum offer accepted by the simulated player (level of aspiration) had significant effects on the pattern of coalition formation, as well as on the mean payoffs of the simulated player. However, opening offer and concession rate of the simulated player did not have significant effects. Their approach is based on the assumption that systematic changes in the behavior of the simulated player correspond to systematic manipulations of process variables. The long-range goal of this approach is to develop a computer program that "mirrors" what the typical subject is likely to do under all possible sequential contingencies. Such a program would represent a "purely descriptive theory" of coalition bargaining, a theory based on a large number of process assumptions.

The study of coalition process is an exceedingly complex and difficult task, and our brief review of coalition research indicates that only a handful of investigators have attempted to analyze process variables. Despite the added complexity, however, the study of process is likely to yield important insights into the nature of outcomes in coalition situations. Such processes would include the effects of power and justice norms (strategic and normative functions) and ultimately may lead to valuable insights regarding laws and regulations for the distribution of rewards to members of society.

ACKNOWLEDGMENTS

The preparation of this article was supported by Research Grant BNS 79-11103 from the National Science Foundation. I thank David Kravitz, Charles Miller, Keith Murnighan, Joan Barth, and Tom Hamilton for their comments and suggestions on earlier drafts of this article.

REFERENCES

Adams, J. S. Toward an understanding of inequity. *Journal of Abnormal and Social Psychology,* 1963, **67,** 422–436.

Anderson, R. E. Status in coalition bargaining games. *Sociometry,* 1967, **30,** 393–403.

Aumann, R. J., & Maschler, M. The bargaining set for cooperative games. In M. Dresher, L. S. Shapley, & A. W. Tucker (Eds.), *Advances in game theory.* Princeton, New Jersey: Princeton University Press, 1964.

Axelrod, R. *Conflict of interest.* Chicago: Markham, 1970.

Birnbaum, M. H. Differences and ratios in psychological measurement. In N. J. Castellan & F. Restle (Eds.), *Cognitive theory* (Vol. 3). New York: Erlbaum, 1978.

Birnbaum, M. H. Comparison of two theories of "ratio" and "difference" judgments. *Journal of Experimental Psychology: General,* 1980, **109,** 304–319.

Blau, P. M. *Exchange and power in social life.* New York: Wiley, 1964.

Bond, J. R., & Vinacke, W. E. Coalitions in mixed-sex triads. *Sociometry,* 1961, **24,** 61–75.

Burhans, D. T. Coalition game research: A reexamination. *American Journal of Sociology,* 1973, **79,** 389–408.

Campbell, D. R., & Stanley, J. C. *Experimental and quasi-experimental designs for research.* Chicago: Rand McNally, 1963.

Caplow, T. Further development of a theory of coalitions in the triad. *American Sociological Review,* 1959, **64,** 488–493.

Caplow, T. *Two against one.* Englewood Cliffs, New Jersey: Prentice-Hall, 1968.

Cartwright, D., & Zander, A. (Eds.). *Group Dynamics,* (3rd Ed.). New York: Harper, 1968.

Chadwick-Jones, J. K. *Social exchange theory.* New York: Academic Press, 1976.

Chertkoff, J. M. Sociopsychological theories and research on coalition formation. In S. Groennings, E. W. Kelley, & M. Leiserson (Eds.), *The study of coalition behavior.* New York: Holt, Rinehart & Winston, 1970.

Chertkoff, J. M. Sociopsychological views on sequential effects in coalition formation. *American Behavioral Scientist,* 1975, **18,** 451–471.

Chertkoff, J. M., & Braden, J. L. Effects of experience and bargaining restrictions on coalition formation. *Journal of Personality and Social Psychology,* 1974, **30,** 169–177.

Crosbie, P. V., & Kullberg, V. K. Minimum resource or balance in coalition formation. *Sociometry,* 1973, **36,** 476–493.

Davis, J. H., Laughlin, P. R., & Komorita, S. S. The social psychology of small groups. *Annual Review of Psychology,* 1976, **27,** 501–541.

Davis, M., & Maschler, M. The kernel of a cooperative game. *Naval Research Logistics Quarterly,* 1965, **12,** 223–259.

DeSwaan, A. *Coalition theories and cabinet formations.* San Francisco: Jossey-Bass, 1973.

Emerson, R. M. Power-dependence relations. *American Sociological Review,* 1962, **27,** 31–41.

Festinger, L. A theory of social comparison processes. *Human Relations,* 1954, **7,** 117–140.

Friend, K. E., Laing, J. D., & Morrison, R. J. Game-theoretic analysis of coalition behavior. *Theory and Decision,* 1977, **8,** 127–157.

Gamson, W. A. A theory of coalition formation. *American Sociological Review,* 1961, **26,** 373–382.(a)

Gamson, W. A. An experimental test of a theory of coalition formation. *American Sociological Review,* 1961, **26,** 565–573.(b)

Gamson, W. A. Experimental studies of coalition formation. In L. Berkowitz (Ed.), *Advances in experimental social psychology* (Vol. 1). New York: Academic Press, 1964.

Guyer, M. J., & Rapoport, A. 2 × 2 games played once. *Journal of Conflict Resolution,* 1972, **16,** 409–432.

Harris, R. J. Handling negative inputs in equity theory: On the plausible equity formulae. *Journal of Experimental Social Psychology*, 1976, **12**, 194–209.

Harris, R. J. Equity judgments in hypothetical four-person partnerships. *Journal of Experimental Social Psychology*, 1980, **16**, 96–115.

Harris, R. J., & Joyce, M. A. What's fair? It depends on how you phrase the question. *Journal of Personality and Social Psychology*, 1980, **38**, 165–179.

Heath, A. *Rational choice and social exchange*. New York: Cambridge University Press, 1976.

Heider, F. *The psychology of interpersonal relations*. New York: Wiley, 1958.

Hoffman, P. J., Festinger, L., & Lawrence, D. H. Tendencies toward group comparability in competitive bargaining. *Human Relations*, 1954, **7**, 141–159.

Homans, G. C. *Social behavior: Its elementary forms*. New York: Harcourt, Brace & World, 1961.

Horowitz, A. D. The competitive bargaining set for cooperative *n*-person games. *Journal of Mathematical Psychology*, 1973, **10**, 265–289.

Horowitz, A. D., & Rapoport, Am. Test of the kernel and two bargaining set models in four- and five-person games. In An. Rapoport (Ed.), *Game theory as a theory of conflict resolution*. Dordrecht, Holland: Reidel, 1974.

Kahan, J. P., & Helwig, R. A. Coalitions: A system of programs for computer-controlled bargaining games. *General Systems*, 1971, **16**, 31–41.

Kahan, J. P., & Rapoport, Am. Test of the bargaining set and kernel models in three-person games. In An. Rapoport (Ed.), *Game theory as a theory of conflict resolution*. Dordrecht, Holland: Reidel, 1974.

Kelley, H. H., & Arrowood, A. J. Coalitions in the triad: Critique and experiment. *Sociometry*, 1960, **23**, 231–244.

Kelley, H. H., & Thibaut, J. W. *Interpersonal relations*. New York: Wiley, 1978.

Komorita, S. S. A weighted probability model of coalition formation. *Psychological Review*, 1974, **81**, 242–256.

Komorita, S. S. Negotiating from strength and the concept of bargaining strength. *Journal for the Theory of Social Behaviour*, 1977, **7**, 65–79.

Komorita, S. S. An equal excess model of coalition formation. *Behavioral Science*, 1979, **24**, 369–381.

Komorita, S. S., & Brinberg, D. The effects of equity norms in coalition formation. *Sociometry*, 1977, **40**, 351–361.

Komorita, S. S., & Chertkoff, J. M. A bargaining theory of coalition formation. *Psychological Review*, 1973, **80**, 149–162.

Komorita, S. S., & Kravitz, D. A. Some tests of four descriptive theories of coalition formation. In H. Sauermann (Ed.), *Contributions to experimental economics: Coalition forming behavior* (Vol. 8). Tubingen, West Germany: Mohr, 1978.

Komorita, S. S., & Kravitz, D. A. The effects of alternatives in bargaining. *Journal of Experimental Social Psychology*, 1979, **15**, 147–157.

Komorita, S. S., & Kravitz, D. A. The effects of prior experience on coalition behavior. *Journal of Personality and Social Psychology*, 1981, **40**, 675–686.

Komorita, S. S., & Kravitz, D. A. Coalition formation: A social psychological approach. In P. B. Paulus (Ed.), *Basic group processes*. New York: Springer-Verlag, 1983.

Komorita, S. S., Lange, R., & Hamilton, T. Effects of level of aspiration in coalition bargaining. In R. Tietz (Ed.), *Aspiration levels in bargaining and economic decision making*. New York: Springer, 1983.

Komorita, S. S., Lapworth, W. C., & Tumonis, T. M. The effects of certain vs risky alternatives in bargaining. *Journal of Experimental Social Psychology*, 1981, **17**, 525–544.

Komorita, S. S., & Meek, D. D. Generality and validity of some theories of coalition formation. *Journal of Personality and Social Psychology*, 1978, **36**, 392–404.

Komorita, S. S., & Moore, D. Theories and processes of coalition formation. *Journal of Personality and Social Psychology*, 1976, **33**, 371–381.

Komorita, S. S., & Nagao, D. H. The functions of resources in coalition bargaining. *Journal of Personality and Social Psychology*, 1983, **44**, 95–106.

Komorita, S. S., & Tumonis, T. M. Extensions and tests of some descriptive theories of coalition formation. *Journal of Personality and Social Psychology*, 1980, **39**, 256–268.

Kravitz, D. A. Effects of resources and alternatives on coalition formation. *Journal of Personality and Social Psychology*, 1981, **41**, 87–98.

Laing, J. D., & Morrison, R. J. Coalitions and payoffs in three person sequential games: Initial tests of two formal models. *Journal of Mathematical Sociology*, 1973, **3**, 3–26.

Lawler, E. J., & Young, G. A. Coalition formation-integrative model. *Sociometry*, 1975, **38**, 1–17.

Leiserson, M. Power and ideology in coalition behavior. In S. Groennings, E. W. Kelley, & H. Leiserson (Eds.), *The study of coalition behavior*. New York: Holt, 1970.

Luce, R. D., & Raiffa, H. *Games and decisions*. New York: Wiley, 1957.

Mazur, A. A nonrational approach to theories of conflict and coalition. *Journal of Conflict Resolution*, 1968, **12**, 196–205.

Medlin, S. M. Effects of grand coalition payoffs on coalition formation in three-person games. *Behavioral Science*, 1976, **21**, 48–61.

Mellers, B. A. Equity judgment: A revision of Aristotelian views. *Journal of Experimental Psychology: General*, 1982, **111**, 242–270.

Merton, R. K. *Social theory and social structure* (Rev. ed.). Glencoe, Illinois: Free Press, 1957.

Michener, H. A., Fleishman, J. A., & Vaske, J. J. A test of the bargaining theory of coalition formation in four-person groups. *Journal of Personality and Social Psychology*, 1976, **34**, 1114–1126.

Miller, C. E. Coalition formation in triads with single-peaked payoff curves. *Behavioral Science*, 1979, **24**, 75–84.

Miller, C. E. A test of four theories of coalition formation: Effects of payoffs and resources. *Journal of Personality and Social Psychology*, 1980, **38**, 153–164.

Miller, C. E., & Crandall, R. Experimental research on the social psychology of bargaining and coalition formation. In P. B. Paulus (Ed.), *Psychology of group influence*. Hillsdale, New Jersey: Erlbaum, 1980.

Murnighan, J. K. Models of coalition behavior: Game theoretic, social psychological, and political perspectives. *Psychological Bulletin*, 1978, **85**, 1130–1153.

Murnighan, J. K., Komorita, S. S., & Szwajkowski, E. Theories of coalition formation and the effects of reference groups. *Journal of Experimental Social Psychology*, 1977, **13**, 166–181.

Murnighan, J. K., & Roth, A. E. Effects of group size and communication availability on coalition bargaining in a veto game. *Journal of Personality and Social Psychology*, 1980, **39**, 92–103.

Murnighan, J. K., & Szwajkowski, E. Coalition bargaining in four games that include a veto player. *Journal of Personality and Social Psychology*, 1979, **37**, 1933–1946.

Nash, J. F. The bargaining problem. *Econometrica*, 1950, **18**, 155–162.

Nash, J. F. Two-person cooperative games. *Econometrica*, 1953, **21**, 128–140.

Psathas, G., & Stryker, S. Bargaining behavior and orientations in coalition formation. *Sociometry*, 1965, **28**, 124–144.

Rapoport, An. *N-person game theory*. Ann Arbor: University of Michigan Press, 1970.

Rapoport, Am., & Kahan, J. P. When three is not always two against one: Coalitions in experimental three-person cooperative games. *Journal of Experimental Social Psychology*, 1976, **12**, 253–273.

Riker, W. H. Bargaining in a three-person game. *American Political Science Review*, 1967, **61**, 91–102.

Roth, A. E. Bargaining ability, the utility of playing a game and models of coalition formation. *Journal of Mathematical Psychology*, 1977, **16**, 153–160.(a)

Roth, A. E. The Shapley value as a von Neumann–Morgenstern utility. *Econometrica*, 1977, **45**, 657–664.(b)

Schelling, T. C. *The strategy of conflict*. London: Oxford University Press, 1960.

Schopler, J. Social power. In L. Berkowitz (Ed.), *Advances in experimental social psychology* (Vol. 2). New York: Academic Press, 1965.

Selten, R., & Schuster, K. G. Psychological variables and coalition forming behavior. In K. Borch & J. Mossin (Eds.), *Risk and uncertainty*. London: Macmillan & Co., 1968.

Shapley, L. S. A value for *n*-person games. In H. W. Kuhn & A. W. Tucker (Eds.), *Contributions to the theory of games* (Vol. 2). Princeton, New Jersey: Princeton University Press, 1953.

Shapley, L. S., & Shubik, M. Method for evaluating the distribution of power in a committee system. *American Political Science Review*, 1954, **48**, 787–792.

Shaw, M. E. *Group dynamics* (3rd. Ed.). New York: McGraw-Hill, 1981.

Stevens, C. M. *Strategy and collective bargaining negotiations*. New York: McGraw-Hill, 1963.

Stryker, S. Coalition behavior. In C. G. McClintock (Ed.), *Experimental social psychology*. New York: Holt, Rinehart & Winston, 1972.

Thibaut, J., & Faucheux, C. The development of contractual norms in a bargaining situation under two types of stress. *Journal of Experimental Social Psychology*, 1965, **1**, 89–102.

Thibaut, J., & Gruder, C. L. Formation of contractual agreements between parties of unequal power. *Journal of Personality and Social Psychology*, 1969, **11**, 59–65.

Thibaut, J., & Kelley, H. H. *The social psychology of groups*. New York: Wiley, 1959.

Uesugi, T. K., & Vinacke, W. E. Strategy in a feminine game. *Sociometry*, 1963, **26**, 75–88.

Vinacke, W. E. Sex roles in a three-person game. *Sociometry*, 1959, **22**, 343–360.

Vinacke, W. E. Power, strategy, and the formation of coalitions in triads under four incentive conditions (ONR Technical Report 3748-02). University of Hawaii, 1962.

Vinacke, W. E., & Arkoff, A. An experimental study of coalitions in the triad. *American Sociological Review*, 1957, **22**, 406–414.

von Neumann, J., & Morgenstern, O. *Theory of games and economic behavior*. Princeton, New Jersey: Princeton University Press, 1947.

Webster, M., & Smith, L. F. Justice and revolutionary coalitions: A test of two theories. *American Journal of Sociology*, 1978, **84**, 267–292.

WHEN BELIEF CREATES REALITY

Mark Snyder

DEPARTMENT OF PSYCHOLOGY
UNIVERSITY OF MINNESOTA
MINNEAPOLIS, MINNESOTA

247

ADVANCES IN EXPERIMENTAL
SOCIAL PSYCHOLOGY, VOL. 18

I. Introduction

The self-fulfilling prophecy is, in the beginning, a false definition of the situation evoking a new behavior which makes the originally false conception come true. The specious validity of the self-fulfilling prophecy perpetuates a reign of error. For the prophet will cite the actual course of events as proof that he was right from the very beginning. Such are the perversities of social logic. (Merton, 1948, p. 195)

This scenario, written several decades ago, suggests that beliefs may influence the course of events in ways that make even false expectations come true. Thus, if I believe that you have a friendly and sociable nature, I might behave in my most charming and likable manner when we spend time together. You, no doubt, would respond in kind to my warm overtures. I, perhaps, would conclude that your friendly and sociable ways were proof that my initial views of your personality had been confirmed. Little would I realize that, had I believed you to be cool and aloof, I probably would have adopted a somewhat more distant and reserved style of interaction. You probably would have treated me to a display of cool and aloof actions that I would have interpreted as validation of my expectation. In either case, you would have "become" the person that I expected to encounter. Yet, in either case, I would not have been aware of the causal role that my own treatment of you had played in generating the very evidence that appeared to fulfill my prior expectations.

The notion that beliefs and expectations can and do create their own social reality is the essence of the self-fulfilling prophecy. It is a notion that has generated diverse empirical attempts by social scientists to document the self-fulfilling nature of beliefs and expectations. And it is a notion that conveys the theme of my own program of empirical and theoretical investigations of the cognitive, behavioral, and interpersonal consequences of individuals' beliefs about themselves and about other people.

In the beginning, what appeared (at the time) to be a conspicuous absence in both theoretical and empirical inquiries into the nature of social beliefs provided the impetus for this program of research. It seemed that most of these inquiries, many of them guided by the attributional perspectives of Heider (1958), Jones and Davis (1965), and Kelley (1973) had focused on the cognitive activities of interpreting information about persons and their behavior. Much was known about the "machinery" of person perception and social cognition (the "how" of making inferences about people's traits and dispositions) but comparatively little was known about the consequences of adopting one belief rather than another. One could only wonder what happened once beliefs were formed. One could only speculate about the ways in which individuals' subsequent thoughts, actions, and interactions are channeled and influenced by their beliefs about other people and by their conceptions of themselves. Indeed, it seemed at the time that theory and research on person perception and attributional processes were in imminent danger of leaving the individual lost in thought, with no machinery that would link thought to action.

These concerns about "conspicuous absences" and "imminent dangers" motivated a journey through the research literature of empirical social psychology, the souvenirs of which were some suggestions that an individual's beliefs about another person might channel social interaction in ways that cause the behavior of that person to confirm the individual's beliefs. Thus, for example, Kelley (1950) found that students who had been told that their instructor would be cold later rated their instructor as colder and more distant than other students in the same class who were told that the same instructor would be warm and friendly. Expectations also affected behavior. Students who believed that the instructor was cold tended to participate less in class discussion than students who believed the instructor was warm. But did the teacher actually behave differently to the two halves of the class? We do not know; other research, however, does suggest that in certain specific contexts one individual's expectations can influence another person's behavior.

In an extensive program of laboratory and field investigations of the effects of experimenters' and teachers' expectations on the behavior of subjects in laboratories and students in classrooms, Rosenthal and colleagues have found that experimenters and teachers, having been led to expect particular patterns of performance from their subjects and students, often act in ways that influence those performances to confirm their initial expectations (e.g., Rosenthal, 1966, 1969, 1971, 1974; Rosenthal & Jacobson, 1968). Although these investigations have received methodological criticism (e.g., Jensen, 1969; Elashoff & Snow, 1971), experimenter expectancy and teacher expectancy effects have been demonstrated sufficiently often (see Rosenthal, 1974, for one frequency count) to attest to their reliability, validity, and social importance.

Empirical research in contexts other than the experiment and the classroom also suggests that one individual's expectations can influence another person's behavior. Jones and Panitch (1971) led one member (the sender) of a dyad to believe that the other member (the receiver) either liked or disliked him. The two members then played a prisoner's dilemma game. Senders who believed that they were playing with a receiver who liked them emitted more cooperative responses than did those who believed that they were playing with a partner who disliked them. Moreover, receivers had more positive attitudes toward the senders in the "like" condition than in the "dislike" condition. Thus, the actions of the senders based on their beliefs about the receivers eventually prompted the receivers to like or dislike the senders.

The prisoner's dilemma game has been the setting for several other investigations of the effects of beliefs on behavior (e.g., Kelley & Stahelski, 1970; Kuhlman & Wimberley, 1976; Miller & Holmes, 1975). Thus, Kelley and Stahelski (1970) found that some individuals believe the world to be composed homogeneously of competitive people. By acting on these beliefs and adopting a competitive stance in the prisoner's dilemma game, these individuals elicited competitive responses from their partners in the prisoner's dilemma situation, whether the partners had cooperative or competitive dispositions. Thus, the feedback that they received validated their beliefs that all people are competitive, even though it was their own behavior that determined their partners' behavior.

As impressive as these demonstrations are, some constraints of the specific situations studied may constitute sources of concern about their relevance to the events of social interaction and interpersonal relationships. Natural social relationships may not be so focused on eliciting specific behaviors as are teacher–learner and experimenter–subject interactions that focus on the clearly defined actions that constitute successful performance in these highly task oriented contexts. Moreover, highly structured social situations such as the prisoner's dilemma game used in so many laboratory investigations of the effects of expectations on behavior may not capture fully the tone and flavor of the beliefs and impressions spontaneously formed in everyday social interaction and the impact of these beliefs on the dynamics of the natural course of interpersonal relationships.

It was with an eye on the dynamic interplay of social beliefs and interpersonal relationships that I began my own attempts to specify the nature of this phenomenon in which beliefs, even ones that initially are wrong, can and do create their own social reality. The focal points of this program of research have been not only *demonstrations* of the pervasive nature of this phenomenon in action but also attempts to chart the underlying social and psychological *processes* by which beliefs translate themselves into reality.

II. Behavioral Confirmation in Social Interaction

The initial investigations of this program of research sought to demonstrate the impact of one individual's beliefs on another person's behavior in contexts designed to mirror as faithfully as possible the spontaneous generation of beliefs and impressions in naturally occurring social interaction and interpersonal relationships. One such context for demonstrating this "behavioral confirmation" phenomenon is provided by first encounters between strangers. When people first meet others, they cannot help but notice certain highly visible and distinctive characteristics, including their sex, race, and physical appearance. Try as they may to avoid it, their very first impressions often are dictated by assumptions about the types of personalities that go along with each of these characteristics.

They may find themselves assuming that they "know" something about the personality of the person they have just met, a person who has yet to say or do anything, just because they "know" what personalities "go with" that person's sex, or that person's race, or that person's appearance. These assumptions, as innocent as they may seem, turn out to have profound effects on the events that transpire between people and the targets of these assumptions.

A. BELIEFS ABOUT APPEARANCE

Consider the case of physical appearance. Many people often assume that the physically attractive possess more socially appealing personalities than the physically unattractive (Dion, Berscheid, & Walster, 1972). As widespread as this belief is, the fact of the matter is that there is little evidence that physically attractive people actually are more likable, friendly, sensitive, kind, sociable, and outgoing than unattractive people (e.g., Berscheid & Walster, 1974).

Nevertheless, research on behavioral confirmation in social interaction has revealed the following scenario of events triggered by the belief that looks and personalities are linked in some meaningful fashion. When individuals first meet other people, they are quick to assume that a physically attractive person is friendly, sociable, and outgoing and that a physically unattractive person is shy, withdrawn, and aloof. In fact, they are quite prepared to make these assumptions without waiting for the other person to say or do anything that might be revealing of that person's true nature. Moreover, individuals have very different ways of treating the attractive and unattractive. These differences in interaction style tend to bring out precisely the behaviors that confirm beliefs about attractiveness. Thus, people thought to be physically attractive actually come to behave in a friendly, likable, and sociable manner, and people thought to be physically unattractive actually come to behave in a cool, aloof, and distant fashion.

In one experiment, Snyder, Tanke, and Berscheid (1977) allowed pairs of previously unacquainted college aged men and women to meet and become acquainted with each other in telephone conversations. Before the conversations began, each man received a Polaroid snapshot of the woman he would meet on the telephone. This photograph, which had been prepared before the experiment, portrayed either a rather physically attractive or a rather physically unattractive young woman. Randomly choosing which pictures to use in each conversation ensured that there was no relation whatsoever between the attractiveness of the woman in the picture and the actual attractiveness of the woman in the conversation.

Even before the conversations began, beliefs about physical attractiveness came into play. In anticipation of their forthcoming meetings, men who looked forward to talking with physically attractive women imagined that they would meet decidedly sociable, poised, humorous, and socially adept beings. Men faced with the prospect of getting acquainted with unattractive women formed images of rather unsociable, awkward, serious, and socially inept creatures. Moreover, the men had very different styles of getting acquainted with women they thought to be attractive and with those they thought to be unattractive. When the woman in the picture was attractive, they treated the woman on the telephone with warmth, friendliness, humor, and animation. However, when the woman in the picture was unattractive, they subjected the woman on the telephone to cold, distant, and reserved treatment.

The behavior of the men, in turn, elicited behaviors on the part of the women that provided behavioral confirmation for the men's initial belief about them. The women who were believed to be physically attractive reciprocated the sociable overtures of the men and actually came to behave in a friendly, likable, and sociable manner. In sharp contrast, the women who were believed to be physically unattractive rejected their partners' treatment of them and adopted cool, aloof, and distant postures during the conversations. These differences in the actual behavior of the women could be discerned even by naive judges who simply listened to tape recordings of only the women's contributions to the conversations. In addition, a sophisticated quantitative analysis (Thomas & Malone, 1979) of the sequential events of these two-person interactions confirmed the key role played by the levels of animation maintained by the men and the women in generating behavioral confirmation outcomes in these conversations.

Clearly, the men in this experiment had been part of a chain of events that produced behavioral confirmation for these beliefs. The critically important role of the men's beliefs in initiating and guiding this chain of events is demonstrated by the fact it was only for those specific attributes on which the men believed attractive and unattractive women to differ that the women demonstrated behavioral confirmation. Although this pattern of specificity between the men's beliefs and the women's behavior suggests the involvement of cognitive mediators in behavioral confirmation processes, one should not infer that all instances of differential treatment of the attractive and the unattractive are mediated by cognitive activities. Indeed, Berkowitz and Frodi (1979) have provided evidence of such differential treatment that seems instead to be the product of affective or emotional responses to attractive or unattractive appearances.

Although in the experiment by Snyder et al. (1977) it was always the men who had the pictures of the women, Andersen and Bem (1981) have shown that even when the tables are turned (when it is the women who have the pictures) many women do lead men to confirm beliefs about their personalities, beliefs formed by the women after seeing pictures of the men. In addition, Andersen and Bem (1981) have found that it is highly sex typed individuals, both males and females, who are most likely to initiate the behavioral confirmation process when faced with the prospect of interacting with other people of attractive or unattractive physical appearance. Although Andersen and Bem (1981) found no evidence that males and females differed in their propensities to initiate behavioral confirmation processes, Christensen and Rosenthal (1982) have found some evidence that males are more likely than females to induce other people to provide behavioral confirmation for their beliefs, and that females are more likely than males to provide behavioral confirmation for the beliefs of other individuals.

These experiments provide some insights into the persistence of stereotyped beliefs about appearances and personalities. The ways that individuals treat other people often lead the attractive and the not-so-attractive people in their lives to confirm their beliefs and expectations. Little wonder, then, that so many people remain convinced that good looks and good personalities go hand in hand. Their own actions have done much to create the appearance of validity for these beliefs. It is experiments such as these that point to the powerful but often unnoticed consequences of social beliefs, the power to influence the course of social relationships in ways that create the illusion of reality. Indeed, other experiments have shown the power of beliefs in diverse domains to cause people to provide behavioral confirmation, even when these beliefs are based upon erroneous assumptions.

B. BELIEFS ABOUT GENDER

There is no denying the existence of beliefs about the sexes. Men typically are assumed to be dominant, independent, competitive, ambitious, and aggressive, and women characteristically are assumed to be submissive, dependent, conforming, affectionate, and sympathetic (e.g., Broverman, Vogel, Broverman, Clarkson, & Rosenkrantz, 1972; Fernberger, 1948; Lunneborg, 1970; Rosenkrantz, Vogel, Bee, Broverman, & Broverman, 1968; Sherriffs, & McKee, 1957; Spence, Helmreich, & Stapp, 1975). These beliefs, as overgeneralized and exaggerated as they may seem to be (and the best evidence is that people believe the sexes to differ in more ways than they really do; e.g., Deaux, 1976; Maccoby & Jacklin, 1974; Tavris & Offir, 1977), can and do assert themselves in relationships between the sexes.

In an experiment, Skrypnek and Snyder (1982) have demonstrated how one individual's beliefs about the nature of the sexes can actually cause the behavior of another person to confirm these beliefs. Pairs of previously unacquainted students interacted in a situation that permitted control over the information that each one received about the other's apparent sex. The two people, located in separate rooms so that they could neither see nor hear each other, communicated by means of a signaling system to negotiate a division of labor for a series of worklike tasks that differed in their connotations of masculinity and femininity.

In two conditions of the experiment, one member of the team was led to believe that the other member of the team was either male or female, respectively. These teams then negotiated (communicating by means of the signaling system) their division of labor of the worklike tasks. In these negotiations, the first members' beliefs about the sex of their partners influenced the outcome of the division of labor. Thus, women whose partners believed that they were collaborating with men actually came to choose relatively many stereotypically masculine tasks, in sharp contrast to those whose partners believed that they were working with women, who came to choose relatively many stereotypically feminine tasks. Moreover, although this behavioral confirmation effect initially was elicited as reactions to overtures made by the first members of the teams, it persevered so that eventually the second members of the teams actually began to initiate behaviors associated with the sex with which they had been labeled by the first members of the teams.

In this experiment, it was possible to separate "real" sex from "apparent" sex and demonstrate that people would come to display behaviors traditionally associated with their apparent sex, even if their apparent sex differed from their real sex. Of course, in everyday life, real and apparent sexes are (with rare exceptions) the same. Nonetheless, this experiment suggests that many sex role behaviors may be the product of other people's beliefs about the sexes. Indeed, Zanna and Pack (1975) have shown how beliefs about sex roles operate in self-presentational situations. They had female undergraduates describe themselves to a very desirable or a rather undesirable male partner. Furthermore, the male possessed one of two differing sets of beliefs about the role of the ideal woman. This information about the partner's beliefs influenced the women's self-presentations. When the partner was desirable, the women expressed agreement with whatever ideology he endorsed, but when the partner was generally undesirable, his viewpoints had little impact on the self-presentational behaviors of the women.

In a subsequent experiment, von Baeyer, Sherk, and Zanna (1981) extended their analysis to include the role of beliefs about sex roles in job interviews. Female job candidates who were to be interviewed by male interviewers learned that the interviewer subscribed either to traditional stereotypes (i.e., the ideal woman should be very emotional, deferential to her husband, home-oriented, and passive) or to their opposites (i.e., the ideal woman should be very independent, very competitive, very ambitious, and very dominant). When the women arrived for their interviews, it was clear that they had dressed to fit the beliefs of the interviewers. Those who expected a traditional interviewer looked decidedly feminine, not only in terms of their overall appearance and demeanor, but also in terms of their choices of accessories and their use of makeup. During the interviews, these same women also offered traditionally feminine answers to questions such as "Do you have plans to include children and marriage with your career plans?"

C. BELIEFS ABOUT RACE

The power of beliefs to generate behavioral confirmation also may be seen in interracial relationships. Word, Zanna, and Cooper (1974) examined the behavior of white interviewers toward white and black job applicants, all of whom had been trained to behave in relatively constant fashion from interview to interview. Measurements of the verbal and nonverbal behavior of the interviewers revealed that black applicants received less immediacy, higher rates of speech errors, and shorter amounts of interview time.

In a second investigation, white confederates were trained to approximate these immediate and nonimmediate interview styles as they interviewed white job candidates. Candidates subjected to the nonimmediate interview styles experienced by blacks in the first investigation performed less adequately and were more nervous than candidates treated to the immediate interview styles experienced by whites in the first investigation.

Considered together, these two investigations suggest that, in interracial interaction, beliefs about the races may constrain the behavior of those involved in ways that cause them to behave in accord with those beliefs. Moreover, the use of job interviews as the vehicle for investigating the behavioral confirmation of beliefs about race suggests that behavioral confirmation processes may be involved in determining who gets which jobs in the first place and in determining actual performance once on the job.

D. BELIEFS ABOUT JOB PERFORMANCE

Are behavioral confirmation processes involved in job selection and job performance? Is it the case that some personnel managers may allow their beliefs to influence the way that they interview job candidates to make it likely that those who fit their beliefs show up better in their job interviews than do job seekers who do not fit their beliefs? For example, when interviewing candidates for the job of counselor (which calls for sensitivity, empathy, and tact), some personnel managers may give female job candidates many opportunities to show their sensitive, empathic, and tactful sides (because, according to prevailing stereotyped beliefs, women are thought to be sensitive, empathic, and tactful) but give male job candidates very few opportunities to show the ways that they, too, prevailing stereotyped beliefs to the contrary, might be capable of sensitivity, empathy, and tact in the counseling situation.

Indeed, investigations of interview strategies suggest that, at least in some contexts, interviewers preferentially inquire about behaviors and experiences thought to be characteristic, rather than those thought to be uncharacteristic, of occupational categories relevant to the interview. Thus, when Snyder, Campbell, and Preston (1982) allowed interviewers to choose questions to ask prospective members of particular occupational categories, these interviewers were particularly likely to choose questions that solicited evidence of the ways in which these prospective members confirmed, rather than disconfirmed, their beliefs about the personal attributes typical of members of these occupational categories. Moreover, in job interviews, applicants may be particularly likely to behave in accord with any hints they receive about the beliefs of interviewers as they strive to survive the screening process and be successful job candidates. In fact, von Baeyer *et al.* (1981) have demonstrated precisely this form of behavioral confirmation in job interviews.

Furthermore, it may be that, even on the job, expectations influence the relationships between supervisors and workers. For example, supervisors who believe that men are better suited to some jobs and women to other jobs may treat their workers in ways that actually encourage them to perform their jobs in the ways dictated by beliefs about differences between women and men. At least one investigation has examined the impact of supervisors' beliefs on workers' performance.

In a vocational training center, King (1971) told a welding instructor that some men in his training program had unusually high aptitude. Although these men had been chosen at random, and although they knew nothing of their designation as high aptitude workers, they showed substantial changes in their performance over the course of the program. They were absent less often than other workers, they learned the basics of the welder's trade in about half the usual time, and they earned higher scores on a comprehensive welding test. These gains were noticed not only by the researcher and by the welding instructor but also by the other trainees who singled out the men as their most preferred co-workers. It seems that the expectations of the welding instructor had influenced the trainees to perform in line with his expectations.

E. INTERNALIZATION AND PERSEVERATION

How stable and enduring are the effects of behavioral confirmation processes? Once a person displays behaviors that confirm another individual's beliefs, for how long will he or she continue to do so? Both theoretical and empirical inquiries have addressed the perseveration of behavioral confirmation beyond the boundaries of the specific context in which it first occurs.

At the theoretical level, this account of perseveration has been offered by Snyder and Swann (1978a). If the behaviors displayed by a person as a result of behavioral confirmation are not overly discrepant from his or her own self-image, they may be internalized and incorporated into his or her self-conception. If internalization occurs, the person then may act on this new self-conception in contexts beyond those that include the individual who originally initiated the behavioral confirmation process.

Empirical research has suggested that internalization and perseveration are likely when behavioral confirmation first occurs in environments that encourage people to regard their new behaviors as representative of underlying traits and dispositions. In their experiment, Snyder and Swann (1978a) observed successive dyadic interactions. In the first interaction, one individual was led to label another person as hostile or nonhostile. Acting upon these beliefs, the individual treated the other person as a hostile or a nonhostile person. The other person soon began to display hostile or nonhostile behaviors. Sometimes, the other person was induced to regard these behaviors as reflections of corresponding inner dispositions, that is, to believe that they actually were hostile or nonhostile types. When this happened, behavioral confirmation extended and persevered beyond the bounds of the original interaction. In a second interaction, with a new and different interaction partner, they behaved in the same hostile or nonhostile manner as they had with the individual who first had labeled them as hostile or nonhostile.

In related investigations, Fazio, Effrein, and Falender (1981) and Riggs, Monach, Ogburn, and Pahides (1983) have demonstrated internalization and perseveration, both on self-descriptions and on a variety of behaviors in subsequent interactions. That the behavioral confirmation process is not limited to the original interaction context in which it first occurs suggests that its impact is neither transitory nor ephemeral. To the extent that people who are the targets of behavioral confirmation processes interact regularly and consistently with individuals who apply the same label to them, the behavioral confirmation process will be a source of regularity and consistency in their social behavior. These people literally will become the people they are thought to be, and their behaviors will reflect the cross-situational consistency and temporal stability that are the defining features of personality traits and dispositions.

III. Behavioral Confirmation: A Theoretical Account

What are the psychological processes that underly and generate behavioral confirmation? The sequential events of the behavioral confirmation process may be viewed in terms of certain critical activities of those who initiate behavioral confirmation processes and of those who provide behavioral confirmation outcomes, activities by which each formulates strategies of action. These conceptual links in the chain of behavioral confirmation can be illustrated concretely with reference to the investigation of the behavioral confirmation of beliefs about physical appearance and personality (Snyder, *et al.*, 1977).

A. BEHAVIORAL CONFIRMATION AS REALITY TESTING

The first link in the chain of behavioral confirmation is that between the first individual's beliefs about the other person (e.g., "she is a sociable person") and the behaviors generated by those beliefs (e.g., "I will be my most charming self"). This link may be viewed as a form of *reality testing*. Beliefs, impressions, and social labels may serve as grounds for anticipating the course of social interaction and may generate behaviors designed to validate or invalidate these anticipations (cf. Kelly, 1955). The formation and validation of these anticipations may be guided by rules of thumb or scenarios involving typical sequences of events and interaction patterns of which the forthcoming interaction may be an instance. Thus, an individual in the Attractive-Picture condition of the Snyder *et al.* (1977) experiment might imagine that "If she is as warm and friendly as I think she is, then she will be a wonderful person to get to know. She'll have all kinds of interesting things to talk about. Why don't I get the relationship off to a good start by getting to know her, and perhaps we'll become friends." He may embellish this imagined scenario with instances from his own life experiences where he has applied this strategy successfully with other people similar in appearance to the person in the picture, instances in which the friendly treatment he now plans for the forthcoming telephone conversation has been a worthy investment of time and effort [cf. Abelson's (1976) discussion of the use of scripts in making decisions and planning behavior].

Having formulated a strategy, the individual then may proceed to act upon this strategy. But these actions themselves may generate behaviors that erroneously confirm and validate belief-based anticipations. For the targets of these actions themselves, no doubt, formulate their strategies of coping with their interaction partners using similar scenarios as guiding rules of thumb (e.g., "If this guy, for no apparent ulterior motive, starts off with so much friendliness, clearly he appreciates my great personality and I should respond in kind and be equally friendly to him") and assimilate their behavior to that of their conversational partners. The process by which targets of behavioral confirmation processes generate their coping strategies is the second key link in the chain of events of behavioral confirmation in social interaction.

Although the substance of their beliefs is somewhat different, the individuals in this experiment may have created for themselves a situation not unlike this one:

> A man construes his neighbor's behavior as hostile. By that he means that his neighbor, given the proper opportunity will do him harm. He tries out his construction of his neighbor's attitude by throwing rocks at this neighbor's dog. His neighbor responds with an angry rebuke. The man may then believe that he has validated his construction of his neighbor as a hostile person. (Kelly, 1955, pp. 12–13)

Both Kelly's hypothetical actor and the individuals in the experiment on behavioral confirmation have played the same causal role in generating the behavioral evidence that erroneously confirms their beliefs, expectations, and labels. The reality of the other person's behavior, the reality that they perceive to exist "out there" in the social world in fact has been constructed by their own transactions with the social world. *Reality testing* has become *reality construction*.

According to the theoretical analysis of behavioral confirmation as reality testing, the activity of individuals who initiate behavioral confirmation is conceptualized as the cognitive formulation and the behavioral testing of anticipatory scenarios. Behavioral confirmation is seen as the reality-constructing consequence of reality testing. Individuals as reality testers employ procedures that constrain the behavior of those with whom they interact in ways that produce behavioral confirmation.

The remaining links in the chain of events concern internalization and perseveration on the part of the targets of behavioral confirmation processes. These links are those that translate targets' newly generated behaviors into internalized self-concepts and that then translate these new beliefs into action in new situations. The link between one's actions and one's beliefs about the meaning of those actions (the link that constitutes internalization) has, of course, been the subject of intensive and productive research on the self-perception and self-attribution processes (cf. Bem, 1972; Jones, Kanouse, Kelley, Nisbett, Valins, & Weiner, 1972).

The nature of the link between beliefs about oneself and one's behavior (the link that constitutes perseveration) is not so clearly specified by the attribution theories (see Bem, 1972, for a discussion of this issue). However, research on the links between attitudes and behavior suggests that new beliefs will be translated into new behaviors to the extent that these beliefs are salient, well articulated, and contain clear behavioral implications, and these beliefs are linked to an "action structure" that makes belief a relevant and appropriate guide to action by endowing beliefs with implications for behavior (Snyder, 1982).

Thus, the targets' rules of thumb during the "internalization" and "perseveration" phases of the behavioral confirmation process may be specific exemplars of the general maxims "I am what I do" and "believing means doing." When these rules of thumb are operative, the outcome is perseveration of behavioral confirmation into new situations with new interaction partners.

B. REALITY TESTING IN SOCIAL INTERACTION

The analysis of behavioral confirmation as reality testing implies that, even if individuals had good reasons to doubt the accuracy of their beliefs about other people, even if they explicitly were to regard their beliefs about other people as hypotheses that may prove accurate or inaccurate, they would continue to act in ways that generate behavioral confirmation for their hypotheses about other people. For example, if, in an investigation of behavioral confirmation, participants were asked to use their getting acquainted conversations to determine whether or not their partners actually had the sociable or unsociable personalities implied by their appearance, these participants would have "hypotheses" that they could test by using their forthcoming interactions as vehicles for collecting "data" relevant to these hypotheses.

Would behavioral confirmation be the outcome of these interactions focused so explicitly on testing the reality of one's beliefs about another person? The analysis of behavioral confirmation as reality testing suggests an affirmative answer to this question, an answer that is provided by an empirical investigation of hypothesis testing in social interaction (Snyder & Swann, 1978b). In that investigation, individuals tested hypotheses about the personal attributes of another person (e.g., that the other person was an extravert, or that the other person was an introvert) by choosing and asking a series of questions of the targets of their hypotheses in conversational interviews.

Specifically, participants learned that they were part of an investigation of how people come to know and understand each other by asking them questions about their likes and dislikes, their favorite activities, their life experiences, and their feelings about themselves. Participants also learned that they would attempt to find out about another person's personality during a conversation in which they could ask questions they thought would help determine whether or not that person had the type of personality outlined on a card provided by the experimenter.

These personality profiles, which had been prepared in advance, provided the participants with hypotheses about the other person. Some participants were assigned to assess whether or not the target's behavior and life experiences matched those of a prototypic extravert (e.g., outgoing, sociable, energetic, confident, talkative, and enthusiastic); other participants, to assess whether or not the target's behavior and experiences matched those of a prototypic introvert (e.g., shy, timid, reserved, quiet, and retiring). Participants then chose 12 questions that they believed would best help them find out whether or not the target's specific beliefs, attitudes, and actions in life situations matched the general characteristics described in the profile. With their choice of questions, participants revealed that they planned to preferentially solicit behavioral evidence whose presence would confirm, rather than disconfirm, their hypotheses. To test the hypothesis that their targets were extraverted individuals, participants were particularly likely to choose to ask questions soliciting manifestations of extraversion (e.g., "What would you do if you wanted to liven things up at a party?"). To test the hypothesis that their targets were introverted individuals, participants were particularly likely to choose to ask questions that solicit manifestations of introversion (e.g., "What factors make it hard for you to really open up to people?").

Moreover, the consequence of these confirmatory hypothesis-testing strategies was behavioral confirmation in social interaction. When hypothesis testers interviewed their targets and collected the data that their hypothesis-testing strategies would provide them, their confirmatory hypothesis-testing strategies constrained the targets of their hypotheses to behave in ways that provided the actual behavioral evidence that would appear to confirm the hypotheses being tested by the hypothesis testers. Targets hypothesized to be extraverts actually presented themselves in more extraverted fashion than did targets hypothesized to be introverts, and these behavioral differences were detectable even by naive judges who listened to tape recordings of only the targets' contributions to the interviews.

Evidently, the targets' answers to the hypothesis testers' questions did provide actual behavioral confirmation for the hypotheses being tested by the hypothesis testers. One possible reason that the targets provided behavioral confirmation is that they regarded the questions being asked of them as reflections of the personalities of their interviewers and, in an attempt to maximize their compatibility with them, offered answers that stressed their similarities to the interviewers, a well-documented self-presentational strategy (e.g., Jones, 1964). Thus, targets who heard questions about their extraversion may have inferred that they were talking with an extraverted interviewer and hence focused on their extraverted activities. Similarly, targets who heard questions about their introversion may have inferred that they were talking with an introverted interviewer and hence restricted their answers to their introverted activities. The end product of these self-presentational activities guided by inferences about the interviewer's personality would, of course, be behavioral confirmation for the hypotheses that guided the interviewer's choice of questions. Support for this interpretation of the target's activities in the behavioral confirmation of hypotheses being tested has been provided by Snyder and Glick (1982).

Evidently, the outcome of the explicit testing of hypotheses in social interaction is behavioral confirmation. Although this outcome is supportive of the *behavioral confirmation as reality testing* analysis, it nonetheless is legitimate to ask how appropriate it is to regard individuals in investigations of behavioral confirmation as reality testers. After all, they were not explicitly instructed to test the accuracy of their beliefs about their interaction partners. Perhaps, rather than testing reality, these individuals simply were coping with the reality of their partner's nature, as they perceived it to be. However, from this theoretical perspective, reality testing is in practice not different from reality coping. When individuals are in doubt about the accuracy of their beliefs about other people, they may test the reality of these beliefs by treating these other people as if these beliefs were accurate. When individuals have no uncertainty about the reality of their beliefs, they (quite reasonably) may cope by treating other people as if they were the persons they are reputed to be. In either case (whether reality testing or reality coping) individuals use their initial beliefs about other people to formulate interaction strategies, and treat other people as if their initial beliefs were accurate. In either case, behavioral confirmation may be the eventual outcome of such "as if" strategies.

IV. A Taxonomy of "Belief Creates Reality" Processes

Investigations of behavioral confirmation in social interaction suggest that, when individuals interact with other people, they often use their preconceived beliefs about them as guides to action. Their actions, in turn, may prompt their interaction partners to behave in ways that confirm the individuals' initial beliefs. As a consequence, individuals' initial beliefs about other people may channel social interaction in ways that cause other people to provide behavioral confirmation for their initial beliefs. That these self-fulfilling consequences of interpersonal beliefs have been demonstrated across diverse types of beliefs and across diverse types of interaction contexts suggests that behavioral confirmation processes are rather general phenomena and that the tendency for beliefs to create their own social realities may be a pervasive one.

Conceptually, the behavioral confirmation process is one in which an individual's actions based upon beliefs about another person cause that other person to confirm the individual's initial beliefs. Operationally, experimental demonstrations of behavioral confirmation in social interaction involve an individual's beliefs about another person as manipulated independent variables and the behavior of that other person as measured dependent variables. Both conceptually and operationally, the behavioral confirmation process may be viewed as but one member of a family of processes whose individual members are defined, on the independent variable side, by the beliefs that initiate these processes and, on the dependent variable side, by the consequences of these belief-initiated activities.

On the independent variable side, behavioral confirmation processes are initiated by beliefs, the targets of which are other people. Clearly, other people are not the only targets of individual's beliefs. Beliefs also may concern one's own personal attributes. Accordingly, it is appropriate to ask whether such beliefs about the self can and do have reality-constructing consequences, and to ask whether individuals may act upon their beliefs about the self in ways that produce evidence that would tend to confirm those beliefs.

Also on the independent variable side, there may exist categorical differences in the nature of the beliefs that initiate reality-constructing processes. In investigations of behavioral confirmation, the beliefs involved were assumptions about the personalities of other people. Thus, for example, there have been demonstrations of behavioral confirmation processes initiated by individuals' assumptions about the kinds of personalities possessed by people of attractive or unattractive appearance, assumptions about the typical personalities of women and of men, and assumptions about the hostile or nonhostile natures of other people (see Section II). Yet, not all beliefs (whether about other people or about the self) are in the nature of assumptions that are accepted without question. Other beliefs are more in the nature of hypotheses, accepted tentatively, open to questioning, and subject to activities designed to verify or falsify those hypotheses. Thus, you may wonder whether or not a friend of a friend is as intellectually inclined as the friend is, whether or not a new student will have the same esteem for you as previous students have had, whether or not you are a truly likable person, or whether or not you have the personal qualities needed for a career in research. Accordingly, it is appropriate to ask whether such hypotheses (whether about other people or about the self) can and do initiate activities that produce evidence that would tend to confirm these hypotheses.

On the dependent variable side, the outcome of behavioral confirmation is manifested in the behavior of the target of an individual's beliefs. It is possible in principle to specify and in practice to investigate another manifestation of processes initiated by an individual's beliefs. That manifestation is information about the target of these beliefs as thought about and as remembered by the individual. Thus, one may ask whether an individual's beliefs can and do influence subsequent cognitive activities such that the individual will be particularly likely to think about and to remember information that bolsters and supports the individual's beliefs. That is, one may ask whether there exist cognitive confirmation processes in addition to behavioral confirmation processes.

Therefore, it is possible to propose three sources of distinguishing features that together may provide a framework for a taxonomy of processes by which beliefs create reality:

1. A distinction about the *target* of the beliefs that initiate these processes (a distinction between an individual's beliefs about another person and an individual's beliefs about his or her own personal attributes).
2. A distinction about the *nature* of the initiating beliefs (a distinction between beliefs as assumptions and beliefs as hypotheses).
3. A distinction about the form of the *consequence* of these belief-initiated activities (a distinction between the target's behavior as it occurs in actual social contexts and the target's behavior as it occurs in thought and memory).

Taken together and considered as orthogonal to each other, these three sources of distinguishing features suggest that there are at least eight identifiable members of the family of processes by which beliefs create reality. These three sources of distinction and the resulting eight "belief creates reality" phenomena are represented in the eight cells of Table I. Although some categories in the taxonomy are better documented than others, there do exist demonstrations of each of the eight "belief creates reality" processes.

A. BEHAVIORAL CONSEQUENCES OF ASSUMPTIONS
    ABOUT OTHER PEOPLE

Evidence for the phenomenon of Cell 1 of the taxonomy of "belief creates reality" processes, defined by an individual's assumptions about another person as the independent variable and the behavior of that person as the dependent variable, is provided by investigations of behavioral confirmation processes (see Section II). In these investigations, one individual's beliefs about another person, even when they were erroneous ones, initiated a chain of events that led the other person to behave in ways that confirmed the first individual's initial beliefs (e.g., Andersen & Bem, 1981; Christensen & Rosenthal, 1982; Ickes, Patterson, Rajecki, & Tanford, 1982; Jones & Panitch, 1971; Kelley & Stahelski, 1970; Kuhlman & Wimberley, 1976; Miller & Holmes, 1975; Rosenthal, 1974; Rosenthal & Jacobson, 1968; Skrypnek & Snyder, 1982; Snyder & Swann, 1978a; Snyder et al., 1977; Swann & Snyder, 1980; von Baeyer et al., 1981; Word et al., 1974; Zanna & Pack, 1975).

Closely related to the consequences of one individual's beliefs about the personal attributes of another person are the consequences of one individual's estimates of another person's beliefs about the first individual. The outcomes of several investigations of this phenomenon suggest that individuals' assumptions

TABLE I

A TAXONOMY OF "BELIEF CREATES REALITY" PROCESSES

Consequences or dependent variable features	Antecedents or independent variable features			
	An individual's beliefs about other people		An individual's beliefs about the self	
	Beliefs as assumptions	Beliefs as hypotheses	Beliefs as assumptions	Beliefs as hypotheses
Target's behavior as it actually occurs	1	3	5	7
Target's behavior as it is remembered	2	4	6	8

about how other people view them affect their behavior in ways that actually cause other people to behave toward them as if they did view them that way.

Farina, Gliha, Boudreau, Allen, and Sherman (1971) measured the impact on psychiatric patients of their belief that others were aware of their psychiatric history. Patients interacted with another individual (actually a confederate) in a cooperative task. Half of the patients believed that their partner knew that they were psychiatric patients. The remainder believed that their partners did not know that they were psychiatric patients. In fact, the confederates did not ever know whether their partners were patients or nonpatients. Nevertheless, believing that others were aware of their status caused the identified patients to feel less appreciated, to find the task more difficult, and to perform rather poorly. Moreover, objective observers perceived them to be more tense, more anxious, and more poorly adjusted than the patients who believed that their partners did not know of their status. Apparently, the belief that others might perceive them as stigmatized individuals caused them to act in ways consistent with such a deviant status.

Moreover, the behavior of individuals who believe that others regard them as stigmatized, in turn, may affect the behavior of others with whom these individuals interact. In particular, empirical research has indicated that individuals who anticipate social rejection from others often bring on the feared rejection. Farina, Allen, and Saul (1968) led college students to believe that they had revealed to another person that they were stigmatized (for example, that they had a history of mental illness). In fact, the other person always received the same neutral information. However, merely believing that another person viewed them as stigmatized influenced the students' behaviors and caused them to be rejected by the other person. Perhaps the stigmatized individuals expected to be viewed negatively by others and rejected by them, and acted in ways that led to this rejection.

These investigations of the behavioral confirmation of stigmatizing labels lend credence to the observations of Goffman (1963) who has written extensively about the plight of stigmatized social groups. The essence of his argument is that people often "force" the stigmatized to play stereotyped roles. For example, he claims that many people want to feel sorry for the handicapped. Therefore, the handicapped can anticipate gains from behaving in ways that evoke pity. The net result is that the handicapped often act out the role that society has laid down for them. In a similar vein, Scott (1969) has written of the blind

> When, for example, sighted people continually insist that a blind man is helpless because he is blind, their subsequent treatment of him may preclude his own exercising the kinds of skills that would enable him to be independent. It is in this sense that stereotypic beliefs are self-actualized. (p. 9)

Evidently, the behavioral consequences of beliefs as assumptions are clearly defined ones. Whether they are initiated by the individual's beliefs about another person or by assumptions about another person's beliefs about him or her, belief-guided activities can and do influence the contributions of both the parties in the course of social interaction with the outcome being behavioral confirmation for the initiating assumptions.

B. COGNITIVE CONSEQUENCES OF ASSUMPTIONS ABOUT OTHER PEOPLE

The phenomenon of Cell 2 of the taxonomy of "belief creates reality" processes is defined by, on the independent variable side of the equation, an individual's assumptions about another person and, on the dependent variable side of the equation, the behavior of that other person as remembered by the first individual. A series of investigations of this phenomenon has revealed that, when an individual attempts to remember previously learned information about another person, the individual will remember and interpret past events in the other person's life history in ways that bolster and support the individual's current beliefs about the other person, even if these beliefs are erroneous assumptions about the other person.

1. The "Betty K" Investigation

Typically, in investigations of this "reconstruction" phenomenon, individuals have read life histories that were followed later by information that induced assumptions about the main character in the life history. The extent to which they remembered the life history in ways that confirmed their current assumptions then were measured. In one such investigation, Snyder and Uranowitz (1978a) had students read identical biographies of a woman named Betty K. One week later they learned something about Betty K's current life-style: Students learned that she was now living with another woman in a lesbian relationship; at the same time, others learned that she was now living with her husband in a heterosexual relationship.

Betty K's life story followed her from birth through childhood, education, and choice of profession. It included facts about her early home life, her relationship with her parents, her social life in high school and in college. The events of Betty K's life were based on beliefs and assumptions about female sexuality held by the student population from which the participants for this investigation were recruited. According to the prevailing image of the lesbian woman, she had an abusive father, never had a steady boyfriend, never dated men, and was rather unattractive. By contrast, the typical image of the heterosexual woman included a tranquil childhood, frequent dates with men, a steady boyfriend, and rather attractive looks. In accord with these beliefs, Betty K had a background rich in events that fit with either image. For example, although she never had a steady boyfriend in high school, she did go out on dates. And, although she did have a steady boyfriend in college, he was more of a close friend than an intimate companion.

To measure the impact of these assumptive beliefs about sexuality, Snyder and Uranowitz (1978a) asked each student to think back carefully over the biography of Betty K that they had read 1 week ago and answer, as accurately as they possibly could, a series of multiple-choice questions about actual events in Betty K's life history. The answers to these objective questions revealed that the students had *reconstructed* the events of Betty K's past in ways that supported their own assumptions and beliefs about her sexual orientation. Those who believed that Betty K was now living a lesbian life-style reconstructed the events of her life to fit with their assumptions about lesbians. For example, they may have remembered the fact that Betty K never had a steady boyfriend in high school, but neglected the fact that she had gone out on many dates in college. Those who believed that Betty K was now living a heterosexual life-style reconstructed the events of Betty K's life to fit with their expectations of heterosexual women. Thus, they may have remembered the fact that Betty K had formed a steady relationship with a man in college, but ignored the fact that this relationship had more the nature of a friendship than a romance. These outcomes occurred in spite of the fact that Betty K's life history was equally rich in events that fit with beliefs and assumptions about the backgrounds of lesbian and heterosexual women.

Further analyses of these outcomes suggested that separate processes of "differential accuracy" and "differential error" contributed to reconstruction. That is, not only were participants better able to identify accurately those facts of Betty K's life that confirmed their assumptions about her sexuality, but also, when they erred in answering questions about Betty K's life, their errors reflected their newly acquired assumptions about her sexuality. Additional evidence suggests that reconstruction is best characterized as the product of an interaction between conceptions of female sexuality and genuine memory for factual events (for details, see Snyder & Uranowitz, 1978a).

Clearly, as historians, the students in these investigations had allowed their preconceptions about lesbians and heterosexuals to dictate the way they wrote and rewrote the life and times of Betty K. This reconstructive activity becomes all the more intriguing when one considers that the beliefs and assumptions on which Betty K's history were based are essentially inaccurate ones. As Money and Erhardt (1972) have concluded "The state of knowledge as of the present does not permit any hypotheses (many psychodynamic claims to the contrary) that will predict with certainty which biographical conditions will ensure that [a] boy or girl will become erotically homosexual, bisexual, or heterosexual" (p. 235). Yet, as long as erroneous beliefs and assumptions about sexuality make it easy to remember evidence that supports these beliefs and assumptions and difficult to bring to mind evidence that questions them, people will continue to cling tenaciously to these erroneous articles of faith.

2. Further "Betty K" Investigations

Three years after the publication of the original Betty K experiment (Snyder & Uranowitz, 1978a), two "failures to replicate" appeared in the published literature (Bellezza & Bower, 1981; Clark & Woll, 1981). Because each of these attempted replications employed the original experimental materials, including the narrative about Betty K and the multiple-choice measure of recognition memory, they obviously cast a cloud over the original Betty K experiment as a demonstration of the reconstructive process. Of course, one could suggest some rather obvious, but nonetheless plausible, candidates for discounting these failures to replicate. Perhaps stereotyped beliefs about the differences between lesbians and heterosexuals had faded (possibly as a result of the increasing visibility and impact of educational campaigns designed to erase these and other stereotypes about sexuality) from the time of the original demonstrations to the time of the attempted replications. And, perhaps, this fading was particularly likely in the state of California (often thought to be a setter of trends in matters of sexuality) where the attempts to replicate occurred. To assess directly each of these possibilities would require appropriate manipulation checks to confirm that subjects who participated in the attempted replications possessed the very same beliefs about sexuality as those who served as the foundation for the Betty K narrative. Unfortunately, neither of the attempted replications contained manipulation checks of this nature. Needless to say, the absence of these critically important manipulation checks makes it difficult to assess the implications of these attempted replications.

It is nevertheless important to recognize that reconstruction prompted by beliefs about sexuality has been demonstrated in procedural paradigms other than that employed in the original investigation and the two attempted replications. One such replication assessed remembering of the facts of Betty K's life with a free-recall measure in place of the recognition memory measure of the original study (Snyder & Uranowitz, 1978c). In this replication, participants read the history of Betty K and later learned either that she was living a heterosexual life-style, that she was living a lesbian life-style, or nothing about her current life-style. They then wrote an essay reporting as many facts about Betty K as they possibly could recall. After direct references to Betty K's sexual life-style had been deleted from the essays, judges classified the essays based on their best estimates of the writer's beliefs about Betty K's sexual life-style. These judges correctly classified essays written by those who believed that Betty K was living a lesbian life-style with substantially better-than-chance accuracy. Judges, however, could not classify ''heterosexual'' or ''no-information'' essays at a rate any better than chance. Evidently, biographers of a purportedly lesbian Betty K recounted her history in ways that communicated their beliefs about her sexual life-style to readers of their essays.

Moreover, evidence of reconstructive activity in thinking about the life history of Betty K is provided by an investigation of retrospective reinterpretation prompted by the newly acquired information about Betty K's sexual lifestyle. Students in one such investigation interpreted the facts of Betty K's life (as they remembered them) in ways that added fresh support and confirmation for their beliefs about her sexual orientation (Snyder & Uranowitz, 1978b). They put their interpretive skills to work when they remembered events that fit their beliefs (for example, one student who accurately remembered that a supposedly lesbian Betty K never had a steady boyfriend in high school confidently pointed to the fact as an early sign of her lack of romantic and sexual interest in men) and when they remembered events that contradicted their beliefs (for example, a student who correctly remembered that a purportedly lesbian Betty K often went out on dates in college was sure that these dates were signs of Betty K's early attempts to mask her lesbian interests and to ''pass'' as heterosexual). In general, as interpreters of Betty K's life, these students construed whatever they remembered (accurately or inaccurately) about Betty K's past as evidence of her emerging sexual orientation.

3. Beyond the "Betty K" Investigations

It also is possible to go beyond these demonstrations and witness reconstructive activities in contexts that do not involve the life history of Betty K and even in those that do not involve beliefs and assumptions about sexuality. In an investigation of reconstruction that abandoned entirely the Betty K biography and focused on the reconstruction of aspects of expressive behavior and self-presentation style, Uranowitz, Skrypnek, and Snyder (1978) had participants watch one of two videotaped conversations between a man and a woman. Each of these interactions had been staged to provide no firm impressions of the two characters. After viewing the videotape, some participants read questionnaires describing the man and the woman in the videotape. One of the items in the questionnaires revealed the character's sexual preferences. All participants learned that the man was heterosexual. Half learned that the woman was heterosexual; half, that she was lesbian.

Participants then reported their retrospective estimates of the impressions they had formed while watching the videotape. Those who learned that the woman was lesbian ''remembered'' that she had seemed to them to be less secure, less sexually warm, less sociable, and less happy. They also were less likely to want her as a friend, less favorable in their overall impressions, and saw themselves as less similar to her. Moreover, when the female character had been labeled after the fact as lesbian, participants "remembered" that she had rarely smiled at the man, hardly flirted with him at all, acted coolly toward him. That is, participants seemed to have reconstructed the impressions that they formed of the target woman during the conversation as if they actually had seen on the videotapes all the expressive behaviors implied by their current assumptions about her sexual orientation. For a related demonstration, see Gross, Green, Storck, and Vanyur (1980).

Moreover, one can move outside the domain of beliefs about sexuality altogether and still witness evidence of reconstructive processes in action. Uranowitz (1981a) had individuals read identical information about another person. This information concerned the social activities engaged in by that person over the course of the past week. Some of these activities were extraverted in character, an equal number of these activities were introverted in character, and other activities were neutral with regard to extraversion and introversion. Two days later, these individuals learned that they were about to interact with the person about whom they previously had read in a social situation for which either a rather extraverted person or a rather introverted person would be particularly appropriate as an interaction partner.

When asked in an independent context to recall the information that they had read about the other person, individuals preferentially recalled behavioral evidence confirming that their partners were the type of persons appropriate to the anticipated interaction. Individuals anticipating interaction in a situation calling for an extravert were particularly likely to remember the extraverted activities and those anticipating interaction in a situation calling for an introvert were particularly likely to remember the introverted activities in which their partner had engaged over the course of the previous week. This reconstructive outcome occurred in spite of the fact that the information these individuals had read had indicated that their interaction partners actually had engaged in equal numbers of extraverted and introverted activities.

Furthermore, just as there is evidence of the reconstructive influence of an individual's beliefs about the personal attributes of another person, so, too, is there evidence of the influence of an individual's estimates of another person's beliefs about the individual on memory for behavioral information relevant to those estimates. Swann and Hill (1981) informed some students that they had been diagnosed by a team of clinicians as emotional types and informed other students that they had been diagnosed as nonemotional types. Still other students received no diagnosis at all. When discrepant from these students' own self-conceptions as emotional or nonemotional individuals, these diagnoses increased the ease with which the students could retrieve from memory information relevant to these diagnostic labels.

These investigations, taken as a set, seem to provide converging evidence for the operation of reconstructive processes in remembering behavioral events. An individual, having adopted particular beliefs and assumptions about another person, will remember and interpret events in that person's past history in ways that bolster and support the individual's current beliefs and assumptions. As a consequence, prevailing beliefs and assumptions will gain added cognitive reality, and even beliefs and assumptions that initially are erroneous and mistaken may gain an illusion of reality from the support and confirmation that are provided by reconstructive processes of thought and memory.

C. BEHAVIORAL CONSEQUENCES OF HYPOTHESES
    ABOUT OTHER PEOPLE

The phenomenon of Cell 3 of the taxonomy of "belief creates reality" processes is defined, on the independent variable side of the equation, by an individual's hypotheses about another person and, on the dependent variable side of the equation, by the actual behavior of that person in social interactions during which the individual attempts to test these hypotheses. The hypotheses that individuals formulate and test in the course of their relationships with other people may be of rather diverse origins. When individuals form first impressions of other people, they may test hypotheses based upon expectations about their newfound acquaintances' personal dispositions (Is this new acquaintance as shy as a mutual friend has led me to believe?). Similarly, when individuals judge familiar people according to novel criteria, they may test hypotheses based upon these newly relevant standards of comparison (Does that friend possess the personal attributes that define the ideal candidate for a career in politics?). Finally, when individuals question the accuracy of existing beliefs about friends, they may test hypotheses based on alternative interpretations of their natures (Is this friend whom I have always liked really as mean tempered as everyone now tells me?).

Having formulated hypotheses about the personal attributes of other people, individuals may proceed to test these hypotheses. In particular, individuals may use their subsequent interactions as opportunities to gather and collect behavioral evidence with which to test these hypotheses. The typical strategy that individuals formulate and enact to test hypotheses in social interaction is that already documented in Section III, the confirmatory strategy of preferentially soliciting behavioral evidence whose presence would tend to confirm rather than to disconfirm the hypothesis under scrutiny (e.g., Snyder & Swann, 1978b).

The commitment to confirmatory hypothesis-testing strategies appears to be a widespread one. It seems to matter hardly at all to individuals where their hypotheses originate (Snyder & Swann, 1978b), how likely it is that their hypotheses will prove accurate or inaccurate (Snyder & Swann, 1978b), whether they are given explicit information about the probable personalities of their targets in addition to the personality type against which they were to test the target (Semin & Strack, 1980), whether the hypotheses explicitly define both confirming and disconfirming attributes (Snyder & Campbell, 1980), whether substantial incentives for accurate hypothesis testing are offered (Snyder & Swann, 1978b), or whether explicit explanations of the potential informativeness of disconfirming evidence are provided (Snyder et al., 1982). In each case, individuals choose to preferentially solicit (by means of the questions that they plan to ask of their targets) behavioral evidence that would tend to confirm their hypotheses (for reviews, see Snyder, 1981c; Snyder & Gangestad, 1981).

Although the hypotheses in this series of investigations always concerned the possible extraverted or introverted nature of another person, the formulation of confirmatory strategies is not limited to hypotheses in this domain. Confirmatory strategies for testing hypotheses about other people have been formulated when individuals have faced the task of testing hypotheses concerning another person's level of dominance or submissiveness (Swann & Giuliano, 1983), another person's level of anxiety (Riggs & Cantor, 1981), another person's level of emotional stability (Sackett, 1980), another person's possession of the attributes of the elderly (Carver & de la Garza, 1982; Rodin & Langer, 1980), or another person's similarity to the modal personality associated with various occupational categories (Snyder et al., 1982; Snyder & Cantor, 1979). Confirmatory hypothesis-testing strategies have been observed even when testing for the projected viability or failure of organizations and business firms (e.g., Kida, 1984).

In addition, the prevalence of confirmatory strategies seems not to be dependent on several features common to most of these investigations. Although most of these investigations have involved hypotheses that were provided explicitly to participants, confirmatory strategies have occurred even when hypotheses about other people are supplied implicitly by features of participants' own personal identities (e.g., Fong & Markus, 1982). Moreover, although most of these investigations employed a task in which individuals chose questions from a set of questions provided to them by the experimenter, the formulation of confirmatory hypothesis-testing strategies is evident even when participants generate their own questions to ask the targets of their hypotheses (e.g., Swann & Giuliano, 1983). Moreover, one need not even employ the question-asking format itself to witness the formulation of confirmatory hypothesis-testing strategies. Rather, it is sufficient simply to ask individuals in a completely unstructured response format to list the types of evidence that they would need to test hypotheses under consideration (e.g., Carver & de la Garza, 1982). And, although in investigations using the question-choosing task, participants have chosen all of their questions in advance of any opportunity to interview the targets of their hypotheses, confirmatory hypothesis-testing strategies occur nevertheless even when individuals choose their questions one at a time and, therefore, can modify their hypothesis-testing strategies in response to the information provided by answers to their questions (Sackett, 1980).

There have been some suggestions (e.g., Trope & Bassok, 1982) that, in question selection tasks, the features that define individual members of the question sets as those that solicit confirmatory evidence and those that solicit disconfirmatory evidence are both the probability of the behavioral evidence solicited by the question (i.e., the likelihood that the behavior in question would be displayed by those who confirm or disconfirm the hypothesis) and the diagnosticity of the behavioral evidence solicited by the question (i.e., the differential likelihood of occurrence of behavior in question in individuals who confirm and those who disconfirm the hypothesis). However, as Swann and Giuliano (1983) have shown, the very act of entertaining a hypothetical belief increases the perceived disparity of evidence that promises to confirm and evidence that would disconfirm that hypothetical belief. Therefore, any concerns about whether individuals differentially prefer confirmatory or diagnostic information are moot, since the two types of information frequently are the same thing in the minds of individuals as hypothesis testers.

D. COGNITIVE CONSEQUENCES OF HYPOTHESES ABOUT OTHER PEOPLE

The phenomenon of Cell 4 of the taxonomy of "belief creates reality" processes is defined, on the independent variable side of the equation, by an individual's hypotheses about another person and, on the dependent variable side of the equation, by the behavior of that other person as remembered by the first individual. This use of remembered behavioral information to test hypotheses about other people reflects the fact that, often in the course of their relationships with other people, individuals acquire considerable amounts of information about the behavior of other people, knowledge that may provide evidence relevant for testing hypotheses about other people.

1. Hypotheses about Particular People

To investigate the processes by which individuals use remembered information about other people in their hypothesis-testing activities, Snyder and Cantor (1979) had individuals read accounts of 1 week in the life of a woman named Jane. Two days later, these individuals used this historical knowledge to test hypotheses about Jane's suitability to apply for either the rather extraverted job of real estate salesperson or the rather introverted job of research librarian. Jane's history was constructed to provide considerable support for either hypothesis. In different situations and with different people she was equally likely to behave in extraverted and introverted fashion. In their hypothesis-testing activities, participants first reported those previously learned facts about Jane that they regarded as relevant to deciding her suitability to apply for the job, and then reported their judgments about her suitability for the job.

To test their hypotheses, participants preferentially reported as relevant factual information that would confirm their hypotheses. To test the hypothesis about Jane's suitability for the job of real estate salesperson, participants were particularly likely to report instances of Jane's extraverted behaviors. To test the hypothesis about Jane's suitability for the job of research librarian, they were particularly likely to report instances of Jane's introverted behaviors. Moreover, after preferentially remembering hypothesis-confirming information, participants came to accept their hypotheses. Having tested a hypothesis about Jane's suitability for one job, participants judged her to be better suited to apply for that job than for the other job. As a consequence of basing their judgments about Jane's personal attributes on the outcome of confirmatory hypothesis-testing activities, what was once only a hypothesis for these individuals became, in their minds at least, a reality.

In related research on the cognitive confirmation of hypotheses about other people, Darley and Gross (1983) examined the consequences of hypotheses about a child's ability level provided by information about her socioeconomic background. Observers watched a videotape of a child taking an academic ability test. Those who believed that she came from a high socioeconomic background later cited evidence from the previously observed ability test to support their judgment that her abilities were well above grade level. By contrast, those who believed she was the product of a low socioeconomic background cited evidence they thought they had gleaned from watching the ability test to validate their judgments that she was below her grade level in academic ability. Darley and Gross (1983) interpreted their findings as suggesting that the information about socioeconomic background, and associated stereotypes, created hypotheses that individuals tested with confirmatory strategies, the outcome of which was false cognitive confirmation for those stereotype-based hypotheses.

Further insight into the dynamics of cognitive confirmation processes is provided by investigations of the processes of explaining and interpreting behavior (e.g., Kulik, 1983; Langer & Abelson, 1974; Zadny & Gerard, 1974). For example, Kulik (1983) has documented the following confirmatory attributional process. When observing and explaining the behavior of another person, individuals attributed behavior that was consistent with their prior conceptions of that person to his or her dispositional properties. At the same time, they attributed inconsistent behavior to pressures of the situation. Both of these attributional tendencies occurred even when circumstantial information indicated such inferences were not normatively warranted. Such confirmatory attributional processes, of course, tend to contribute to the perpetuation of any hypotheses that initiate them. To the extent that confirmatory behavioral evidence is accepted and given credence and disconfirmatory behavioral evidence is explained away, individuals will be adding to their stock of hypothesis-confirming evidence but not to their store of hypothesis-disconfirming evidence.

Confirmatory strategies for using remembered information to test hypotheses also characterize the attempts of individuals to evaluate the accuracy of other people's beliefs about them. In an examination of these activities, Swann and Read (1981a) provided participants either with the hypothesis that another person held favorable attitudes toward them or with the hypothesis that another person held unfavorable attitudes toward them. They then provided participants with the opportunity to test these hypotheses by listening to a tape recording of a set of statements (some of which were positive and some of which were negative) that the other person supposedly had made about them. Some time later, they asked participants to recall as many of their partner's evaluative statements as they possibly could.

Participants who hypothesized that their partners held favorable attitudes toward them remembered substantially more positive statements than negative statements. At the same time, participants who hypothesized that their partners held unfavorable attitudes toward them tended to remember more negative statements than positive statements. Evidently, participants preferentially remembered information about their partners' supposed behaviors that would tend to confirm their hypotheses about their partner's attitudes toward them. A related experiment (Swann & Read, 1981a) suggests that the locus of this confirmatory outcome is not to be found in differences in initial attention to the favorable and unfavorable statements. Rather, the locus of the phenomenon is likely to be found either in differential encoding or in differential retrieval of the positive and negative statements.

A phenomenon closely related to the use of remembered information to test hypotheses about people is that of incrimination through innuendo. Wegner, Wenzlaff, Kirker, and Beattie (1981) investigated the effects of incriminating innuendo offered by news media on impressions of the targets of innuendo. In their investigations, innuendo headlines (e.g., "Is Bob Talbert linked with Mafia?" "Is Andrew Winters connected to Bank Embezzlement?") caused readers to form distinctly negative impressions of the targets of these innuendos. One interpretation of the power of innuendos in actual news media is that innuendos constitute hypotheses about their targets (e.g., that an elected official may be active in organized crime), hypotheses that induce readers to preferentially remember previously reported news that would confirm these hypotheses (e.g., any and all previous hints of criminal activity, however slight the hint, on the part of that elected official). Having preferentially remembered the news that confirms the innuendo-based hypotheses, and not that which disconfirms it, readers of incriminating innuendos may then be swayed by them and adopt negative attitudes toward the targets of innuendos.

2. Hypotheses about Categories of People

The same preferential thinking about events that confirm hypotheses may also be evident when individuals are asked to contemplate the validity of propositions about human nature. Snyder and Gangestad (1982b) asked individuals what types of evidence they would seek to test the following hypothesis about human nature: Women are particularly susceptible to flattery and thus tend to comply with requests when smiled at and when given compliments. The evidence relevant to testing this hypothesis falls into the four categories defined by the compliance rates of, respectively, females who are flattered, females who are not flattered, males who are flattered, and males who are not flattered. Virtually all participants indicated that they would seek evidence of the compliance rate of females who are flattered, evidence that (if flattery induces compliance) would confirm the hypothesis. At the same time, substantially fewer participants indicated that they would seek evidence about the compliance rate of males who were observed and/or evidence of the compliance rate of targets who are not flattered. In fact, only one-third of the participants in this investigation indicated that they would seek all four types of evidence.

Needless to say, few individuals would ever actually carry out a formal survey of the compliance rates of women and men when flattered or not flattered. Nevertheless, in their attempt to bring to mind instances of previously observed behavior of friends and acquaintances that might be relevant to testing these hypotheses, many individuals might bring to mind precisely those instances that fall into the categories of evidence that participants in this investigation indicated they would seek in order to test the hypothesis. Thus, individuals who contemplated the proposition that women are particularly susceptible to requests accompanied by flattery might be particlarly likely to think of those times when they have observed women complying with requests when flattered, but somewhat less vigilant to searching their memories for instances of women complying with requests when not flattered or instances of the susceptibility of men to requests accompanied and not accompanied by flattery. Accordingly, such individuals would be more likely to encounter, in their memories, evidence that appears to confirm rather than evidence that appears to disconfirm this hypothesis about human nature.

In fact, other research on the testing of hypotheses about categories of people and their associated behavioral tendencies suggests precisely this outcome. Snyder and Gangestad (1982b) asked participants to recall information about people they have known in their own lives relevant to testing one of four hypotheses: (1) that endomorphs, as opposed to ectomorphs, tend to be relaxed and sociable rather than restrained and anxious, (2) that endomorphs, as opposed to ectomorphs, tend to be restrained and anxious rather than relaxed and sociable, (3) that ectomorphs, as opposed to endomorphs, tend to be relaxed and sociable rather than restrained and anxious, and (4) that ectomorphs, as opposed to endomorphs, tend to be restrained and anxious rather than relaxed and sociable. Results indicated that participants selectively reported instances that tended to confirm, rather than disconfirm, their hypotheses. Further analyses showed that this general effect occurred both within the immediate domain of the hypothesis and the comparison domain of the hypothesis. Thus, for instance, given the hypothesis that endomorphs, as opposed to ectomorphs, tend to be relaxed and sociable rather than restrained and anxious, participants reported more instances of endomorphs who were relaxed and sociable than of endomorphs who were restrained and anxious. At the same time, participants reported greater numbers of ectomorphs who were restrained and anxious than ectomorphs who were relaxed and sociable. Finally, participants' assessments of the truth or falsity of the hypotheses were sensitive to their tendency to report more confirmatory than disconfirmatory instances.

The consequences of confirmatory activities in thought and memory, whether the targets of these activities are specific people or categories of people, are that attempts to assess the accuracy of hypotheses about other people will make it all the more likely that beliefs that begin as hypotheses will come to be accepted as facts, even when there may exist considerable amounts of evidence that would disconfirm those beliefs, evidence that may go undetected by confirmatory strategies for thinking about and remembering information with which to test these hypotheses.

E. BEHAVIORAL CONSEQUENCES OF ASSUMPTIONS
    ABOUT THE SELF

The phenomenon of Cell 5 of the taxonomy of "belief creates reality" processes is defined, on the independent variable side of the equation, by an individual's assumptions about himself or herself and, on the dependent variable side of the equation, by the actual behavior of that individual and other people with whom he or she interacts. With respect to the influence of assumptions about the self on the individual's own behavior, there exists considerable evidence that individuals often take actions that provide them with opportunities to act upon and maintain features of their conceptions of self. And, with respect to the influence of assumptions about the self on the behavior of other people, there exists substantial evidence that individuals often act in ways that elicit behaviors from others supportive of their own conceptions of self.

1. The Actions of Self

Research on the behavioral consequences of features of self-conception suggests that individuals who regard themselves as extraverts, more so than those who regard themselves as introverts, seek out stimulating social situations that involve assertiveness, competitiveness, and intimacy, and that provide opportunities to engage in extraverted behaviors (Furnham, 1982). Similarly, those who regard themselves as sensation seekers seek out sensation-providing leisure situations (Zuckerman, 1974) and those who think of themselves as authoritarians gravitate toward authoritarian educational settings (Stern, Stein, & Bloom, 1956). Moreover, individuals who believe that their own actions can influence their outcomes look for situations in which their outcomes are determined by their own skills; at the same time, individuals who believe that their own actions cannot influence their outcomes look for situations in which their outcomes are determined by chance (Kahle, 1980).

In addition, individuals who regard themselves as competent, intelligent people strive to protect, preserve, and sustain their images of self-competence by strategic "self-handicapping" actions that make it easier for them to externalize (i.e., explain away) their failure and to internalize (i.e., take credit for) their successes (e.g., Jones & Berglas, 1978; Berglas & Jones, 1978). Among these self-handicapping strategies are those practiced by persistent gamblers who tend to accept their wins at face value but invest considerable time and effort in explaining away their losses (Gilovich, 1983), a self-handicapping strategy whose use may contribute to the billions of dollars lost every year at casinos and racetracks. Also among these self-handicapping strategies is the reporting of symptoms of physical illness and other physical complaints in circumstances in which poor health could legitimize poor performance, a self-protective strategy that seems to be particularly characteristic of hypochondriacal individuals (Smith, Snyder, & Perkins, 1983).

Finally, high self-monitoring individuals, who regard themselves as pragmatic creatures who strive to mold and tailor their self-presentational behavior to social and interpersonal cues to situational appropriateness, gravitate toward social situations that permit them to act upon their pragmatic sense of self, and low self-monitoring individuals, who regard themselves as principled beings who strive to enforce consistency and correspondence between their social behavior and underlying attitudes and dispositions, gravitate toward social situations that permit them to act upon their principled sense of self (Snyder, 1979, 1982b, 1983; Snyder & Gangestad, 1982a; Snyder & Kendzierski, 1982).

In each case, individuals appear to seek out social situations that will foster and encourage the behavioral expression of features of their conceptions of self. To the extent that they succeed in regularly and consistently spending time in these situations, and to the extent that these situations promote the regular and consistent display of behavioral manifestations of these features of their self-conceptions, these individuals will come to create and enforce congruence between their beliefs about themselves and their behavior in social contexts.

2. The Actions of Other People

A clearly defined example of the influence of one individual's conception of self on the behavior of other people is that reported by Kelley and Stahelski (1970), in which individuals who conceived of themselves as competitively oriented behaved toward other people in ways that elicited from them competitive actions, even if those other people were not by nature disposed to compete. In a similar vein, Fong and Markus (1982) have demonstrated that individuals who were "schematic" in the domain of extraversion (i.e., regarded extraverted behaviors as typical of and important to them) preferentially solicited manifestations of extraversion in other people. In addition, Swann and Read (1981b) have demonstrated that individuals who conceive of themselves as assertive and those who conceive of themselves as emotional will take actions designed to solicit behavioral evidence from others that confirms their self-conceptions within the domains of assertiveness and emotionality. They seem sufficiently motivated to solicit this social feedback that they will do so even at some monetary costs to themselves (Swann & Read, 1981b).

A particularly intriguing manifestation of this phenomenon is provided by the interpersonal dynamics of depression. Coyne (1976b) has argued that depressed individuals behave in ways that arouse hostility, resentment, and rejection in other people. In a demonstration of this process, Coyne (1976a) arranged for clinically depressed patients to converse with nondepressed nonpatients. After these conversations, the nondepressed nonpatients themselves ended up feeling depressed, anxious, hostile, and rejecting toward the depressed patients. More recently, Strack and Coyne (1983) have documented the same processes with persons drawn from a "normal" population who were experiencing depressed mood states. They, too, provoked anxious, depressed, and hostile feelings in those who conversed with them and were rejected by their conversation partners. Similar scenarios and outcomes have been observed by Hammen and Peters (1978) and by Howes and Hokanson (1979). In addition, in the domain of anxiety, Riggs and Cantor (1981) have found that individuals who conceive of themselves as anxious interact with other people in ways that cause them, too, to show signs of being anxious people.

F. COGNITIVE CONSEQUENCES OF ASSUMPTIONS
   ABOUT THE SELF

The phenomenon of Cell 6 of the taxonomy of "belief creates reality" processes is defined, on the independent variable side of the equation, by an individual's assumptions about himself or herself and, on the dependent variable side of the equation, by that individual's remembering of behavioral information relevant to those beliefs. Research on this phenomenon suggests that, as historians of their own lives, individuals are particularly likely to remember those events that are congruent with their current conceptions of themselves, including their currently held attitudes (e.g., Bem & McConnell, 1970; Ross, McFarland, & Fletcher, 1981; Wixon & Laird, 1976), their current statements about their actions (e.g., Bem, 1966; Maslach, 1971), their current mood states (e.g., Bower, 1981; Isen, Shalker, Clark, & Karp, 1978; Laird, Wagener, Halal, & Szegda, 1982; Snyder & White, 1982), and their currently dominant motives (e.g., McAdams, 1982).

1. The Effects of Current Attitudes

One week after reporting their attitudes on an issue of concern to them, students in an experiment reported by Bem and McConnell (1970) wrote essays opposing their own attitudes. Those who wrote their essays under conditions of relatively free choice (of the form offered in "forced compliance" situations) shifted their attitudes in the direction of their essays. Immediately after writing their essays, some of these students had to remember the attitudes they had expressed 1 week earlier. These students "recalled" not their "old" attitudes they actually had reported, but attitudes that reflected their "new" attitudes formed after writing their counterattitudinal essays. This outcome, in which current attitudes have influenced the remembering of previous expressions of attitudes, has been replicated by Wixon and Laird (1976).

In addition, Ross *et al.* (1981) and Ross, McFarland, Conway, and Zanna (1983) have offered further evidence of the influence of currently held attitudes on the remembering of personal histories. For example, in each of two studies, Ross *et al.* (1981) first manipulated participants' attitudes by means of persuasive messages and then had them recall past behaviors relevant to the newly formed attitudes. Thus, for example, participants who formerly held positive attitudes toward the effects of toothbrushing but who now had been persuaded that frequent toothbrushing actually was quite dangerous and could harm the enamel and gums recalled fewer instances of toothbrushing in the previous week than participants who had been exposed to messages supporting frequent brushing of the teeth. This influence of newly acquired attitudes, whereby individuals preferentially remember those of their previous actions that support their current attitudes, seems to be particularly characteristic of individuals low in self-monitoring (Snyder, 1979), for whom consistency between attitudes and behavior typically is substantial (e.g., Snyder, 1982c) and relatively atypical of high self-monitoring individuals for whom attitudes and behavior often are unrelated in a wide variety of domains.

2. The Effects of Current Statements

Closely related to these demonstrations of the influence of current attitudes on the remembering of the past are demonstrations of the effects of one's current statements about one's actions on memory for one's actual actions. The clearest demonstration of this phenomenon is Bem's investigation of false confessions (1966). Students participated in an experiment, supposedly on lie detection, in which they first crossed out specified words on a list, and then learned to tell the truth in the presence of a "truth light" and to tell lies in the presence of a "lie light." They then were required to state that they previously had crossed out some words and not crossed out other words. When these "confessions" were false, but had been made in the presence of the truth light, participants came to believe in their false confessions. They committed more errors of recall and expressed less confidence in the accuracy of their recall than they did after either false confessions uttered in the presence of the lie light or after making no confessions at all.

In a replication of this experiment, Maslach (1971) verified the effect of the truth light on false confessions. It produced more errors of recall after false confessions. However, in her experiment, the truth light also produced more errors of recall after true confessions, although not to the same extent that it did after false confessions. This pattern of findings suggests that the effects of the truth light may not be so much one of inducing individuals to accept the truth of their current statements but rather one of inducing individuals to be less vigilant about verifying the truth or falsity of their current statements. Nevertheless, whatever the precise mediator of the false confessions effect, the fact is that, as a consequence of their false confessions made in truth-telling circumstances, these participants evidently came to "remember" that they actually had performed the actions to which they now confessed.

3. The Effects of Current Mood States

Based upon the outcomes of several investigations, it appears that individuals preferentially remember those past events and past experiences whose affective quality is congruent with their current mood states. To demonstrate the impact of current mood states on the remembering of the past, Snyder and White (1982) induced individuals to experience the moods of elation or depression and then permitted them to reminisce about the events of their lives. Individuals in an elated mood were particularly likely to remember the pleasant events and the happy experiences of their lives. By contrast, individuals in a depressed mood were particularly likely to remember the unpleasant events and the sad experiences of their lives.

Taken together with related demonstrations by Isen et al. (1978) who have demonstrated the influence of winning games on the recall of previously learned positive words, these findings by Teasdale and Fogarty (1979) who have demonstrated the influence of happy and sad mood states on the speed of retrieval of pleasant memories, by Bower (1981) who has demonstrated the influence of hypnotically induced pleasant and unpleasant mood states on the remembering of personal episodes, and by Laird *et al.* (1982) who have demonstrated the effect of mood changes induced by manipulating facial expressions on recall of previously read material, all provide support for a proposition offered by, among others, Freud (1914/1901) and Bartlett (1932).

One potential consequence of the preferential remembering of mood congruent events is the perpetuation of current mood states. For example, the more unhappy experiences that a depressed person recalls, the more reasons that he or she may feel he or she has for being depressed. It may even be that attempts to understand and to cope with one's moods by thinking about the events that could account for one's moods may have the unintended effect of consolidating and perpetuating one's moods. In addition, attempts to help others understand and cope with their moods (in particular, their depressed moods) by encouraging them to talk about relevant events in their lives also may serve unintentionally to consolidate and perpetuate their mood states.

4. The Effects of Motives

In an exploration of autobiographical memory, McAdams (1982) examined the links between individuals' dominant motives and the themes that occur in their accounts of the events of their lives. To do so, McAdams first identified (by means of the Thematic Apperception Test) individuals for whom interpersonal intimacy and personal power were characteristically dominant motives. He then collected open-ended autobiographical recollections fro 1 these individuals and coded them for themes of interpersonal intimacy and personal power. He found that individuals who were high in intimacy motivation remembered experiences of intimacy (e.g., love and friendship, sharing, helping and being helped) to a greater extent than individuals low in intimacy motivation. Similarly, individuals high in power motivation remembered experiences of power (e.g., strength, impact, vigor, fame, recognition) more so than did individuals low in power motivation.

Clearly, for present purposes, it is tempting to interpret these findings in terms of individuals' current motives directing the remembering of autobiographical events. Yet, given the correlational nature of these findings, the possibility that it is the remembering of particular autobiographical events that influences individuals' current motives must also be recognized. What is needed is an experimental investigation in which particular individual motives are systematically aroused or manipulated, and the expectations of these experimentally induced motives on the remembering of the events of one's life are then assessed.

G. BEHAVIORAL CONSEQUENCES OF HYPOTHESES ABOUT THE SELF

The phenomenon of Cell 7 of the taxonomy of "belief creates reality" processes is defined, on the independent variable side of the equation, by an individual's hypotheses about himself or herself and, on the dependent variable side of the equation, by the actual behavior of that individual and other people with whom he or she interacts for purposes of testing these hypotheses.

The effect of individuals' hypotheses on their own subsequent behavior is demonstrated by studies reported by Sherman (e.g., 1980; Sherman, Skov, Hervitz, & Stock, 1981). For example, Sherman (1980) had individuals offer hypothetical predictions about their own future behavior. Although these hypothetical predictions typically were at odds with base rates for typical behaviors in the situations involved, the very act of offering these hypothetical predictions led individuals to behave in accord with their hypothetical predictions. Because their own actions provided behavioral confirmation for their hypotheses about themselves, the errors of their hypotheses effectively turned into self-erasing errors.

The effects of individuals' hypotheses on the behavior of others with whom they interact are demonstrated by a pair of studies reported by Swann (Swann & Hill, 1982; Swann & Read, 1981a). In each case, individuals learned that another person did not share their views of themselves. Thus, in the Swann and Hill study, some individuals who regarded themselves as dominant and forceful learned that they did not seem to another person to be the dominant and forceful type. And, in the Swann and Read study, individuals who regarded themselves as rather likable learned that another person just might regard them as dislikable. Effectively, these messages turned what had been assumptions about themselves into hypotheses about themselves. That is, participants were forced to recognize that it was but a hypothetical possibility that they really were the forceful, dominant types or that they really were the likable types that they thought themselves to be. In subsequent social interactions, these individuals behaved in ways clearly designed to bolster and confirm their own cherished conceptions of themselves, both in their own eyes and in the eyes of their interaction partners and any observers of the interaction. And they succeeded. In the Swann and Hill study, individuals who had had their assumptions about their forceful, dominant nature turned into hypotheses were observed by outsiders to behave in all the more dominant and forceful manner. And, in the Swann and Read study, individuals who had had their assumptions about their likable natures turned into hypotheses elicited particularly positive reactions from their interaction partners.

H. COGNITIVE CONSEQUENCES OF HYPOTHESES ABOUT THE SELF

The phenomenon of Cell 8 of the taxonomy of "belief creates reality" processes is defined, on the independent variable side of the equation, by an individual's hypotheses about himself or herself and, on the dependent variable side of the equation, by that individual's remembering of behavioral information relevant to those hypotheses. To examine this phenomenon, Snyder and Skrypnek (1981) investigated the ways that individuals test hypotheses prompted by the courses of action they must choose. Specifically, they explored the processes by which individuals decide whether or not they have the personal attributes that define the ideal candidates for particular jobs.

One source of information with which to test hypotheses about job suitability is knowledge about one's own personal characteristics and psychological attributes, one's own interests and preferences, one's own abilities and skills, one's own past behaviors and prior activities. That is, individuals may search for answers to the question "What do I know about myself that would help me make judgments about my own job suitability?" In their investigation, Snyder and Skrypnek (1981) had participants test either a hypothesis about their suitability to apply for a job that required the attributes and aptitudes of a "masculine" personality (e.g., one who is athletic, independent, and competitive, and has leadership ability, organizational ability, and supervisory ability) or a hypothesis concerning their suitability to apply for a job that required the attributes and aptitudes of a "feminine" personality (e.g., warmth, understanding, cheerfulness, playfulness, compassion, cooperativeness, and sensitivity).

Participants in this investigation first reported everything that they knew about themselves that they considered relevant to assessing their suitability for the job under consideration. They then reported their judgments of their own suitability for that job. In these hypothesis-testing activities, participants were particularly likely to report evidence of their suitedness for the job in question (that is, evidence that would confirm hypotheses about their job suitability); by contrast, they were particularly unlikely to report evidence that would indicate their unsuitedness for the job (that is, evidence that would tend to disconfirm hypotheses about their job suitability). Moreover, to the extent that they preferentially reported hypothesis-confirming evidence of their suitedness for the job, they were particularly likely to accept hypotheses about their job suitability.

In related work on testing hypotheses about the self, Pennebaker and Skelton (1981) investigated the effects of hypotheses on the experience of physical symptoms. In one of their investigations, individuals listened to a signal after they were provided with the hypothesis that the signal would increase, decrease, or have no effect on skin temperatures. The effects of these hypotheses were that participants preferentially monitored these changes in skin temperature that would confirm their hypotheses, and proceeded to report changes in their own skin temperature that confirmed their hypotheses.

The potential consequences of these confirmatory approaches to testing hypotheses about the self are that hypotheses about the self may gain considerable inertia. The very act of considering the possibility that one may be qualified for a job may leave one convinced of his or her actual suitability for the job. The very act of contemplating one's possible symptoms may leave one convinced that one actually possesses the symptoms and the disorders associated with them. What begin as hypotheses, conjectures, and possibilities may end up as realities.

V. Disconfirmation Outcomes

Of what consequence are an individual's beliefs? Whether the target of those beliefs is another person or the self, whether those beliefs are held as assumptions or as hypotheses, the message is the same. Beliefs initiate activities that provide both behavioral and cognitive confirmation for themselves. Any consideration of confirmation outcomes immediately raises the issue of disconfirmation outcomes. Does there exist a behavioral disconfirmation process in which an individual's actions cause the target person to behave in ways that disconfirm the individual's beliefs? And does there exist a cognitive disconfirmation process in which an individual is particularly likely to bring to mind and remember information that would disconfirm the individual's beliefs about the target person? Both behavioral disconfirmation and cognitive disconfirmation outcomes have been documented in investigations of the consequences of beliefs. Moreover, disconfirmation outcomes initiated by beliefs as assumptions and by beliefs as hypotheses have been documented.

A. DISCONFIRMING BELIEFS AS ASSUMPTIONS

1. Cognitive Disconfirmation

At least one cognitive disconfirmation outcome has been documented in the domain of reconstructive remembering processes prompted by current beliefs. Uranowitz (1981b) had students rate the compatibility of engaged couples, using pictures and interest statements of each couple's members as guides. In fact, the members of these couples had been paired so that half were matched on the basis of looks, and half were matched on the basis of interests. Two days later, the participants read an essay, supposedly to be used by the psychology department, that described the results of interpersonal attraction research in very categorical, reactance-arousing ways. They were then asked to rematch the members of the couples they had rated earlier, based upon their memories of who went with whom. Those who read an essay stating categorically that psychologists *know* that people *only* use looks in mate selection reacted against the essay and seemed to bend over backward to disconfirm that contention by using *interests* as their primary strategy in the matching task. By contrast, those who had read that psychologists know for an absolute fact that people are attracted to each other solely on the basis of interests bent over backward to use the *photos* as the basis for their matching task. Those who read more qualified essays showed no such reactance-based disconfirmatory reconstruction of what they had learned about the engaged couples.

There also exists evidence for the behavioral disconfirmation of beliefs as assumptions. Under what circumstances can actions based upon one individual's impressions of another person cause that person to behave in a manner that disconfirms the individual's beliefs? For example, when can treating people as if they were warm and sociable actually make them noticeably cool and aloof? Operationally, a behavioral disconfirmation outcome is one in which social interaction creates a *negative relationship* between one individual's beliefs and another person's behaviors, in contrast to a behavioral confirmation outcome which operationally is one in which social interaction creates a *positive relationship* between one individual's beliefs and another person's behavior.

2. Behavioral Disconfirmation in Instructional Contexts

One analysis of the origins of both behavioral confirmation and behavioral disconfirmation outcomes has been provided by Swann and Snyder (1980). Their account has focused on the link between an individual's beliefs about an interaction partner and that individual's decisions about how to behave during their interaction. They have suggested that an individual's decisions about how to translate general beliefs about the other person into a specific pattern of self-presentation behaviors often are based upon "theories" about the qualitative nature of the general beliefs to be translated into action.

To illustrate their point, they have offered the example of individuals in supervisory or teaching roles who turn to a theory about the nature of ability in planning their instructional strategies. One instructor may rely on an "environmental" theory of ability, a theory that assumes ability to be a direct product of effective instruction by teachers. Such a theory of the extrinsic nature of ability would lead this instructor to adopt a directive approach for his or her teaching activities. Another instructor may rely on a "maturational" theory of ability, a theory that assumes ability to emerge naturally and spontaneously from the development over time of students' competencies. Such a theory of the intrinsic nature of ability would lead this instructor to adopt a nondirective approach for his or her teaching activities.

Instructors' theories of ability may interact with their beliefs about their students when it comes time to choose a teaching strategy. Thus, an instructor who works with the extrinsic theory of ability may plan this teaching strategy for a student believed to have considerable natural ability: "If this student is so high in ability, then I will do all that I can to ensure that this student reaches full potential by devoting lots of instructional effort to teach this student many skills.'' Instructors who employ this extrinsic theory in teaching tasks that involve the acquisition of trainable skills will probably generate *behavioral confirmation* for their initial beliefs about their students. Students believed to be high in ability will outperform those believed to be low in ability because only they will have been taught the skills necessary to perform the task. By contrast, an instructor who works with the intrinsic theory of ability may plan this teaching strategy for a student believed to be high in native ability: ''If this student is so gifted, then to ensure that this student develops full potential I will leave this student alone to develop natural capabilities without my interference while I work with other students who really need me as a teacher.'' Instructors who employ this intrinsic theory in tasks that involve the acquisition of trainable skills may generate *behavioral disconfirmation* outcomes. Students believed to be high in ability may perform more poorly than those believed to be low in ability precisely because they never are taught the skills they need to succeed in the tasks at hand.

In support of this analysis, Swann and Snyder (1980) reported the following empirical investigation. Some individuals (''instructors'') were asked to teach a card trick to two other people (''pupils''). Prior to the training period, instructors were introduced to either the theory that ability is produced by extrinsic factors such as careful and thorough instruction or the theory that ability emerges spontaneously from intrinsic factors such as pupils' unstructured experiences with the task. All instructors were led to believe that one of their pupils was relatively high in ability and the other was relatively low in ability. Instructors operating with the extrinsic theory of ability used their best teaching method with pupils believed to be high in ability and thereby produced behavioral confirmation for their initial beliefs. Pupils believed to be high in ability outperformed those believed to be low in ability. By contrast, instructors operating with the intrinsic theory of ability used their best teaching method with pupils they believed to be low in ability and thereby produced behavioral disconfirmation for their initial beliefs. Pupils believed to be low in ability outperformed those believed to be high in ability.

3. Behavioral Disconfirmation
in Social Relationships

Although they developed and investigated their analysis in the context of educational and instructional situations, Swann and Snyder (1980) have pointed out the ways in which the same processes that link individuals' beliefs about other people to their strategies for interacting with them may generate behavioral confirmation and behavioral disconfirmation outcomes in a wide range of situations in which one individual invokes preconceived beliefs about another person. They have offered the example of an individual who anticipates interaction with a person believed to be cold and hostile. In that situation, some individuals might invoke a reciprocating self-protective theory of coping with social relationships: "To protect myself from any possible embarassment or pain, I will be just as cold and hostile as that person will be." To the extent that the other person responds in kind to that individual's hostile overtures, behavioral confirmation will be the outcome of their interaction. This scenario is precisely the one that occurred in the experiment by Snyder and Swann (1978a): people whose interaction partners regarded them as hostile types came to display more hostility than people regarded by their interaction partners as nonhostile types.

Yet, in such situations, one need not adopt the reciprocating theory of coping. Rather, one could invoke a compensatory theory of dealing with a social situation involving a reputedly cold and hostile person. Individuals operating with this theory would plan this self-presentational strategy: "To ensure that this interaction proceeds comfortably, I will be especially friendly and talkative to make up for that person's coolness." If the interaction partner returns these friendly advances, his or her behavior will constitute behavioral disconfirmation for his or her allegedly cold and hostile temperament.

This form of behavioral disconfirmation produced by compensatory theories of social interaction may account for the findings of Bond (1972). In his study, women who had been expected to be cool and aloof became warm and talkative in interaction with those who held these expectations. One interpretation of these findings begins with the assumption that the holders of these expectations believed that it was their responsibility to maintain an active conversation. Thus, when they interacted with another person whom they believed to be cool and aloof, they attempted to compensate for the shyness of their partners by behaving in an especially warm and friendly manner. Their partners then reciprocated their warmth and friendliness, thereby providing behavioral disconfirmation for the initial expectation that they would be cool and aloof in conversation.

In addition, a similar process may account for the activities of androgynous women who, when interacting with allegedly attractive or unattractive partners in an experiment by Andersen and Bem (1981), behaved in ways that led allegedly unattractive targets to behave in a more socially appealing manner than allegedly attractive targets, thereby producing a behavioral disconfirmation outcome. Perhaps these non-sex-typed individuals bent over backward to be friendly and sociable toward those of lesser attractiveness to demonstrate their liberation from an interpersonal orientation of being more attuned to other people's physical qualities than to their personalities, an orientation that they might have associated (with some justification, as the research by Andersen & Bem, 1980, does suggest) with the type of sex-typed individual they seek not to be.

Similar compensatory processes may have been at work in the investigation of Swann and Hill (1982), who had participants play a two-person game in which the players alternated between a dominant "leader" role or a submissive assistant role. During a break between games, one player (actually a confederate of the experimenter) informed the other player that she believed her to be or that she did not believe her to be the forceful, dominant type. When the confederate's beliefs challenged the player's own self-perceived dominance or nondominance, the players behaved in ways designed to disconfirm the confederate's beliefs. Perhaps to compensate for the threatening views of the player, self-perceived dominants who believed that their partners regarded them as submissive behaved in particularly dominant fashion, and self-perceived submissives who believed that their partners regarded them as dominant behaved in especially submissive ways. These behaviors, which provided behavioral disconfirmation for the player's beliefs about how the other player viewed her, were visible even to outside objective observers who formed impressions of the players congruent with their displays of dominance or submission.

Further support for the role of these two theories for handling interpersonal situations in generating behavioral confirmation and behavioral disconfirmation outcomes has been provided by Ickes et al. (1982). They found consistent patterns of behavioral and self-report evidence for the operation of a reciprocity strategy (in which individuals adopted a friendly attitude to one thought to be a friend, and thereby produced a behavioral confirmation outcome) and a compensation strategy (in which individuals maintained a friendly posture with one expected to be unfriendly, and thereby produced a behavioral disconfirmation outcome) in unstructured, face-to-face social interactions.

Taken together, the intrinsic and extrinsic theories of ability as well as the reciprocating and compensatory theories of social interaction appear to be members of a set of theories on which individuals rely in translating their beliefs about other people into modes of treatment of these people. By specifying the theories with which individuals operate in acting upon interpersonal beliefs it seems to be possible to predict and explain when behavioral confirmation outcomes and when behavioral disconfirmation outcomes will occur in social interaction.

B. DISCONFIRMING BELIEFS AS HYPOTHESES

Although confirmatory strategies seem to typify the activities of individuals as hypotheses testers (for a review, see Snyder & Gangestad, 1981), this rule is not without its rare exceptions. At least two procedures, one relatively cognitive in nature, the other relatively motivational in nature, have succeeeded in inducing individuals to abandon confirmatory strategies for testing hypotheses about other people.

1. The Cognitive Procedure

The relatively cognitive procedure is one developed by Snyder and White (1981), who reasoned that confirmatory hypothesis-testing strategies may reflect the fact that individuals typically define the hypothesis-testing task as one of determining the extent to which the hypothesis under scrutiny is true. That is, individuals routinely may define the hypothesis-testing task as a verification task. Therefore, they induced individuals to regard the task of testing hypotheses about other people as a falsification task, that is, as one of determining the extent to which the hypothesis under scrutiny was not true. These individuals formulated disconfirmatory hypothesis-testing strategies of preferentially soliciting hypothesis-disconfirming evidence with which to test their hypotheses.

From this perspective, the rarity with which individuals formulate disconfirmatory strategies for testing the hypotheses about other people provided to them in investigations of hypothesis-testing processes probably reflects the fact that they tend not to define the task of testing hypotheses in terms of building the case against hypotheses. Instead, it may be that individuals typically tend to define the hypothesis-testing task as one of preferentially building the case in support of hypotheses by soliciting and accumulating hypothesis-confirming evidence. The existence of this confirmatory philosophy of science is suggested also by findings that individuals regard confirmatory evidence as more convincing and probative (e.g., Lord, Ross, & Lepper, 1979) as well as more relevant and informative (e.g., Snyder & Campbell, 1979) than disconfirming evidence. By encouraging them to abandon this confirmatory "philosophy of science" in favor of a disconfirmatory philosophy of science, it is possible to induce individuals to put aside their confirmatory hypothesis-testing strategies and adopt disconfirmatory ones.

2. The Motivational Procedure

The relatively motivational procedure for encouraging individuals to abandon confirmatory hypothesis-testing strategies is one developed by Snyder et al. (1982). This procedure emerged from an attempt to identify motivational aspects of hypothesis-testing processes by considering the social and interpersonal context within which hypothesis-testing activities occur in social interaction. Specifically, Snyder et al. (1982) suggested that testing hypotheses in social interaction may provide opportunities for hypothesis testers to engage in impression management activities. Theory and research on impression management have emphasized the lengths to which individuals can and will go to control the impressions that they convey to other people in social interaction (for reviews, see, for example, Schlenker, 1980; Snyder, 1981a; Tedeschi, 1981). They reasoned that, if the hypothesis-testing situation constitutes an impression management situation, then it may be possible to harness the motivational forces of impression management to influence the behavior of individuals in the hypothesis-testing situation.

When individuals use social interaction to test hypotheses about other people, they are not only gathering information with which to make judgments about other people but also transmitting information to other people that may form the basis for judgments that other people will make about them. In particular, the questions that individuals choose to ask to test hypotheses about other people may form the basis on which other people will form impressions of those individuals. Moreover, by their choices of questions to ask, individuals may influence or manage the impressions that they transmit to other people in the context of their hypothesis-testing activities.

To the extent that individuals restrict their choices to questions that solicit behavioral evidence from one domain (in this case, to questions that solicit hypothesis-confirming evidence), they may convey the image of being closed-minded individuals who have prejudged the personalities of other people to whom those questions are directed. On the other hand, to the extent that individuals choose to ask questions that solicit behavioral evidence from diverse behavioral domains (in this case, questions that solicit hypothesis-confirming and hypothesis-disconfirming evidence), they may convey the image of being open-minded individuals who are willing to suspend judgment until they have given other people the opportunity to reveal diverse facets of their personalities.

It follows from this line of reasoning that, if individuals were sensitized to the impression management implications of the strategies by which they test hypotheses in social interaction, they might abandon confirmatory evidence-gathering strategies (which may convey the impression that they are closed-minded individuals) in favor of strategies that gather both confirmatory and disconfirmatory evidence with equal diligence (strategies which convey the impression that they are open-minded individuals). Indeed, in an empirical investigation, participants who were sensitized to the impression management implications of their hypothesis-testing activities planned to assess the accuracy of hypotheses by asking questions that solicited confirming evidence and questions that solicited disconfirming evidence in numbers that did not differ from each other. If anything, their question choices suggest a slight tendency to bend over backward in these circumstances and preferentially solicit disconfirming evidence.

In addition, an extension of research on hypothesis testing in social interaction suggests that individuals will act in ways that generate behavioral disconfirmation for hypotheses that challenge or threaten central aspects of their own personal conceptions of self. Swann (1978) examined the processes by which individuals test hypotheses about what other people may or may not have believed about them. He arranged for pairs of previously unacquainted participants (a "self" and a "partner") to engage in getting acquainted conversations. Some of the selves were led to form the hypothesis that their partners might like them, other selves were led to form the hypothesis that their partners might dislike them, and other selves were not led to form any hypothesis about their partner's feelings for them. The selves' hypotheses about their partners' evaluations of them interacted with their own conceptions of themselves as likable or dislikable individuals to influence the partners' ultimate reactions to the selves. Selves who hypothesized that their partners might dislike them, but who regarded themselves as likable individuals, treated their partners in ways that elicited most favorable reactions from their partners. By contrast, selves who hypothesized that their partners might like them, but who regarded themselves as dislikable individuals, treated their partners in ways that elicited the most unfavorable reactions from partners. Evidently the activation of hypotheses that their partners might not share their attitudes toward themselves motivated selves to act in ways that led the partners to disconfirm the selves' hypotheses about the partners' sentiments.

VI.   The Nature of Beliefs

In light of the outcomes of these investigations of the cognitive, behavioral, and interpersonal consequences of beliefs, what can be said about the nature of beliefs? It appears that beliefs (whether they are assumptions or hypotheses) about people (either the self or other people as targets of beliefs) are actively involved in initiating and guiding the course and outcome of social interaction and the remembering and interpretation of events relevant to these beliefs.

A.   SOCIAL BELIEFS AS SOCIAL SCENARIOS

What is it about beliefs about people that accounts for the active, initiatory role that they play in guiding and influencing subsequent thought and action? One theoretical possibility is suggested by an elaboration of the analysis (originally presented in Section III,A) of the role of ''scenarios'' in behavioral confirmation processes. It may be that beliefs about people contain within them anticipations, theories, or scenarios of events. These events are those that the individual estimates are likely to have occurred in the past behaviors of targets of those beliefs and scenarios of events that are likely to occur in the future behavior of the targets of these beliefs.

When individuals think about the targets of their beliefs, these theories may guide the formation of scenariolike anticipations of what information is likely to characterize these targets and these scenarios actively guide the gathering and interpreting of information about the targets of their beliefs. Similarly, when individuals anticipate their forthcoming interactions with the targets of their beliefs, these theories may guide the formation of scenariolike anticipations of what events are likely to occur as the interactions unfold, and these scenarios actively guide the individual's interactional strategies. To the extent that these anticipations or "theories" guide subsequent thoughts about the target and subsequent social interaction involving the target, the reality-constructing impact of beliefs in the cognitive, behavioral, and interpersonal domains are likely, if not inevitable, consequences of the active and initiatory nature of beliefs about people.

That these consequences more typically provide confirmation rather than disconfirmation suggests that the guiding scenarios are more likely to be as-if scenarios, in which the target acts in accord with the individual's beliefs, than as-if-not scenarios, in which the target violates the individual's beliefs. Indeed, a variety of considerations suggest that it may be easier to construct as-if scenarios than as-if-not scenarios. In particular, in a wide variety of cognitive tasks, people are more likely to use—are more facile in using and are more responsive to— positive instances or occurrences than negative instances or nonoccurrences (e.g., Gollob, Rossman, & Abelson, 1973; Hovland & Weiss, 1953; Jenkins & Ward, 1965; Smedslund, 1963; Wason & Johnson-Laird, 1972). To the extent that as-if scenarios, which involve positive instances and occurrences of targets behaving in accord with beliefs and hypotheses, more readily come to mind than as-if-not scenarios, then it becomes all the more likely that these as-if scenarios will guide subsequent thought and interaction involving the targets of beliefs and hypotheses (for evidence of the influence of scenarios on behavior see Gregory, Cialdini, & Carpenter, 1982). The directive influence of as-if scenarios may then generate samples of evidence, either in thought or behavior, in which confirming evidence will be overrepresented and disconfirming evidence will be underrepresented.

B. THE SOCIAL NATURE OF SOCIAL BELIEFS

Moreover, investigations of the reality-constructing consequences of social beliefs make clear just what it is that is inherently and fundamentally *social* about social beliefs. That is, these investigations sensitize us to the links between social beliefs and social reality. Social beliefs can and do create their own social reality. The very events of the social world (in particular, the behaviors of the targets of social beliefs, both as they appear in memory and in social interaction) may be products of preconceptions about the social world (in particular, assumptions and hypotheses about the characteristic nature of particular types of people). Social beliefs are *social* beliefs precisely because of their intimate involvement in the construction and the reconstruction of social reality in ongoing and continuing social relationships. Social beliefs are *social* beliefs precisely because of the links they create between the domain of thought and the domain of action. It is because of these links between thought and action that beliefs about the social attributes of people are fundamentally and inherently different from beliefs about the physical attributes of objects. Acting on beliefs about objects and physical events does not influence the reality of those objects and events in the same way that acting on beliefs about people and social events does influence the reality of those people and their behavior. For example, a sedan does not become a sportscar because I think of it as one and try to handle it as one, but a person may become friendly and sociable because I believe him to be, and treat him as if he were, that type of person.

That people are not objects, and that beliefs about people differ from beliefs about objects, has considerable implications for the ways that students of social cognition and person perception approach their subject matter. That beliefs about people are *social* beliefs precisely because of their intimate involvement in the construction of social reality in ongoing relationships means that social beliefs cannot be studied meaningfully in static circumstances of minimal personal involvement. This approach prevents us from witnessing the intimate interplay between social beliefs and social behavior in ongoing interpersonal relationships. By attending to the influence of beliefs on the unfolding dynamics of continuing sequences of social interaction, it is possible to appreciate the ways by which individuals *create* the information and events that they encounter and attempt to understand in their social worlds. That is, events in the social world may be as much *effects* of individuals' beliefs as they are the *causes* of these beliefs. This viewpoint has implications for diverse theoretical issues.

C. BELIEFS ABOUT TRAITS AND CONSISTENCY IN BEHAVIOR

From this perspective, it becomes easier to appreciate individuals' stubborn tendency to fashion images of others largely in trait terms (e.g., Jones & Nisbett, 1972), despite the poverty of evidence for the pervasive cross-situational con-sistencies in social behavior that the existence of true traits would demand (Mischel, 1968). Even though any target person's behavior may, overall, lack the trait defining properties of cross-situational consistency, the actions of an-other individual guided by beliefs may produce consistency in the samples of behavior available to that individual. Individuals' impressions of other people may cause them to behave in consistent *traitlike* fashion for them. In that sense, individuals' trait-based impressions of other people are veridical, even though the same person may behave or be led to behave in a fashion perfectly consistent with opposite beliefs held by other individuals with quite different impressions of that individual. Thus, individuals may not err when they fashion their images of other people in dispositional or trait terms. They only err to the extent that they underestimate the extent to which the consistencies and regularities that they observe in others are a product of their own impression-based treatment of other people.

If this viewpoint is correct, then some redirection of the search for cross-situational consistency (the defining feature of "personality traits") is in order. The unit of analysis and search must become the "individual, belief, and target" unit. That is, assessments of the extent of traitlike cross-situational stability in a particular target's social behavior must take into account the role of particular individuals and their beliefs about the target in creating stability across particular "individual, belief, and target" domains. In fact, it was possible in one experiment (Snyder & Swann, 1978a), to observe the socialization of a "trait" of hostility in targets in the course of their successive interactions with different individuals.

As a conceptual parallel to such individual-generated cross-situational consistencies, there may also exist target-generated patterns of cross-situational consistencies. Targets who hold salient and well-articulated images of themselves in particular domains may proceed to act out such images across diverse situations and therefore create cross-situational *traitlike* organizations in their social behavior. In each case, that of individual-generated cross-situational consistency and that of self-generated consistency, the principle is the same. The organization of behavior across situations may be, in part, the product of the self-fulfilling influence of beliefs on behavior.

D. "ACCURACY" AND "ERROR" IN BELIEFS

From this perspective, notions about "errors" and "biases" in attributional processes may take on new meaning. Heider's (1958) observation that we often underestimate the impact of situational forces and overestimate the role of dispositional causes has been confirmed repeatedly (e.g., Bem, 1967; Jones & Harris, 1967). Social perceivers seem quite willing to perceive dispositional causes for behavior that (at least in the eyes of the experimenter) is a clear product of obvious situational pressure. Similarly, self-perception can be led astray in cleverly contrived misattribution experiments (e.g., Davison & Valins, 1969; Nisbett & Schachter, 1966). In such misattribution experiments, actors "erroneously" infer dispositional causes for their behavior when in fact their behavior really is a product of experimental manipulations of their situations.

However, research on the consequences of beliefs suggests that, over time, such errors become "self-erasing" errors. For example, individuals in experiments on behavioral confirmation were induced (by the experimental manipulations) to adopt erroneous beliefs about targets. However, as a result of interaction guided by these initial impressions, targets' behavior came to behaviorally confirm and validate these initially erroneous impressions. Initial errors erased themselves, not because individuals became aware of the inaccuracy of their initial impressions, but because the social world changed to conform to the individual's view of it. Thus, the initial accuracy or inaccuracy of beliefs and attributions may be a moot point. For, over time, even errors may create their own reality.

E. THE SPECIAL CASE OF STEREOTYPED SOCIAL BELIEFS

That beliefs may create their own reality helps explain the persistence of so many clearly erroneous social stereotypes. For example, there exist widely shared stereotypes about, among other things, sex, age, race, ethnicity, nationality, religion, sexuality, occupation, and social class. But such stereotypes are often highly inaccurate. How is it, then, that erroneous stereotypes can continue to exist and be resistant to change? Research on the impact of belief on the dynamics of social relationships suggests one answer to this puzzling question.

As long as people have faith in their stereotypes, they may treat other people in ways that actually elicit from them behaviors that support those stereotypes. By acting upon their stereotyped images of others, people may lead other people who may not really fit those stereotypes to behave in accord with these stereotypes. If, based upon erroneous stereotypes, people treat other people in ways that actually bring out behaviors that support those stereotypes, they may never get the opportunity to discover the ways in which some of their stereotypes may be wrong. If people assume that physically attractive people are friendly, sociable, and outgoing and thus treat them in ways that bring out the friendly, sociable, and outgoing in them, they may never see that some attractive people might really be shy, reserved, and aloof types. If people assume that other people are passive, dependent, and conforming just because they are women and therefore maneuver women into roles that demand passive, dependent, and conforming behaviors, they may never discover that some women might otherwise have chosen roles that permit active, assertive, and independent action. In each case, by acting upon their stereotyped assumptions about human nature, people can and do lead others who may not really fit those stereotypes to behave in accord with those stereotypes.

Moreover, research on hypothesis testing in social interaction suggests that, even if individuals were to develop sufficient doubt about the accuracy of their stereotypes that they might proceed to test them, they would be likely to "discover" all the evidence that they need to confirm and retain their stereotyped beliefs about human nature. And, in the end, they may be left with the secure feeling that these stereotypes must be correct because they have survived (what may seem to them) perfectly appropriate and even rigorous procedures for assessing their accuracy. For elaboration of the nature and implications of this analysis of the perpetuation of social stereotypes, see Snyder (1981b).

However, this analysis, if carried to its logical conclusion, leads to a puzzling state of affairs. If, by acting as if false stereotypes were true, people lead others to act as if those stereotypes were true, why then do these stereotypes not come to be true? Why, for example, have researchers found so little evidence that attractive people actually are, in general, as friendly, sociable, and outgoing and that unattractive people actually are, in general, as shy, withdrawn, and aloof as dictated by the stereotype that links looks and personality? Surely, it seems to follow that if what happens in experiments on behavioral confirmation happens on a large scale in people's lives, there would be more evidence for the validity of stereotypes.

There is, though, a resolution of this apparent paradox of stereotypes being both true and not true. At least in the case of the "beautiful people are good people" stereotype, the explanation has something to do with the old adage that "beauty is in the eye of the beholder." Very few people have the kind of looks that virtually everyone agrees is very attractive or very unattractive. Instead, most people fall somewhere in between these extremes, in the vast middle ground where they have the kind of looks that makes them rather attractive to some people but somewhat less attractive to other people. What this means is that when they spend time with those who find them attractive, those other people will tend to bring out their most sociable sides; but, when they are with those who find them less attractive, those other people will tend to bring out their less sociable sides. Although their actual physical appearance does not change, they will present themselves quite differently to their admirers and to their detractors. For their admirers they become attractive people, and for their detractors they become unattractive people.

This mixed pattern of behavior, in which most people, in different situations and with different people, will be both sociable and unsociable, both outgoing and shy, both warm and aloof, will prevent the development of any general, overall ties that bind physical attractiveness and personality, the kinds of overall ties that would constitute genuine evidence for the validity of the stereotype. For these reasons, it seems quite possible that stereotypes can create for themselves the illusion of reality in one-to-one situations without also gaining a general validity that makes them accurate for all people, at all times, and in all circumstances. Such may be the power of stereotyped social beliefs. Even when they are wrong, they may create and sustain their own reality, but that reality is one that is limited to those interpersonal relationships in which stereotypes work their way.

VII. Conclusions

It is a basic and an undeniable fact of social life that we form impressions of other people whom we encounter in our day-to-day lives. In our relationships with others, we want to know not only what they do, but why they do what they do, to feel that we understand what motives, intentions, and dispositions underlie an individual's actions. Indeed, as a direct result of generations of theory and research on impression formation and person perception, investigators have learned a great deal about how individuals process information to form beliefs and impressions of other people. Accordingly, there exists considerable knowledge about the antecedents of social beliefs.

But of what consequence are our beliefs and impressions of other people? What happens once impressions have been formed? How are our subsequent thoughts, actions, and interactions channeled and influenced by our impressions of others? It is to such concerns that empirical and theoretical research on the cognitive, behavioral, and interpersonal consequences of social beliefs has been addressed. Guiding that research has been the hope that, by understanding the consequences of social beliefs, it would be possible to understand the very nature of social beliefs.

Empirical investigations have been designed to chart the processes by which an individual's beliefs can and do initiate cognitive, behavioral, and interpersonal activities that influence the reality of those beliefs. These investigations have suggested that, whether individuals regard their beliefs as assumptions or as hypotheses, whether their beliefs concern themselves or other people, social beliefs can and do channel the remembering of past events and the unfolding of future events in ways that determine both the subjective and the objective reality of their beliefs. The practical implications of these reality-constructing consequences of social beliefs are considerable, both at the level of individual lives and at the level of society. (For discussion of the involvement of these processes in, among other things, the development and treatment of psychopathological conditions, the origins of inequities in educational and occupational opportunities, the roots of deviance and criminality, and the dynamics of prejudice and discrimination, see Snyder, 1981b,c; 1982a).

The theme, then, of this psychology of beliefs is this: The things that individuals believe exert powerful influences on the ways that they and other people live their lives. Beliefs and impressions do not exist in a vacuum. Instead, the processes of social thought are intimately woven into the fabric of social interaction and interpersonal relationships. The events of our lives are very much a reflection of our beliefs about ourselves and about other people in our social worlds. It is in this sense that beliefs can and do create reality.

ACKNOWLEDGMENTS

Research on the consequences of beliefs and the preparation of this manuscript have been supported by National Science Foundation Grants SOC 75-13872, BNS 77-11346, and BNS 82-07632 to Mark Snyder.

REFERENCES

Abelson, R. P. Script processing in attitude formation and decision making. In J. S. Carroll & J. W. Payne (Eds.). *Cognition and social behavior.* Hillsdale, New Jersey: Erlbaum, 1976.

Andersen, S., & Bem, S. L. Sex typing and androgyny in dyadic interaction. *Journal of Personality and Social Psychology,* 1981, **41,** 74–86.

Bartlett, F. C. *Remembering: A study in experimental and social psychology.* Cambridge: Cambridge University Press, 1932.

Bellezza, F. S., & Bower, G. H. Person stereotypes and memory for people. *Journal of Personality and Social Psychology,* 1981, **41**(5), 856–865.

Bem, D. J. Inducing belief in false confessions. *Journal of Personality and Social Psychology,* 1966, 3(6), 707–710.

Bem, D. J. Self-perception: An alternative interpretation of cognitive dissonance phenomenon. *Psychological Review,* 1967, **74,** 183–200.

Bem, D. J. Self-perception theory. In L. Berkowitz (Ed.), *Advances in experimental social psychology* (Vol. 6). New York: Academic Press, 1972.

Bem, D. J., & McConnell, H. K. Testing the self-perception explanation of dissonance phenomena: On the salience of premanipulation attitudes. *Journal of Personality and Social Psychology,* 1970, **14,** 23–31.

Berglas, S., & Jones, E. E. Drug choice as an externalization strategy in response to noncontingent success. *Journal of Personality and Social Psychology,* 1978, **36,** 405–417.

Berkowitz, L., & Frodi, A. Reactions to a child's mistakes as affected by her/his looks and speech. *Social Psychology Quarterly,* 1979, **42**(4).

Berscheid, E., & Walster, E. Physical attractiveness. In L. Berkowitz (Ed.), *Advances in experimental social psychology* (Vol. 7). New York: Academic Press, 1974.

Bond, M. H. Effect of an impression set on subsequent behavior. *Journal of Personality and Social Psychology,* 1972, **24,** 301–305.

Bower, G. H. Emotional mood and memory. *American Psychologist,* 1981, **36,** 129–148.

Broverman, I. K., Vogel, S. R., Broverman, D. M., Clarkson, F. E., & Rosenkrantz, P. S. Sex-role stereotypes: A current appraisal. *Journal of Social Issues,* 1972, **28,** 59–78.

Carver, C. S., & de la Garza, N. H. *Schema-guided information search in stereotyping of the elderly.* Unpublished manuscript, University of Miami, Coral Cables, Florida, 1982.

Christensen, D., & Rosenthal, R. Gender and nonverbal decoding skill as determinants of interpersonal expectancy effects. *Journal of Personality and Social Psychology,* 1982, **42**(1), 75–87.

Clark, L. F., & Woll, S. B. Stereotype biases: A reconstructive analysis of their role in reconstructive memory. *Journal of Personality and Social Psychology,* 1981, **41**(6), 1064–1072.

Coyne, J. C. Depression and the response of others. *Journal of Abnormal Psychology,* 1976, **85,** 186–193. (a)

Coyne, J. C. Toward an interactional description of depressions. *Psychiatry,* 1976, **39**(1), 28–40. (b)

Darley, J. M., & Gross, P. H. A hypothesis-confirming bias in labeling effects. *Journal of Personality and Social Psychology,* 1983, **44,** 20–33.

Davison, G. C., & Valins, S. Maintenance of self-attributed and drug-attributed behavior change. *Journal of Personality and Social Psychology,* 1969, **11,** 25–33.

Deaux, K. *The behavior of women and men.* Monterey, California: Brooks/Cole, 1976.

Dion, K., Berscheid, E., & Walster, E. What is beautiful is good. *Journal of Personality and Social Psychology,* 1972, **24,** 285–290.

Elashoff, J. D., & Snow, R. E. *Pygmalion reconsidered.* Worthington. Ohio: Charles A. Jones, 1971.

Farina, A., Allen, J. G., & Saul, B. B. B. The role of the stigmatized in affecting social relationships. *Journal of Personality,* 1968, **36,** 169–182.

Farina, A., Gliha, D., Boudreau, L. A., Allen, J. G., & Sherman, M. Mental illness and the impact of believing others know about it. *Journal of Abnormal Psychology,* 1971, **77,** 1–5.

Fazio, R. H., Effrein, E. A., & Falender, V. J. Self-perceptions following social interaction. *Journal of Personality and Social Psychology,* 1981, **41**(2), 232–242.

Fernberger, S. W. Persistence of stereotypes concerning sex differences. *Journal of Abnormal and Social Psychology,* 1948, **43,** 97–101.

Fong, G. T., & Markus, H. Self-schemas and judgments about others. *Social Cognition,* 1982, **1,** 191–204.

Freud, S. *The psychopathology of everyday life.* New York: Macmillan, 1914 (originally published, 1901).

Furnham, A. Personality and activity preference. *British Journal of Social and Clinical Psychology,* 1982.

Gilovich, T. Biased evaluation and persistence in gambling. *Journal of Personality and Social Psychology,* 1983, **44,** 1110–1126.

Goffman, E. *Stigma: Notes on the management of spoiled identity.* Englewood Cliffs, New Jersey: Prentice-Hall, 1963.

Gollob, H. F., Rossman, B. B., & Abelson, R. P. Social inference as a function of the number of instances and consistency of information presented. *Journal of Personality and Social Psychology,* 1973, **27,** 19–33.

Gregory, W. L., Cialdini, R. B., & Carpenter, K. M. Self-relevant scenarios as mediators of likelihood estimates and compliance: Does imagining it make it so? *Journal of Personality and Social Psychology,* 1982, **43,** 89–99.

Gross, A. E., Green, S. K., Storck, J. T., & Vanyur, J. M. Disclosure of sexual orientation and impression of male and female homosexuals. *Personality and Social Psychology Bulletin,* 1980, **6**(2), 307–314.

Hammen, C. L., & Peters, S. D. Interpersonal consequences of depression: Responses to men and women enacting a depressed role. *Journal of Abnormal Psychology,* 1978, **87**(3), 322–332.

Heider, F. *The psychology of interpersonal relations.* New York: Wiley, 1958.

Hovland, C. I., & Weiss, W. Transmission of information concerning concepts through positive and negative instances. *Journal of Experimental Psychology,* 1953, **45,** 175–182.

Howes, M. J., & Hokanson, J. E. Conversational and social responses to depressive interpersonal behavior. *Journal of Abnormal Psychology,* 1979, **88**(6), 625–634.

Ickes, W., Patterson, M. L., Rajecki, D. W., & Tanford, S. Behavioral and cognitive consequences of reciprocal versus compensatory responses to pre-interaction expectancies. *Social Cognition,* 1982, **1,** 160–190.

Isen, A. M., Shalker, T. E., Clark, M., & Karp, L. Affect, accessibility of material in memory, and behavior: A cognitive loop? *Journal of Personality and Social Psychology,* 1978, **36,** 1–12.

Jenkins, H. M., & Ward, W. C. Judgment of contingency between responses and outcomes. *Psychological Monographs,* 1965, **79,** (1, Whole No. 594).

Jensen, A. R. How much can we boost IQ and scholastic achievement? *Harvard Educational Review,* 1969, **39,** 1–123.

Jones, E. E. *Ingratiation.* New York: Appleton-Century-Crofts, 1964.

Jones, E. E., & Berglas, S. Control of attributions about the self through self-handicapping strategies: The appeal of alcohol and the role of underachievement. *Personality and Social Psychology Bulletin*, 1978, **4**, 200–206.

Jones, E. E., & Davis, K. E. From acts to dispositions: The attribution process in person perception. In L. Berkowitz (Ed.), *Advances in experimental social psychology* (Vol. 2), New York: Academic Press, 1965.

Jones, E. E., & Harris, V. A. The attribution of attitudes. *Journal of Experimental Social Psychology*, 1967, **3**, 1–24.

Jones, E. E., Kanouse, D., Kelley, H. H.. Nisbett, R. E., Valins, S., & Weiner, B. *Attribution: Perceiving the causes of behavior.* New York: General Learning Press, 1972.

Jones, E. E., & Nisbett, R. E. The actor and the observer: Divergent perceptions of the causes of behavior. In E. E. Jones, D. Kanouse, H. H. Kelley, R. E. Nisbett, S. Valins, & B. Weiner (Eds.), *Attribution: Perceiving the causes of behavior.* New York: General Learning Press, 1972.

Jones, S. C., & Panitch, D. The self-fulfilling prophecy and interpersonal attraction. *Journal of Experimental Social Psychology*, 1971, **7**, 356–366.

Kahle, L. R. Stimulus condition self-selection by males in the interaction of locus of control and skill–chance situations. *Journal of Personality and Social Psychology*, 1980, **38**, 50–56.

Kelley, H. H. The warm–cold variable in first impressions of persons. *Journal of Personality*, 1950, **18**, 431–439.

Kelley, H. H. The process of causal attribution. *American Psychologist*, 1973, **28**, 107–128.

Kelley, H. H., & Stahelski, A. J. The social interaction basis of cooperators' and competitors' beliefs about others. *Journal of Personality and Social Psychology*, 1970, **16**, 66–91.

Kelly, G. A. *The psychology of personal constructs.* New York: Norton, 1955.

Kida, T. The impact of hypothesis-testing strategies on auditors' use of data. *Journal of Accounting Research*, 1984, in press.

King, A. S. Self-fulfilling prophecies in training the hard-core: Supervisors' expectations and the underprivileged workers' performance. *Social Science Quarterly*, 1971, **52**(1), 369–378.

Kuhlman, D. M., & Wimberley, D. L. Expectations of choice behavior held by cooperators, competitors, and individualists across four classes of experimental game. *Journal of Personality and Social Psychology*, 1976, **34**, 69–81.

Kulik, J. A. Confirmatory attribution and the perpetuation of social beliefs. *Journal of Personality and Social Psychology*, 1983, **44**, 1171–1181.

Langer, E. J., & Abelson, R. P. A patient by any other name . . . : Clinician groups difference in labeling bias. *Journal of Consulting and Clinical Psychology*, 1974, **42**, 4–9.

Laird, J. E., Wagener, J. J., Halal, M., & Szegda, M. Remembering what you feel: Effects of emotion on memory. *Journal of Personality and Social Psychology*, 1982, **42**(4), 646–657.

Lord, C. G., Ross, L., & Lepper, M. R. Biased assimilation and attitude polarization: The effects of prior theories on subsequently considered evidence. *Journal of Personality and Social Psychology*, 1979, **37**(11), 2098–2109.

Lunnenborg, P. W. Stereotypic aspects in masculinity–femininity measurement. *Journal of Consulting and Clinical Psychology*, 1970, **34**, 113–118.

Maccoby, E. E., & Jacklin, C. N. *The psychology of sex differences.* Stanford, California: Stanford University Press, 1974.

McAdams, D. P. Experiences of intimacy and power: Relationships between social motives and autobiographical memory. *Journal of Personality and Social Psychology*, 1982, **42**(2), 292–302.

Maslach, C. The "truth" about false confessions. *Journal of Personality and Social Psychology*, 1971, **20**(2), 141–146.

Merton, R. K. The self-fulfilling prophecy. *Antioch Review*, 1948, **8**, 193–210.

Miller, D. T., & Holmes, J. G. The role of situational restrictiveness on self-fulfilling prophecies: A theoretical and empirical extension of Kelley and Stahelski's triangle hypothesis. *Journal of Personality and Social Psychology,* 1975, **31,** 661–673.

Mischel, W. *Personality and assessment.* New York: Wiley, 1968.

Money, J., & Ehrhardt, A. A. *Man and woman: Boy and girl.* Baltimore: Johns Hopkins Press, 1972.

Nisbett, R. E., & Schachter, S. Cognitive manipulation of pain. *Journal of Experimental Social Psychology,* 1966, **2,** 227–236.

Pennebaker, J. W., & Skelton, J. A. Selective monitoring of physical sensations. *Journal of Personality and Social Psychology,* 1981, **41**(2), 213–223.

Riggs, J. M., & Cantor, N. *Information exchange in social interaction: Anchoring effects of self-concepts and expectancies.* Unpublished manuscript, Gettysburg College, 1981.

Riggs, J. M., Monach, E. M., Ogburn, J. A., & Pahides, S. Inducing self-perceptions: The role of social interaction. *Personality and Social Psychology Bulletin,* 1983, **9,** 253–260.

Rodin, J., & Langer, E. Aging labels: The decline of control and the fall of self-esteem. *Journal of Social Issues,* 1980, **36**(2), 12–29.

Rosenkrantz, P. A., Vogel, S. R., Bee, H., Broverman, K. K., & Broverman, D. M. Sex-role stereotypes and self-concepts in college students. *Journal of Consulting and Clinical Psychology,* 1968, **32,** 287–295.

Rosenthal, R. *Experimenter effects in behavioral research.* New York: Appleton-Century-Crofts, 1966.

Rosenthal, R. Interpersonal expectations: Effects of the experimenter's hypothesis. In R. Rosenthal & R. L. Rosnow (Eds.), *Artifact in behavioral research.* New York: Academic Press, 1969.

Rosenthal, R. Teacher expectations and their effects upon children. In G. S. Lesser (Ed.), *Psychology and educational practice.* Glenview, Illinois: Scott, Foresman, 1971.

Rosenthal, R. *On the social psychology of the self-fulfilling prophecy: Further evidence for Pygmalion effects and their mediating mechanisms.* New York: M.S.S. Inf. Corp. Modular Publications, 1974.

Rosenthal, R., & Jacobson, L. *Pygmalion in the classroom.* New York: Holt, Rinehart & Winston, 1968.

Ross, M., McFarland, C., Conway, M., & Zanna, M. P. Reciprocal relation between attitudes and behavior recall: Committing people to newly formed attitudes. *Journal of Personality and Social Psychology,* 1983, **45,** 257–267.

Ross, M., McFarland, C., & Fletcher, G. J. O. The effect of attitude on the recall of personal histories. *Journal of Personality and Social Psychology,* 1981, **40**(4), 627–634.

Sackett, P. R. *The interviewer as hypothesis tester: The effects of impressions of an applicant on subsequent interviewer behavior.* Unpublished manuscript, University of Kansas, 1980.

Schlenker, B. R. *Impression management: The self-concept, social identity, and interpersonal relations.* Monterey, California: Brooks/Cole, 1980.

Scott, R. A. *The making of blind men.* New York: Russell Sage Foundation, 1969.

Semin, G. R., & Strack, F. The plausibility of the implausible: A critique of Snyder and Swann. *European Journal of Social Psychology,* 1980, **10,** 379–388.

Sherman, S. J. On the self-erasing nature of errors of prediction. *Journal of Personality and Social Psychology,* 1980, **39**(2), 211–221.

Sherman, S. J., Skov, R. B., Hervitz, E. F., & Stock, C. B. The effects of explaining hypothetical future events: From possibility to probability to actuality and beyond. *Journal of Experimental Social Psychology,* 1981, **17,** 142–158.

Sherriffs, A. C., & McKee, J. P. Qualitative aspects of beliefs about men and women. *Journal of Personality,* 1957, **25,** 451–464.

Skrypnek, B. J., & Snyder, M. On the self-perpetuating nature of stereotypes about women and men. *Journal of Experimental Social Psychology,* 1982, **18,** 277–291.

Smedslund, J. The concept of correlation in adults. *Scandinavian Journal of Psychology,* 1963, **4,** 165–173.

Smith, T. W., Snyder, C. R., & Perkins, S. C. The self-serving function of hypochondriacal complaints: Physical symptoms as self handicapping strategies. *Journal of Personality and Social Psychology,* 1983, **44,** 787–797.

Snyder, M. Self-monitoring processes. In L. Berkowitz (Ed.), *Advances in experimental social psychology* (Vol. 12). New York: Academic Press, 1979.

Snyder, M. Impression management: The self in social interaction. In L. S. Wrightsman & K. Deaux (Eds.), *Social psychology in the eighties.* Belmont, California: Brooks/Cole, 1981. (a)

Snyder, M. On the self-perpetuating nature of social stereotypes. In D. L. Hamilton (Ed.), *Cognitive processes in stereotyping and intergroup behavior.* Hillsdale, New Jersey: Erlbaum, 1981. (b)

Snyder, M. Seek, and ye shall find: Testing hypotheses about other people. In E. T. Higgins, C. P. Herman, & M. P. Zanna (Eds.), *Social cognition: The Ontario symposium on personality and social psychology.* Hillsdale, New Jersey: Erlbaum, 1981. (c)

Snyder, M. Self-fulfilling stereotypes. *Psychology Today,* July 1982, 60–68. (a)

Snyder, M. *Understanding individuals and their social worlds.* Invited address, American Psychological Association, Washington, D. C., 1982. (b)

Snyder, M. When believing means doing: Creating links between attitudes and behavior. In M. P. Zanna, E. T. Higgins, & C. P. Herman (Eds.), *Consistency in social behavior. The Ontario Symposium* (Vol. 2). Hillsdale, New Jersey: Erlbaum, 1982. (c)

Snyder, M. The influence of individuals on situations: Implications for understanding the links between personality and social behavior. *Journal of Personality,* 1983, **51,** 497–516.

Snyder, M., & Campbell, B. H. *Testing hypotheses about other people: The hypothesis-tester's philosophy of science.* Unpublished research, University of Minnesota, 1979.

Snyder, M., & Campbell, B. H. Testing hypotheses about other people: The role of the hypothesis. *Personality and Social Psychology Bulletin,* 1980, **6,** 421–426.

Snyder, M., Campbell, B., & Preston, E. Testing hypotheses about human nature: Assessing the accuracy of social stereotypes. *Social Cognition,* 1982, **1,** 256–272.

Snyder, M., & Cantor, N. Testing hypotheses about other people: The use of historical knowledge. *Journal of Experimental Social Psychology,* 1979, **15,** 330–342.

Snyder, M., & Gangestad, S. Hypothesis-testing processes. In J. H. Harvey, W. Ickes, & R. F. Kidd (Eds.), *New directions in attribution research* (Vol. 3). Hillsdale, New Jersey: Erlbaum, 1981.

Snyder, M., & Gangestad, S. Choosing social situations: Two investigations of self-monitoring processes. *Journal of Personality and Social Psychology,* 1982, **43,** 123–135. (a)

Snyder, M., & Gangestad, S. *Testing hypotheses about human nature: The design of experiments.* Unpublished research, University of Minnesota, 1982. (b)

Snyder, M., & Glick, P. *The role of the target in hypothesis-testing.* Unpublished research, University of Minnesota, 1982.

Snyder, M., & Kendzierski, D. Choosing social situations: Investigating the origins of correspondence between attitudes and behavior. *Journal of Personality,* 1982, **50,** 280–295.

Snyder, M., & Skrypnek, B. J. Testing hypotheses about the self: Assessments of job suitability. *Journal of Personality,* 1981, **49,** 193–211.

Snyder, M., & Swann, W. B., Jr. Behavioral confirmation in social interaction: From social perception to social reality. *Journal of Experimental Social Psychology,* 1978, **14,** 148–162. (a)

Snyder, M., & Swann, W. B., Jr. Hypothesis-testing processes in social interaction. *Journal of Personality and Social Psychology,* 1978, **36,** 1202–1212. (b)

Snyder, M., Tanke, E. D., & Berscheid, E. Social perception and interpersonal behavior: On the self-fulfilling nature of social stereotypes. *Journal of Personality and Social Psychology*, 1977, **35**, 656–666.

Snyder, M., & Uranowitz, S. W. Reconstructing the past: Some cognitive consequences of person perception. *Journal of Personality and Social Psychology*, 1978, **36**, 941–950. (a)

Snyder, M., & Uranowitz, S. W. *Reconstructing the past: The role of interpretive processes in reconstruction.* Unpublished research, University of Minnesota, 1978. (b)

Snyder, M., & Uranowitz, S. W. *Reconstructing the past: An investigation of interpersonal biography.* Unpublished research, University of Minnesota, 1978. (c)

Snyder, M., & White, P. Testing hypotheses about other people: Strategies of verification and falsification. *Personality and Social Psychology Bulletin*, 1981, **7**, 39–43.

Snyder, M., & White, P. Moods and memories: Elation, depression, and the remembering of the events of one's life. *Journal of Personality*, 1982, **50**(2), 149–167.

Spence, J. T., Helmreich, R., & Stapp, J. Ratings of self and peers on sex-role attributes and their relation to self-esteem and conception of masculinity and femininity. *Journal of Personality and Social Psychology*, 1975, **32**, 29–39.

Stern, G., Stein, M., & Bloom, B. *Methods in personality assessment: Human behaviour in complex social settings.* New York: Free Press, 1956.

Strack, S., & Coyne, J. C. Social confirmation of dysphoria: Shared and private reactions to depression. *Journal of Personality and Social Psychology*, 1983, **44**, 798–806.

Swann, W. B., Jr. *The interpersonal nature of self-conceptions.* Unpublished doctoral dissertation, University of Minnesota, 1978.

Swann, W. B., Jr., & Giuliano, T. Confirmatory search strategies in social interaction. Unpublished manuscript, University of Texas at Austin, 1983.

Swann, W. B., Jr., & Hill, C. A. *Some cognitive consequences of threats to the self.* Unpublished manuscript, University of Texas at Austin, 1981.

Swann, W. B., Jr., & Hill, C. A. When our identities are mistaken: Reaffirming self-conceptions through social interaction. *Journal of Personality and Social Psychology*, 1982, **43**, 59–66.

Swann, W. B., Jr., & Read, S. J. Acquiring self-knowledge: The search for feedback that fits. *Journal of Personality and Social Psychology*, 1981, **41**(6), 1119–1128. (a)

Swann, W. B., Jr., & Read, S. J. Self-verification processes: How we sustain our self-conceptions. *Journal of Experimental Social Psychology*, 1981, **17**, 351–372. (b)

Swann, W. B., Jr., & Snyder, M. On translating beliefs into action: Theories of ability and their application in an instructional setting. *Journal of Personality and Social Psychology*, 1980, **38**, 879–888.

Tavris, C., & Offir, C. *The longest war: Sex differences in perspective.* New York: Harcourt Brace Jovanovich, 1977.

Teasdale, J. D., & Fogarty, S. J. Differential effects of induced mood on retrieval of pleasant and unpleasant events from episodic memory. *Journal of Abnormal Psychology*, 1979, **88**, 248–257.

Tedeschi, J. T. (Ed.). *Impression management theory and social psychological research.* New York: Academic Press, 1981.

Thomas, E. A. E., & Malone, T. W. On the dynamics of two-person interactions. *Psychological Review*, 1979, **86**(4), 331–360.

Trope, Y., & Bassok, M. Confirmatory and diagnosing strategies in social information gathering. *Journal of Personality and Social Psychology*, 1982, **43**, 22–34.

Uranowitz, S. W. *The reconstruction of social behavior: Cognitive and motivational determinants.* Unpublished doctoral dissertation, University of Minnesota, 1981. (a)

Uranowitz, S. W. *The influence of reactance arousal on reconstruction.* Unpublished research, University of Minnesota, 1981. (b)

Uranowitz, S. W., Skrypnek, B. J., & Snyder, M. *Reconstructing the past: The role of stereotypes in remembering observed social information.* Unpublished research, University of Minnesota, 1978.

von Baeyer, C. L., Sherk, D. L., & Zanna, M. P. Impression management in the job interview: When the female applicant meets the male (chauvinist) interviewer. *Personality and Social Psychology Bulletin,* 1981, **7**, 45–52.

Wason, P. C., & Johnson-Laird, P. N. *Psychology of reasoning: Structure and content.* London: D. T. Batsford, 1972.

Wegner, D. M.. Wenzlaff, R., Kirker, R. M., & Beattie, A. E. Incrimination through innuendo: Can media questions become public answers? *Journal of Personality and Social Psychology,* 1981, **40**, 822–832.

Wixon, D. R., & Laird, J. D. Awareness and attitude change in the forced-compliance paradigm: The importance of when. *Journal of Personality and Social Psychology,* 1976, **34**(3), 376–384.

Word, C. O., Zanna, M. P., & Cooper, J. The nonverbal mediation of self-fulfilling prophecies in interracial interaction. *Journal of Experimental Social Psychology,* 1974, **10**, 109–120.

Zadny, J., & Gerard, H. B. Attributed intentions and informational selectivity. *Journal of Experimental Social Psychology,* 1974, **10**, 34–52.

Zanna, M. P., & Pack, S. J. On the self-fulfilling nature of apparent sex differences in behavior. *Journal of Experimental Social Psychology,* 1975, **11**, 584–591.

Zuckerman, M. The sensation seeking motive. In B. Maher (Ed.), *Progress in experimental personality research* (Vol. 7). New York: Academic Press, 1974, 79–148.

INDEX

A

Accuracy of social perception, 161–162
Achievement motivation, 60, 64
Acquiescence, 23
Affection, 19–20
Agreement effects, 92–116
  being liked interpretation, 106–109
  being right interpretation of, 103–106
  size of, 109–110
Analysis of variance, 100–102
Androgyny, 16, 61, 64
Anti-competitive theory, 186
Appearance, 251–253
Assumptions about other people, 264–271
Assumptions about self, 277–282
Attentiveness, 23
Attitude similarity, 186
Attraction effects, 92–116
  being liked and, 109
  size of, 109–110
Attraction reciprocity, 157–160
Attractiveness, see Appearance
Autonomy, 5

B

Balance theory, 89–140
  agreement effects, 92–116
  assumption of $p-o$ similarity, 102–103
  attraction effects, 92–116
  generalized tetrahedron formulation, 121–123
  implicitness–explicitness of balance inferences, 115–116
  Jordan paradigm, 90–119
  and logic, 136–137
  and pleasantness, 111–113
  and self-esteem, 113–115

and social influence, 116–119
  three-sign balance effects, 99–102
  Wiest tetrahedron, 119–136
Bargaining theory, 198–200, 214, 238
  in multivalued games, 217–219
Behavioral confirmation
  as reality testing, 258–259
  in social interaction, 250–257
  theory, 257–262
Being-liked interpretation, 106–109
Being-right interpretation, 103–106
Beliefs, 247–305
  accuracy in, 295–296
  about appearance, 251–253
  about consistency in behavior, 294–295
  disconfirming, see Disconfirmation
  error in, 295–296
  about gender, 253–254
  about job performance, 255–256, 284
  nature of, 292–297
  about race, 255
  social, 292–294
  stereotyped, 293–297
  taxonomy of, 262–285
  about traits, 294–295
Bem Sex Role Inventory (BSRI), 16
Block design, 151–152
Block–round robin design, 152–153
BSRI, see Bem Sex Role Inventory

C

Checker-board design, 151
Circle design, 151
CLalt, see Comparison level for alternatives
Coalition
  bargaining, see Coalition bargaining
  definitions of, 184–185

CONTENTS OF OTHER VOLUMES